GOD AND GREATER BRITAIN

GOD AND GREATER BRITAIN

Religion and National Life in Britain and
Ireland 1843–1945

John Wolffe

London and New York

First published 1994
by Routledge
11 New Fetter Lane, London EC4P 4EE

Simultaneously published in the USA and Canada
by Routledge
29 West 35th Street, New York, NY 10001

© 1994 John Wolffe

Typeset in 10 on 12 point Garamond by
Computerset, Harmondsworth, Middlesex
Printed and bound in Great Britain by
Biddles Ltd, Guildford and King's Lynn

British Library Cataloguing in Publication Data
A catalogue record for this book is available from the British Library

Library of Congress Cataloging in Publication Data
Wolffe, John
God and Greater Britain : religion and national life in Britain and Ireland,
1843–1945 / John Wolffe
p. cm.
Includes bibliographical references and index.
1. British Isles—Church history—19th century. 2. British Isles—Church
history—20th century. I. Title
BR743.W65   1994
274.1′08—dc20   93-38980 CIP

ISBN 0-415-03570-8

CONTENTS

CONTENTS

ILLUSTRATIONS

FIGURE

PLATES

TABLES

PREFACE

The idea for this book began to germinate in 1977, when, in that pleasant oasis between school and university, I was walking in the rain in the north-west Highlands of Scotland. The party was somewhat demoralized by the weather, and to keep our spirits up we began to sing:

> And did those feet in ancient time
> Walk upon England's mountains green?
> And was the holy Lamb of God
> On England's pleasant pastures seen?
> And did the Countenance Divine
> Shine forth upon our clouded hills?
> And was Jerusalem builded here
> Amid these dark Satanic mills?

We moulded William Blake's lines to our own situation: 'England' became 'Scotland' and 'clouded', 'bloody rainy'. No doubt countless others have sung and adapted these lines in comparable circumstances, a practice that represents a blending of the religious and the secular and of the 'English' and 'British' that is all the more striking for being usually entirely unconscious. Indeed, confusion of this kind reflects not chance muddled thinking, but rather longstanding cultural patterns.

During subsequent years of undergraduate and postgraduate historical study, which involved research in all the component nations of the United Kingdom, my fascination with the place of religion in the social, political and cultural life of these islands gathered momentum. In my doctoral thesis, published as *The Protestant Crusade in Great Britain, 1829–60* (Oxford, 1991), I examined, among other things, the connections between organized anti-Catholicism and British national identities. The present book represents an advance towards a more general interpretation. It crosses the conventional divide between monograph and textbook. A wide and complex subject is explored not in a systematic, even fashion, but through deeper investigation of particular themes, by way of particularly illuminating specific evidence and incidents. It is my hope that the result will be of interest to specialist, student and 'general reader' alike. I have tried to avoid assuming prior knowledge in the reader, but in order to keep this objective compatible with moderate length, it has often been necessary to be ruthlessly selective in the coverage. Those who need more information are directed to the works cited in the footnotes and to the suggestions on further reading.

This book also explores the interface between 'ecclesiastical' or 'church' history and 'mainstream' history. This task has been made easier by the development in recent years of a school of 'religious' history which has moved far beyond the bounds of conventionally defined Christian institutions and theologies. At the same time historians in other fields have shown a growing sensitivity to religious factors. Nevertheless this process still seems to me to be capable of further constructive advance. In doing this I am not attempting to imply that religion explains everything; rather to provide a counterweight to any continuing tendency to marginalize it, and to assist those students of political, social, and cultural history who find themselves forced by the logic of their sources to enter a territory they find unfamiliar. At the same time I hope to indicate further potentialities in the study of religion itself.

In the second half of the book the theme is developed in a particular way through examination of the interplay of religion with national consciousness in the two large islands of Ireland and Great Britain lying off the north-west coast of Europe. I have in the title resurrected the term 'Greater Britain' which had some currency in the late nineteenth century. The phrase was originally used to refer to imperial possessions on a global scale, but I use it with ironically evocative intent to point up the cultural and political prominence of the concept of 'Britain' in these islands. 'Greater Britain' was a state of mind – which was of course vigorously contested – rather than an objective geographical description, and it is for that reason that I prefer it to 'British Isles', which is readily interpreted in both ways and hence gives understandable offence in Ireland. My aim is to indicate how religion contributed to sustaining the legitimacy and coherence of 'Greater Britain', which was often in revealing confusion with what might be termed 'Greater England'. Accordingly it is necessary to concentrate particularly on England, the most populous and powerful of the nations in the archipelago. At the same time the Irish, Scottish and Welsh alternatives demand careful consideration and the reasons for their relative degrees of effectiveness must be explored. Constraints of space, available material, and competence (I speak neither Gaelic nor Welsh) nevertheless limit the extent to which some lines of enquiry can be pursued. The intention is not, however, to explore all possible ramifications of the subject, but rather to set out an overall framework and to fill in some illustrative sections of it.

I approach my task, I trust, in a spirit of humility rather than of iconoclasm, aiming to complement rather than negatively to criticize the work of others, and very mindful of the manifold debts I have incurred. The ideas for this book took shape during the five stimulating years I spent in the Department of History at the University of York, an assemblage of scholars and students which is both 'religious' and 'British' in the most positive sense of those often derogatory words. I also very gratefully acknowledge the support of the British Academy during the two years that I held one of their postdoctoral fellowships, and the encouragement and assistance of colleagues in the Faculty of Arts at The Open University since my move there in 1990. More specifically, I have gained much from the comments of David Bebbington, David Hempton, James Macmillan, Andrew and Amanda Norman, and my mother, Mary Wolffe, who have all read the manuscript, made numerous helpful suggestions, and saved me from many errors. I appreciate the patience and encouragement of Claire L'Enfant at Routledge, and the unstinting assistance of Wendy Clarke and other secretarial staff at The Open University. I am moreover, very conscious of those wider and deeper influences which have made this book possible, from older relatives who have provided that living link with the past essential to any historian; from friends who have shared in the geographical and intellectual explorations reflected here; and from students at York and The Open University whose ideas, questions and blank incomprehension have all in different ways contributed to my own understanding. I thank them all, but blame none of them for any remaining deficiencies.

John Wolffe
The Open University, September 1993

ACKNOWLEDGEMENTS

The permission of the following to reproduce copyright material is gratefully acknowledged:

The British Museum for engravings of *The Great Day of His Wrath* and *The Light of the World*;

Faber & Faber Ltd for lines from T. S. Eliot's 'Little Gidding' and Edwin Muir's 'Robert the Bruce';

Harcourt Brace and company for excerpt from T. S. Eliot's 'Little Gidding' in *Four Quartets*, copyright 1943 T. S. Eliot and renewed 1971 by Esme Valerie Eliot;

Oxford University Press for translated lines from Gwenallt and for lines from Edwin Muir's 'Robert the Bruce';

Scottish Academic Press for lines from 'A Drunk Man Looks at the Thistle';

Victor Gollancz Ltd for translated lines from Gwenallt.

1

INTRODUCTION

Religion and nationhood in modern Britain

As the trains from the north-east rumble across the Victorian viaduct into Leeds station they pass the parish church, built between 1838 and 1841, a prominent symbol of the self-assertion of the Church of England in a northern industrial town. It is recorded that on an ordinary early spring Sunday evening in 1851 the church was filled to capacity with 3,000 people, several hundred of whom were standing in the aisles.[1] The traveller who leaves the train at Leeds will emerge from the station into the bustle of City Square and will be confronted with further reminders of the role of religion in urban life. On the eastern side of the square is the conspicuous Mill Hill Unitarian Chapel, constructed a few years after the parish church, imitating its style and in conscious rivalry with it; to the west is a line of statues of local worthies, which includes W. F. Hook, the energetic vicar during whose incumbency the parish church was rebuilt.

An hour's drive north of Leeds in the very different landscape of Upper Wharfedale one finds, amidst the fields and fells, the beautiful medieval church of Hubberholme. Like almost all old churches, however, it has not been left untouched by the nineteenth and twentieth centuries. In particular, a prominent monument records the career of George Andrew Hobson, a civil engineer who had family ties with that quiet Yorkshire village and who went at the high tide of British imperialism to superintend the construction of the railway-bridge over the River Zambezi below the Victoria Falls. Part of the inscription reads:

In this and other ways he helped to further the building up of the British Empire whose interests were dear to his heart. A practical Christian, brave, faithful, modest and single-minded, pure in heart and duty – Blessed are the Pure in Heart for they shall see God.

1

The images can be multiplied and are apparent today to anyone who travels around the British Isles with their eyes open. The townscapes of Guildford, Liverpool and Truro are dominated by Victorian or post-Victorian cathedrals. In Scotland the diverse buildings of the Presbyterian denominations, from the grandiose churches of 'Holy Corner' in Edinburgh to the small meeting places of Highland congregations, serve as reminders of the equally prominent place of religion north of the Border. Nonconformist chapels survive across Wales, mute testimony to their prominence in the social and cultural life of the communities of the principality in the Victorian and Edwardian eras. The simple buildings of Primitive Methodism are still to be found in the depths of the English countryside. Across the Irish Sea the two cathedrals of Armagh, set on their opposing hills, serve as striking symbols of the depth and divisiveness of religious labels. At the seat of government, the statesmen commemorated within the walls of Westminster Abbey and the grave of the Unknown Warrior underline the pervasive role of religion in the rituals of the nation, in war and in peace, and its place in the joys and the griefs of communities and individuals. Assessments of the exact significance of such visual evidence will vary considerably, especially when it is examined in conjunction with the documentary sources that form the usual raw material of historical research. Nevertheless it provides an appropriate starting point for this book: church buildings and monuments not only indicate both the pervasiveness and the variety of religion in the period with which we are to be concerned but also remind us that its legacy, however utilized, is with us still.

The central theme of this book is the interaction between religion in its various manifestations, and forms of community, national and imperial identity, culminating in the vigorous nationalism of the early twentieth century. This is naturally a story in which the organized churches played a significant part, but this is not to be a study in conventional 'church' or 'ecclesiastical' history. Rather it is an examination of the broader force of religion which, as will be shown in due course, can be seen as operating in numerous unofficial and unorthodox manners. In a moment we shall turn to look more closely at some key concepts, but at the outset it is worth formulating some further questions which will help to focus enquiry and point to the general shape of the argument.

First, what did the people of the United Kingdom really believe about fundamental problems of life, death, God and personal identity, those issues which are generally labelled as 'religious'? This is an extremely difficult question for the historian to answer, overlaid as it is with the need to disentangle personal conviction from records which are likely to be more informative about official teachings and outward appearances. The forms of official and outward religion are very revealing in themselves in indicating much about the power structures and shared values of society. Furthermore, in the absence of other evidence, active participation in them is the best indication we have of the attitudes of individuals. However, such participation would mean different things to different people at different times, and it should not be assumed without careful investigation that non-involvement in organized religion implied a lack of personal belief.

Second, what contribution did religion make to the formation of group identities, in terms of local communities, political parties and nations? In recent years scholars have increasingly moved away from viewing social class as a general organizing principle, so the exploration of such an alternative approach has a wide historical relevance. It is noteworthy that even historians with Marxist sympathies, who might have been expected to have adhered most closely to materialist interpretations, have become increasingly interested in religion. As the editors of an important recent volume put it:

> The cultural revolution of the 1960s has perhaps made socialists more ready to admit the power and autonomy of the imaginary, to consider belief systems as a *primum mobile* which structure and constitute action rather than passively reflecting it. It has made us more sensitive to the ways in which belief acts, not so much as a reflection of material interests, but as an independent cultural force.[2]

Third, a development of the previous question is to ask how religion shaped the general pattern of British history in the nineteenth and twentieth centuries. Set in a wider historical context, Britain appears distinctive and unusual in respect of its political and social stability. Between the mid-nineteenth and the mid-twentieth centuries France and Russia experienced violent revolutions; the United States and Spain were ravaged by civil wars; Germany and Italy were 'unified' and, later, succumbed to dictatorships; and the Habsburg and Ottoman Empires disintegrated. Earlier generations of historians from Elie Halévy to E. P. Thompson have argued that religion in general and Methodism in particular were of crucial importance in preventing revolution in Britain in the late eighteenth and early nineteenth centuries. Our present concern is not so much with that now rather hackneyed debate, but with a later period during which the rise of nationalism in Europe added the threat of territorial fragmentation to that of political and social up-heaval. How does an understanding of religious history help to explain why in Scotland, Wales and the north-east of Ireland cultural and political identification with Britain continued to prove stronger than more localized nationalism? How did religion contribute to that high point of national self-confidence which saw the acquisition of a world-wide empire, and the dogged waging of two total wars? How, on the other hand, was religion related to the most dramatic discontinuity in the history of the United Kingdom state, the ending in 1921 of the Union with the twenty-six counties of southern and western Ireland?

Finally, how satisfactory is it to accept the conventional view of the twentieth century as a period of inexorable 'secularization' in which religion became more and more marginal to community and national life? If Britain is compared with the United States, Poland, or South Africa, or, within our own frame of reference, with Ireland, broad generalizations about the decline of religion in the modern world become less satisfactory. To what extent is it valid to think in terms of changes in the nature of religion rather than of its retreat to the wings of the historical stage? And in what ways was the history of religion in twentieth-century Britain a reflection of specific features of the national experience?

These groups of questions set an agenda for the book and they will be addressed in turn in the chapters that follow. Chapters 2, 3 and 4 are concerned with different aspects of the context of belief, initially through an examination of the formative influences on Victorian reli-gion; and subsequently through an analysis of the varieties of official and unofficial religion and the encounters between them. This discussion will also begin to address the second question posed above by drawing connections to social and community identities. Chapter 5 opens the second part of the book in which links to other processes of historical change are more explicitly addressed, first through a number of verbal 'snapshots' of the situation in the mid-nineteenth century, and then in subsequent chapters by way of an examination of politics, culture, imperial mentalities, and the impact of war. In this analysis discussion of the relationship between religion and identity will be developed, and the implications pursued for the nature of 'Britishness', the place of Ireland, Scotland and Wales within the United Kingdom, and national responses to the wider world. The material here collected will lay the foundation for exploration in the concluding chapter of the final set of questions relating to secularization.

Historical periodization should never be rigid especially when, as in this book, we are concerned with currents of belief and influence that did not abruptly appear or disappear. Nevertheless the chronological limits indicated in the title provide some indication of the shape of the argument. As we shall note in more detail in subsequent chapters, 1843 was a highwater mark in the prominence of religion in the early Victorian period. The Church of Scotland was disrupted, the Repeal campaign in Ireland reached its climax, controversy raged over the role of the churches in education, and spiritual concerns loomed large in the discussion of social problems and international relations. Such were some indications of the formative influence religion was to have on national life during the next century. The year 1945 will be a much more familiar date to the secular historian, marking the last great triumph of the British Empire, and presaging the decline of the structure of interlinked religious and political ideas with which it had been associated.

The remainder of this chapter is designed to provide a theoretical and historiographical explanation of the terms used and the approach adopted. The reader who is content to take this discussion as read – at least for the present – may prefer to skip these sections and proceed directly to Chapter 2.

1. APPROACHING THE HISTORY OF RELIGION

Historians of religion have been noticeably coy about defining the scope of their enquiries. Peter Lake confesses himself 'no more capable of defining religion than . . . of defining history' while Patrick Collinson views the question 'what is religion?' as one 'with which anthropologists are more familiar than historians'.[3] Such caution is understandable, but it means that once the scholar ventures beyond the defined territory of ecclesiastical institutions, the ground covered by traditional 'church history', he or she does not encounter any clear frontiers. This can have considerable advantages, and is certainly a check against the simplistic pigeonholing of subtle human beliefs and experiences, but it can also be a source of confusion. Moreover, it has been observed that historians' assumptions about the nature of religion have far-reaching implications for the character of their work, which are all the more insidious if they remain unspoken.[4] Accordingly, with the intention of providing something of a conceptual map for the chapters that follow, we shall briefly examine some influential definitions of religion as they have been applied to historical enquiry. The definitional and conceptual problems to be addressed lie at the interface of at least six disciplines in addition to history: anthropology, philosophy, psychology, religious studies, sociology and theology. Accordingly any viewpoint will be a personal and potentially debatable one, inevitably simplifying some of the issues and reducing complex ambiguities in the hope of at least achieving an approach that is comprehensible and a tool that is usable for historical analysis.

In classical Latin the word *religio* was used of reverence for the gods or holy things, a usage revived in the context of Christian humanism in the fifteenth century. The effect of the division of western Christendom in the sixteenth century was to give the word its application to specific institutionalized bodies, Protestant or Roman Catholic 'religions'.[5] However, such frameworks of belief and ecclesiastical authority did not operate in isolation in early modern Britain: under the 1688 political settlement 'the Protestant religion', in a Presbyterian form in Scotland and an Anglican one elsewhere, played a key role in the structures of the state and local communities. 'Religion' thus came in effect to be viewed as the ideological cement of society as well as a specific theological framework of belief. The Church of England's 1662 Holy Communion liturgy spoke of 'godly and quiet' governance and linked 'the punishment of wickedness and vice' closely to 'the maintenance of thy [God's] true religion and virtue'. In 1828 the Duke of Newcastle, a staunch political conservative, wrote of the necessity

> above all things in Religion . . . to have a standard and fixed point, that standard I consider to be Christ and that fixed point the Church of England inculcating to the letter and the purest spirit the doctrine of our Saviour and the whole word of God.[6]

Newcastle subsequently attributed the political and social turmoil of the early 1830s to changes in the religious constitution of the country. He held that political stability could only be restored through a return to 'the revered Religion of our wise forefathers.'[7]

Meanwhile, however, alternative perceptions were gaining ground, stimulated most directly by the Evangelical Revival of the eighteenth century. 'Religion' became less a matter of adherence to an institutional and social structure; more a matter of personal conviction and experience. Thus a Methodist evangelist in Norfolk in the 1830s wrote of one of his converts who had professed to be 'a very godly man' that 'he had never . . . had any light, or religious feeling' before his conversion.[8] It was religion in this subjective, intensely personal sense that the American evangelist Charles Finney had in mind when he published his

Lectures of Revivals of Religion (1835), which was tremendously influential in Britain. In articulating his own understanding of religion the Duke of Newcastle had derided evangelical preachers as 'spiritual upstarts'; but by 1892 the definitional boot was on the other foot in a *Punch* cartoon in which a disillusioned Methodist local preacher announces to the vicar that 'For the future, I chucks all religion, and I goes to Church'.[9] Perceptions still differed, however, as expressed in an exchange in one of J. M. Barrie's novels, published in 1892 but set earlier in the century, in which the Auld Licht minister's mother advises him on the kind of woman he should marry:

> 'A truly religious wife would be a great help to you.'
> 'Religious,' Gavin repeated slowly. 'Yes, but some people are religious without speaking of it. If a woman is good she is religious.'[10]

The personal experiential understanding of religion profoundly influenced one of the earliest social scientific approaches to the problem. In 1901–2 William James, a psychologist and philosopher at Harvard University, delivered the Gifford Lectures in Edinburgh entitled *The Varieties of Religious Experience*. He argued that the starting point for the study of religion must be individual spirituality rather than ecclesiastical structures or schemes of dogmatic theology. James defined religion as 'the feelings, acts, and experiences of individual men in their solitude, as far as they apprehend themselves to stand in relation to whatever they may consider the divine'.[11] The subsequent lectures focused on correspondingly individualistic aspects of religion, such as the 'sick soul', conversion and saintliness, and had very little to say about ecclesiastical institutions and the social implications of belief.

A decade later, on the other hand, Émile Durkheim's seminal sociological study, *The Elementary Forms of the Religious Life*, dwelt rather on the underlying reality of social entities and on religion as a development from them. He defined 'religion' as 'the system of symbols by means of which Society becomes conscious of itself; it is the way of thinking characteristic of collective existence'. (Examples of such 'systems of symbols' might be the rituals expressing the dignity and coherence of a state, such as Trooping the Colour and the opening of Parliament, or the regular customs marking out the lives of institutions and families, from school speech days to Christmas lunch.) Durkheim also offered a more specific development of his definition, but one that still emphasized the communal nature of religion:

A religion is a unified system of beliefs and practices relative to sacred things, that is to say, things set apart and forbidden – beliefs and practices which unite into one single moral community called a Church, all those who adhere to them.[12]

Thus Durkheim, by exploring the manner in which religion cemented social ties, seemed to be giving a new twist in a scientific context to eighteenth-century and earlier ideas of religion as the lynch-pin of order and cohesion in human affairs.

In some respects James's and Durkheim's approaches were at opposite poles, the former emphasizing individual experience, the latter collective belief and practice. However, they both represented an approach to the understanding of religion that left transcendent theological questions open or even consigned them to irrelevance. At the same time they provide a theoretical justification for extending the study of religion well beyond the analysis of formal religious institutions, which may have little connection with the 'experience of individual men in their solitude' and only be a small part of the 'system of symbols by which society becomes conscious of itself'.

A further important approach emerged from the thought of the German theologian Paul Tillich (1886–1965) who defined religion as 'being grasped by an ultimate concern', by which he meant 'taking something with ultimate seriousness, unconditional seriousness', 'demanding a decision of our whole personality'. As with James's and Durkheim's approaches this was something much wider than 'an organized group with its clergy, scripture and dogma'. In particular Tillich included within his definition of 'ultimate concern' ideologies such as nationalism or Communism 'which claim the loyalty or veneration of their followers with the intensity sometimes of the theistic religions'. These he termed 'quasi-religions' or 'secular faiths', causes with an ideological structure and cultural power analogous to recognized religions, which became the mainspring of the actions of communities and individuals.[13]

Accordingly we see narrow definitions of religion in terms of specific ecclesiastical structures co-existing with broader definitions which relate religion to personal experience, 'society', or other forms of intense ideological conviction. This provides a framework in which the historian can operate, one which may be understood in terms of a series of widening definitions. In the narrowest sense, that of traditional ecclesiastical history, 'religion' denotes a particular defined institutional structure; in other words, in the case of Christianity, a church. This body defines in some way the nature of the beliefs to which its members are expected to subscribe, beliefs which, in general, relate to the deity and a systematic understanding of the supernatural. Churches may vary greatly in their size and nature of their organization, from single congregations adhering to strict autonomy from outside authority, acknowledging no superior but God, to complex hierarchical bodies such as the Church of England and the Roman Catholic Church. For a person to be 'religious' in this sense they need to be identified in some verifiable way with a church, whether through formal membership or by means of attendance. There is likely to be an ambivalence towards supernatural claims made outside official channels, memorably expressed by Bishop Butler when he told John Wesley that 'the pretending to extraordinary revelations of the Holy Ghost is a horrid thing, a very horrid thing'.[14] Ecclesiastical institutions, having established themselves as the interpreters and facilitators of the relationship between humankind and God, will not welcome perceived manifestations of the supernatural which challenge their authority and do not fit into their existing conceptual frameworks. Religion in this narrow institutional sense is termed in this book 'official religion'.

In Britain such official religion can also be characterized in broader terms as 'Christianity', the sum of churches, the perceived but not defined common ground between the different institutional bodies that profess 'Christian' belief, as opposed to other major world religions. The concept of 'Christianity' may also identify the dominant religious ethos of the whole society and culture. The tightness with which Christianity is defined has changed over time: in the eighteenth century in Britain it was readily equated with 'Protestantism', excluding Roman Catholics, or even (in England) the Church of England, excluding non-Anglicans. By the later nineteenth century the concept had become sufficiently fluid for it to be compatible with the toleration of minorities of atheists, agnostics and adherents of other world religions, notably Jews. During the twentieth century the concept of Britain as a 'Christian' country arguably began to give way to a perception of it as religiously pluralistic. With reference to the period with which we are concerned, however, 'Christianity' serves as the most appropriate general characterization.

Christianity, however, has not been expressed only in official institutionalized terms, and those professing to be committed Christians have not always been directly affiliated to churches. Such people perhaps have held an individualistic understanding of religious experience, or claimed to have received direct divine revelation which has placed them at odds with ecclesiastical authority. Such 'rebels' against existing churches may in due course be the founders of new organized structures: the institutionalization and formalization of Methodism in the late eighteenth and early nineteenth centuries is a good example of this process. Thus the unofficial became official.

At the same time there was a wider spectrum of what we shall call in this book 'unofficial religion', constituting a broad range of beliefs, still with supernatural references, but going well beyond the framework of orthodox Christianity. Such forms of religion are more readily observed than categorized. There is a very real danger of giving a loaded application to terms such as 'superstition', 'magic', and 'popular religion'. Historians, moreover, have been somewhat over-enthusiastic about drawing firm distinctions of uncertain validity.[15] Nevertheless some cautious distinctions can be made. 'Magic' was defined by Tillich as 'the practice of influencing living beings or not living beings without using physical causality'.[16] Its scope is thus perceived as limited, not necessarily implying any belief in a deity or an integrating general structure of ultimate concern. A 'superstition' can be similarly characterized as a limited and isolated belief: the practice of touching wood or reading a horoscope may well occur quite independently of other aspects of an individual's beliefs and worldview.

Such distinctions should not be rigidly applied. For example, although in theological terms there is a clear distinction to be drawn between a prayer directed to God and a spell directed at a material person or object, the working of the individual consciousness in a given historical context was more ambivalent. Tillich noted that 'magic elements creep into all religions, even the highest', a view supported by Keith Thomas's interpretation of the Reformation as an endeavour to purge the magical from religion.[17] Conversely, ideas labelled as magical or superstitious may well acquire a religious quality when they are part of a wider structure of belief. Thus observance of Hallowe'en can be anything from an opportunity for playing with pumpkins to an expression of deeply-held 'occult' convictions. Research on superstition in the 1960s suggested that there were indeed those who adhered to such 'alternative' frameworks of belief.[18] There are thus good *a priori* grounds for thinking that in the more distant past such unofficial religion existed. However, the ideas of relatively poorly educated people, such as the nineteenth-century Irish peasantry, have been vulnerable to dismissive treatment, associated with the impact of a literate culture with rationally integrated structures of theology on an oral culture whose modes of understanding may be no less coherent on their own terms, but are very differently expressed. For example, in June 1832 a schoolteacher derided the credulity of the 'lower classes' who had transmitted sticks and turf across the length and breadth of Ireland as a protection against cholera. But for the people concerned this form of communication was presumably far more meaningful than the written word and was a consistent part of a state of mind in which immediate concrete divine intervention was readily expected.[19] One person's 'credulity' or superstition could be a central part of another's religion.

Further broadening of the definition of religion employs the ideas of Tillich and Durkheim to move beyond relationships to the divine and supernatural to incorporate other areas of human ideology and experience which seem to be of equal or even greater social importance and emotional power, and will in this book be termed 'quasi-religion'. The concept of ultimate concern expresses the individualistic and ideological approach to such beliefs, which are often articulated in language suggesting unconditional commitment. The Irish national anthem is a good example of this much wider phenomenon:

> Soldiers are we, whose lives are pledged to Ireland;
> Some have come from a land beyond the wave;
> Sworn to be free, no more our ancient sireland
> Shall shelter the despot or the slave.
> Tonight we man the *bearna baoghail*
> In Erin's cause, come woe or weal,
> 'Mid cannon's roar and rifle's peal
> We'll chant a soldier's song.[20]

Durkheim's concept of a system of symbols emphasizes rather the collective dimension of quasi-religion, the rituals and practices that give society its cohesion. Just as ultimate concern may give rise to language reminiscent of official religion the expression and assertion of such ties may come to parallel its practice. A notable example of this is in the use of the sense of the 'sacred', the idea that certain objects, places, or even people, have a special significance and hence are set apart from the outside world for particular functions. This is a particular feature of the more Catholic forms of official Christianity which accord reverence to church buildings, images, relics and the priesthood, but can also be noted in national and communal life even when divorced from an explicit Christian context. Instances of this include the status accorded to flags and military insignia; the placing of monuments in public places; and the use of processions in drawing attention to the distinctiveness and apartness of royalty and the holders of civic and public office.

We have thus identified three broad categories – official religion, unofficial religion, and quasi-religion[21] – but have emphasized the extent to which they merge into each other in a manner that makes the inflexible application of such terms inappropriate. Moreover particular events and circumstances can validly be understood in a variety of different ways. For example, a marriage in church is at one and the same time a manifestation of the theological and liturgical convictions of official Christianity; a focus for a variety of unofficial beliefs and practices; and a powerful ritual expressing certain profound convictions and social solidarities. An important historical instance was the burial of the Unknown Warrior at Westminster Abbey on Armistice Day 1920. This was both a powerful quasi-religious affirmation of the solidarity of British society after the trauma of war; an expression of a range of unofficial religious beliefs about the war and those who had lost their lives; and a ritual instigated by ecclesiastics seeking to bring these diverse spiritualities under the umbrella of official Christianity. The ambiguities were well symbolized by the location of the dead soldier's grave, immediately inside the main doors of the Abbey, where the inside world of official religion met the exterior ones of unofficial and quasi-religion.[22]

Faced with such complexity, historians have been reluctant to define and categorize. At the same time, the malleable nature of theoretical understandings of religion has given scope for great versatility of scholarly endeavour: as Rosemary O'Day has put it, 'Religious history is a compendium of many games'.[23] Historians of the early modern period, studying an era when the social and political significance of organized religion was undeniable, have played these games with particular facility. While study of ecclesiastical institutions continued, Keith Thomas's *Religion and the Decline of Magic* (1971) opened up the study of forms of unofficial religion that had only very loose affinities with orthodox Christianity. Others brought the techniques of social history to bear on the analysis of organized religious structures or sought to earth the historical study of religion in the investigation of ordinary human communities. The result has been at times to make religion appear as the pivot of the history of society.[24]

In relation to the centuries since the Reformation, the sphere of religion might at first sight appear a more limited one. The tendency of much historical writing has been to examine the development of a particular Christian tradition largely in isolation from its wider social context. The traditionally celebratory nature of accounts such as Bernard Ward's multi-volume history of the Roman Catholic Church in the late eighteenth and early nineteenth centuries[25] has given way to cooler and more critical evaluations. However, even relatively recent work – for example, Owen Chadwick's *Victorian Church* (2 vols, London, 1966, 1970) – has still been exposed to the charge of perpetuating complacent official denominational myths.[26] Nevertheless, an increasing number of scholars have begun to widen and redirect the focus of enquiry by examining the social impact of official religion and exploring the varieties of unofficial religion prevalent in the eighteenth, nineteenth and twentieth centuries.[27] Investigations of this kind have stimulated some social historians to place religion much closer to the centre of their analysis than had hitherto been the case.[28] At the same time religion has also come to be perceived as a central force in intellectual and political history.[29]

The intention in subsequent chapters is to summarize and build on the conclusions of such recent work. At the same time the objective is further to test the boundaries of religious history by tracing the development of forms of quasi-religion in the nineteenth and twentieth centuries. It will be suggested that such structures of ultimate concern and symbolic meaning were often in Britain and Ireland not so much a reaction against pre-existing forms of official and unofficial religion, but rather an evolution from them. In order to illustrate and explain this point further we now turn to discuss one specific example of a quasi-religion which will become a particular focus of discussion in the later chapters of this book.

2. RELIGION AND NATIONHOOD

In relating religion to nationhood one is obliged to engage with a further complex range of concepts and definitions. In particular, 'nationalism' has attracted widespread historiographical attention, which has under-lined the difficulty of subjecting the word to precise and generally agreed definition. It would be unrealistic even to begin to survey all the relevant literature here, but some general points need to be made before the discussion is specifically related to the history of religion.

'Nationalism' has been generally distinguished by historians from relatively diffuse and limited states of mind which can be conveniently labelled 'national identity' and 'patriotism'.[30] At its most basic level national identity can be perceived as simply a neutral reference point identifying the nation to which an individual or community belongs. Historically it stretches back a long way, certainly to the medieval era, to the point at which people began to define themselves as 'English' or

'French'. Thomas Arnold, Headmaster of Rugby and briefly Regius Professor of Modern History at Oxford in the early 1840s, put it like this:

> We, this great English nation, whose race and language are now overrunning the earth from one end of it to the other, – we were born when the white horse of the Saxons had established his dominion from the Tweed to the Tamar. So far we can trace our blood, our language, the name and actual divisions of our country, the beginnings of some of our institutions. So far our national identity extends, so far is history modern, for it treats of a life which was then, and is not yet extinguished.[31]

As the tone of this quotation illustrates, the assertion of national identity potentially implied the erection of barriers and a spirit of exclusiveness: for example, Arnold himself believed strongly that the Irish were an entirely separate race from the English.[32] When identities overlapped or were held simultaneously such strident assertion of them could lead to tensions and conflicts within and between individuals. The seriousness of these depended on the context: for most inhabitants of England, in the nineteenth century as at the present day, a sense of being simultaneously 'English' and 'British' presented few practical problems. In Scotland and Wales, and above all in Ireland, the question of whether to identify primarily with the smaller national entity or with the all-encompassing 'British' state was a much more acute and divisive one.

Patriotism, defined by the *Oxford English Dictionary* as defending or being zealous for one's 'country's prosperity, freedom or rights' is also a more complicated concept than it might appear at first sight. In some respects the idea would seem to be summed up by the cosy complacency of an early nineteenth-century children's hymn:

> Now pray we for our country,
> That England long may be
> The holy and the happy –
> The beautiful and free:[33]

For others it has been perceived as relating particularly to the promotion of national interests in the international sphere.[34] However, in the late eighteenth and early nineteenth centuries patriotism was associated with more internally divisive resonances, being the label given to radical political programmes which at the time were far from attracting national consensus. It was in this context that Samuel Johnson offered his celebrated definition of patriotism (1775) as 'the last refuge of the scoundrel', and a newspaper entitled *The Patriot* (1792) saw its purpose as being to uphold liberty, 'a reform of abuses, and an *equal Representation of the people*' against alleged 'gigantic strides to despotism and arbitrary power'.[35] A contrasting use of the word is encountered in a pamphlet of 1839 by John Cumming, a Presbyterian minister, who perceived patriotism as missionary endeavour to convert the un-churched population of Britain to Christianity.[36] Within the political sphere too the concept proved malleable: in 1867 Disraeli spoke of the Conservative Party as being 'supported by the fervour of patriotism', by which he clearly meant something rather different from the Radicals.[37] Patriotism, in sum, was a fluid and versatile sentiment which could readily be redefined, and defies simplistic categorization. Linda Colley has recently observed:

> Becoming a patriot was a political act, and often a multi-faceted and dynamic one. We need to stop confusing patriotism with simple conservatism, or smothering it with damning and dismissive references to chauvinism and jingoism. Quite as much as any other human activity, the patriotism of the past requires flexible, sensitive and above all, imaginative reconstruction.[38]

The concept of 'nationalism' has been taken to imply a more focused set of attitudes and actions, although here too precise definition has proved difficult. The word itself was, unlike 'patriotism', not widely used in nineteenth-century Britain, and even in relation to continental Europe it sometimes has the appearance of an ideal category imposed by historians rather than a concept readily espoused and understood by contemporaries. In the broadest terms it might be defined as conscious and deliberate efforts, by political, economic, social or cultural means, to develop and assert a perceived national identity, generally through the sustaining or creation of a corresponding nation state. Its emergence is usually located in a particular historical context, late eighteenth- and early nineteenth-century Europe, where, it is held, the requisite preconditions for its development were first in place. These conditions included the emergence of 'modern' bureaucratic state structures; a consciousness following the French Revolution of the sovereign people as a political entity; improved communications and growing economic interdependence between regions; more widespread literacy leading to the standardization and imposition of national languages; and the cultural impact of Romanticism asserting a national spirit in literature, art, and music, in contrast to the cosmopolitanism of the Enlightenment era. Within this general framework particular historians and political scientists have developed distinctive constructions and emphases. Two recent examples include John Breuilly's perception of nationalism as 'primarily . . . a form of politics' and Benedict Anderson's more cultural conception of the nation as an 'imagined community', and nationalism as the assertion of a 'fraternity that makes it possible over the last two centuries, for so many millions of people, not so much to kill, as willingly to die for such limited imaginings.' [39]

Writers on nationalism have thus in practice not separated definition of the concept from explanation of how, when, and why it emerged. Accordingly discussion on whether nationalism existed in other historical contexts – say ancient Greece, the early Islamic Middle East, or sixteenth- and seventeenth-century England – is likely to be foreclosed by the assertion that it cannot have done because the requisite historical conditions were not in place. Such an approach is defensible in that it averts the danger of comparative analysis sliding into meaningless generalization, but it also precludes the open-minded investigation of relevant parallels and precedents. More specifically the continental European orientation of much work on nationalism – focused, for example, on German writers, French politicians, and Italian revolutionaries – has perpetuated the implicit assumption that nationalism was weak or non-existent in Britain/England, especially because of the absence of such radical manifestations as the revolutions of 1848.[40] By contrast, nationalism has much more readily been identified as a force in Irish history, although often in a manner somewhat detached from the wider European context.[41]

As long ago as 1926 the American scholar Carlton J. H. Hayes set out a case for viewing nationalism in religious terms. He wrote of the underlying influence of man's fundamental 'religious sense' and suggested that nationalism paralleled many features of organized religion, including unconditional commitment and ritual observance. It was syncretistic, drawing on the extensive nominal Christianity of the western world. Hayes concluded that 'Nationalism has a large number of particularly quarrelsome sects, but as a whole it is the latest and nearest approach to a world-religion'.[42] It is strange that such insights were not taken up by subsequent students of nationalism. A more widespread approach in recent books has been to characterize nationalism 'as a kind of modern substitute for religion', while perplexity is expressed about the instances where organized Christianity and nationalism (for example, in Ireland and South Africa) have flourished in the same countries.[43] If, however, nationalism is perceived as developing out of religion rather than straightforwardly replacing it, such apparent anomalies become much more comprehensible.

There are, moreover, important points of contact between the manner in which nationalism has been conceptualized and the more general definitions of religion discussed above. If nationalism, at least in its more developed forms, is perceived as an ideology that can inspire the life and death commitment of millions of men and women it is indeed legitimate to describe it as a quasi-religion of ultimate concern in the terms of Tillich's definition. At the same time nationalism has also been held to have generated extensive ritual and symbolic expressions of the nation which can been seen as religious in Durkheimian terms. There is considerable evidence to support such an interpretation of German nationalism in the period between 1870 and 1945.[44] Nationalism indeed has recently been interpreted as manifesting all the functional dimensions that can be attributed to religion, namely ritual, myth, experience, ethical implications, doctrine, organization, and material statements in art and architecture.[45]

There are further reasons for believing that a fruitful avenue to the investigation of national consciousness in Britain and Ireland is likely to be by way of religion. The character of their organized religion is one of the most obvious factors distinguishing the British from many continental Europeans, and from the majority of the Irish. In the Catholic countries of Europe the universal claims of Rome could make religion appear an anti-national force and nationalism was apt to be correspondingly secular in character. In Britain (as in Holland and Scandinavia) the legacy of the Reformation was a religious framework less readily susceptible to such reaction. Indeed anti-Catholicism of a Protestant rather than secular kind was one of the most conspicuous expressions of national sentiment, which, during the eighteenth century, served to undergird British identity.[46] This religious basis for the nation was reinforced by a sense of being specially favoured by God: for instance in 1839 George Croly argued that Roman Catholics should not have been admitted to Parliament because, 'There is the strongest reason to believe, that as Judaea was chosen for the especial guardianship of the original Revelation; England has been chosen for the especial guardianship of Christianity'.[47] Moreover Anglicanism as a variety of Christianity did not exist outside Britain and Ireland until it was exported to the colonies and the Empire, but within these islands it enjoyed considerable prominence, above all in the links between the state and the Church of England. The national divisions of 'Greater Britain' were also associated with distinctive religious identities. The Presbyterianism of

Scotland and Ulster and the Nonconformity of Wales were associated with noticeable cultural and political differences, albeit subsumed within an overarching Protestantism. The Roman Catholicism of much of Ireland pointed to a more fundamental divergence. Detailed analysis and refinement of this picture will follow in later chapters.

At least in the earlier part of the period examined in this book, if contemporaries themselves understood anything at all by the use of the word 'nationalism' in a British context, they were likely to give it a religious application, relating to special divine choice or privileging of a particular nation. Such explicit contemporary usage need not necessarily limit the historian, but it is important and suggestive evidence. George Stanley Faber, in a theological treatise published in 1836, attributed the origin of the concept to the seventeenth-century philosopher John Locke and defined it as, 'The election of certain whole nations into the pale of the visible Church Catholic, which Election, however, relates purely to their privileged condition in this world, extending not to their collective eternal state in another world'.[48] This was presumably the idea the anti-Catholic leader Hugh McNeile had in mind when he delivered a speech entitled 'Nationalism in Religion' to the Protestant Association in May 1839. He called for Christian endeavours to support the nation, particularly in resisting the 'papal system'. Following Faber and Locke, McNeile referred to Chapter 9 of Paul's Epistle to the Romans in which the apostle wrote (vv. 1–5) of his sorrow for the Israelites, his 'brethren' and 'kinsmen by race', the heirs of the covenants and promises of God. Jesus himself had wept over Jerusalem and it followed that 'we cannot allow our spirituality as Christians entirely to supersede our patriotism as Britons'.[49] More commonly, however, the religious resonances of the word 'nationalism' were negative ones: in 1873 John Henry Newman asserted that Christianity abhors 'pure nationalism', which he associated rather with the theocracy of the Islamic Caliphate, a system 'as congenial to the barbarian as Christianity is congenial to man civilized'.[50] In 1880 the author of a hostile assessment of the Elizabethan Church wrote of it using persecution to maintain 'the new system of nationalism in religion'.[51]

In conclusion, we can enunciate some hypotheses which will be more fully explained, substantiated and developed in the chapters that follow. Religion, it is suggested, was an important building block of national identity in Britain and Ireland. Moreover it was often in a religious context that explicitly nationalist ideas were stated. Meanwhile, it will be argued, religious organizations had a substantial impact on society during the nineteenth and early twentieth centuries. Their endeavours were not always, or even usually, successful in terms of the extension of official religion on its own terms, but they did diffuse very widely a generalized religious consciousness of an unofficial or quasi-religious kind. Among much of the population this state of mind did not imply institutionalized or theologically defined commitment, but it did indicate a receptivity to religious language and emotions. In such a context varieties of nationalism that expressed themselves in broadly religious terms proved to have a powerful appeal. The merging of religion and nationalism reached its climax in the early twentieth century as the United Kingdom engaged in a major war and Ireland experienced revolution and partition. Such are the bare bones of an argument which must now be fleshed out in greater detail.

2

A STRANGE WARMING?
The formation of Victorian religion

This chapter constitutes a brief survey of the major forces that shaped the contours of religious and national life in Britain and Ireland in the period leading up to the mid-nineteenth century. It is designed to provide essential background and context for subsequent more detailed analysis of later developments. In the first two sections an account will be given first of evangelicalism and then of Catholicism. These were the most dynamic varieties of official Christianity in the early nineteenth century, and, both in positive and negative respects, they had a particularly formative impact on the period that followed. In the final section of the chapter the preceding discussion will be set in the context of the wider development of religious and national life in the early nineteenth century.

1. EVANGELICALISM

The conventional version of the history of evangelicalism takes us back to a May evening in 1738 when John Wesley went unwillingly to a religious meeting at Aldersgate Street in the City of London. He heard a reading from Martin Luther's preface to the Epistle to the Romans. Wesley's own journal records what happened:

> About a quarter before nine, while he was describing the change which God works in the heart through faith in Christ, I felt my heart strangely warmed. I felt that I did trust in Christ, Christ alone for salvation; and an assurance was given me that he had taken away *my* sins, even *mine*, and saved me from the law of sin and death.[1]

Wesley's strange warming remains one of the most familiar expressions of that movement which became known as the Evangelical Revival. It symbolized a new mood and style in Christianity which he did an immense amount to promulgate himself. Wesley's own famous description of the experience thus became an inspirational version of a central feature of subsequent evangelical self-consciousness and spiritual experience. The significance of this event, like that of many other perceived turning points in history, can, however, easily be exaggerated. In 1738 Wesley was already in his mid-thirties, an ordained Anglican clergyman, and someone who had for many years been striving for more intense experience of God and a zealous Christian ministry. His conversion was certainly a new beginning for him, releasing those formidable energies that contributed so greatly to the development of Methodism, but it was much more a fulfilment than a repudiation of his past life. Moreover the movement with which Wesley was associated was already gathering momentum in 1738 quite independently of his own contribution: the leading Welsh revivalist Howell Harris later pungently observed that 'all knew Mr Whitefield was the first field-preacher in England, and the work was in the fields in Wales long before'.[2] Indeed the tide that was flowing transcended the influence and control of any single individual.

What was 'the Evangelical Revival' and how do we explain it? 'Evangelical' is a problematic word which has a range of meanings in different historical contexts, but it is used here to denote a form of Protestantism where strong emphasis is placed upon the need for conversion, which might be gradual, but was frequently virtually instantaneous. Whereas John Wesley apparently remained sufficiently self-possessed to note the time, other converts had much more dramatic experiences. In February 1742 a young woman became very distressed during the minister's sermon at Cambuslang church near Glasgow and was taken to the manse in a semi-hysterical state, saying that her sins were so many that Christ would not receive her. Following exhortation and prayer, however, she said:

> Christ says to me, 'He will never leave me nor forsake me . . . he is telling me, He hath cast all my Sins behind his back. . . . My Beloved is the chief among ten thousand, yea he is altogether lovely. O Sirs, will ye come to Christ . . .'[3]

This is a good illustration of the normative features of an evangelical conversion, in which an acute and oppressive sense of sinfulness gave way to an equally intense experience of forgiveness and of personal encounter with Christ. Converts might fear hell and judgement but their deepest emotion was positive realization of the love of Christ. This love was perceived as having been expressed supremely in Christ's death on the Cross, held to constitute an atoning sacrifice diverting God's wrath from the sins of humankind. This was the theology expressed in one of the greatest hymns written by John Wesley's younger brother Charles:

> And can it be that I should gain
> An interest in the Saviour's blood?
> Died he for me, who caused his pain;
> For me who him to death pursued?
> Amazing love! how can it be,
> That thou, my God, shouldst die for me![4]

Evangelicals were like other Protestants in maintaining a deep reverence for the Bible, but differed from them in having a particularly powerful desire to share the Gospel message and experience with others.[5] (Evangel*icals* were thus often active evangel*ists*, proclaimers of the Gospel, but the two words must not be confused.)

The phrase 'Evangelical Revival' is conventionally used with reference to a period in the second quarter of the eighteenth century when evangelical ideas and religious experience emerged with considerable vigour in a wide range of English- and German-speaking countries over a geographical range from Eastern Europe to the American frontier. In an American context the alternative label of the 'Great Awakening' is also used. The word 'revivalism' has more specific connotations. This implies a particularly intense form of evangelicalism, in which numerous people share a conversion experience at the same time, perhaps in the same meeting or service. This may be accompanied by powerful emotional, spiritual and psychological effects such as weeping or ecstasy. For example, in 1835 at Bala in North Wales 'strong men [fell] down dead like logs of wood, their limbs stiffened, their eyes glaring'.[6] The initial revivalist movements of the 1730s and 1740s eventually lost momentum, but there was an important second wave in the 1790s which lasted into the nineteenth century. Similar phenomena continued to recur, notably in the 1830s and 1840s, in 1859, in a spiritual stirring that was especially strong in Ulster, and in the Welsh revival of 1904–5. Accordingly although the original Great Awakening had occurred more than a century before the opening of the period surveyed in this book, its continuing legacy and inspiration is very relevant to our concerns.

The broader use of the word 'revival' begs questions: it implies that the religious movement of the eighteenth century was a recovery of a form of Christianity that had been in eclipse since the era of the Reformation, or perhaps even since the early church. In fact while it indeed drew on an eclectic range of influences from the past, it combined them with genuinely innovative features, and resulted in patterns of religious experience, theology and observance that, taken as a whole, had no obvious historical precedents. Some threads of influence can be traced back to the Reformation as mediated particularly through the English Puritanism of the seventeenth century, but evangelicals were generally much more activist in their outlook than the Puritans had been and enjoyed substantially greater assurance of the reality of their faith and their salvation. Even where Calvinist influence remained strong it did not produce the kind of introspective fatalism that fostered religious doubts and inhibited evangelistic effort.[7] Moreover the beliefs of John Wesley and his immediate followers were Arminian rather than Calvinist, which means that they held that salvation was in theory available to all humanity, not only the elect. Wesley had spent his formative years in high church Anglican circles, where close-knit voluntary societies for moral and spiritual discipline had attracted extensive support in the early eighteenth century. There were direct personal links between these societies and early Methodism.[8] Meanwhile in Scotland and Ireland the evangelical movements of the eighteenth century drew on currents of intense spiritual experience within the Presbyterian tradition that can be traced back to the Six Mile Water revival in Ulster in 1625.[9] Such diverse indigenous influences were combined with further currents from outside the British Isles, from the contemporary movements in North America, and equally significantly in continental Europe. Indeed the first stirrings of revival have been traced to Silesia, and the Moravians significantly identified a religious group in Britain with the name of the region of Central Europe from which its initial adherents had originated. It was at a Moravian meeting that John Wesley was converted and he shortly afterwards visited the movement's headquarters at Herrnhut in Saxony.[10]

Just as numerous streams of influence flowed together to produce the river of the Evangelical Revival, it subsequently divided to form an equally complex delta of influences. In institutional terms evangelicalism was not in itself an organized form of religion, but rather a mode of thinking and acting. A political analogy may be helpful here. Socialism as a broad movement has generated numerous institutions, sometimes at odds with each other, and in similar fashion evangelicalism had a variegated impact on the structures of British religion. It is true that the evangelical movement was directly linked to the formation of a whole new family of denominations, the Methodists, and, in the late eighteenth and early nineteenth centuries, it would be true to say that all Methodists were evangelicals. But the reverse was *not* true: not all evangelicals were Methodists. Methodism was in its origins a society within the Church of England, and other Anglicans became evangelicals seemingly independently of Methodist influence. Evangelicals were also to be found in existing dissenting bodies such as the Baptists and the Independents. These groups taken as a whole were increasingly influenced by the new movement. In Scotland and Ireland evangelicalism was frequently contained under the umbrella of Presbyterianism, although institutional splits did arise from its influence. The point is illustrated in Figure 1. The variety of the institutions that mediated evangelicalism to society themselves heightened regional and national diversity. The Anglican 'Clapham Sect' in south London was very different in ethos from Cornish Methodism and from Nonconformity in Birmingham and Leeds, let alone the Presbyterianism of the Scottish Highlands and of rural Ulster, and the chapels in the Welsh valleys. Nevertheless an overarching sense of evangelical common ground survived, as was evident in the aspirations that led to the formation of the Evangelical Alliance in 1846. A resolution of the Congregational Union in October 1843 recognized 'with great joy . . . renewed proofs of the essential unity of the evangelical churches of the Protestant Reformation'.[11]

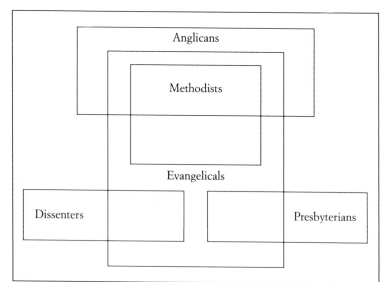

Figure 1 Denominational interrelationships of the Evangelical Revival

The very diversity of evangelicalism renders statistical assessment of its impact a difficult matter. Methodist numbers provide some indication of trends. Growth was initially quite modest: when membership figures were first recorded in 1767, the total for the British Isles was 25,911, together with an unknown number of Welsh-speaking Calvinistic Methodists, for whom figures for this date are not available. The remainder of the eighteenth century saw substantial if fluctuating increases, with the impact of revivalist outbreaks clearly apparent, above all in 1794 when Wesleyan Methodist membership in Great Britain increased by 13.52 per cent in a single year. In 1800 the total recorded number of Methodists (still excluding the Calvinistic Methodists) was 115,370. It is noteworthy this included a relatively significant minority of 19,292 in Ireland. In Scotland, on the other hand, the impact of revival was contained within the Presbyterian churches and there were only 1,041 Methodists in 1800. The first half of the nineteenth century was a period of continuing substantial growth: Wesleyan Methodist numbers in England increased from 88,334 in 1800 to 319,770 in 1846; Primitive Methodism, formed as a result of a further revivalistic surge around 1810, had over 100,000 members by 1850. In Wales the earliest available figures record 37,576 Calvinistic Methodists in 1838, at which date there were also 16,053 Wesleyan Methodists in the principality.[12] Such figures suggest that, far from losing momentum after its first two generations, evangelicalism's true success as a mass movement occurred in the decades around 1800 rather than in the mid-eighteenth century. Moreover Methodist membership figures understate the numbers of those who had some contact with the societies, let alone, as we noted in the previous paragraph, the many thousands of evangelicals to be found in other denominations.

Beyond such complex but tangible relationships to the structures of official religion were wider linkages of cultural influence. By the mid-nineteenth century there were many people who had imbibed certain evangelical ideas and attitudes while not identifying wholeheartedly with the movement. The future Roman Catholic cardinal, John Henry Newman, came under evangelical influence as a teenager, and recalled half a century later 'the inward conversion of which I was conscious, (and of which I am still more certain than that I have hands and feet)'.[13] Even those who explicitly rejected evangelicalism could not ignore it, as is evident in the novels of Charles Dickens, Anthony Trollope, and, above all, George Eliot.

The emergence of evangelicalism in the eighteenth century was therefore a cornerstone of the pattern of British and Irish religion in the nineteenth century. It is accordingly instructive to consider a little more closely why the movement gathered and sustained its strength. In so doing one encounters a central dilemma for the historian of religion: how does one do justice to the movement's own claims to legitimacy in 'other-worldly' terms – that its growth was quite simply a product of the outpouring of the Holy Spirit – while working within the 'this-worldly' framework and evidence of historical investigation? It would be too crude to see the response to such a problem as merely a matter of personal belief: the intellectual issues are much more complex. On the one hand a believing historian may hold a theological conviction that God is generally active in history, but refuse to make specific claims to discern the hand of the Holy Spirit because these cannot be verified in terms of recognizable evidence. On the other hand it is possible to acknowledge the practical power of religious experience while remaining sceptical or agnostic regarding its origins. Accordingly in practice the two perspectives can converge in an acknowledgement that the men and women involved in the revival movements felt they were encountering spiritual forces outside themselves, and that this generated an excitement that was, in the short term at least, self-sustaining. It is no abdication of responsibility on the part of the historian, but a recognition of the limits of his proper sphere, to suggest that the source of these convictions can be left for debate among psychologists, theologians and philosophers.

The historical problem is rather how such motivation internal to individuals related to pressures external to them. The limits of interpretation can be defined by outlining two radically different, but not irreconcilable, views which we shall label the 'heroic' and the 'materialist'. The 'heroic' approach dominated the earlier historiography of the Evangelical Revival and implied that it was made by the energy and devotion of a number of 'great men', such as John Wesley, George Whitefield, Howell Harris (in Wales), and Jonathan Edwards (in North America). Emphasis is placed on potent images of self-sacrifice, such as Whitefield's premature death from exhaustion and Wesley's continued hard work into advanced old age. This version of events is a species of 'official history', represented in writings like those of John Wesley Bready, who implied that his namesake had almost singlehandedly transformed the spritual and moral condition of England.[14] Although the weaknesses in such an approach are very much apparent, it still should not be rejected out of hand. The commitment and energy of the leading figures in the revival was undeniable. In May 1742 George Whitefield began preaching to large crowds at Moorfields in London, but, hearing news of revival in Scotland, he hastened north and was shortly preaching to vast gatherings there at almost every hour of the day and night.[15] Furthermore the revivalists showed enormous courage and dedication in refusing to be deflected from their work by the considerable opposition that they encountered. This sometimes culminated in outright physical violence.[16] In addition this perspective is helpful in focusing attention upon one of the most characteristic features of the Evangelical Revival: the role played by itinerant preachers. Distortion can arise, however, if one concentrates only on the major figures, and forgets the role of the numerous obscure preachers who transmitted evangelical teachings. The geographical range of Whitefield's activities was exceptional, but his working day can hardly have been longer than that of ordinary Wesleyan Methodist ministers in the nineteenth century who were expected to labour for between ninety and a hundred hours a week.[17] The crucial contributions made by women must also be acknowledged. Selina, Countess of Huntingdon, played an important role in the diffusion of Calvinistic Methodism until her death in 1791; in a subsequent generation Hannah More was a central influence in spreading evangelicalism in the Church of England. At a lower social level too women were sometimes energetic as lay preachers and organizers of local classes and chapels, particularly within Primitive Methodism, which developed from 1810 as a result of a new phase of popular revivalism.[18] In short, if the 'heroic' perspective is modified to constitute a more generalized acknowledgement of the role of individual agency it still has much to commend it.

Nevertheless there are limits to the usefulness of this approach. For one thing it tends to obscure the extent to which the movement spread by permeation rather than dramatic confrontation. This was especially true within the Church of England, where evangelicalism remained a force even after Methodism set itself decisively on the road to separation around the time of Wesley's death in 1791.[19] More importantly perhaps, the heroic view is difficult to reconcile with the varying responses to evangelicalism at different times and places: if the preacher and the organization were constant factors, why should their impact differ?

The 'materialist' approach starts rather with the social and economic circumstances and presents the phases of revival as a reflection of these. In 1906 the French historian Elie Halévy first pointed out that the emergence of Methodism in the late 1730s and early 1740s coincided with a period of economic crisis. Desperation in terms of earthly prospects drove men and women to other-worldly beliefs, explanations and activities: hence they were receptive to evangelical revivalism.[20] A related approach favoured by more recent historians links the success of evangelical groups to the social dislocation accompanying the transition to an urban, industrial society. The loss of familiar ties and social order induced a state of *anomie*, a sense of disorientation and lack of purpose and role in a community. This state of mind was relieved by the intense experience of conversion and of subsequent integration into a chapel or church community.[21] Moreover the physical and emotional stress of work in early industrial factories produced psychological pressures which, in a memorable phrase coined by Edward Thompson, were relieved by the 'psychic masturbation' of participation in emotionally intense Sunday worship.[22]

Such approaches are helpful but they also leave much unexplained. Later periods of revival did not correlate so readily with economic crisis. Although circumstances in the 1790s and the 1840s might seem to support the view that material deprivation enhanced receptivity to evangelicalism, the evidence is at best ambivalent.[23] It is true that evangelicalism worked in early industrial communities to overcome anonymity and isolation, but it was also successful in some districts where the pace of change was relatively slow and community ties were not disrupted to the same extent.[24] A model of socio-economic causation that could explain all these variations would have to be significantly more complex than any hitherto advanced. At the same time, the broad correlation between the growth of evangelicalism and the socio-economic changes of the Industrial Revolution is undeniable and the impression that periods of revivalist enthusiasm often coincided with phases of particular social crisis appears well founded.

In a rounded explanation of the growth of evangelicalism the 'heroic' and 'materialist' perspectives appear not as incompatible but as complementary. A recognition of the importance of individual agency is not inconsistent with the acknowledgement that its impact was contingent on favourable social conditions. Moreover, as was indicated in Chapter 1, a community's outward forms of religious expression are likely to reflect a wide range of individual attitudes and motivations. The triggers were almost infinitely variable in the kaleidoscope of human personality and social experience. Generalization is accordingly unwise, but particular occurrences admit of more specific emphasis. For example, Whitefield's charismatic preaching was central to the revival of 1742 in Scotland, whereas a revival in Cornwall in 1799 can be convincingly related to a period of uncertainty in the local copper-mining industry.[25]

These stimuli were mediated to the individual through a web of circumstances and cultural values. The uncertainty of life was seldom far from the eighteenth- and nineteenth-century consciousness and reminders of mortality might kindle a search for a framework in which to make sense of the feared unknown beyond the grave. In July 1744 an alcoholic, shaken at seeing the gravestone of an acquaintance in Cambuslang churchyard, was so desperate for spiritual counsel that he immediately went to see the minister, interrupting him at his dinner.[26] Such fears were all the more potent when they swept through whole communities, sometimes in response to the danger of life-threatening diseases, as in the cholera epidemics of 1832 and 1849.[27] Awakening sexuality and a longing for emotional fulfilment could also be a powerful trigger: there is ample evidence that conversions most frequently occurred in the years of adolescence or young adulthood.[28] The Welsh hymnwriter William Williams of Pantecelyn wrote in 1777 of Methodist societies as 'a company of lively and daring young men; and a bevy of young girls at the peak of their strength and vigour'.[29]

The broader interplay of evangelicalism with culture was a complex mixture of confrontation and assimilation. Evangelicals placed themselves in firm opposition to the perceived dissipation and paganism of popular mores. Inevitably this stance frequently led, initially at least, to hostile reactions. Nevertheless in the longer term a process of accommodation can be discerned. In 1828 when the people of the fishing village of Mousehole in west Cornwall experienced revival they continued to mark Midsummer but with religious services rather than the traditional rituals. In many parts of the British Isles Methodism proved to be a fertile source of such spiritual and communal substitutes for earlier customs, and even proved able to co-exist with unorthodox folk beliefs.[30]

A parallel process can be detected in high culture. At first sight the intense Christianity of George Whitefield (1714–70) might seem poles apart from the sceptical philosophy of his near contemporary David Hume (1711–76). Here indeed was a conflict of ideas as sharp as the confrontation of values that occurred when Whitefield's preaching at Moorfields challenged the surrounding fairgoers. Nevertheless, although some strands in eighteenth-century thought were very much at odds with evangelicalism, other aspects of the Enlightenment cast of mind were by no means inconsistent with religious revival. Despite Hume's considerable influence, the sceptical side of Enlightenment thought was much less strong in Britain – as in Germany – than in France.[31] Evangelicals, for their part, might be sympathetic to some beliefs which were very much at odds with the Enlightenment, but on the other hand there was a readiness to stress the rational and empiricist pedigree of their own fundamental convictions. Wesley himself wrote that 'religion and reason go hand in hand'; his evangelical contemporaries welcomed the study of science and nature as providing additional evidence of divine glory and power.[32] Thomas Chalmers, the leading Scottish evangelical of the first half of the nineteenth century, affirmed the value of intellectual progress because he saw it as reinforcing awareness of humanity's need for God.[33] Evangelicalism continued to be responsive to cultural trends: while rational 'enlightened' modes of thought endured, there were signs from the 1820s that some evangelicals at least were becoming receptive to the more dramatic and emotional perceptions of history and human experience that were arising from Romanticism. In the theological sphere this expressed itself particularly in the heightened expectation of cataclysmic divine intervention in human affairs.[34]

Thus in the opening decades of Victoria's reign the evangelical movement remained a dynamic and broadly based religious force, combining spiritual energy, institutional diversity and cultural sensitivity. Arguably it was now passing the peak of its influence, but its impact on the lasting framework of British and Irish religious and social life was unmistakable.

2. CATHOLICISM

The word 'catholic' in its most general sense simply means 'universal' and can be used outside a specifically religious context. In its narrowest sense, usually qualified as 'Roman Catholic', it refers to the Church of which the Pope is the earthly head. In an intermediate sense it refers, in a manner analogous to evangelicalism, to a broad strand in religious thought which cannot be limited to a single institution, and, in nineteenth- and twentieth-century Britain has claimed a prominent place in the Anglican as well as the Roman Church. In essence the distinguishing feature of Catholics in this broad sense of the word is a belief in the divine authority of the visible Church, given greater weight in proportion to the authority of the Bible and 'private judgement' than is the case with evangelicals and other Protestants. It follows that clergy and bishops are accorded greater reverence, and that salvation for the individual lies not so much in an internalized personal conversion as in faithful participation in the rites of the Church and in deference to its authority.

It would seem therefore that in its basic nature Catholicism is a form of religion more emphatically official in its nature than evangelicalism.

However, such a judgement has to be qualified by recognition of the scope for variation within a broadly Catholic framework: issues such as the precise nature of authority, forms of worship and the place of saints could all become matters of considerable controversy. Ecclesiastical structure was always strong but it did not determine everything. A further qualification arises from study of unofficial religion. In Ireland before the famine, rural beliefs often owed as much to a supernaturalist folklore as to official Roman Catholicism; in later nineteenth-century urban Roman Catholicism it is clear that religious participation owed a great deal to the need to find a focus for communal identities.

For much of the period between the Reformation and the nineteenth century Catholic ideas were subordinate in the Church of England, which perceived itself in explicitly Protestant terms. Accordingly the history of Catholicism becomes essentially the history of Roman Catholicism, which was at a low ebb at the time of the emergence of evangelicalism. Roman Catholic numbers were fairly stable during the seventeenth and eighteenth centuries, but they still appeared to be a weak, marginalized and sometimes persecuted minority. In the late eighteenth century there were probably around 80,000 Roman Catholics in England and about 30,000 in Scotland.[35] In general these were concentrated in relatively remote areas, coastal Lancashire, the uplands of Northumberland, Durham and Yorkshire, the Enzie of Banff in north-east Scotland, the West Highlands and the Hebrides. There were pockets of Roman Catholicism in other areas, such as the Welsh Borders and the West Midlands, but they were very thinly spread in the south of England and in central Scotland, and there were hardly any at all in Wales and south-west England. In total contrast, in Ireland, a country with a population of around 6 million in the early nineteenth century, Roman Catholics outnumbered Protestants in a ratio of approximately four to one.

The distribution of Roman Catholics in areas remote from central authority reflected the difficulty experienced by sixteenth- and seventeenth-century governments in imposing a Protestant religious settlement. The survival of Roman Catholicism owed a lot to the role of the small, but significant, number of gentry and nobility who remained loyal to the faith, supported priests and protected Roman Catholic tenants and dependants on their estates. The implication of this was that Roman Catholicism was socially a very diverse community, with an aristocratic element as well as a noticeable presence among the middle and lower orders of society. This social diversity increased further in the late eighteenth century when the impact of industrialization, particularly in Lancashire, brought urban life and commercial activities to a number of English Roman Catholics. In Ireland, by contrast, although there was a Roman Catholic presence in the higher levels of society, it was a disproportionately small one.

In his study of English Roman Catholics in the period between the Reformation and the Industrial Revolution, John Bossy argues that Roman Catholicism in this period should be regarded as a variety of religious dissent, comparable to other groups who rejected the Established Church of England, such as Baptists and Quakers. He points out that, in the main, Roman Catholics in the eighteenth century were concerned not to confront Protestants, but to have a quiet life, living in harmony with their neighbours and not antagonizing the government. They were accordingly restrained in their religious activity and politically loyal to the British state.[36] There is a good deal of truth in this argument, but in two important respects Roman Catholicism did differ very substantially from Protestant dissent. First there was a strong perception, attributable particularly to the international organization of the Roman Catholic Church, that it presented a fundamental challenge to the British state and way of life. Second, the weakness of the Roman Catholic community in England and Scotland has to be set in the context of the overwhelming numerical strength of Irish Roman Catholicism.[37] These two points will be explored in turn.

The sense that Roman Catholicism was presenting a serious threat to the state was understandable in the sixteenth and seventeenth centuries. Pius V's Bull of 1570 released Elizabeth's subjects from their allegiance and was followed by the Spanish Armada, the Gunpowder Plot, and fears of Roman Catholic influence during Charles I's reign. In the late seventeenth century the imaginary Popish Plot of 1678 led to a frenzy of anti-Roman feeling, and, under James II, a serious attempt was made to restore the country to Roman Catholicism. Accordingly after 1688 the succession to the throne was confined to Protestants: George I and his heirs owed the Crown to the exclusion of numerous Roman Catholics who came before them in terms of strict hereditary right. The Jacobite Rebellions of 1715 and 1745 were intended to restore the Roman Catholic Stuarts and hence kept hostility alive. Although English Roman Catholics did not give them much more than token support, their loyalty was still called into question. In Scotland, moreover, Roman Catholic sympathy for the Stuarts was genuine and active at least until after 1745.[38] Hence, until the end of the eighteenth century penal legislation in theory precluded Catholics from worshipping and in practice excluded them from most areas of public life.

From the 1760s onwards government suspicions were decreasing and the relaxation of the penal legislation came on to the political agenda. On the other hand popular fear of Roman Catholics remained strong, fuelled by garbled popular tradition relating to sixteenth- and seventeenth-century events. This showed little sign of declining significantly when the Jacobite threat receded. The explosive potential of such attitudes became dramatically apparent in the Gordon Riots in London in 1780, as a result of which 285 people were killed, 173 wounded, more than 450 arrested and thirty-five executed.[39] Such a historic context of truly ferocious hostility was an important aspect of the position of Roman Catholics in nineteenth- and twentieth-century Britain.

In Ireland the Roman Catholic majority suffered during the eighteenth century from the application of similar penal laws to those constraining the Roman Catholic minority in Britain. Discriminatory legislation on land tenure and inheritance meant that during the century the proportion of Irish land owned by Roman Catholics declined to 5 per cent.[40] Active participation in government and public life was effectively limited to the Protestant minority, particularly those who conformed to the Established Church of Ireland. The Parliament in Dublin, in existence until the Union of 1800, was a wholly Protestant institution. However, although such structures ensured that Irish Roman Catholics were politically impotent, the vast majority of them stayed loyal to their faith. The ancient hierarchy of bishops and the parochial structures were maintained in competition with the Anglicans. Indeed, as the century went on, there were signs that far from withering away in the face of persecution, the Roman Catholic Church was modestly gaining in religious vitality.[41]

During the early nineteenth century interconnections between Britain and Ireland grew stronger. In part this was for constitutional reasons: the abolition of the separate Parliament in Dublin in 1800 led to a consciousness of Britain and Ireland as a united political unit. In this, taken as a whole, Roman Catholics were still a minority, but a substantial rather than a negligible one, roughly a quarter of the population of the United Kingdom. At approximately the same time, for social and economic reasons, the trickle of immigration to Britain in the eighteenth century began to swell into a steady stream, and eventually in the 1840s to a deluge. Given the pre-existing culture of suspicion of Roman Catholics in Britain contemporary perceptions of this influx inflated its significance even further.

Around the end of the eighteenth century Roman Catholicism in Britain, like evangelicalism, entered a period of spectacular growth: between 1800 and 1850 the proportion of Roman Catholics in the population increased from 1.2 per cent to 4.06 per cent at a period when overall population was growing at a very rapid rate.[42] This was accompanied by important changes of ethos. It should be noted that English Roman Catholic numbers were themselves rising significantly, even without the Irish influx. This was partly due to natural increase but also reflected the fact that, in areas where Anglican church provision was weak, Roman Catholics were able to make some converts from nominal Protestantism.[43] In England the Roman Catholic community became increasingly urbanized, but without traumatic discontinuities. There was a consequent shift in the leadership away from the gentry – more influential in a rural environment – to the priests, who now became increasingly self-assertive. In the early nineteenth century, however, there were significant tensions between clergy and congregations who did not submit readily to clerical domination.[44] In Scotland, on the other hand, the indigenous Roman Catholic population was probably stagnant or even declining, and the geographical and social changes in the community were more dramatic. From the early nineteenth century the growing industrial and urban centres of the central belt began to attract Roman Catholic migrants from the Highlands as well as from Ireland: one calculation indicates that between 1755 and 1851 the proportion of Roman Catholics in the population of Inverness-shire fell from 19 per cent to 11.2 per cent, while in Lanarkshire it rose from nothing to 12.5 per cent.[45]

The scale of such changes was greatly increased by immigration from Ireland. It has been calculated that between 1780 and 1850 the English Roman Catholic population of four Lancashire towns rose from 5,000 to over 20,000, but during the same period the numbers of Irish rose from a negligible figure to 100,000, outnumbering the English by five to one by 1850.[46] This obviously changed the social composition of the Church, giving it a much larger proportion of members among the poor and very poor than it had previously possessed. As the impoverished Irish person became the normative image of a Roman Catholic this also heightened the impression that the religion was un-British, socially disruptive, and potentially politically subversive. Indigenous English and Scottish Roman Catholics, keen to demonstrate their own social and political respectability, thus viewed the Irish influx with mixed feelings.

The early nineteenth century also saw spiritual and devotional developments, which reflected the greater self-confidence that came

from increasing numbers. Roman Catholics came to be more conspicuous in their conduct of worship, and more uncompromising in the
assertion of their religious identity. In their attitudes to Protestants they
were increasingly likely to work for their conversion rather than merely
seek peacefully to co-exist with them. Prayers for the conversion of
England became a regular feature of devotion which, as a whole, became
more intense and unmistakably Catholic.[47] This development needs to
be seen in Britain in the context of the Evangelical Revival as reflecting a
parallel search for a more authentic expression of God. In a European
perspective it was a part of that wider development of a more Italianate
devotion and theology throughout the Roman Catholic Church, usually
known as 'Ultramontanism', meaning 'from beyond the Alps'. A further
expression of this was the growth of religious orders in Britain, mainly
among women, but to some extent involving men as well. The number
of monasteries and nunneries increased steadily during the nineteenth
century, although most were small in size, apart from the few large
abbeys such as Ampleforth and Downside.

In Ireland too the early nineteenth century was a period of increasing
Roman Catholic vigour. The gradual relaxation of the penal laws
facilitated organization and boosted morale, while bishops and clergy
became more conscientious and efficient in their leadership and ministry. In 1795 a college was set up at Maynooth in County Kildare for the
training of priests, thus removing the necessity for them to study abroad
and thereby enhancing corporate spirit and sensitivity to Irish conditions. There was extensive evidence of popular piety and support for the
Church, even if this was not always expressed through regular observance of the forms of official Catholicism. The widespread commitment
of the people was strikingly illustrated by the extensive church-building
that occurred in the second quarter of the nineteenth century, which
was all the more remarkable as this was a period of acute economic
difficulty, poverty and social turmoil.[48]

In the 1830s and 1840s there were increasing signs that Catholicism as
a broader religious tendency was gaining some ground outside the
Roman Catholic Church. In the early eighteenth century Catholic
concepts had had some currency among the Non-Jurors who had
refused to swear the oath of allegiance to William and Mary in 1688 and,
in Scotland, among Episcopalians. There had also been lingering signs
of a Catholic style of devotion in the Church of England itself, although
these disappeared by the middle of the century. Meanwhile the Non-
Jurors died out and Episcopalianism in Scotland declined to become a
tiny remnant. From around 1800, however, the Episcopal Church north

of the Border, with its strong sense of catholicity, began to revive. There was a corresponding resurgence in the high church wing of the Church of England, represented particularly by a group dubbed the Hackney Phalanx (from the place of residence of Joshua Watson, its most prominent lay supporter), several of whom became bishops.[49] In general this early nineteenth-century generation of high churchmen, although reverencing tradition and concerned to improve the conduct of worship and pastoral care, stopped well short of explicit identification with a Catholic concept of the Church of England. Nevertheless it was fertile soil in which the Oxford (or Tractarian) Movement, the commencement of which is conventionally dated to 1833, could take root. An address to the Archbishop of Canterbury, drawn up in the early days of the movement, did not use the word 'Catholic', but well illustrated a sense of the Church of England deriving its authority from ancient tradition rather than a Protestant appeal to the Bible:

> we are especially anxious to lay before your Grace the assurance of our devoted attachment to the Apostolical Doctrine and Polity of the Church over which you preside, and of which we are Ministers; and our deep-rooted attachment to that venerable Liturgy, in which she has embodied in the language of ancient piety, the Orthodox and Primitive Faith.[50]

A few years later J. H. Newman specifically articulated a theory of the Church of England as Catholic but not Roman. He saw this as representing a legitimate strand in the Church's history, but admitted that 'it still remains to be tried whether what is called Anglo-Catholicism . . . is capable of being professed, acted on, and maintained . . . or whether it be a mere modification or transition-state either of Romanism or of popular Protestantism'.[51] In 1845 Newman himself, after a long struggle between his vision of catholicity and his loyalty to the Church of England, converted to Roman Catholicism. On the other hand other adherents of the Oxford Movement found it possible to maintain a Catholic view of the Anglican Church. This gradually gained ground during the Victorian era.

In a sermon in 1851 Newman, now a Roman Catholic priest, eloquently portrayed the progress of his adopted creed during the previous half-century. He characterized the Roman Catholics of his boyhood as 'the pebbles and *detritus* of the great deluge . . . a set of poor Irishmen, coming and going at harvest time . . . perhaps an elderly person . . . grave and solitary, and strange . . . an oldfashioned house of gloomy appearance'. By contrast, the present was a time of 'second spring', an almost miraculous rebirth of Catholicism in England.[52] The perception betrayed the fact that Newman was initially an outsider to the Catholic revival, and the reality, as we have seen, was somewhat more gradual and prosaic.[53] Nevertheless the concept of a 'second spring' still has importance for understanding contemporary perceptions: those living through the period often seemed to believe that something strikingly new was happening. Suddenly Roman Catholics began to think that they could carry all before them and, conversely, Protestants began to feel threatened by the vitality and growth of a group that had traditionally incurred their suspicion.

The early Victorian period thus saw considerable rivalry between the two dynamic religious forces discussed in this chapter. Competition first gathered momentum in Ireland in the 1820s where evangelical efforts to promote a 'second Reformation' by the conversion of 'papists' not surprisingly came into conflict with the increasingly energetic Roman Catholic Church. The confrontation had extended to Britain by the 1830s. One consequence was that the two movements began to define themselves more specifically against each other, a tendency especially apparent among evangelicals. This process was reinforced by the growth of Catholic ideas in the Anglican Church, which was liable to be perceived by evangelicals as 'Romish' infiltration and led them to feel that they were engaged in a struggle for the soul of the Church of England itself. By the mid-nineteenth century they were frequently presenting themselves as the true guardians of the Protestant tradition stemming from the Reformation, defined in opposition to Rome. In the associated polemics, differences of theological and practical emphasis were firmly asserted: private judgement stood against the authority of the Church; the Bible against tradition; clerical marriage against celibacy.[54]

Nevertheless Catholicism and evangelicalism had more in common than their adherents were ready to acknowledge. Both were enjoying considerable expansion, a reflection of their shared capacity to stimulate religious responses at a wide variety of intellectual, social and emotional levels. Above all, each in different ways could give a powerful stimulus to the defining and strengthening of community, both at local and national levels. Such communities were given wider legitimacy and significance by the capacity of each movement to set them in the context of a wider whole, either the universal Catholic Church, or the worldwide invisible fellowship of those who had secured salvation through the Cross of Christ. The processes involved will be explored more fully in later chapters, but first the political and religious context of the early nineteenth century must be more fully outlined.

3. RELIGION AND POLITICS AFTER THE FRENCH REVOLUTION

An early Victorian writer claimed that after 1789 'the triumph of atheism in France restored Christianity to England'.[55] Implicit in this judgement is the assumption that before 1789 Christian conviction and observance were at a low ebb. We have indeed seen, in the previous sections of this chapter, how both evangelicalism and Catholicism, initially movements at the margins of eighteenth-century religion, entered an important phase of growth around 1789, and came to be formative influences on church life in the Victorian era. However, before discussing the interconnections between religion and political circumstances in the years after the French Revolution, some brief consideration needs to be given to the wider character of Georgian religion. Was it really as nominal and decayed as Victorian critics suggested?

The dominant tone of religion in the eighteenth century was set by the Established Churches[56], which were particularly closely linked to the state in this period. The Establishment was Anglican in England, Ireland, and Wales, and Presbyterian in Scotland; but throughout the British Isles it was a central part of the mechanisms of government and society. Bishops were political appointments and peers of the realm; the more substantial of the lower clergy were landowners and magistrates. In Scotland the kirk session was an active agent of moral and social discipline. One of the most influential theoretical articulations of this situation was that set out by William Warburton in 1736 in a work whose argument was well summarized by its title: *The Alliance between Church and State, or the Necessity and Equity of an Established Religion and a Test-Law Demonstrated, From the Essence and End of Civil Society, upon the Fundamental Principles of the Law of Nature and Nations.* Warburton justified Establishment, conceived as a contract between the two entities of Church and state, as a pragmatic arrangement which benefited both parties. The Church gained protection and privilege; the state the support of religion for its own institutions and its assistance in maintaining the stability of civil society. The precise form and teachings of the Church were not at issue: thus there was no inconsistency in having a Presbyterian Establishment in Scotland and an Anglican one elsewhere.[57] At the end of the century the concept of partnership was merging into one of 'indissoluble union', at least in the eyes of Edmund Burke. He believed that in his countrymen's minds 'Church and State are ideas inseparable . . . and scarcely is the one ever mentioned without the other'.[58]

The dominant theological accompaniment to such a constitutional framework was a retreat from the dogmatic certainties of the seventeenth century to a frame of mind labelled as 'latitudinarian' or 'moderate', the latter term being more current in Scotland. The emphasis of preachers was liable to be on reason rather than revelation, and on morality rather than spirituality. Worship was generally restrained, the celebration of Holy Communion infrequent and liturgical practice austere. High church advocacy of a stronger spiritual authority for the Church and a more conscientious and disciplined piety was, however, more influential in the Church of England than has often been recognized.[59] Moreover evangelicals within the Established Churches began to make their presence felt, even if they remained very much in a minority.

Nevertheless there was undeniably a marked difference between the ethos of the Georgian Church and that of the Victorians. However, this acknowledgement does not constitute an endorsement of the value judgements made by its critics. It is true that concrete charges can be made to stick, in matters such as unjustifiable pluralism (holding of more than one post), neglect of pastoral responsibilities and poor maintenance of churches, but the underlying issue was a conflict in religiosity, or ways of being religious.[60] Later Catholics and evangelicals, with their own sharply defined creeds, looked at the past and perceived diffuse theology, perfunctory worship, and accommodation to the world and its pleasures. A more sympathetic evaluation might applaud theological accessibility and social realism. Certainly the 'moderate' approach to Christianity could bear fruit in considerable influence for the church. A notable example of this was in the Edinburgh Enlightenment in the third quarter of the eighteenth century, where the Church of Scotland, led by William Robertson, had an extensive political and cultural impact.[61]

The French Revolution, in conjunction with the Industrial Revolution, undoubtedly helped to stimulate new and revived forms of religious activity. Attacks on the Roman Catholic Church in France led many of its clergy to seek refuge in Britain where they were generally welcome and, as the perceived victims of persecution, helped to inspire a growth in public sympathy for their co-religionists.[62] The new political contours of Europe meant too that Roman Catholics at home were no longer perceived as a major threat to the state. Accordingly there were partial relaxations in the penal laws, and even financial support for Roman Catholicism not only at Maynooth College, but also, for a brief period, in Scotland.[63] Such developments helped to support the modest prosperity of the Roman Catholic community in Britain and quicken the morale and ambitions of their brethren in Ireland. Meanwhile, as we have seen, the 1790s were a period of rapid growth in popular evangelicalism, in a climate where a sense of political crisis reinforced the social dislocation arising from industrialization in producing potent preconditions for revival. At the same time fear of disorder, immorality and 'atheism' were conducive to a favourable cultural and political climate for the crusade of William Wilberforce and other Anglican evangelicals for the amelioration of morals and behaviour. Hannah More's popular novels and pamphlets had an extensive impact in diffusing such attitudes lower in the social scale. From this period we can thus trace the blending of evangelicalism with other potent forces in national culture in the defining of codes of socially accepted conduct.

To a limited extent these strengthening currents in the religious life of Britain around 1800 were favourable to the maintenance of the eighteenth-century order of things. Roman Catholics in England and Scotland, for the moment at least, continued politically quiescent. Evangelicals such as More and Wilberforce advanced moral reform as the obverse of social conservatism. They remained, moreover, steady supporters of the Establishment of religion. As late as the 1830s Thomas Chalmers, influential in England as well as in Scotland, was still an earnest advocate of the maintenance of state support for the Church. Methodists too were frequently ready supporters of the existing relationships between Church and state: strongly conservative strands in John Wesley's thinking shaped the views of the next generation of Wesleyans under the long ascendancy of Jabez Bunting during the first half of the nineteenth century.

Nevertheless, in the longer term the new wine of religious movements that claimed intense commitment from their adherents could not readily be contained within the old wineskins of a constitutional fabric in which the authority of the Church was so closely intertwined with the interests of the state. Institutional and social changes fundamentally undermined the viability of the Burkean concept of the relationship between religion, state and society. Although the revivalism of the 1790s and early 1800s was partly contained within the conservative fabric of Wesleyan Methodism, it also stimulated more radical tendencies. These initially found expression in the secession led by Alexander Kilham in 1797 to found the Methodist New Connexion, which explicitly repudiated the political loyalism of the Wesleyan majority. The larger Primitive Methodist Connexion which took shape from 1811 also implied a rejection of Establishment, although here regarded more in its religious than its political aspect. More generally, the rapid growth of all forms of Nonconformity between the 1790s and the 1820s produced a situation where the monopolistic status of the Established Churches would inevitably come under ever closer scrutiny. A growing awareness that an anomaly existed in England and Wales, and to a lesser extent in Scotland, also served by association to raise consciousness of the longstanding situation in Ireland where the privileged status of Anglicanism in the eyes of the state implied estrangement between the government and the great majority of the people.

An indication of the tensions that existed came with the Revolutionary and Napoleonic Wars. Evangelical loyalty to the state was not so strong that it overcame a prior obligation to shape a response to war in Christian terms. Among dissenters a sense of war being an unmitigated evil was strong, and prayers were often for peace rather than for victory. Their central preoccupation remained evangelism and moral reform.[64] Even Anglican evangelicals had ambivalences about Britain's position: war was seen as a depraving influence, and endeavours to restore the perceived moral and religious corruption of the old order in Europe did not inspire their enthusiasm.[65] Further evidence of attitudes emerges from sermons preached on the death and funeral of Lord Nelson in 1805 and 1806. A preacher in Chelsea acknowledged the nobility of seeking fame and of honouring national worthies, but still recognized that 'some may deem war incompatible with the spirit or letter of Christianity' and suggested that after Nelson had received his fatal wound the Christian had superseded the hero.[66] At West Cowes John Styles similarly upheld the appropriateness of recognizing secular distinction. Nevertheless Nelson's death was a sign of the danger of relying too much on the arm of flesh, and only the Christian who overcame the world could achieve the true 'imperishable fame' that eluded generals, statesmen and admirals. Fearing lest he had inadvertently conceded too much to terrestial glory, he then added a preface to the printed version stressing that the leading principle of life was to know nothing but Christ crucified.[67] In London, John Townsend, a dissenting minister, contrasted the death of Nelson, 'a sacrifice to his zeal for his country' with that of St Stephen, 'a martyr to his zeal for the cause of Christianity'; he also complained at the profane behaviour of the crowds at the funeral, and regretted the continuing calamity of a war which was attributable to the lust of men's hearts. All three examples imply a disjunction between Christian and national loyalties which contrasts significantly with Burke's claim that the ideas of Church and state were inseparable in people's minds.[68]

On the other hand the very insistence of some preachers on distinguishing Christian commitment from secular heroism reflected the manner in which many of their compatriots were venerating Nelson as a focus of patriotism. For some the manner of his death gave him an almost Christlike quality.[69] A similar tendency was apparent in veneration for the monarchy. The jubilee of George III in 1809 was marked by extensive celebrations which included numerous church services; in 1817 the death in childbirth of Princess Charlotte, only legitimate daughter of the Prince Regent, stirred an intense public grief reflecting an incipient quasi-religious cult of royal women.[70] Such attitudes were to recede somewhat in the 1820s with the return of peace and a noticeable decline of the popularity of the royal family after the death of George III, but, as we shall see, they were to resurface powerfully at the end of the century.[71]

Revolution and war in Europe were also a powerful stimulus to millennial speculation. Amidst the ruin of the old order Britain was felt to be specially preserved by God and to have a central role in the fulfilment of divine purposes now hastening on to their climax. Such national privileges were felt to carry a corresponding burden of responsibility to spread the Gospel and promote the moral improvement of humankind.[72] This sense of accountability was apparent in the considerable growth of overseas missionary endeavour from the 1790s, and in the campaigns to abolish the slave trade (successful in 1807) and colonial slavery (1833). Such was the frame of mind of William Wilberforce, expressed in a pamphlet in 1823:

> Let us not presume too far on the forbearance of the Almighty. Favoured in an unequalled degree with Christian light, with civil freedom, and with a greater measure of national blessings than perhaps any country upon earth ever before enjoyed, what a return would it be for the goodness of the Almighty, if we were to continue to keep the descendants of the Africans, whom we have ourselves wrongfully planted in the western hemisphere, in their present state of unexampled darkness and degradation![73]

At the same time, evangelicalism also contributed to the articulation of Welsh and Scottish alternatives to a 'British' sense of identity. The growth of Nonconformity in Wales was particularly vigorous and gave the principality a distinctive religious ethos, with the Church of England widely regarded as an alien institution. The chapels, particularly in the indigenous Calvinistic Methodist denomination, also fostered a Welsh language culture. In Scotland the increasing strength of evangelicalism in the Church of Scotland was, as we shall see in a later chapter, an important factor leading to the Disruption of 1843 in which the distinctive spirit of Scottish religion was vigorously reaffirmed.

Ireland presented a very different kind of picture, but there too the 1790s were a significant watershed in the relationship between religion and national identity. The last two decades of the eighteenth century saw a growth in Irish national consciousness which showed some signs of bridging divisions between Protestants and Roman Catholics. The Society of United Irishmen, founded in Belfast in 1791 to campaign for Parliamentary reform, declared that 'no reform is practicable, efficacious or just, which does not include *Irishmen* of every religious persuasion'.[74] Presbyterians, who shared some of the grievances of Roman Catholics against the Anglican Establishment, were prominent in the movement. The efforts of the United Irishmen reflected the influence of French-style secular republicanism and culminated in rebellion in 1798. However, the rising was weakened by the mutual suspicions of Protestants and Roman Catholics and its failure was followed by the development of an increasingly close alignment between nationalism and Roman Catholicism. Protestants lost enthusiasm for republicanism while Roman Catholics came to identify with specifically confessional movements such as Ribbonism (agrarian secret societies) and the Catholic Association of the 1820s.[75] Meanwhile in 1795 in south Armagh, the Orange Order had been formed as a focus for the mutual defence of Protestants in the face of perceived Roman Catholic terrorism. The insecurity of the years around 1798 contributed to a climate in which evangelical revivalism flourished in Ulster, thus reinforcing the distinctive religious and political identity of the province.[76] Thus as the nineteenth century opened the sectarian polarities that were to dominate subsequent decades of Irish history were coming increasingly into focus.

When the Dublin Parliament was abolished in 1800 it had initially been intended that Roman Catholics would now be given the right to sit in the united Parliament, with the position of the Protestant minority in Ireland secured by the weight of the Protestant majority in Britain. In the event George III refused to countenance this arrangement, and Emancipation was postponed for nearly thirty years. For the next three decades Roman Catholics in Britain and Ireland and a significant body of Protestant political sympathizers campaigned hard for Emancipation. Indeed, especially in the 1820s, the issue was seen as the fundamental question in British politics. Ultimately in 1828 the Irish Roman Catholic leader Daniel O'Connell won a Parliamentary by-election in County Clare. O'Connell had been legally permitted to stand, but as a Catholic he was not able to take the oath required of MPs and so could not take his seat. Faced with the danger of a major crisis if O'Connell's success were to be paralleled across Ireland at a general election, the Duke of Wellington's government decided on a strategic retreat. Emancipation was enacted early in 1829, permitting Roman Catholics henceforth to sit in Parliament and hold nearly all public offices.

Emancipation was a crucial stage in the process of Roman Catholic revival and growth. Political measures do not necessarily in themselves mean a great deal, but in this case the Roman Catholic community on both sides of the Irish Sea had been investing considerable efforts of time and money for a sustained period. Accordingly eventual success, although it only directly affected the lives of the élite, was a tremendous boost to morale, reinforcing the encouragement that came from numerical growth and a more intense spirituality. Roman Catholics now felt that they could look forward to a continued increase in strength and influence. In retrospect Emancipation was the beginning of a sustained period of Roman Catholic growth and consolidation in mid-nineteenth century Britain. There was a corresponding hardening in anti-Catholicism among evangelicals. The preconditions for this already existed in theological trends which were leading to a sharpened sense of the imminence of divine judgement and of conflict between good and evil, and hence to a need uncompromisingly to confront perceived religious error. While many evangelicals – including members of the Established Churches as well as Nonconformists – had initially supported Emancipation as a matter of civil justice, with its passage they began to feel increasingly insecure. As the state was no longer exclusively Protestant, and Catholicism – both Roman and Anglican – was on the increase, they came to see themselves as responsible for the guardianship of the Reformation heritage and thus developed a more dogmatic and trenchantly anti-Catholic tone.[77]

Moreover, in the triumph of the Emancipation campaign, Roman Catholic Ireland was serving notice to Britain that it expected to be treated as far more than a colony, and that it expected to retain and develop its own identity. Emancipation was a political victory in the face of the tendency of Protestants to view the Union with Britain as the basis for establishing an integrated Protestant empire in which Irish Roman Catholics would either be converted or continue indefinitely as second-class citizens. Before 1829 this Protestant dream seemed attainable; after 1829 it looked completely impossible. Meanwhile the direct link developed with the Roman Catholic Church, which O'Connell enlisted to help stir up support for his cause, underlined the significant change in the dominant character of Irish nationalism. The events of the 1820s can thus be seen as an early and powerful example of the force of nationalism when reinforced by organized Christianity.

Emancipation also significantly changed the constitutional basis of the British state, especially when it is viewed in conjunction with the repeal of the Test and Corporation Acts in 1828, which secured full civil participation for Nonconformists. Dissenters, unlike Roman Catholics, had not been excluded from national life in practice, but the ending of their theoretical political disabilities was still a significant concession, albeit a relatively uncontentious one. These measures recognized the logic of the religious changes apparent since the 1790s. No longer was government exclusively Anglican and Protestant. A sense that dramatic change had occurred emerges clearly from the diary of the Duke of Newcastle, one of the staunchest opponents of the measure:

A minister of the Crown has dissolved the Constitution, the pride, the boast, the bulwark of the country. . . . The Act of Settlement has been laughed at. The Act of Union with Scotland scouted and violated. The King, who has *sworn* to do otherwise has personally given his assent to the rescission of those acts which placed his family on the Throne of England – and here we are . . . a prey to the most tormenting anxiety for the future, with an ocean of difficulties before us and threatened mischiefs of the utmost magnitude surrounding us on all sides.[78]

Such language might seem somewhat hysterical but it reflected a not inaccurate perception that Emancipation was initiating an era of constitutional change. In the short term the political situation was destabilized in a manner which contributed directly to the crisis that led to the passing of the Reform Act in 1832; in the long term controversy and legislation relating to the privileges of the Established Churches and the role of religion in relation to state and society was to continue for many decades. Above all, Emancipation meant that simple equations between Protestantism and patriotism were now much more likely to be contested.[79]

Awareness of changed circumstances was very apparent during the 1830s. In all parts of the United Kingdom opponents of the Established Churches felt encouraged to press home an advantage, while supporters suffered a crisis of morale and identity. In Ireland further changes were not slow in coming. The Irish Church Temporalities Act of 1833 scaled down the resources of the Church of Ireland in the light of the fact that it only held the loyalty of around a tenth of the population. This was widely perceived as a betrayal, and heightened Anglican anxieties in Britain as well as in Ireland. These were expressed particularly in the emergence of the Oxford Movement, initiated on 14 July 1833 when John Keble, in an assize sermon at Oxford, denounced the Irish Church Act as a symptom of 'national apostasy'. The subsequent divisive ferment of ideas among high churchmen reflected uncertainty over whether the Anglican Church's future security was to be found primarily in tenacious maintenance of its remaining links with the state, or rather in the assertion of its status as a branch of the universal Catholic Church. The latter course might imply disestablishment or even *rapprochement* with Rome.

A parallel dilemma faced evangelicals. For some in England and Ireland security lay in forceful proclamation of the Protestant character and mission of the British nation as anchored by the national Church and sustained by its reinvigorated evangelical ministry.[80] Similarly in Scotland the initial response of evangelicals in the Established Church to increasing pressure for disestablishment was to redouble their own pastoral and political efforts in order to outflank opponents.[81] Such approaches inevitably increased the distance between themselves and evangelical Nonconformists. Such an outcome was resisted by those who saw their prime loyalty as being not to the Establishment, but to an identity as evangelicals which was shared with Nonconformists.[82] There was also a growing feeling, finding striking expression in the Scottish Disruption of 1843, that loyalty to the state connection might compromise the integrity of Christian witness.

A further set of responses to the changes in the constitutional position of religion came from more liberal thinkers. A seminal influence was provided by the poet and philosopher Samuel Taylor Coleridge, the author of 'Kubla Khan' and 'The Ancient Mariner'. In his *Constitution of Church and State* (1830)[83] he presented a view of the national Church as something much wider than the institutional Church of England, as encompassing the whole sum of the nation's cultural and spiritual activity. Its prime function was to civilize rather than to Christianize. Another advocate of meeting the crisis by broadening the nature of the

Church was Thomas Arnold, headmaster of Rugby, immortalized in fiction in *Tom Brown's Schooldays* (1857), written by his pupil Thomas Hughes. In *The Principles of Church Reform* (1833) he argued that the key to the continuing existence and value of the Established Church would be to make it as open as possible, potentially encompassing all Englishmen by theological flexibility and accommodation of different preferences in relation to styles of worship and religious practice. Arnold believed that Church and state should merge into each other, an ideal realized in microcosm in his own administration of Rugby in which the offices of headmaster and chaplain were combined in his own person. It has been suggested that such 'liberal Anglican' views were reflected in the ecclesiastical and Irish policies of the Whig governments of the 1830s, which can be interpreted as attempts to broaden the base of the connections between Church and state.[84]

In the half-century before 1843 the fabric of religious life in Britain and Ireland underwent very considerable change. The impact of evangelical revival and resurgent Catholicism diversified the range of religious options and reshaped relationships between religion and national consciousness. The implications of these changes will become further apparent in subsequent chapters, first as we consider in Chapters 3 and 4 the place of religion in the lives of ordinary people and local communities; and subsequently in assessing its relationship to national political and cultural life.

3

GOD MADE THEM HIGH OR LOWLY?

Official religion

At Saltaire in Yorkshire, Titus Salt, manufacturer of woollens and worsteds and Liberal MP for Bradford from 1859 to 1861, constructed in the 1850s a model village for his workforce. At its heart, directly opposite the mill, stands the Congregational Church, a grandiose neoclassical building clearly asserting the dominance of Salt's patriarchal Nonconformity in the social and moral order he wished to reinforce. The dominant chapel and mill were complemented by an institute for the educational cultivation of the workforce. The village was laid out on a grid plan in which streets named after members of the Salt family intersect with others commemorating royalty. Larger houses for foremen and mill management were interspersed with the smaller houses for the workforce, thus ensuring that the hierarchy of the mill was maintained in the street.

Saltaire is a particularly graphic example of the extent to which the buildings and institutions of official religion were often a key part of the social structure of local communities. In particular it serves as a powerful visual reminder that official religion included not only state-supported churches – the Church of England, the Church of Ireland, which retained its links with the state until 1870, and the Church of Scotland – but also organized Nonconformity. Chapels which originated in unofficial dissenting protest against Established religious authority had often by the Victorian period come to play a pivotal role in the social hierarchy of their respective communities. Roman Catholicism too was becoming very much an official religion in this sense by the middle of the century, with the formalization of its organization in the restoration of the hierarchy of bishops in 1850, and the development of increasingly ambitious and enduring church-building. The legacy of the evangelical and Catholic growth analysed in the preceding chapter was thus great diversity in the character of official religion. It was linked to a wide range of political and constitutional attitudes and, as we shall see, cut across some social distinctions even while it served to reinforce others.

The purpose of this chapter and the next one is to examine the institutions and reality of religion, particularly in local communities, during the Victorian years and afterwards. The material is organized on the basis of the categories of official and unofficial religion which were explained in Chapter 1.[1] In this chapter there will be a discussion of formal religious institutions and the extent and nature of their support. We shall first survey the various branches of official religion, examine their social significance and consider the manner in which they changed during the period. Then in the second section of the chapter we shall investigate the available evidence for the numerical strength of official religion. In Chapter 4 the religious attitudes – or lack of them – of those not connected with the organized churches will be explored under the heading of 'unofficial religion', and the changing nature of these beliefs in the face of the vigour of institutional religion will be examined. This consideration of religion as it impinged on everyday life is an essential preliminary for the analysis of its relationship to national affairs, which will follow in subsequent chapters.

1. THE VARIETIES OF OFFICIAL RELIGION

The Church of England and Ireland provides the obvious starting point for this account. At the beginning of our period it was formally linked with the state in all parts of the British Isles except Scotland, and had an important role to play in local and national power structures. It was a hierarchical institution headed by four archbishops: Canterbury was by far the most important, having jurisdiction over virtually the whole of England south of the Trent and nearly the whole of Wales. The province of York was relatively much smaller, consisting of the northern counties of England and the Isle of Man. The Irish hierarchy was also headed by two archbishops, Armagh and Dublin, although before the reforms of 1833 there had been four. The next tier of administration was provided by the diocesan bishops, of whom, not counting the archbishops, there were twenty-five in England and Wales in 1850, and ten in Ireland. In addition the Isle of Man had its own bishop.

Within the dioceses there were various intermediate levels of jurisdiction, particularly archdeaconries and rural deaneries, but the basic building blocks of the Church's organization were the parishes, which varied tremendously in size. At one extreme the numerous old churches which survive in historic towns such as Exeter, Norwich or York are a reminder that parishes there were very small, covering perhaps only a few hundred square yards. These reflected the density of population in walled cities in the medieval era. At the other extreme in sparsely populated moorland and mountain districts parishes could be many miles across, while even in settled agricultural districts they were often large or awkward in shape and included more than one village.

A general awareness of the institutional and geographical organization of the Church leads to two observations. First, there was an aspiration to maintain a presence in every corner of the country. Herein was the reason for the numerical strength of the Irish hierarchy which, even after the reforms of 1833 had reduced it substantially, still seemed disproportionate in a country in which only 10.7 per cent of the population was Anglican.[2] The ideal of an Established national Church was that it should be responsible for all the people, even those who were apathetic or hostile towards it. Second, however, the historic inflexibility of Anglican structures were, in England and Wales, a major root of the Church's difficulty in making this constitutional theory a social and religious reality. At diocesan level there had been some changes in the late 1830s, but many bishops still had responsibilities beyond the capability of even the most energetic of men: the diocese of Exeter covered the whole of Devon and Cornwall; the bishop of Lincoln was responsible for Derbyshire and Nottinghamshire as well as for Lincolnshire. The only new dioceses to be created before the last quarter of the century were those of Ripon and Manchester. At the parochial level too, although change was under way by 1850, it was still belated and retarded by legal and administrative difficulties.

Such is the context in which the position of the Church of England in local communities needs to be seen. The conservative ideal was that the parish should itself be a coherent community, dominated by the squire and parson in the countryside; and in the towns by the vicar and the leaders of civic and commercial life. Certainly this ideal did exist in some parishes, but by the nineteenth century probably in no more than a small minority. The key problem was that many parishes were not of a viable size and geography for the ideal to be a reality, especially in view of the changes in population and the nature of society that had occurred since they had been set up centuries earlier. Some parishes, especially in former medieval walled towns, were too small. In York the movement of population outside the walls was already well under way by the early Victorian period and some city-centre churches were far from full. Talk of the amalgamation of parishes was already in the air.[3] The problem of redundant churches in historic cities has been a more long-term one than is often appreciated and arose originally as much from changing patterns of residence as from decline in religious adherence. Moreover in city centres people could choose from a whole range of churches within easy walking distance, so the coherence of a parish as a community that both lived and worshipped together was very limited. Ironically, at the same time as city-centre churches lacked congregations, growing populations in suburbs suffered from a lack of Anglican church accommodation. York again provides a good example, with problems which had to be remedied by the construction of churches like St Paul's, Holgate, in 1851, and St Clement's in 1872–4.[4] Thus even where the Church was superficially strong, in practice it was struggling to maintain an effective and consistent presence.

The problems were much more acute in areas removed from the traditional ecclesiastical centres, particularly in large and populous parishes. There were numerous instances, typically but not exclusively in the north of England, where parishes that had originally consisted of large tracts of moorland or waste around a single settlement were now becoming areas of dense industrial and urban development. Leeds in the mid-sixteenth century was, by modern standards, a large village with a population of some 3,000, mostly living close to the medieval parish church on the banks of the river Aire. By 1841 not only had the population of the parish increased to over 150,000, but many of these people lived in substantial townships at a considerable distance from the parish church. New churches were built for them, but the whole remained one parish: technically the new churches were known as 'chapels of ease', subordinate to the jurisdiction of the parish church, but provided for the ease of the people so that they did not regularly have to travel to the parish church for services. However, until the parish was divided in 1844 these separate churches were not allowed to obtain the degree of legal independence that would have enabled them to develop as genuine centres of local community according to the Anglican ideal.[5] Population shifts could also produce difficulties in agricultural districts. For example, a report on the Vale of York parish of Moor Monkton in 1845 observed that: 'The Church of this place is most inconveniently situated for the population of the Parish – It is about half a mile from the Village of Moor Monkton . . . and two and a half miles from Hessay, a populous hamlet in the Parish'.[6]

If the gap between Anglican aspirations and realities was thus starkly apparent in England, it was even more dramatic in Wales and Ireland. The diocese of Llandaff, covering many of the South Wales valleys, faced in particularly extreme form the problems of adaptation to the needs of an increasingly urbanized society. Ancient parochial division did not correspond to contemporary patterns of settlement. Clergy, such as the vicar of Aberdare in 1849 with one church and one curate pastoring 12,000 people dispersed over a parish ten miles by six, had an impossible task.[7] In the south of Ireland the Church found itself ministering to increasingly dispersed and embattled Anglican minorities, with no realistic prospect of making much impact on the Roman Catholic majority. In the 1860s 486 of the Church of Ireland's 1,518 benefices had a hundred or less church members.[8] In the north of Ireland needs and resources were rather better balanced than in most other parts of the United Kingdom, but the phenomenally rapid growth of Belfast gave rise to pressures similar to those apparent in English industrial centres.[9]

Scotland differed markedly from the other parts of the British Isles in that the Established Church there was Presbyterian not Anglican. Some isolated chapels apart, the Church of England did not have an organized presence north of the Border. The Scottish Episcopal Church was a distinct body with its own traditions, although it gradually grew much closer to the Church of England with which it is nowadays in full communion. Within Scotland it remained a minority and technically Nonconformist form of religious affiliation, greatly overshadowed by the Church of Scotland which retained its links with the state and since 1690 had adopted a Presbyterian form of organization. This meant that the Church was governed not by bishops but by a hierarchy of courts and assemblies, from the kirk session in each parish, through the presbytery covering the town or district, and the synod with regional jurisdiction, to the General Assembly, the supreme body which meets in Edinburgh each May to legislate and settle appeals from the lower courts. The participation of ministers and lay elders at all levels of church government contrasted with the Church of England where such participation in decision-making was virtually non-existent before the second half of the nineteenth century, and Convocation, the Church's 'Parliament' had not been active since 1717. In Scotland, on the other hand, in the absence of a lay Parliament in Edinburgh since the Union of 1707 the General Assembly served as an important expression of Scottish identity and a forum for debate. Thus in both legal and political terms the general assembly represented a significant focus of jurisdiction and engagement.

The Church of Scotland resembled the Church of England in that it sought to maintain a territorial parochial organization in all corners of the country. Historically its role in the community had been even greater than that of its southern neighbour, with responsibilities relating to local government, social welfare and education. Like the Church of England it was under strain from the growth of population associated with the Industrial Revolution and the changing pattern of settlement, and found it difficult to respond because of institutional and legal difficulties. Unlike the Church of England it had to live with the sudden and direct consequences of a major split in 1843.[10] The seceding Free Church of Scotland also saw itself as an institution with a national status and scope, although it had cut its formal links with the state. In competition with the Church of Scotland it sought to maintain a presence and jurisdiction in all parts of Scotland, and in some areas, especially in the Highlands, it commanded the support of the overwhelming majority of the churchgoing population.

In evaluating the role of organized religion in local communities it is important to recognize the implications of the claims of the Church of England (in Wales and Ireland as well as England), the Church of Scotland, and the Free Church of Scotland to be truly national churches with a role in every community in the country. The fact that at times such claims looked very unrealistic did not stop them being made, and their potential for producing division when they were contested was considerable. The aspirations of the Established Churches also had significant implications for their social composition. Generally speaking the Church of England, and to a lesser extent, the Church of Scotland, bound up as they were with the structures of social and political authority, were likely to be dominated by the social élite: the landed aristocracy, the gentry and substantial farmers in the country; the civic dignitaries and professions in the towns. Poorer people were made to feel that the Church legitimated the structures that kept them in a subordinate situation. The most striking illustration of this was the private pew system which operated in many nineteenth-century churches: pews were rented by individuals and families and those who could not afford to rent were liable to be consigned to the side aisles or the back of the building. In many churches there was very little free space for those who did not rent pews, and such seating as there was would be associated with a considerable stigma of inferiority. The layout and size of pews also reflected the social hierarchy, although by giving the more prosperous parishioners a physical stake in the church they may well have helped to sustain their identification with it. In Glasgow at least the socially exclusive effects of the system increased during the first half of the nineteenth century as rents were increased.[11]

Nevertheless it would be wrong to infer that the Established Churches did not receive a significant degree of support from the working classes. Evidence for some Glasgow churches in the middle of the nineteenth century suggests that the membership of the three Church of Scotland churches in the sample included 78.6 per cent of artisans and unskilled labourers, as opposed to 54.3 per cent for the non-Established churches. The Church of Scotland was relatively attractive because its moral discipline and financial demands tended to be less onerous.[12] A similar point has been made in relation to the Church of England in later nineteenth-century Lancashire where 'a widespread temperamental disaffinity between Nonconformity and popular manners' gave some credence to Anglican claims to be the true 'church of the people'.[13]

During the Victorian period, moreover, the Established Churches did feel an increasing sense of responsibility and mission to the poorer people in society. This stemmed in part from an instinct for self-preservation in the face of political attack, which obliged them to demonstrate that they were not neglecting their historic role. Social fears blended here with political unease: in 1840 Sir Robert Inglis in urging Parliament to promote more money for church-building, stated bluntly that, 'The Church is the most effective restraint upon crime: and a well-administered parochial superintendence is the most complete and efficient police of any country'.[14] Increasing energy also reflected the impact of the activism and zeal which stemmed from the evangelical and Oxford movements. The standard Anglican response was to build and rebuild churches: 929 in England between 1841 and 1850; 820 between 1851 and 1860; 1120 between 1861 and 1870.[15] New churches were more likely to have a substantial provision of free seats for the working classes and were frequently deliberately situated in poorer districts. In Scotland there had been a great surge of church-building by the Church of Scotland in the 1830s under the leadership of Thomas Chalmers, when about 200 churches had been constructed. In the subsequent aftermath of the Disruption of 1843 Free Church congregations had to build themselves new places of worship, thus further substantially enlarging the overall number of churches in Scotland, although in the cities these were prone to be situated so as to serve the middle rather than the working class.[16] Similarly in South Wales the Anglican Church began belatedly but energetically to respond to the needs of a greatly increased population, a development that is linked particularly to the appointment of Alfred Ollivant to the see of Llandaff in 1850.[17] The Victorian era saw particularly extensive church-building in Wales, with the number of Anglican places of worship increasing from 1,040 in 1831 to 1,867 in 1906, and correspondingly widespread rebuilding and extension.[18]

The Victorian era also saw substantial reforms in the organization of the Church of England. In 1835 Sir Robert Peel had set up the Ecclesiastical Commission (the ancestor of the present-day Church Commissioners) to recommend improvements. Legislation was subsequently passed to revise diocesan boundaries; to redistribute revenues where they were most needed; and severely to restrict pluralism, which had frequently led to neglect and injustice. Subsequently the New Parishes Act of 1843 simplified the legal procedures involved in dividing densely populated or unwieldy parishes. The Church of Ireland similarly underwent substantial reforms between 1800 and 1870, partly through the efforts of its own leaders; partly, especially in the aftermath of the legislation of 1833, by the will of government. There was a steady increase in the number of benefices and churches.[19]

Although much of the legal basis for reforming the Church of England was already in place before 1850, its implementation on the ground took several decades. Readers of Anthony Trollope's Barsetshire novels will be familiar with the tensions there depicted between the old and the new during the 1850s and 1860s. Much depended on the energy and efficiency of individual bishops whose impact was likely to be limited by the scale of the task before them. It was not until the 1870s and 1880s that the number of dioceses was significantly increased, and only after the First World War that the modern figure of forty-one dioceses in England and six in Wales was reached. During the same period the Church gradually acquired a stronger central organization, starting in the 1850s with the revival of the Convocations of Canterbury and York, the assemblies of the clergy which had not met other than formally since the early eighteenth century. The idea of lay participation gained ground through Church Congresses which took place annually from 1862. Laymen were represented in the Convocations from 1886 and the structure was reorganized with the creation of the Church Assembly in 1919, which was itself replaced by the General Synod in 1970.

In turning to consider the situation of Nonconformity in local communities we must first remember that we are dealing with a category that was very diverse institutionally and theologically, with several dozen different groups. Not only were there Congregationalists (at an earlier date known as Independents), Baptists, Presbyterians, Methodists, Unitarians, Quakers and, from the 1880s, the Salvation Army, as well as other smaller groups, but several of these categories were significantly divided among themselves. This was especially true of the Methodist tradition which in 1850 comprised Wesleyans, the original mainstream; Primitive Methodists, more working-class in composition; Bible Christians, concentrated in the rural West Country; the Methodist New Connexion; the Protestant Methodists; the Wesleyan Methodist Association; and the Wesleyan Reformers. The last three named amalgamated in 1857 to form the United Methodist Free Churches.[20] There was also a significant division between Particular and General Baptists. There is no space here to trace the development and characteristics of these different denominations in specific detail, but some trends and categories will be discussed.[21]

Nineteenth-century Nonconformity was the product of widely diverse historical events. The Baptists and Congregationalists had their origins in conscientious dissent from the Anglican religious settlements of the sixteenth and seventeenth centuries, but they were also shaped in important ways by the spiritual and theological consequences of the Evangelical Revival, and the social and economic impact of the Industrial Revolution. Meanwhile the English Presbyterians who, like their Scottish counterparts, had initially been orthodox Calvinists, in the eighteenth century followed a rather different path: they were influenced not so much by the Evangelical Revival as by the more liberal and secular strands of Enlightenment thought. So they moved to the Unitarian position, in which the doctrines of the Trinity and the divinity of Christ are played down, and much of the doctrinal framework of mainstream Christianity accordingly modified. Unitarians tended to do particularly well out of the economic growth of the late eighteenth and early nineteenth centuries, and emerged as an important force in the society of many commercial and industrial centres. However, lacking the expansionist zeal of more evangelical groups, they did not increase their numbers. Subsequently in the later nineteenth century orthodox Presbyterianism began to re-establish itself in England. Apart from the Unitarians, the only other long-standing religious group which did not expand in the nineteenth century was the Society of Friends (Quakers).

Some Nonconformist groups had already by 1850 formed an upper middle-class social élite in large industrial and commercial towns such as Birmingham, Leeds and Manchester. In the south and in cathedral cities they were more likely to be overshadowed by Anglican aristocratic and professional classes. Denominationally these groups were likely to be Unitarian, Congregationalist or sometimes Wesleyan Methodist. They built grand chapels and civic buildings to display their wealth and power. Their Scottish counterparts were Free Church and United Presbyterian who, it has been suggested, represented new wealth, whereas the Church of Scotland was supported rather by the more staid and settled elements of the middle class.[22] In the north of Ireland orthodox Presbyterians, strongly influenced by Scotland, came to play something of a similar role. These Nonconformist urban élites were Liberal in politics, as they wanted to see the remaining privileges of the Established Churches removed, but in their social attitudes they were frequently deeply conservative. They conceived of society as a hierarchy in which religion was a crucial spiritual and moral cement, but a hierarchy in which the Nonconformist industrialist or entrepreneur, rather than the Anglican squire or parson, was the dominant figure. Their chapels were not necessarily socially exclusive and the lower middle class and artisans were often active members, but they served as a channel for the exercise of power and prestige by those who possessed the greatest wealth. Like Anglican places of worship they were frequently sustained by pew rents and, although the social order this represented might be more fluid than in the parish church it was none the less very tangible. This social vision is reflected in the model villages a number of industrialists built for their employees. Saltaire was followed later in the century by Bournville near Birmingham, associated with the Cadbury chocolate factory; and Aintree in Lancashire, built by William Hartley for the workforce at his jam factory. On a larger scale, late nineteenth-century Nonconformists in cities such as Birmingham cultivated what has been dubbed the 'civic gospel', a vision of the city itself as a large community fulfilling the Word of God in providing public services and social discipline for its inhabitants.

However, the majority of Nonconformity in the mid-nineteenth century existed in a more modest social context, drawing the core of its support from a rather lower stratum of society, the lower middle class and upper working class. The Primitive Methodists indeed originated as a more predominantly working-class denomination, especially strong among miners and agricultural labourers. Nonconformity of this kind tended to emerge among those who were either physically remote from the parish church, or socially and culturally alienated from it. The chapel would then become an important focus of the community. This kind of Nonconformity could be found both in the countryside and in industrial settlements in most parts of Britain. In Scotland Presbyterian groups which had seceded from the Established Church were more widespread than the Methodists and Baptists who were its mainstay in England.[23] In Ireland, on the other hand, Methodism was a principal catalyst of revivalist popular evangelicalism. In Wales such lower-class Nonconformity was at its most developed and influential. The weak hold of the Church of England in the principality combined with the strong impact of evangelicalism on the industrializing society of the valleys of the south to produce villages and towns in which the chapels were the central focus of the community. Furthermore in early industrial Wales evangelical Nonconformist networks were an important link between town and countryside. Men moving in search of work whether on a seasonal or permanent basis were likely to bring with them a letter of recommendation committing them to the care of the local chapel.[24] In addition to the growth of the Calvinistic Methodists, later the Presbyterian Church of Wales, there was also considerable lower-class support for the Baptists and the Congregationalists.

As the nineteenth century wore on such chapel communities, in both England and Wales, tended to move upwards in the social scale. This progress can be followed in the changing size and pretensions of their places of worship. At the beginning of the Victorian period these were usually simple, small, and inexpensive buildings, but by the end of the nineteenth century all bodies of Nonconformists were building much grander chapels which emulated the pretensions of the Unitarians, Wesleyans and Congregationalists. A good example of this is provided by the small west Yorkshire town of Hebden Bridge which lacked an Anglican church until 1832 and was dominated by Baptists. Both the Particular (Calvinist) and General (Arminian) traditions were prominently represented. The former built their first chapel in 1777, but replaced it in 1857 with the larger Hope Chapel, still one of the most prominent buildings in the main street. Meanwhile the General Baptists built a succession of chapels at Birchcliffe on a hill above the town, culminating in 1898–9 with a very elaborate and imposing building that effectively displayed the wealth of the congregation.[25] At a fairly early stage in the nineteenth century affiliation to organized religion had come to be associated with a perceived division within the working class between the 'respectable' – God-fearing, moral, law-abiding and clean-living – and the remainder, seen as hard-drinking, sexually promiscuous and potentially disorderly. During the Victorian period 'respectability' became more diffused among the working class, but existing religious groups tended to become more socially exclusive. By 1900 Nonconformity as a whole was becoming more predominantly middle-class in character, a process associated with continuing urbanization, which meant that even smaller towns such as Hebden Bridge developed greater prosperity and social stratification.

These changes were accompanied by a counterpart to the reform and reorganization undergone by the Church of England during the Victorian era, as Nonconformity increasingly acquired more coherent and nationwide structures. Methodism had always possessed a hierarchical organization with the circuit system in the localities and the conference at the centre, although among the smaller Methodist groups this was less authoritarian in its operation than among the Wesleyans. Baptists and Congregationalists, on the other hand, had originally lacked central organization: the latter's older name of Independents indicated their emphasis on the principle of autonomy of the local congregation. However, the formation of the Baptist Union in 1813 and the Congregational Union in 1832, in which year the Baptist Union was reorganized, provided the foundation for growing denominational coherence. This trend continued throughout the rest of the century and was paralleled among Methodists and Presbyterians by gradual reunification among the groups which had divided at various times from the main stem. The General Assembly of the Presbyterian Church in Ireland had been formed in 1840 by the merging of the Synod of Ulster and the Secession Synod, which dated back to the 1740s. In Scotland the consolidation of various dissenting Presbyterian groups led in 1847 to the formation of the United Presbyterian Church which itself was to combine with the Free Church in 1900. Eventually the resulting United Free Church rejoined the Church of Scotland in 1929.[26] In English Methodism a similar process reached its conclusion in 1932 when the Wesleyans, the Primitives, and the United Methodist Churches joined to form a single body. From the 1890s the moves towards consolidation went beyond individual denominations with the formation in 1896 of the National Council of Free Churches, an ancestor of the modern Free Church Federal Council which was set up in 1940. The sense of a 'Free Church' identity itself suggested a growing institutional maturity and self-confidence when compared with the earlier words 'dissent' and 'Nonconformity'.

New revivalist and sectarian movements developed during the Victorian era and did something to fill the social gap left by the growing prosperity and institutionalization of mainstream Nonconformity. Prominent among them was the Salvation Army which became an important religious force in the three decades before the First World War: membership increased from under 5,000 in 1877 to 115,000 in 1911.[27] Although in some respects the outlook of its founder, General Booth, was a deeply conservative one, the Salvation Army still possessed a strong emotional appeal blended with genuine social concern. This made it attractive to that lower-class constituency which existing Nonconformity, even in its originally more popular forms, now tended in practice to exclude.

The final major division of official Christianity, the Roman Catholic Church, has already been extensively discussed in the previous chapter. Two key developments in 1850 served, both in practical and symbolic terms, to strengthen its growing institutional maturity. First, in England and Wales a territorial hierarchy of twelve bishops, headed by the Archbishop of Westminster, was set up. This replaced the looser and more provisional system whereby Roman Catholics had, since the Reformation, been led by vicars-apostolic, holding episcopal rank, but having jurisdiction over districts rather than dioceses. The new bishops avoided titles then held by Anglicans, thus implicitly accepting their possession of the historic sees, and took their names from towns such as Birmingham, Clifton (Bristol), Hexham and Salford. Although these titles were made illegal by the Ecclesiastical Titles Act of 1851, this was never effectively enforced and was repealed in 1871. The hierarchy was subsequently expanded to the modern total of five archbishops and fifteen bishops, not counting auxiliaries. Meanwhile the Scottish hierarchy was restored in 1878. At a lower level of organization the relatively loose structure of the missions of earlier days developed into a rich and energetic parish life, with numerous social and educational as well as religious activities which provided an important focus for Irish communities in Britain. There was extensive building activity, and the increasingly large and elaborate Roman Catholic churches of the Victorian era are testimony to a greatly enhanced confidence and sense of stability. The effect of all this was to strengthen the position of the Roman Catholic Church in Britain and render it, as numbers grew further, a significant force in local and regional life.

Second, although the discontinuities were less apparent than in England and Wales, 1850 was also an important symbolic date in the history of the Roman Catholic Church in Ireland. That year saw the arrival in Ireland of Paul Cullen, Archbishop of Armagh from 1850 and of Dublin from 1852, an authoritarian Ultramontane who was to dominate Irish Catholicism until his death in 1878. Also in 1850 an episcopal synod at Thurles in County Tipperary agreed a code of discipline which marked the culmination of the preceding period of reform. Meanwhile in the aftermath of the tragic loss of life and emigration that had occurred in the great famine of 1846–7, the Church now found that its resources were more equal to the demands being made upon them and effective pastoral control became easier. During the second half of the nineteenth century Mass attendance reached near universal levels that were maintained for much of the twentieth century, and the Roman Catholic Church correspondingly gained in social and political influence.

During our period the only substantial organized non-Christian religious group in Britain was the Jewish community. The Jews numbered 25,000 in 1800; 35,000 in 1850; and 60,000 by 1880.[28] Much the largest concentration of Jews was in London, but, by the turn of the century there were also significant communities in Cardiff, Dublin and Glasgow, and in a number of English provincial cities. During the thirty years before the First World War immigration from Eastern Europe greatly increased Jewish numbers, to some 300,000 in 1914, an influx which can be compared with the impact of the Irish on Roman Catholicism in Britain a generation before. In other respects too the experience of official Judaism during the Victorian era resembled that of Christian churches. Like the Roman Catholics, Jews gradually acquired full civil rights and enhanced status in the wider community, a process which culminated in the Emancipation Act of 1858, which gave them the right to sit in Parliament. At the same time British Jewry developed and strengthened its internal organization, under the leadership of Nathan Marcus Adler who was elected to the newly created office of Chief Rabbi in 1844 and his son Hermann, who succeeded him in 1891. The Adlers established the Chief Rabbinate as an office with considerable authority to exercise religious discipline and arbitrate in disputes. The process of centralization was reinforced by the formation of the United Synagogue in 1870. Socially British Jewry was very diverse, and became more so with the immigration of the late nineteenth century. Until the 1880s, however, it was disproportionately middle-class and throughout the period power lay with an élite of financiers, merchants and professional men, whose influence ensured an exclusiveness in many synagogues comparable to that of the unreformed Church of England or the Unitarians. This reached its apogee in the secession of some Jews in the capital to form the West London Reform Synagogue of British Jews, a movement which owed as much to social élitism as to theological and liturgical difference.[29]

There was also a growing number of other religious groups, both on the fringes of Christianity and representing other major world religions, which set up at least a token presence in Britain. Mormon missionaries first arrived at Liverpool in 1837 and enjoyed significant initial success before numbers declined again in the 1850s because of mass emigration to America; Spiritualism became established in 1852; Christian Science was imported to England in 1897. Islam initially developed around visitors and more permanent residents from the Indian subcontinent who came to Britain for political, professional or commercial reasons, as well as Arab sailors who settled in ports such as Liverpool and South Shields. A mosque was built at Woking in 1889 and there was significant organizational activity in Liverpool at the turn of the century.[30] There was a Sikh temple in London by 1900, and the Buddhist Society, drawing its support from the indigenous population rather than immigrants, was founded in 1924.

Nonconformity and Roman Catholicism in Britain had played a central role in the new community structures emerging in the wake of industrialization, and the Established Churches, after a slow start, were by the second half of the nineteenth century showing a capacity to reform and adapt themselves. However, over the period as a whole there was a tendency for official religion to become more official in the sense that it acquired greater bureaucracy and centralization. The long-term result was to weaken the ties between religious bodies and the local communities in which they had had their birth. A revealing example of the tensions this could produce is provided by the case of the north Yorkshire fishing village of Staithes where Methodist reunion in 1932 failed to diminish the strength of the community structures around the two competing chapels: as late as the 1970s plans for rationalization stirred strong hostility and had to be abandoned. The villagers felt their identity and community to be threatened by the denominational bureaucracy.[31] At the same time, newer religious bodies, whether orthodox Christians like the Salvation Army or more exotic creeds like the Mormons, faced, despite a measure of success, an uphill struggle in developing support in communities where clear social and value structures already existed.

At the same time, as the nineteenth century wore on, the increasing formalization and standardization of official religious structures provided the basis for a strengthening national consciousness in ecclesiastical life. Congregations might still retain a strong sense of local identity, but for the leaders at least this was balanced by an awareness of being part of a larger whole. Roman Catholic reform in Ireland; Anglican Church Congresses; the development of the Free Church ethos in England; and Presbyterian reunion in Scotland were all symptoms and catalysts of this process. Herein, as we shall see in subsequent chapters, lay the potential for official religion to become an important vehicle for nationalism.

2. THE DIMENSIONS OF RELIGIOUS PARTICIPATION

The measurement of involvement in organized religion is a complex and controversial business. In this section two complementary approaches will be used. There will first be an analysis of a unique survey, the Census of Religious Worship of 1851, which, for all its limitations, provides a snapshot of the pattern of attendance on one Sunday at the beginning of our period. Unfortunately, however, although there were some local unofficial surveys at later dates, the exercise was never repeated on a nationwide basis. Subsequently, in tracing the patterns of change over subsequent decades we shall use series of membership and other statistics. Discussion of Ireland will be postponed to the end of the section, because the different nature of the available evidence renders it impossible to make direct comparisons with England, Scotland and Wales.

On Sunday 30 March 1851 all places of religious worship in England, Scotland, and Wales were asked to make a return of various information, including the seating capacity of the building and, most interestingly for our purposes, the number of people who attended each service on that day. There was no question on the composition of church attenders by age group and gender. The information provided was somewhat patchy, particularly in Scotland, but it permits the compilation of Tables 3.1 and 3.2.

It is important at the outset to note that these figures all relate to *attendances* not individuals: in other words, when someone went to church more than once on census Sunday he or she was counted twice, or even three times. Hence, although at first sight it might seem that 60.8 per cent of the population of England and Wales and 60.68 per cent of that of Scotland attended public worship, this was not the case, and this figure represents an upper limit. The lower limit is provided by the numbers at the best-attended service, that in the morning, which was 25.9 per cent of the population of England and Wales. Common sense suggests that we should take a figure somewhere towards the middle of this range, but judgements about this are inevitably arbitrary. Accordingly one cannot be more specific than to say that the census returns indicate that probably between a third and a half of the population of Britain attended worship on that day.

There are considerations which suggest that the census figures underestimate the influence of organized religion. Attendance on a given Sunday is not the same as a count of those linked with the institution. There would obviously have been significant numbers of people unable

Table 3.1   1851 Religious Census – England and Wales[a]

(a) Total attendances (in thousands)

Service time	Numbers	% of population
Morning	4,643	25.9
Afternoon	3,191	17.8
Evening	3,066	17.1
Total	10,896	60.8

(b) By denomination

	Attendances	% of population	% of attendance
Church of England	5,292,551	29.52	48.57
Protestant Nonconformists	5,167,824	28.83	47.43
Roman Catholics	383,630	2.14	3.52
Mormons	35,626	0.20	0.33
Jews	6,030	0.03	0.06
Others	10,405	0.06	0.1

(c) Local samples

Counties	Population	Attendance as % of population	By denomination C of E	RC	NC
Devon	567,000	70.5	56.9	0.9	42.6
Oxfordshire	170,000	69.0	58.5	1.2	40.3
Lancashire	2,031,000	44.1	42.6	16.3	41.1
West Riding	1,366,000	52.9	34.2	2.9	62.9

Towns	Population	Attendance as % of population	By denomination C of E	RC	NC
Exeter	32,818	84.5	64.7	0.9	34.4
York	36,303	62.3	43.2	10.5	46.3
Bristol	137,328	56.7	44.9	5.9	49.2
Sheffield	135,310	32.1	34.3	9.2	56.5
Merthyr Tydvil	63,080	88.5	6.0	4.3	89.7[b]

Notes:

a This table and the subsequent ones have been compiled on the basis of figures in the printed reports of the Census (*Parliamentary Papers*, 1852–3, lxxxix (England and Wales) and 1854, lix (Scotland)) and summaries of it in Robert Currie, Alan Gilbert and Lee Horsley, eds, *Churches and Churchgoers: Patterns of Church Growth in the British Isles Since 1700* (Oxford, 1977), pp. 216–19; John D. Gay, *The Geography of Religion in England* (London, 1971), pp. 22–4; B. I. Coleman, *The Church of England in the Mid-Nineteenth Century* (London, 1980), pp. 40–1. It should be noted that the national (but not local) figures given are after 'correction' by Horace Mann, the editor of the published census returns, who added an estimate for places of worship that failed to make a return. The number of these was fairly small in England and Wales, although higher in some districts; but it Scotland it was much larger, amounting in the case of the Church of Scotland to 32 per cent of churches. Accordingly the figures for Scotland need to be viewed with particular caution.

b In order to simplify this table Mormons have been counted as Nonconformists. In most cases their numbers were non-existent, or negligible, but in Merthyr they amounted to a significant 4.32 per cent of total attendances.

Table 3.2   1851 Religious Census – Scotland[a]

	Attendances	% of population	% of attendances
Church of Scotland	566,409	19.61	32.87
Free Church	555,702	19.24	31.71
Other Presbyterian	369,451	12.79	21.09
Episcopalians	43,904	1.52	2.50
Roman Catholics	79,732	2.76	4.55
Other Nonconformists	134,056	4.64	7.65
Mormons	3,407	0.12	0.19
Jews	35	0.0012	0.0019
Total	1,742,687	60.68	

Note:

[a] See note a to Table 3.1 for discussion of the limitations of these statistics.

to attend due to youth, age, illness, or essential work; and others may well have been deterred by the inclement weather. Furthermore if we assume that 30 March 1851 was a typical Sunday, and this is itself debatable, it does not follow that the same people attended every week. One Yorkshire clergyman wrote on his form: 'many who attend this Place of Worship attend *frequently* but not regularly'.[32] There is no way of judging how widespread this 'frequent' (but less than weekly) attendance was, but it seems not unreasonable to suggest that appreciably over half the total population attended at least one service in the course of a month.

The figures are rather less treacherous as an indication of relative strengths, whether between denominations or in comparing different regions and localities. The most obvious conclusion to be drawn from Table 3.1 (b) is that while the Church of England had marginally more worshippers than all the Nonconformist denominations put together, it did not have an absolute majority. The statistics could, at least in England, be interpreted as a vindication of its privileged status, especially if the Nonconformist bodies were to be considered separately, in which case the next largest single group was the Wesleyan Methodists, with 1,544,528 worshippers.[33] Nevertheless the Anglican claim to be genuinely the church of the whole population looked somewhat threadbare. Note too the very low level of Jewish attendances counted on the Sabbath, Saturday 29 March, probably reflecting the perceived exclusiveness of synagogues at this date: 3,500 represented only 16 per cent of the ethnically Jewish population.[34]

Table 3.1 (c) provides some indication of the geographical and social factors affecting attendance. First, there was a difference between north and south. Both the southern counties listed had substantially higher overall attendances and a noticeably larger proportion of Anglican ones than the two northern counties. The same is broadly true of the towns, although here a second factor comes into play, namely size and level of industrial development. Thus one can contrast York with Sheffield and Exeter with Bristol, both pairs within a hundred miles of each other, but showing significantly different experiences. Third there is a comparison to be made between town and country, although here the results are more ambiguous. The cathedral cities of Exeter and York had higher and more Anglican attendances than the county areas adjoining them, Devon and the West Riding respectively. On the other hand Sheffield's figures were lower than those for the West Riding. Note too the substantial regional inequalities in the distribution of Roman Catholics.

This sample is generally an accurate reflection of the broader picture. Urbanization usually told against church attendance and there was a broad inverse correlation with the size of the town. On the other hand southern towns, even including London, generally had higher church attendances than would fit this rough rule of thumb, and historic and cathedral cities were the most churchgoing and Anglican of all, more so sometimes than their rural hinterland. It can be inferred that, for towns, an important factor was not just size but rate of growth: in places like Sheffield which had been the boom towns of the Industrial Revolution there was a large proportion of recent migrants. These, it seems, were less likely to be attracted to public worship than a more settled population, and here too the problem of inadequate resources, both of buildings and of clerical manpower, was most acute. It is also clear that, although attendance was usually higher in the countryside than in the towns, even there it was very far from universal.

The tables also serve to demonstrate the distinctiveness of the Welsh and Scottish experiences. Wales as a whole had a much higher rate of attendance than England, equivalent to 83.4 per cent of the population in South Wales, and 86.6 per cent in North Wales.[35] When the English figures are taken separately from the Welsh the attendance there comes down to 59.1 per cent of the population.[36] Moreover the figures for Merthyr Tydvil indicate that in this instance at least industrialization worked, if anything, to the advantage of organized religion. Here the numerical ascendancy of Nonconformity over the Church of England was overwhelming, and, even over the principality as a whole, Anglicanism was very much a minority religion. Within Nonconformity, Baptists and Congregationalists were stronger in the south, while in the north Methodists alone had more than half the total attendances.

Roman Catholicism was still under-represented, although numbers were increasing due to Irish immigration in Glamorgan, reflected in the Catholic attendances for Merthyr which exceeded the average for England and Wales.

Whereas Wales differed from England in the level and distribution of attendances, Scotland had a very similar rate of participation, but a totally different institutional structure. Taken as a whole Presbyterians dominated with 84.5 per cent of total attendances, but the impact not only of the Disruption but also of earlier secessions was very apparent, in weakening the position of the Church of Scotland. Nevertheless allegiance to the Established Church was still significantly greater than in Wales. Episcopalians were no more than a significant minority, already exceeded in numbers by the Roman Catholics who were being swelled by Irish immigration. The relative weakness of non-Presbyterian dissent, comprising Baptists, Congregationalists, Methodists and others, is also striking. The overall figures conceal substantial regional variation within Scotland. The Church of Scotland was weak in the major cities, with only 16 per cent and 20 per cent of recorded attendances in Edinburgh and Glasgow respectively.[37] The north and the Western Isles were almost exclusively Free Church; for example, 85.44 per cent of recorded attendances in Ross and Cromarty.[38] The Catholic presence was greatest on Clydeside, but also significant in other towns including Edinburgh and Dundee, although very small in rural Scotland, except for some pockets of long-standing Scottish (rather than Irish immigrant) Catholicism in the north-east and the Highlands.

These then are some of the broad patterns which can be discerned in the results of the 1851 Census. However, it must be stressed that throughout Britain the experience of adjacent and apparently similar localities could differ considerably. When plotted on a map indicators of religious practice and affiliation can often look like a random patchwork quilt. Thus in explaining them due weight has to be given to factors other than the socio-economic composition of an area, in particular to the personality of religious leaders and the experience of different church and chapel groups. An energetic Anglican parson could substantially enhance his church's position; periods of revivalism could lead to a legacy of very strong Nonconformity, particularly Methodism. One of the most important conclusions to be drawn from study of the religious census is thus the sheer diversity of local experience, which organized religion both reflected and helped to shape.

The contemporary conclusion of Horace Mann that the working class was generally absent from public worship should not automatically be endorsed. Overall attandances were high enough to imply that a proportion at least of the lower strata in society must have been present. Moreover, when specific regions and localities are examined, the evidence that this was so is reinforced.[39] On the other hand there were still numerous absentees, and the indications are that while the skilled artisan groups frequently attended churches or chapels, the unskilled and the destitute stayed away. Moreover failure to attend church did not necessarily imply an absence of religious belief, a point which will be explored further in the next chapter.

It remains to develop the current discussion by considering the pattern of change over the rest of our period by means of membership statistics. Two important limitations must first be noted. First, although statistics are available for most Nonconformist denominations, some important religious groups, notably Roman Catholics and Anglicans, did not have any formal membership. One is thus obliged to resort to figures such as records of baptism, confirmation, communicants, or in the twentieth-century Church of England, electoral roll membership. All these can be valid and helpful on their own terms but comparison becomes a difficult and somewhat subjective process. Second, membership figures may not reveal all that much about the numbers regularly attending worship or participating in the other activities under the auspices of religious organizations. The tendency was for membership to be smaller than attendance in the nineteenth century, but larger in the twentieth. This was a significant change which means that membership should not be used too simplistically as an indicator of changes in a denomination's strength over time.

Tables 3.3, 3.4 and 3.5 present membership and other figures at twenty-year intervals for some of the major denominations. The figures are given in numerical terms and as a percentage of the population of the relevant country at the census taken during the year in question. There are some gaps where no usable information is available: in some instances this has been filled with statistics relating to another neighbouring year, as stated in the notes to the tables.

These tables serve to indicate the most important trends. In England all the sample denominations continued to grow in absolute numbers, at least until the Edwardian period, but, as the percentages make clear, Nonconformists were beginning to lose ground relative to population before the turn of the century. The Church of England continued to gain proportionately as well as absolutely for a decade or two longer.[40] However, in numerical terms the most successful religious group in the twentieth century has clearly been the Roman Catholics. Again, the

Table 3.3   Church membership in England[a]

	Church of England[b]	Methodists	Congregationalists	Roman Catholics[c]
1851		435,971	165,000	900,000
		2.58%	0.98%	5.02%
1871		570,198		
		2.51%		
1891	1,490,000	690,691		1,375,000[d]
	5.42%	2.51%		4.67%
1911	2,293,000	786,330	288,075	1,710,000
	6.74%	2.31%	0.85%	4.74%
1931	2,288,076	788,020	286,277	2,206,244
	6.05%	2.09%	0.76%	5.65%
1951	1,847,998[e]	681,181	207,152	2,808,596
	4.44%	1.64%	0.50%	6.42%

Notes:
a This table and the two following it summarize information derived from Robert Currie, Alan Gilbert and Lee Horsley, eds, *Churches and Churchgoers: Patterns of Church Growth in the British Isles Since 1700* (Oxford, 1977), pp. 128–66, to which source the reader who requires further detail is referred.
b Easter communicants.
c From estimates by clergy; including Wales as well as England, and as a percentage of the population of England and Wales.
d Figure for 1892.
e Figure for 1950.

Table 3.4   Church membership in Wales

	Church in Wales[a]	Calvinistic Methodists[b]	Congregationalists
1851		52,600[c]	60,000[c]
		5.23%	5.96%
1871		93,276	
		7.63%	
1891	111,249	137,415	130,112[d]
	7.35%	9.08%	8.59%
1911	159,252	183,647	168,814
	7.86%	9.08%	8.33%
1931	185,484	185,234	161,737
	8.58%	8.57%	7.48%
1951	176,723[e]	157,124	143,613
	8.13%	7.23%	6.61%

Notes:
a Institutionally part of the Church of England until it was disestablished in 1921.
b Known as the Presbyterian Church of Wales from 1933.
c Figure for 1848.
d Figure for 1890.
e Figure for 1956.

Table 3.5   Church membership in Scotland

	Church of Scotland	Other Presbyterian	Roman Catholic	Episcopalian	Baptists and Methodists
1871	436,147	426,689			15,067
	12.98%	12.70%			0.45%
1891	599,531	527,431[a]	343,000[b]	91,740	20,656[c]
	14.89%	13.10%	8.52%	2.28%	0.51%
1911	714,915	506,096	546,000[d]	142,464	33,452
	15.02%	10.63%	11.47%	2.99%	0.70%
1931	1,260,620	27,616[e]	607,000	133,752	36,168
	26.03%	0.57%	12.53%	2.76%	0.75%
1951	1,273,027	32,850[f]	748,463	103,598	33,499
	24.98%	0.64%	14.69%	2.03%	0.66%

Notes:
a Includes 1890 figures for Reformed Presbyterians and Original Secession.
b Figure for 1892.
c There is no figure available for Primitive Methodists in 1891 and accordingly the mean of the figures for 1871 and 1911, calculated at 1673, has been added to the available Baptist and Wesleyan figures.
d Figure for 1913.
e Includes 1935 communicants figure for Free Church.
f Includes 1953 figures for Reformed Presbyterians and Original Secession: 1957 figure for Free Church.

figures given can mislead in as much as they are a summation of the parish priests' returns of estimated numbers in their parishes, a figure likely to include the nominal and entirely passive to a greater extent than do the series for other denominations. Continuing immigration from Ireland also helped to keep the numbers bouyant. Nevertheless even if the absolute numbers should be scaled down somewhat the trend is significant, showing the capacity of the Roman Catholic Church to retain and even extend its support at a period when otherwise the position of major religious groups was weakening. During the interwar period Anglicans and Nonconformists maintained their absolute numbers – indeed the peak figure of 2.39 million Anglican Easter communicants was not reached until 1927 – but clearly became a reduced proportion of the total population. After the Second World War this relative decline became an absolute reduction in numbers.

There was a broadly similar pattern in Wales, although here Nonconformity almost held its own in proportional as well as absolute terms until the First World War. However, the Anglican Church was also growing strongly in this period, and, unlike Nonconformity, sustained this in the interwar years, even overtaking the Calvinistic Methodists as the largest single denomination. Its peak number of communicants was not reached until 1938. As in England, the Second World War was followed by general decline.

It was in Scotland that the loss of momentum in the non-Established churches was most apparent. The Free Church and the United Pres-byterians were in absolute as well as relative decline before the First World War, in spite, or perhaps because of, their amalgamation in 1900 to form the United Free Church. The Church of Scotland, on the other hand, gained ground in the late nineteenth century, and continued to do so even after the First World War. The figures for 1931 and 1951 are of course inflated by the reunion of 1929, but it is striking that in 1931 the enlarged Church of Scotland was supported by a marginally higher proportion of the population than had been all the Presbyterian groups put together in 1911. Indeed the numerical peak of Church of Scotland membership, at 1,319,574, was not to be reached until 1956.[41] Roman Catholicism in Scotland showed a similar pattern of enlargement to that in England and came to form an even more substantial proportion of the population. Smaller religious groups generally prospered in the early twentieth century. The Scottish Episcopal Church shared in some of the growth of the Church of England in the period before the First World War, although it then suffered a particularly substantial loss of ground in the subsequent decades. The residual dissenting Presbyterian churches and the small groups of non-Presbyterian dissenters – of which Baptists and Methodists are here taken as representative – enjoyed a more sustained expansion which lasted at least until the 1930s.

The preceding discussion has been descriptive rather than explana-tory, but the time has now come to draw out some implications which will be explored further in subsequent chapters. The figures given above indicate that in all parts of Britain, organized Christianity, taken as a whole, continued until the Second World War to maintain approx-imately the same level of adherence as it had done in the late Victorian period. When the memberships of the sample denominations are added together, it emerges that in England and Wales there was only minimal decline proportional to population, from 14.64 per cent in 1911 to 14.55 per cent in 1931 in England;[42] and from 25.02 per cent in 1891 to 24.63 per cent in 1931 in Wales. In the Scottish sample overall adherence even rose, from 39.3 per cent in 1891 to 42.64 per cent in 1931. In 1931 the total proportion of the population with some recorded church affiliation amounted to at least 18.89 per cent in England, 38.52 per cent in Wales and 43.74 per cent in Scotland.[43] Certainly not all members were regular attenders, and in Scotland it appears that attendance was declining even while membership was still rising. On the other hand membership figures do not include children, who would often have been regular if involuntary worshippers. The readiness of such substantial sections of the population to identify with organized religion implies that it remained a significant focus for their sense of identity. This was especially so in Scotland and Wales where higher levels of religious affiliation in the twentieth century were an important aspect of their distinctiveness from England.

This is the overall context for examination of the relative fortunes of the different religious groups. There were internal institutional and spiritual factors which help to explain some of the trends: these include the impact of belated reform and reorganization on the Church of England and its counterparts and the effect of the Revival of 1904–5 in retarding the decline of Welsh Nonconformity. However, over the period as a whole the more successful churches fell into two categories. First, there were the Church of England, the Church of Scotland and the Church in Wales after disestablishment, which served as points of reference for people's sense of national identity within the British state. Second, there were churches which were able to maintain a close identification with the structure of particular geographically concentrated and socially coherent communities. The Roman Catholic Church was by far the most important example of this, but the resilience of small

Table 3.6 Religious affiliation in Ireland (as percentage of population)

	Population	Roman Catholic	Episcopalian	Presbyterian
All Ireland				
1834	7,754,100	80.9	10.7	8.1
1861	5,798,750	77.70	11.95	9.02
1891	4,704,750	75.40	12.75	9.46
1911	4,420,214	73.36	13.04	9.97
Free State[a]				
1911	3,139,688	89.6	7.9	1.5
1926	2,971,992	92.6	5.5	1.1
1946	2,955,107	94.3	4.2	0.8
Northern Ireland				
1911	1,250,531	34.4	26.1	31.6
1926	1,256,561	33.5	27.0	31.3
1951	1,370,921	34.4	25.8	29.9

Source: Robert Currie, Alan Gilbert and Lee Horsley, eds, *Churches and Churchgoers: Patterns of Church Growth in the British Isles Since 1700* (Oxford, 1977), pp. 220–2.
Note:
a The twenty-six southern counties were known as the Irish Free State until they became the Republic of Ireland in 1949.

Presbyterian groups, particularly in the Highlands and Islands, also illustrates the point. Mainstream English Nonconformity had been in such a position in the nineteenth century, but by the First World War the coherence of chapel communities was weakening.

Irish religious statistics are more scanty, and different in nature from those for England, Scotland and Wales. The 1851 religious census did not extend to Ireland, and there is a lack of membership statistics collected by the religious denominations themselves. On the other hand in 1834 the Commissioners of Public Instruction calculated the strengths of the different religious groups at that time and, from 1861 onwards censuses for Ireland, unlike those for Britain, included a question on religious affiliation. These results permit the compilation of Table 3.6, which summarizes results for the major religious groups.

The three groups listed above accounted for all but a small minority of the Irish population. The remainder consisted mainly of other Protestant denominations, of which the Methodists were much the most numerous, although by the turn of the century there were also a few thousand Jews. A striking feature of the returns is how few people identified themselves as having no conventional religious belief, only 146 in the whole of Ireland in 1861.[44] This did not mean that all the remainder were actively involved but it still showed the extent to which religious labels could define the population. Moreover the available evidence indicates that among Catholics, from the later nineteenth century until at least the 1970s, actual church attendances amounted to over 90 per cent of the nominally Catholic population.[45] Among the Presbyterian population commitment was nothing like so high, but it

Table 3.7   Presbyterian Church in Ireland: communicants

	Number	As % of total population	As % of Presbyterians returned in Census
1864[a]	122,790	2.12	23.46
1891	102,735	2.18	23.08
1911	105,962	2.40	24.05
1926	109,748	2.60	25.76
1951[b]	126,902	2.93	29.23

Source: Robert Currie, Alan Gilbert and Lee Horsley, eds, *Churches and Churchgoers: Patterns of Church Growth in the British Isles Since 1700* (Oxford, 1977), pp. 132–5.
Notes:
a Calculation based on 1861 Census.
b Calculation based on 1946 Census for Free State; 1951 Census for Northern Ireland.

was steadily increasing during the first half of the twentieth century, as is shown in Table 3.7.

Ireland with its polarized communities provides an extreme example of the tendency we have already noted in Britain for official religion to maintain strong support where it is associated with social structure and identity. Table 3.6 also serves to indicate some of the changes over time. The proportion of Roman Catholics in the population declined somewhat in the later nineteenth century because Catholics were over-represented in the social groups more affected by post-famine depopulation and emigration. The figures for 1911 show the nature of the geographical distribution of religious allegiance on the eve of partition. Note that in this respect the difference between the Free State and the north increased in the twentieth century as the Protestant population in the south declined. The Church of Ireland accounted for the majority of southern Protestants.

In concluding this chapter cautions about the perspective here offered need to be reiterated. Institutional and statistical history offer an essential skeleton for the understanding of the official religious presence in the life of Britain and Ireland, but such an approach on its own lacks flesh and human depth. Statistics in particular have a seductiveness which can cause one all too easily to forget the diversity of motives and beliefs, social and spiritual, which led men, women and children to attend services on that early spring day in 1851, or to enrol themselves in the membership of the various denominations. Official religion was strongest numerically when it was linked into a wider system of cultural values and so we need to be alert to the possibility that people could participate for very unofficial motives: in other words, the act of attending public worship did not necessarily imply subscription to the parson's or the minister's theological standpoint. Conversely, non-participation could cover a whole spectrum of attitudes, from strong identification of a kind – such as participation in activities other than Sunday services – not recorded in the statistics, through sympathetic apathy, to more or less articulate hostility. Thus we shall turn in the next chapter to examine more closely the attitudes of ordinary people towards religion.

4

OUTSIDE THE SHEEPFOLD?

Unofficial religion

One New Year's Eve in mid-Victorian London the two Anglo-Catholic clergy ministering at the the new church of St Alban's, Holborn, had retired to bed, but found their slumbers disturbed by a crowd gathering in the street outside. One of them, Arthur Stanton, recalled that:

> the bell of the Clergy House was perpetually rung and the demand shouted, 'Aint you going to have a service?' So . . . I got up and and opened the church and let the people in. They filled the church to the doors, and ever afterwards the service was con-tinued, and without announcement or bell the church is always full . . . the poorest come – all the poor – and come in a way they come at no other time; God won't bless them in the year, they think, if they don't.[1]

The clergy had been reluctant to hold a New Year service hitherto because they believed it to be without 'Catholic precedent'. It is an ironic reflection on the efforts of Victorian churchmen to draw the working classes to public worship that on this occasion a service was packed to the doors in spite rather than because of their efforts. Herein lies telling evidence of the existence of an unofficial religious conscious-ness that was independent of official religion and had a life of its own.

The subject of this chapter is the substantial proportion of the population who had only a weak link with institutional religion, or no connection at all. There is an immediate problem of evidence. The focus of attention, in the nineteenth century at least, is the less well educated and literate strata of society; people who accordingly seldom recorded their beliefs and perceptions. There is furthermore the general difficulty of writing the history of something that is by definition unorganized: there are no institutional records and few points of reference. Certainly there has been no lack of investigation, discussion and speculation on the beliefs – or lack of them – of the unchurched, but such evidence all too often has its built-in bias. Contemporary politicians, churchmen, ecclesiastical reformers, even self-conscious secularists, all had their own concerns. More recent and disinterested researchers have had their methodological difficulties. Victorian folklorists, in their efforts to record the customs and superstitions of rural Britain and Ireland, were better at noting the range of traditional beliefs than at evaluating the extent of their influences. Twentieth-century social scientists and poll-sters have had to struggle to avoid intellectual imprisonment by their own questionnaires, as these are prone to impose an external and potentially misleading pattern on people's beliefs. It would be unrealis-tic to suppose that such difficulties in the raw material can be wholly overcome.

The chapter will be divided into three sections. In the first we shall examine unofficial religion in pre-industrial rural society. The encoun-ter between unofficial and official religion will be analysed in the second section, in the context of the socio-economic changes associated with industrialization and urbanization, and the wider impact of Victorian religious reform and revival. Finally, there will be an examination of some of the new forms of unofficial religion that developed in the later Victorian decades as a result of this encounter, and continued well into the twentieth century. This threefold division is made for convenience of analysis and it must be emphasized that in reality the changes that took place were uneven in their impact and all three phases existed in parallel. On the one hand vigorous official religion in the form of Methodism and evangelical Anglicanism had been confronting popular beliefs in industrializing communities since the late eighteenth century; on the other a traditional rural structure of belief was still very much in evidence around 1900 in more remote areas such as Thomas Hardy's Wessex.

1. FOLK RELIGION AND CUSTOM

The term 'folk religion' is a potentially loaded one and, like the word 'superstition', is used in a rather patronizing sense to denominate beliefs that are implicitly presented as inaccurate, outdated, or incoherent. In the present context, however, 'folk religion' is viewed as something very different from superstition – as an integrated structure of supernatural belief and practice, consistent on its own terms but reflecting the semi-literate and pre-industrial culture in which it was based. Only when the overall framework disappeared could its isolated remnants in, say,

Hallowe'en traditions, be fairly dismissed as superstitions. The word 'custom' is used to denote a broader category of practices, those without any clear supernatural reference, but which still reflected the ultimate concerns and symbolic structures of the community.

The results of the 1851 Religious Census discussed in Chapter 3 indicated that in the countryside participation in official religion was far from universal. Moreover even in the Anglican ideal of a village, dominated by the squire and the parson, where there was universal church attendance, it did not follow that the personal beliefs of those present in the pews corresponded to the teachings of orthodox Christianity. It is clear from the work of Keith Thomas and others that the Protestant Reformation in the sixteenth and seventeenth centuries did not eliminate an alternative structure of popular convictions concerning magic and witchcraft.[2] The imprint of such beliefs remained significant especially in the remoter areas of rural England, in the Highlands of Scotland, where the kirk was unable to establish a strong presence and, above all, in Ireland. Here in the eighteenth century neither indolent Anglican clergy nor the repressed Roman Catholic Church was in a position to gain the consistent adherence of the population to its teachings.

Folk religion in nineteenth- and twentieth-century Britain has received limited historical study and one is accordingly heavily dependent on evidence and information from geographically limited sources, notably the South Lindsey area of Lincolnshire for the nineteenth century and the fishing village of Staithes on the northern coast of Yorkshire for the twentieth century.[3] Both are away from the main centres of population and cultural influence and accordingly may not be typical of the whole country. By the same token, however, they may well serve as a stronger 'link with the past' than more centrally situated districts. For Ireland research is more widespread geographically but focused chronologically on the pre-famine period: specific evidence is scanty on the extent to which the structure of belief then prevalent persisted into the later nineteenth century and beyond.[4]

The structure of folk religion was defined not by any abstract theological structure but rather by the passage of time, the long-term sequences of the life-cycle of the individual and the relatively short-term routine of the seasons of the year. This implies that it will flourish best in a stable and coherent community strongly influenced by the routines imposed by nature, where the individual is well known to a whole village, and seedtime and harvest, summer and winter, shape the whole pattern of work and leisure. This naturally implies that agricultural villages had the most strongly ingrained folk religion, although a fishing village such as Staithes met many of the same criteria, with the added factor of the influence on life of the mighty natural force of the sea.

In many respects folk religion was built round the rites and practices of official Christianity, but interpreting and developing them in an alternative fashion. This was particularly apparent in the practices associated with the life-cycle of the individuals. The rites of passage – baptism, confirmation, marriage and funeral – were the focus for considerable unofficial religious belief and even people not normally linked to the churches regarded these as important stages in their lives. Views on baptism well illustrate the differences between the interpretations placed by the clergy and the laity on the same event. For the clergy it might either be a sacramental regeneration of the soul of the child, or a formal entry into the Church of Christ. In folk religion the ceremony lacked any specific theological content: it was rather an occasion of 'christening' or 'naming,' giving a name to a child, entitling him or her to a Christian burial, and bringing to an end a period in which the child was not fully accepted as a part of the community. It was also seen as a security for good luck in life and a protection against illness.[5] In relation to confirmation the divergence was even more marked: for the Anglican clergy this was a solemn ceremony in which the teenager renewed in his or her own name the vows made on their behalf at baptism, and became a fully fledged member of the Church. For the young person and probably for their parents as well, it was a kind of symbolic rite of entry into adulthood. In mid-nineteenth-century Lincolnshire many confirmees marked their new status by going straight from the church to the public house.[6] In Yorkshire around 1900 confirmation was regarded as marking the end of schooling and the beginning of adult employment. For many it represented the conclusion of Sunday School and church attendance, which were seen as an aspect of childhood rather than the beginning of fuller adult participation.[7]

Marriage as a ceremony was generally left as the preserve of official religion, and folk belief and custom centred rather on wider matters of courtship and sexuality. There were, for example, widespread practices in Lincolnshire whereby young people, especially girls, sought to foretell the identity of their future partners. For example, a house key would be fastened in a Bible which was then rested on a finger while the girl recited the names of men she knew. When the Bible spun round it indicated that she had named her husband-to-be.[8] This illustrates two features of folk religion. First it was bound up with a stable community in which everyone is known: the possibility that the girl will not yet have met her future husband is apparently not considered. Second, the physical attributes of official Christianity – in this case the Bible, but in others Communion bread or church buildings – were held to have miraculous powers.

Even in pre-industrial and rural Britain popular sexual mores did not conform to the standards of official religion. The illegitimacy rate in England and Wales in the early and mid-nineteenth century was around 6 per cent of live births,[9] low by modern standards, but when allowance is made for shot-gun marriages, contraception (however crude), and occasions when sexual relations did not result in pregnancy, still implying quite widespread pre- and extra-marital intercourse. In the eyes of the clergy the marriage ceremony was, in sexual terms at least, the point at which the relationship was initiated; in the eyes of their parishioners it was probably often the stamp of communal and official approval on a relationship that had already had its physical side. Such at least would seem to have been the case in rural Yorkshire in 1900 according to an Anglican parson who complained of the 'want of purity' in his parish 'and the little sense of the gravity of such sins (through custom) before marriage'.[10] However, over England and Wales as a whole the illegitimacy rate had fallen by 1900 to around 4 per cent, a sign perhaps of a more effective imposition of official moral standards. In Scotland illegitimacy was nearly 8 per cent in 1855 and charges of fornication were still brought before kirk sessions, a sign that even those formally associated with the churches were by no means immune from this sin. In Ireland, by contrast, illegitimacy rates were much lower, at 3.8 per cent when first recorded in 1864 and 2.7 per cent in 1900, and it seems that premarital intercourse, especially if it resulted in pregnancy, was much less socially acceptable.[11] On the other hand strict standards of sexual behaviour contrasted with an uninhibited strain in conversation and manners. Moreover, at least in the pre-famine period, precise regulations of marriage by parents and priests was not infrequently resisted by couples who eloped or adopted the unofficial, but widely accepted, practice of clandestine marriage, conducted by suspended clergy and others.[12]

It was in response to death that official and unofficial religion came closest together, each contributing their part to interlinked rites and social customs. These procedures ensured the decent disposal of the corpse, assisted those who were grieving with emotional, practical and spiritual support, and reaffirmed the solidarity of the community. The churches provided the funeral ceremony and the burial, but folk religion added initial portents of the death and rituals such as telling honey-bees of the death of their owner, in the belief that if the bees were not so informed either they would die or there would be another human death in the household. This procedure was reportedly performed over much of England in the Victorian period.[13] Unofficial religion also gave considerable attention to the treatment of the body, through rituals designed to protect the living from contamination by the dead, while also providing an occasion for final symbolic reconciliation with the deceased. Thus in early twentieth-century Staithes bodies were laid out, watched over round the clock, and visited by relatives and friends.[14] Such practices were only a faint shadow of the wake as it had been marked in nineteenth-century Ireland. Here considerable festivities, including drinking and games loaded with sexual innuendos, often took place in the presence of the corpse. This custom has been interpreted as placating the spirit of the deceased by a final feast in his or her honour, or as a reassertion of the vitality of the community in the face of the disruption arising from bereavement. Unlike other Irish unofficial religion it was sufficiently culturally resilient to survive immigration to Britain, but on both sides of the Irish Sea, it gradually declined in the later nineteenth and twentieth centuries, surviving if at all, in more restrained forms analogous to that operating in Staithes.[15]

The annual sequence of the calendar generated numerous further beliefs and practices, in which, significantly, the high points for unofficial religion did not readily correspond to those of the official Christian liturgical year. It is true that there were some common points of focus. Thus Good Friday was treated with reverence by South Lindsey people, but not so much for the theologically orthodox commemoration of Christ's crucifixion as for being associated with a sense of power that made it a good day for planting crops and caused hot cross buns to protect houses from fire.[16] Christmas was certainly celebrated, in England at least, but as much as an occasion for social conviviality as for spiritual observance. Folk customs and beliefs blended with Christian ones, a process apparent in the content of carols such as 'The Cherry Tree' in which the biblical incident (Matthew 1:19) when Joseph finds Mary to be pregnant and accordingly hesitates to marry her is linked to non-Christian ideas of the cherry as a symbol of fertility.[17]

More generally, however, the high points for unofficial religion were marginal to official religion, as was illustrated at the beginning of the chapter. In twentieth-century Staithes the New Year was still being ritually introduced into houses which had to be clean before midnight by a 'first-footer', always a man.[18] In Victorian South Lindsey a rich range of unofficial beliefs were central on 24 April, St Mark's Eve, including the expectation that the devil rode around on a pig and renewed the power of witches. The church building itself became a focus for unorthodox practices, including watching at midnight for portents of the marriages and deaths that were to occur in the community during the coming year.[19] Similarly Hallowe'en (31 October) might appear superficially to be linked to All Saints' Day on 1 November, but in reality drew on traditions ultimately derived from the ancient Celtic festival of Samhain which were sustained by the playfulness of children.[20] Ireland was especially rich in festivals with Celtic origins, which sometimes survived well into the twentieth century. St Bridget's Day (1 February) might be linked to the commemoration of a Christian saint and marked with the wearing of crosses, but it had its origins in Imbolc, the Celtic festival of the beginning of spring. Similarly, St John's Eve (23 June) was the festival of Midsummer, celebrated by the lighting of bonfires and rituals to ward off evil and bring good luck, and surviving in County Galway at least until the middle of the twentieth century. Lughnasa, marking the beginning of the harvest, proved particularly tenacious, and resilient to even superficial Christianization.[21]

The impression that unofficial religion only assimilated official religion selectively, and on its own terms, is confirmed by attitudes to the clergy. Even in England there were occasional instances where magical powers were attributed to Anglican parsons, and in Ireland the idea that Roman Catholic priests had, for example, the power to cure the sick, was probably rather more widespread.[22] A further illustration of the kind of interaction that occurred is the relationship in Ireland between Roman Catholic pilgrimages and unofficial 'patterns'. These latter were gatherings held at places held to be sacred, most commonly holy wells. There was likely to be a link to the feastday of a saint associated with the place, but the devotional practices that occurred were not necessarily sanctioned by ecclesiastical authority, and clergy often criticized the unseemliness of the more festive aspects of the proceedings. The continuing influence of pre-Christian Celtic tradition was again very much apparent.[23]

Unofficial interpretations of official religious occasions merged into forms of wholly non-Christian belief. Witchcraft was still quite widely feared in the nineteenth century, although it did not attract anything like the paranoid and persecuting hostility that it had attracted in the seventeenth century.[24] In Ireland strong popular belief in fairies persisted well into the nineteenth century: they were held to inhabit particular bushes which were left undisturbed even in the middle of cultivated fields. There was the further conviction that fairies could steal a child away and replace him or her with a changeling, which as late as 1895 led to a woman in County Tipperary being burnt to death because she was held to be a fairy child.[25]

Instances of unofficial religion could be multiplied, but the time has come to suggest some conclusions, bearing in mind the framework suggested in Chapter 1. The most salient feature of the unofficial religion here surveyed was an absence of any abstract theology or claims to internalized spiritual experience. Encounters with the supernatural had only a limited significance; for example, in providing a specific insight into the future. The essence of folk religion was ritual and symbolism, designed to ward off evil, bring good luck and cement the solidarity of the community. Its coherence came not from any intellectual scheme but from its integration with the physical environment, the annual round and the landmark events of human life in a stable community. Its relationship to official religion was an ambivalent one: on the one hand certain dates, artefacts and persons provided a common focus, but the associated practices and interpretations varied substantially. It can be inferred that the make-up of the unofficial religion of the nineteenth century in this respect reflected the legacy of previous attempts by the Church to bring popular belief under the umbrella of orthodox Christianity. We must now turn to consider the further phase in this encounter between the official and the unofficial that occurred during our period.

2. RECHRISTIANIZATION

A consciousness that popular religious belief was at best sub-Christian and at worst pagan began increasingly to trouble churchmen in the early nineteenth century. In rural areas not yet touched by industrialization there was at least reassurance to be derived from the existence of formal ties between the church and the population, even if the reality of spiritual life fell short of the ideals of official Christianity. Even this cold comfort was denied to the clergy facing the problems of recently industrialized areas. These often lacked both places of worship to form a focus for the community and the stable cultural and social structures that were an essential prerequisite for folk religion.

At the beginning of our period Britain's shift from the predominantly rural society of the eighteenth century to the primarily urban one of the twentieth had reached its middle point, with the population approximately equally divided between town-dwellers and inhabitants of the country. The recent and rapid nature of the urbanization which had taken place is indicated by the fact that in 1851 nearly half the inhabitants of the largest English and Scottish towns were migrants to them. By 1900, however, three-quarters of the British population lived in towns and urban communities which had become much more stable and well established.[26] Much of Ireland remained, by contrast, a predominantly rural and small town society, but the rapid growth of Belfast and the migration of many thousands of Irish to British cities meant that they too experienced a similar transition.

The discontinuity between rural and urban life should not be overstated. Seasonal migration of labour and the initial development of some industrial settlements as overgrown villages in hitherto rural areas meant that in the mid-nineteenth century the socio-economic distinction between town and country was by no means clear cut. Likewise, there were points of continuity between rural and urban religious beliefs. In particular, the rites of passage continued to play a part in the lives of all but the most impoverished and dehumanized of the urban poor. Nevertheless many of the other factors that sustained unofficial religion in the countryside were lacking in the towns. The rhythm of the agricultural year was absent; so were the fairy bushes, holy wells and other features of the landscape that fuelled Irish popular belief. Above all, initially at least, there was a lack of those shared traditions and that long-term acquaintance with one's neighbours which could provide a basis for meaningful communal rituals and folk religion. The effect was to water down and reduce the content of existing unofficial religion, although it was not wiped out entirely. In Ireland, moreover, at the same time that the growth of British towns was at its most rapid, the socially traumatic experience of the famine of 1847 probably left around a million people dead and drove several millions more into emigration, many to Britain, but even more to North America. The population left behind was static and even declining in numbers; more prosperous in material terms, but with the vigour of pre-famine folk religion noticeably impaired.

It is against this background of widespread and profound social change that we need to see the relationship between official and unofficial religion as it developed during the period. The widespread indifference that surrounded the institutional churches is best understood not so much as a rejection of religion in the broad sense, but as a loss of familiar points of reference and a reluctance to identify with unfamiliar structures, especially when these were associated with varying degrees of social exclusiveness.

In some instances new structures of belief emerged from a powerful fusing of official and unofficial religion. The best example of this has already been discussed in the previous two chapters. During the early nineteenth century the catalytic impact of revivalist preachers on communities experiencing social change could lead to the formation of new values and beliefs based on Nonconformist chapels and reflecting the teachings of official Christianity. Early Primitive Methodism in particular drew on rich strains of folk religion and recast them in its own image.[27] A further example of this process is provided by the impact of evangelical revivalism in the Scottish Highlands in the first half of the nineteenth century, transforming a society which had only weak ties to official religion into one of the strongholds of the Free Church.[28] By 1850, however, communities had largely ceased to be radically transformed by events of this kind: certainly revivalism continued, notably in 1859 and in the Sankey and Moody campaigns of the 1870s, but now it tended to win over individual converts without dramatically changing wider social and cultural structures.

Churches were sometimes willing during the later nineteenth century to countenance the limited assimilation of modified folk religion. One notable example of this is the 'invention' of the Harvest Festival. The harvest supper and related celebration had been a prominent feature of pre-industrial village life, but not one in which the churches had played any significant part. In 1843 R. S. Hawker, vicar of Morwenstow in Cornwall, introduced a harvest thanksgiving service. The innovation spread rapidly. It had reached Anglican churches in Lincolnshire by 1858 and was being adopted by their Methodist neighbours in the 1860s.[29] In country churches it proved an effective substitute for the now-declining traditional harvest supper; meanwhile in the towns it appealed to those who felt a nostalgic attraction to the rural life they or their ancestors had left behind. Something of a similar process can be discerned in the development of Christmas, with the Church coming to sanction and indeed promote aspects of the folk religion surrounding the festival. For example, it was Edward White Benson, the first Bishop of Truro, who in the late 1870s, devised the Festival of Nine Lessons and Carols.[30] This liturgy became the blueprint for twentieth-century 'traditional' carol services in which carols reflecting folk religion were freely associated with those expressing more orthodox Christian theology. Similarly any liturgical unease felt by clergy over the celebration of Watch Night services on New Year's Eve gave way, as we have seen, under popular pressure. It was reported that in Edwardian London 'men and women who never attend any place of worship will crowd out of the public houses on New Year's Eve and fill the biggest churches in the immediate neighbourhood'.[31]

The dominant reaction of the churches nevertheless was that unofficial attitudes to religion as they stood were not valid and acceptable. The working classes were seen as requiring rechristianization, to be brought within the fold of official Christianity. Working from this standpoint most Victorian proponents of institutional religion, although they might modify the presentation of their message in order to make it more accessible, were certainly not prepared to make concessions of substance or to seek to build on features of folk religion. The underlying assumption was that human beings were inherently sinful and alienated from God. They could rectify this and obtain salvation only through submission to the discipline of the Church (the Catholic emphasis) and personal faith in Christ (the Protestant emphasis).

The initial policy to be adopted, by the Established Churches in particular, was simply to build more churches, to provide clergy for them and hope that these increased resources and greater physical proximity to working-class dwellings would be sufficient in themselves to achieve the desired end. By 1850 the limitations of this approach were already apparent, and the religious census confirmed that, although there were local shortages of church accommodation, elsewhere pews were empty while their potential occupants stayed away. So further strategies assumed considerable importance.

From the second quarter of the nineteenth century onwards, the efforts of the Protestant clergy were complemented in the towns by those of numerous lay workers. The London City Mission (LCM), founded in 1835, was employing 375 men in 1860. The organization was supported by evangelical Anglicans and Nonconformists and the task of the agents was defined by Protestant evangelical priorities. They were to read and expound the Bible to anyone prepared to listen, calling upon them to consider the state of their souls and to be converted to Christ. They spent their working lives visiting repeatedly closely defined districts of about 500 families, situated in the poorest quarters of the capital. Assuming that there were on average two adults in each family, it can be estimated that the LCM alone was in contact with some 375,000 people, not counting children, more than 10 per cent of the population of the capital at that date. Moreover when the agents of other organizations – 119 Scripture readers and 137 women employed by the Ranyard Bible Mission – are added, it is clear that a substantial proportion of the London working classes was being exposed to evangelistic endeavours of this kind.[32] Activities on a similar proportionate scale were under way in other cities: for example, in 1864 the Glasgow City Mission was employing fifty-two men and its efforts were complemented by an extensive range of other agencies that sought to draw the poor of Scotland's largest urban centre into church.[33] Such constant activity was the unspectacular background to the dramatic but relatively short-term work of Sankey and Moody and other evangelists. During subsequent decades the impetus shifted somewhat from domestic visitation to the erection of mission halls, designed to complement the work of the churches through catering for specifically working-class congregations.

This evangelical missionary endeavour had its Catholic counterpart in the work of religious orders, including the Passionists, Redemptorists and Rosminians, at its height in both Britain and Ireland between the 1850s and the 1870s. As among evangelicals, preaching was a key tool. Catholic theology was reflected in the centring of missions on the development of the spiritual and devotional life of the parish, and the emphasis was on drawing people into regular attendance and practice of the faith rather than on internalized conversion. The church was made attractive by colourful decoration and elaborate and emotional cere- monies which contrasted with the dreariness of daily life. Similar procedures were adopted by the Anglo-Catholic (or ritualist) wing of the Church of England which had developed in the wake of the Oxford Movement. Churches were set up to provide a strongly visible devo- tional focus in working-class areas while some clergy began to share houses together in order to provide a base for endeavours like those of the Roman Catholic religious orders. Parish missions were held, notably in London in the 1860s and 1870s.

Mission increasingly became linked to a wider range of philanthropic activities. The Bible Society, founded in 1804, came to see the mass distribution of cheap copies of the Scriptures as a means to the improvement of the social and moral condition of the poor, as well as being a basis for securing their spiritual salvation.[34] Other activities, such as the direct relief of distress, the provision of housing and medical facilities for the poor, and the 'rescuing' of prostitutes were undertaken not only as ends in themselves but also because they provided potential openings for the Gospel. Such was the motivation behind the endeav- ours of the Earl of Shaftesbury (1801–85) both in promoting more humane legislation and in his numerous involvements with voluntary societies, which he related to the 'single object' of his life, 'the advance- ment of [God's] ever-blessed name, and the Temporal and eternal welfare of all mankind'.[35]

Education was a particularly important vehicle for disseminating official Christianity. During the first half of the nineteenth century the churches had been at the forefront of the development of day schools in England and Wales, seeing them as a key part of their evangelistic strategies. Obviously reading was an essential tool for knowledge of the Bible and understanding of the extensive spiritual and moral literature now directed at the working classes. In the education provided by the churches religion was not merely accorded considerable prominence, but was seen as the foundation of all other knowledge. In Scotland the link between religion and education was even stronger. Schools had traditionally been closely controlled by the Church, and all Presbyterian groups took educational responsibilities seriously. Something of their motivation is conveyed by the following extract from the report of a United Presbyterian mission in Glasgow:

> [Christian hopes] for the wider diffusion throughout the masses of the sanctifying and elevating influences of the Gospel, must chiefly rest on the religious training of the rising generation, and it is of the highest moment that benevolent Christian effort be especially directed to the right education of those who . . . might otherwise grow up in ignorance and ungodliness.[36]

Opposition from the churches delayed the introduction of a system of state education until 1870 in England and Wales and 1872 in Scotland. Although in some respects the position of the churches in education weakened thereafter, religious influences still remained important. Schools run by churches and chapels continued and could receive government grants; in Scotland the board (state) schools could provide denominational education supported by the rates if a local decision was taken to that effect. Although the board schools in England and Wales were allowed to provide only nondenominational education, this still had a strong religious content.[37] Moreover the position of religion in schools was, if anything, strengthened by subsequent legislation. The Education Act of 1902 permitted local school boards to use ratepayers' money to finance denominational schools and a similar provision was made for Scotland in an Act of 1918. The Church of England and the Roman Catholics were the main beneficiaries of these measures.[38] This system was further reinforced in England and Wales by the 1944 Act which also required, for the first time, that every school day should begin with collective worship. In Ireland meanwhile an attempt in the 1830s to set up a nondenominational national system of education proved unsuccessful in the medium term, and during the second half of the century all schools became, in effect, segregated on religious lines and strongly influenced by the churches.

The influence of day schools was complemented by Sunday Schools, first popularized by Robert Raikes from 1780, and widespread by the later nineteenth century. Initially Sunday Schools provided a rudimentary general education and were not necessarily directly controlled by the churches. They were open to adults as well as children. During the Victorian period the gradual development of widespread weekday elementary education facilitated a shift to a more specifically religious emphasis in the Sunday Schools. At the turn of the century attendance was widespread in England and Wales and, significantly, parents who were not themselves regular church attenders still sent their children to Sunday School. There were 5,514,820 scholars enrolled in 1907, corresponding to a proportion of 76.6 per cent of those aged between five and fourteen.[39] The figure began to fall thereafter. Even so, a sample of working-class Hull residents indicates that sixty-three out of sixty-eight of those born before about 1925 had attended Sunday School; and seventy-nine out of ninety-seven of those born between about 1926 and 1955.[40] In Scotland participation was also very substantial, although never perhaps quite on the scale prevailing south of the Border, and it had already started to fall noticeably before the First World War.[41]

By the end of the nineteenth century, philanthropic and educational activities had diversified into extensive networks of classes, meetings and societies, designed to reinforce the faith and institutional loyalty of Sunday congregations, but also providing a regular weekday point of contact with those who did not normally attend public worship. Associated with active churches were a range of literary and educational clubs, mothers' meetings, guilds for young people, social welfare structures, sports facilities and the like. In 1900 an overworked vicar in Reading observed that 'Each class and sometimes each section, and, sometimes each profession wanted something specially done for themselves'.[42] Such activities had considerable appeal in urban environments where alternative sources of entertainment were limited and state and municipal provision still restricted. By 1900 church organizations were becoming institutionalized on a national scale in bodies such as the Boys' Brigade, the Girls' Friendly Society, the Young Men's/Women's Christian Association, and the Mothers' Union, all of which enjoyed substantial support. The Scouts and Guides followed early in the new century. The Roman Catholic Church, both in Britain and Ireland, was particularly assiduous in developing organizations of this kind, offering devotional stimulus and practical support, and providing its adherents with rich community structures that could meet all their needs – material, social and spiritual. For example, during the second half of the nineteenth century St Patrick's, Soho, had parish schools and clubs for children; a meeting for women which offered practical advice on domestic matters as well as pious edification; and a Brotherhood for men, which functioned as a friendly society paying sickness and death benefits, while also promoting the spiritual growth of its members.[43] A further illustration is provided by the St Vincent de Paul Society in Glasgow, a lay organization that offered an extensive range of social welfare services within a religious framework.[44]

This brief outline of some of the strategies adopted by official Christianity conveys an impression of a formidable energy and commitment, which brought the churches into at least some contact with virtually the whole of the population of Victorian and early twentieth-century Britain. Even in the interwar period, although much of this machinery had now declined somewhat from its peak, it still remained very substantial. It remains, however, to evaluate its effectiveness in achieving its objectives, and to explore the nature of the religious attitudes that emerged in the wake of all this activity.

3. 'DEVOTIONAL REVOLUTION', DIFFUSIVE CHRISTIANITY AND SECTARIANISM

The nature of unofficial religion in the predominantly urbanized and industrialized society of the late nineteenth and twentieth centuries is best analysed by considering four sets of responses to the missionary endeavours of institutional religion, the two extremes of acceptance and rejection, and two middle courses of diffuse assimilation and sectarian identification.

First, there were the occasions when official religion apparently met with very substantial success. Energetic Anglican clergy could build up strong working-class congregations, an achievement reached by different routes by evangelicals, such as William Champneys at St Mary's, Whitechapel, and by Anglo-Catholics, like Arthur Stanton at St Alban's, Holborn.[45] At times of revival Nonconformity could enjoy noticeable if short-lived extensions of its influence, and a preacher of the calibre of Charles Haddon Spurgeon could draw vast congregations over a long period. Such successes depended heavily on the local circumstances and personalities involved.

Roman Catholicism in Britain and Ireland was particularly successful in bringing about a large-scale, profound, and sustained transformation of unofficial religion. It has been argued that the aftermath of the famine saw a 'devotional revolution' in Irish Catholicism; a shift from folk religion to Ultramontane orthodoxy, and from widespread non-practice to almost universal mass attendance, supported by a range of elaborate and colourful devotional practices.[46] A similar process occurred among Irish immigrants in Britain. Faced with large populations who only had weak links with the Church, clergy threw themselves into active pastoral endeavours assisted by parish missions and extensive education and social institutions. During the second half of the nineteenth century a pattern of much more extensive practice and involvement developed. Mass attendance never attained the remarkably high levels prevailing in Ireland itself and priests were constantly worrying about the 'leakage' of professed Catholics. Nevertheless chapels still operated with considerable effectiveness as a key focus of the Irish subculture.

The concept of 'devotional revolution' has given rise to considerable scholarly debate, which has focused on the question of how far developments following the famine were foreshadowed in the first half of the nineteenth century. In the present context, however, our concern is with assessing the nature of the end product. The superficial impression that the Roman Catholic Church remodelled unofficial religion in its own image needs to be qualified by the recognition that official Catholicism also changed considerably at the same time. Although the shift from pre-Victorian relative passivity to vigorous Ultramontane authoritarianism stemmed largely from the internal dynamics of the Church, it was also in part a direct response to awareness of the perceived substandard religion of the laity. Certainly change reflected increased discipline and commitment on the part of the clergy and, in Ireland, related to the effect of the famine in reducing the strain on the resources of the Church. However, it has been suggested, an important psychological effect of the famine and emigration was to reinforce a widespread crisis of fear and loss of identity among the survivors, which was resolved by official Catholicism.[47] There is a parallel here with the flowering of revivalist Methodism among the early industrial working classes in England and Wales.

This general structural argument can be reinforced by further consideration of the nature of post-famine Catholicism. Certainly folk religion declined, but, as we have seen, it was a long time a-dying. Moreover, at the same time, Catholicism was being reshaped 'from below' as well as 'from above'. In 1879 there was an apparition of the Virgin at Knock, followed by miraculous cures at the site, and the subsequent development of this remote County Mayo village as a major pilgrimage centre.

The process came to receive tacit official Catholic acceptance, but the point is that it arose not from the imposition of the teaching of the Church, but from a popular piety in which a strong sense of place and of the reality of the miraculous were still very potent.[48] In Britain there were no Knocks, but there was the development of what has been termed 'vulgar piety': crude, colourful and emotive ceremonial that fed on the culture of a people for whom religion was still more a matter of communally significant shared ritual than of theological creeds and internalized spirituality.[49]

The development of Judaism in Britain at the end of the nineteenth century merits attention in this context, because it represents a more extreme example of the tendency we have noted in Roman Catholicism for new religious structures to emerge in spite of, rather than because of, the attitudes of an official leadership. The large numbers of im-poverished East European immigrants who arrived in the later nineteenth century formed their own organizations, the *chevroth* (singu-lar *chevra*). These met in humble, often rented, surroundings and reflected the limited material resources of their members, but were the focus for an intensely committed spirituality and religious discipline. It was reported of Jews in Leeds in 1889 that 'it is the very poorest who keep the religious statutes the strictest . . . the poorer the man the more strictly he adheres to those laws; it is a notorious fact'.[50] The *chevroth* also provided educational and social welfare facilities. The relationship between the immigrants and the established leadership of Anglo-Jewry was an uneasy one, as prosperous Jews were embarrassed by the material poverty and spiritual wealth of their co-religionists, while the immi-grants resented the social exclusiveness and religious lukewarmness of the existing synagogues. However, as the Jewish community gradually developed greater overall cohesion, it was religion outside the official structures that stirred a revitalization of spirituality and official religious practice.

Second, there was the opposite reaction, the explicit rejection of supernaturalist religion which developed in the secularist movement. This owed some initial inspiration to the legacy of Thomas Paine and other late eighteenth-century radical thinkers, and took firmer organ-izational shape in the early Victorian period. Moral and theological criticism of Christian orthodoxy was linked to social and political attacks on the existing power structure. Secularists formed societies, held meetings and circulated literature, but did not become more than a minority movement. Even at its peak in the 1880s the National Secular Society only had six thousand members and there were at most 100,000 sympathizers. Ironically, but significantly, their institutions tended sociologically to behave in a fashion not unlike Nonconformist chapels, with a similar social base among artisans and the lower middle class. They sang secular hymns, held Sunday Schools and offered a range of leisure activities.[51] Moreover active commitment to secularism was very much an individual matter, often a reaction against earlier equally strong identification with Christianity, and it seldom mobilized whole communities.[52] In short, in repudiating official religion secularists mirrored it as well as confronting it.

Third, the majority of the British population thus remained between the two extremes of explicit acceptance and explicit rejection, and held to modified forms of unofficial religion. Protestant missions enjoyed only limited success in terms of drawing the poor into explicit conversions and active involvement in the Church. However, although there were people who forcefully rebuffed the missionaries, the more widespread reaction appears to have been polite indifference associated with a readiness at least to listen to what they had to say.[53] In the 1890s a missionary reported: 'The Gospel is a great power with the people at the time. They will thank you for speaking to them and mean well, but soon forget'.[54] A similar point can be made about the impact of the religious tone of day and Sunday School education: the evidence of oral history and autobiographies implies that most children did not react strongly to it either way, but rather were brought to regard Christianity in a neutral way as a natural feature of their social and cultural landscape.[55] The networks of ancillary church societies also demonstrated a tension between objectives and achievements. For the official leadership they were conceived of as a means to strengthen popular support for their core religious objectives, but, for many, participation was simply an end in itself. Writing of his youth in the 1860s and 1870s, the Labour cabinet minister George Lansbury recalled that then 'there was no social life outside religious organizations'.[56] Arguably, therefore, the churches were themselves inadvertently reinforcing a perception of religion as concerned not with transcendent spiritual claims, but with do-goodery and moral regulation.[57]

The term 'diffusive Christianity' has been coined to characterize the attitudes of the bulk of the British population in the late nineteenth and early twentieth centuries.[58] By this is meant a vague non-doctrinal kind of belief: God exists; Christ was a good man and an example to be followed; people should live decent lives on charitable terms with their neighbours, and those who do so will go to Heaven when they die. Those who suffer in this world will receive compensation in the next.

The churches were regarded with apathy rather than hostility: their social activities made some contribution to the community. Sunday School was felt to provide a necessary part of the upbringing of children, and the rites of passage required formal religious sanction. Association was maintained by attendance at certain annual and seasonal festivals, but weekly participation in worship was felt to be unnecessary and excessive. Women and children were more likely than men to be regularly involved, but this did not imply that adult males were hostile; merely – it can be surmised – that they tended to see themselves as the main breadwinners, and felt that women should therefore represent the family's interests in the religious arena.[59] The emphasis was on the practical and the communal rather than the theological and the individual. This unofficial religion was more derivative of official religion than pre-industrial folk religion and lacked the same rich range of alternative beliefs. There is accordingly some foundation for the judgement that around 1900 the British people were, albeit in a diffuse and passive sense, closer to Christian orthodoxy than they had ever been in their history.[60]

As active involvement with official religion declined in the first half of the twentieth century, it can be inferred that a corresponding penumbra of diffusive Christianity was left behind. In 1909 it had been observed that: 'The tide is ebbing within and without the churches. The drift is towards a non-dogmatic affirmation of general kindliness and good fellowship, with an emphasis rather on the service of men than on the fulfilment of the will of God'.[61] In 1931 the vicar of St Lawrence, York, expressed his surprise 'that so many parishioners who seem thoroughly well-disposed to both Church and clergy yet do not come to Church as regular worshippers'.[62] By this date the kind of benevolent neutrality adopted by many among the Victorian working classes in the wake of missionary and philanthropic activity had begun to spread to those artisan and middle-class groups who had earlier been the mainstay of churches and chapels. A valuable indication of people's attitudes to religion at the end of our period is provided by a survey of an unnamed London borough conducted by Mass Observation in the mid-1940s. Generalized Christian belief was widespread: two-thirds of men and four-fifths of women believed in the existence of God; 44 per cent of men and 60 per cent of women acknowledged Christ to be 'more than a man'; 28 per cent of the sample had been to church within the last six months. The vast majority, including 73 per cent of non-believers, thought religion should be taught in schools, if only to give children a stable ethical foundation. However, there was much confusion and inconsistency. On the one hand a substantial proportion of professed non-believers admitted to praying, at least in times of crisis; on the other hand numerous Church of England churchgoers (but noticeably fewer Roman Catholics and Nonconformists) doubted key dogmas such as life after death or the divinity of Christ. There were also indications of the ambivalent impact of religion in schools: clergy commented that education was concluded at a point before young people could face up to religious issues in an adult fashion, and that accordingly all their exposure to Christianity had not equipped them with any real understanding. Conclusions were summarized as follows:

> Belief or non-belief is becoming more and more a purely private affair. Belief is becoming less and less associated with any recognised religious system, and believers correspondingly less acquainted with religious dogma or the outline of religious ethics. Ostensibly many people's religion to-day is one they have 'worked out for themselves.' In fact, this means in most cases that it is based on a narrower acquaintance with its sources than before. It is not a new religion, but an incomplete version of the old, commanding less faith, covering a less wide field.[63]

In other words, the diffusive had become even more diffuse. Note also what has probably been the distinctive feature of the twentieth century, the decline of a sense that religion, whether official or unofficial, has a communal dimension and an increased emphasis on its limitation to the private sphere.

Nevertheless even in the mid-twentieth century something of the separation between official and unofficial religion can still be discerned. Mass Observation noted that 36 per cent of its sample saw religion primarily in terms of *beliefs*, faith and God; while 32 per cent placed the emphasis rather on *conduct*, doing good to others, the remainder demonstrating only a negative or incoherent conception.[64] This broadly corresponds to the distinction we have noted above, between institutions stressing internalized adherence to specific dogmas on the one hand, and unofficial religion in which tangible and visible actions were more important on the other. A further survey, conducted in the 1960s, also led to the suggestion that there were different ways of being religious: on the one hand active church involvement associated with an orthodox Christian framework of belief; on the other occasional church attendance linked to a markedly 'superstitious' view of life.[65]

Finally, there was the sectarian outcome. This denotes an identification between religious labels and community identities in a manner that led to outright polarization and confrontation between different groups. The most obvious example was the conflict between Protestants and Roman Catholics in the north of Ireland, Lancashire, the west of Scotland and elsewhere, but the concept is also applicable to areas where there was separation between the Established Churches and Nonconformity. Sectarianism linked the characteristics of successful official religion to those of diffusive Christianity. On the one hand it reflected genuine divergences among the organized churches and was associated with high levels of active official religious commitment. On the other hand it mobilized those whose understanding of orthodox Christian teaching might be very small, but who still identified strongly with religious categories as defining the basic nature of their communities.

The manner in which late nineteenth- and twentieth-century sectarianism linked official and unofficial religion was a logical outcome of the various factors which had contributed to its development. Anti-Catholicism in Britain had deep roots in popular culture which can be traced back to the Reformation era and which still found expression in the Victorian period in the widespread celebration of Guy Fawkes Day. Similarly, in Ireland communal identities and traditions had been forged in the conflict of the seventeenth century and were reinforced at the end of the eighteenth century by the emergence of organized agrarian secret societies such as the Protestant Orange Order and the Roman Catholic Defenders. Urbanization in the course of the nineteenth century was frequently associated with spatial and occupational segregation between Protestants and Roman Catholics, notably in Belfast, Glasgow and Liverpool. This reinforced group solidarity and perceptions of the other creed as alien and hostile. Antagonisms were both expressed and reinforced by outbreaks of outright violence. Meanwhile both revivalist Protestantism and Ultramontane Roman Catholicism were exerting their influence, urging their adherents to eschew the spiritual dangers of contact with adherents of 'false religion' and seeming to sanction confrontation in the cause of salvation.[66]

The institutions and influence of official religion were thus an important foundation for sectarianism, but other structures had played a crucial role in sustaining the equation between creed and community. The Orange Order, formed in Ulster in 1795, suppressed in 1836, but reviving again from the 1850s, was a central focus of Protestant identity in Lancashire and in Scotland as well as in the north of Ireland. In its rules and constitution the Order affirmed a strong identification with the official teaching of the churches, but the membership did not necessarily live up to their professions, and in practice the Orange Lodge with its prayers, ritual and 12 July processions could become a substitute for church involvement.[67] Likewise, in Glasgow, the Old Firm soccer rivalry of (Roman Catholic) Celtic and (Protestant) Rangers originated with respective official religious involvements in the formation of the clubs, but acquired a life of its own, as the popular appeal of football grew in the early twentieth century. The sectarian identities of the clubs hardened in the interwar period.[68]

Rivalries between Anglican and Nonconformist were seldom as deep seated or intense as those between Protestant and Catholic, but they did have a similar tendency to co-opt those with only a tenuous commitment to official religion in the cause of group solidarity. This tendency was especially apparent in the industrial towns of northern England. Church and chapel stood at the symbolic centre of competing networks of social, educational, cultural and political activity. These were not infrequently reinforced by the attitudes of rival Nonconformist and Anglican employer élites who transmitted their own religious identities to their workforces through the patronage of schools and places of worship. A Nonconformist schoolmaster in Stalybridge in 1876 felt that his school was looked on 'as part of [the] works'.[69] Whitsun marches by schools were a particularly public show of rival identities, as at Ashton in the late nineteenth century:

> We 'walked' . . . in a state of intense consciousness both of self and schism. I have said 'schism' because the proceedings were indeed frankly and unblushingly sectarian. We who were Dissenters 'walked' in the morning . . . the Church had seized the afternoon.[70]

This was an environment in which even the non-churchgoer would be likely to identify strongly with one side or the other. Its implications for political life will be further explored in Chapter 6.

The relatively small extent of organized secularism in comparison to the wide assimilation of diffusive Christianity and the considerable force of sectarian identification leads to the conclusion that the most significant alternative to official Christianity in nineteenth- and early twentieth-century Britain was not explicit secularity but rather unofficial religion. Social dislocation reduced the variety and power of many of the beliefs held in pre-industrial society, but these were slow to disappear completely. Meanwhile the nineteenth century saw a new phase in a process whereby unofficial religious consciousness accepted some of the forms of official religion, but set them in a very different framework from that usually held by the clergy. It was this divergence that led to the widespread perception, among both contemporaries and historians, that Victorian efforts to Christianize society had 'failed'. Such an evaluation may well reflect an accurate appreciation of the divergence between official objects and achievements, but is liable to obscure the very real impact that the efforts of the Church had had. They had diffused religious sentiment in the making of the urbanized society of nineteenth-century Britain. Compared with earlier phases of unofficial religion, however, that sentiment had less of the magical and more of the pragmatic; a weaker relationship to time and place, and a stronger connection to institutions and associations. Above all, the explicitly supernatural content was becoming more attenuated. It is thus appropriate to suggest that by the end of the nineteenth century unofficial religion was merging into quasi-religion, in the terms of the definitions set out in Chapter 1. The significance of this development will become more apparent in the later chapters of this book as we examine the power of religion as a basis for political identification, cultural influence and military mobilization, all of which contributed to the development of nationalism.

5

HIGH TIDE OF FAITH?

Religion and Nationhood around 1850

On 18 May 1843 the General Assembly of the Church of Scotland met at St Andrew's Church in Edinburgh amidst customary pageantry and unusual excitement. After some of the preliminary formalities had been completed, the moderator, Dr David Welsh, departed dramatically from the normal procedure by reading a protest against the 'violation of the terms of the Union between Church and State in this land' and announcing that he and his supporters would be 'separating in an orderly way from the Establishment'. A vivid eye-witness account takes up the story:

> The Moderator laid the Protest on the table – lifted his hat – turned to the Commissioner, who had risen – and bowed respectfully to the representative of Royalty, an act which seemed to many as if the true old Church of Scotland were then and there bidding farewell to the State which had turned a deaf ear to her appeals. Leaving the chair, Dr Welsh moved towards the door. . . . Man after man rose, without hurry or confusion, and bench after bench was left empty, and the vacant space grew wider as ministers and elders poured out in long procession. Outside in the street, the great mass of spectators had long been waiting in anxious anticipation, and when at last the cry arose, 'They come! they come!' and when Dr Welsh, Dr Chalmers, and Dr Gordon appeared in sight, the sensation, as they came forth, went like an electric shock through the vast multitude, and the long deep shout which rang along the street told that the deed had been done.[1]

When calculations were made it transpired that 454 of the Kirk's 1,195 clergy had solemnly and publicly left the Established Church to form the Free Church of Scotland.[2] This was no mere storm in an ecclesiastical tea-cup, but a movement that struck at the heart of one of Scotland's key national institutions. Subsequent months saw the creation, in a remarkably short space of time, of a new church with a presence in every part of Scotland, supported solely from the commitment and financial resources of its own adherents.

This event was the first, and in some respects the most dramatic, of a series of occurrences in the decade around 1850 which form the subject of this chapter. This discussion will serve to illustrate aspects of the relationship between religion and nationality in Britain and Ireland in the middle of the nineteenth century and provide a context for examination of subsequent developments in the following chapters. The present chapter will fall into two sections. In the first we shall examine three events, one each in Scotland, Ireland and Wales, which serve to indicate the links between religion and national identity: respectively, the Disruption, the Repeal campaign of 1843 and the 'treason of the Blue Books' in 1847. Second we shall turn to some events of the early 1850s, the outcry against 'papal aggression' in 1850–1, public responses to the death of the Duke of Wellington in 1852 and the outbreak of the Crimean War in 1854. These will demonstrate that despite the ample evidence of division on national and religious lines in mid-nineteenth-century Britain, the forces operating to promote cohesion were, in general, also powerful.

1. HOLY NATIONS?

The Disruption of the Church of Scotland was a climax resulting from the working out of a variety of tensions and pressures in the Scottish ecclesiastical system. For ease of analysis these can be categorized under three headings: legal and constitutional difficulties; the impact of evangelicalism; and personal factors, particularly the role played by Thomas Chalmers, the dominant Scottish churchman of his day who had a powerful vision of the place of the Church in local and national communities.

The specific disputes that culminated in the Disruption related to patronage. The right of the Crown, institutions such as town corporations and individual lay people, particularly local squires and nobility, to appoint ministers to Church of Scotland parishes had been briefly abolished in 1690, but after the Union of 1707 was restored by the Westminster Parliament in 1712. Even if a congregation disliked an appointee its members could not reject him, provided his qualifications and morals were satisfactory. This had led to a variety of secessions from the Church during the eighteenth century. In the 1820s and 1830s resistance to the system increased and in 1834 the General Assembly passed the so-called Veto Act which declared that an appointment should be set aside if a majority of communicant male heads of families in the parish dissented from it. The civil courts refused to accept the legality of the congregational veto, and a series of involved lawsuits followed as appointees rejected by the parishioners appealed successfully to the Court of Session and the House of Lords. By the early 1840s the consequences of this conflict of jurisdictions were resulting in chaos in some parishes, notably in the presbytery of Strathbogie in Banffshire. Here seven ministers deposed by the Church for implementing an earlier civil court judgement were ministering in competition with clergy recognized by the Church.

The legal dispute was inextricably enmeshed with a second factor, the consequences of the Evangelical Revival in Scotland. As in England, the movement was in part contained within the Established Church, and in part contributed to secession from the Church of Scotland and the strengthening of dissenting groups. These latter, however, generally remained Presbyterian in organization. Thus by the 1820s evangelicals were both challenging the Church of Scotland from outside, and operating as an increasingly powerful group within it. The largest body of dissenters, the United Secession Church, formed in 1820 from the amalgamation of groups originating in the eighteenth century, in 1839 had 361 congregations and a following of 261,345, 10 per cent of the population of Scotland.[3] The United Secession Church was predominantly evangelical in character and especially strong in the towns, notably Glasgow. Thus, especially when the existence of further smaller bodies is taken into account, there was substantial numerical pressure on the Church of Scotland. Moreover from around 1830 dissenters became aggressively voluntaryist; in other words, they demanded the elimination of the privileged state connections of the Established Church. The movement reflected secular influences such as the contemporary demand for liberal political reform and free trade, but in the conviction that disestablishment was the essential preliminary for the effective preaching of the Word, successful evangelistic effort and the working of the Holy Spirit, evangelical priorities were very much apparent.

Evangelicals inside the Church of Scotland were stirred into greater self-assertion partly in a desire to outflank this challenge from outside. If the Established Church could show itself to be an effective and faithful evangelistic agency then much of the voluntaryist case would be answered. At the same time evangelicals within the Kirk had their own considerable dynamic. As a party in the General Assembly and elsewhere they confronted the moderates, who adhered to the more relaxed theological standpoint characteristic of the mainstream of the Church in the eighteenth century, and believed strongly in the value of the state connection and the unrestricted right of lay patrons as a check to populism and inequality among congregations. Evangelicals on the other hand saw the moderates as offering only a chilly theology and accepting constraints on the Church which compromised its spiritual integrity and curtailed its evangelistic effectiveness and its capacity to respond to its rivals. Hence the legal disputes over patronage served as a focus for much wider disputes over the whole nature of the Church of Scotland and its connection with the state. This was further evident in the unfolding during the decade or so before the Disruption of the conflict over patronage in parallel with other evangelical campaigns. The passing of the Veto Act by the General Assembly in 1834 reflected the attainment of evangelical ascendancy and it was in the same year that the Church launched a sustained endeavour to promote church extension, meaning the building and endowment of new places of worship in populous districts. This heightened conflict with dissent and also increased the stresses in the Church's relationship with governments that found it was politically expedient to take account of dissenting concerns. Accordingly no state money for church-building was forthcoming. Moreover in 1839 and 1843 court decisions effectively deprived the new churches which had been built by public subscription and donation of any independent legal status, thus severely curtailing their effectiveness. A further impetus to evangelical dissatisfaction with the Established Church came from 1839 onwards as a result of revival movements reflecting particularly the influence of the American, Charles Finney.[4] These encouraged a climate of opinion in which Establishment ties seemed dispensable and radical change was conceivable and even desirable as part of the coming of a new millennial age.

The third factor which catalysed the other forms leading to the Disruption was the personal ideas and influence of Thomas Chalmers (1780–1847), the key leader of the evangelical party and subsequently of the Free Church. This is of course not to deny the role of other individuals, merely to focus on the man whose contribution was of the most crucial importance. A moderate in his youth, Chalmers was converted to evangelicalism around 1810 and came to fame between 1815 and 1823 as a parish minister in Glasgow. He associated the zealous preaching of Christianity with a vision for creating and sustaining a parish as a mutually supportive community in which religious commitment would be the cement of a social structure. The welfare and security of all would be sustained through the charitable impulse of Christianity. The nation as a whole would become a godly commonwealth made up from these local communities. Chalmers was giving an evangelical cast to traditional Scottish and Calvinist ideas of the role of the Church in local society and his ideal, despite the questionable extent of its practical success, attracted widespread interest and enthusiasm both in Scotland and elsewhere. The idea that a community should order itself free from state intervention also dovetailed with the *laissez-faire* doctrines that were enjoying considerable currency at this time. It is possible to see events in the Church of Scotland in the two decades before the Disruption as reflecting the endeavour to realize Chalmers's vision: the campaign for church extension as a means of ensuring that parish communities would be of a manageable size; patronage disputes as reflecting the anxiety that they should have autonomy and spiritual independence. Certainly Chalmers himself played a leading role in both campaigns. In 1838, moreover, he appeared on a London platform to deliver his influential *Lectures on the Establishment and Extension of National Churches* in which he vigorously defended them as the surest means to national spiritual elevation and social cohesion. There is accordingly at first sight something more than a little perplexing in Chalmers's subsequent leadership of the Disruption, but it is explained by his conviction reached by 1843 that the Church of Scotland in its existing form was so compromised and hamstrung that it was incapable of realizing the social and spiritual aspirations he had for it. As perceived by Chalmers the Free Church, which unlike any previous Protestant Dissenting group sought to sustain a national territorial parochial structure, was not a rejection of the principle of a national church but rather an endeavour to create a true godly commonwealth on a restored foundation.

Was the Disruption a nationalist movement? A case can certainly be made that it was, in so far as it stemmed from self-assertion by a substantial body of Scottish opinion in the face of indifference, incomprehension and downright opposition at Westminster. It was also an emphatic rejection of the Patronage Act of 1712 which had seemed to infringe the terms of the Union with England. Moreover the landlords who, as patrons, were a focus of Free Church opposition, were frequently more Anglicized than the congregations. On the other hand the Disruption occurred at the expense of an institution which, for all its limitations in the eyes of the seceders, was still distinctively Scottish, and the legal conflicts which had precipitated the split were in general between the Church and the highest court in Scotland itself, the Court of Session. Furthermore, although popular engagement in the Disruption was considerable and certainly reflected a sense of identification with Scotland, there is little sign of the kind of nationalist language that attributes a spiritual character to the nation independent of its religion. When the seceders explained their position it was in orthodox Christian terms, as was only to be expected from a new Christian denomination. Nevertheless that very assertion of Christian orthodoxy could be associated with a statement of Scottish distinctiveness, as in a poetical tribute to Chalmers written on his death in 1847:

> Scotland, I love thee! Every blade of grass
> That waves above thy martyrs' graves so dear.
> I love thy Sabbath rest – thy Bible lore –
> Thy sanctuaries – thy sacraments – thy psalms –
> Thy testimony – bearing for the truth –
> Faithful contendings for the Word of Life
> For Christ, His Cross, His crown and covenant.
> Scotland, with thee I mourn thy patriot gone –
> Him whose high mental powers and moral worth
> Gave thee pre-eminence o'er other lands –
> Lands favoured more with verdant fruitful fields.
> A nation's strength consists not in its gold –
> Its merchandise – its valleys, rocks and hills –
> Its wide-spread lakes – its rivers, groves and meads –
> But in the might and moral magnitude,
> Of holiness within the deathless mind.[5]

The impulses that lay behind the Disruption, the assertion of spiritual integrity and independence and the vision of the Christian community and godly commonwealth, thus had the potential to feed into cultural currents that flowed well beyond the specific evangelical context enunciated by Chalmers. In the short term however, after the great outpouring of energy and sacrifice associated with the creation of the Free Church, there was a certain loss of momentum. The Free Church tended to recede from Chalmers' vision into a vigorous but ultimately limited denominational life and the division of the Scottish Church for the remainder of the nineteenth century proved in the long run to weaken its social and cultural credibility. Meanwhile there was little sign of a more fully developed secular nationalism.

Three days after the stirring events at St Andrew's, Edinburgh, a crowd estimated at 300,000 gathered near the Rock of Cashel, that startling cathedral-crowned hill which rises abruptly above the countryside of southern Tipperary. Cashel had been the seat of the ancient kings of Munster and remained the titular ecclesiastical centre of southwest Ireland. The historical and religious resonances of the site were prominent in the minds of the organizers of the monster meeting, one of a series of some forty rallies held during 1843 to promote the campaign led by Daniel O'Connell to obtain the repeal of the legislative union between Britain and Ireland. The climax of the Cashel meeting was reached when the veteran Liberator himself delivered a compelling oration to his ecstatic followers, but it is notable that the chair had been taken by a Roman Catholic archdeacon and two of the supporting speakers had been clergy, one of whom saw the 'finger of the Almighty' in the Repeal agitation. The other, the Revd Dr Burke, parish priest of Clonmel, referred to the Rock of Cashel 'once the dwelling of sanctity and learning' as a strong reminder of the past glories of their country, which 'should infuse into the heart of every Irishman a desire to see those glories revived, and their country elevated once more to the dignity of a nation'.[6] Similarly close links between the Repeal movement, the Roman Catholic Church and the religious consciousness of the people were apparent at a later meeting in the series, at the Hill of Tara, twenty-five miles north of Dublin, on 15 August 1843, the Feast of the Assumption. Tara had been the capital of the pre-Christian High Kings of Ireland and, much more recently, the burial place of some of the insurrectionists ('Croppies') killed in the suppression of the rising of 1798. The emotive resonances of the site were further reinforced by Thomas Moore's lines 'The harp that once thro' Tara's Halls . . .', the melody of which was played by a harper who preceded O'Connell's carriage as he approached the rally. The attendance was estimated as close to a million. The local Roman Catholic clergy headed by John Cantwell, the Bishop of Meath, gave the meeting their strong support, as indicated by a substantial clerical presence on the platform. Open air masses were said on the Hill of Tara itself and, although these were ostensibly to provide for the devout away from home on a holy day, the proximity of the altar to the grave of the Croppies hinted at links between religious and national consciousness. In his speech O'Connell began with an extended attack on the Union as constitutionally invalid and economically detrimental and followed this by expressing the hope that Ireland would benefit from the Church's prayers. Bishop Cantwell took a prominent part in the proceedings at a subsequent dinner: his health and that of the Catholic priests of Ireland was proposed and he responded with a vigorous speech.[7]

Some observers at the time were struck by the parallels that could be drawn between O'Connell's Repeal movement and Chalmers's Free Church of Scotland. The *Inverness Courier* compared the 'champion of Ireland and of Catholic Europe' with 'the pride of Presbyterian Scotland'.[8] Certainly there were similarities. Both were concerned with institutions central to the identity of their respective nations; both reflected the personality and vision of leaders of great personal charisma and influence; both mobilized an impressive degree of popular support; both obtained the passionate engagement of large numbers of clergymen. Above all, both gave substance to the view that broadly religious motivation and inspiration was a major force in the national life of both Scotland and Ireland at this time. Nevertheless, if we are properly to understand the contrasting dynamics and significance of that religious presence in the two countries, two key distinctions need to be made. First, Repeal, unlike the Free Church, was led by a layman for avowedly political purposes. Granted that O'Connell was a committed son of the Roman Catholic Church, the agenda still reflected secular as well as ecclesiastical priorities. Second, as the above descriptions of the Cashel and Tara meetings serve to indicate, the religious dimensions of the Repeal movement went outside the strictly official teaching of the Church to encompass unofficial and even quasi-religious ritual and the symbolic exaltation of national identity and tradition. At the same time the Roman Catholic presence remained very strong.

Since the victorious conclusion of the Emancipation campaign in 1829 O'Connell had been a crusader waiting for a new cause. Repeal was his ultimate objective, but he recognized that in the early 1830s it would not command the same degree of support as Emancipation. In particular, the Roman Catholic bishops would have been more reluctant to throw their support behind a movement with a less obviously religious character. Accordingly Irish politics and agitation in the 1830s were focused on issues which were less all-encompassing: reform in 1833 of the Protestant Church of Ireland to render it less offensive to the Roman Catholic majority; educational provision; and the campaign against tithes which were commuted to a rent charge in 1838. These were issues on which it was relatively easy to consolidate the alliance with the Roman Catholic Church forged during the 1820s, but, by the same token, they served to reinforce alienation between the Protestant and Catholic communities and to diminish O'Connell's potential to be a truly national leader able to transcend the sectarian divide.

Hence, when, in April 1840 O'Connell ultimately decided to launch an active campaign for Repeal, he faced difficulties on two fronts, problems which were reflected in the limited impact made in early months. The hesitations of the priests proved to be much the lesser obstacle. The decade since 1829 had seen a significant shift in the balance of power in the Church away from older men trained on the continent before 1795 towards younger Maynooth-educated clergy. The former were generally reluctant to assume a political position in opposition to the government; the latter were often closer to the mood of the Irish people and had fewer hesitations. They were led by the formidable John MacHale, who had been appointed Archbishop of Tuam in 1834. The lower clergy proved even more ready to identify themselves with Repeal than the bishops, a reflection not only of their pastoral response to the condition of their parishioners, but also of the ambivalences of their status as leaders of peasant society. Although they were accorded considerable respect and perceived as vested with a patriarchal authority, this did not preclude their parishioners from defying their wishes in relation to particular social practices and political involvements. So, as the Repeal movement gathered momentum some clergy found themselves pushed by the people into participation. As a *Times* reporter put it, 'the priests, if they are to guide, must, like the helm of the ships, be also prepared to follow'.[9] There remained a minority of bishops, of whom Daniel Murray, the Archbishop of Dublin, was the most prominent, who continued to refuse to identify themselves with the agitation, but as a generalization the perception that the Church was firmly identified with the Repeal cause was an accurate one. In the eyes of Sir James Graham, Home Secretary in the Conservative government of Sir Robert Peel, 'It is a religious struggle, directed by the R. Catholic Hierarchy and Priesthood . . . and I very much doubt whether any political considerations enter much into the causes or objects of this strife'.[10]

Graham was, however, overstating the case. It was undeniable that Roman Catholic commitments and organizational structures contributed very substantially to the agitation, but this must not obscure the aspiration of O'Connell and others to found their campaign on a broader base. The 1842 Report of the National Repeal Association had called on Protestants to join in 'genuine Irish patriotism' and in February 1843 O'Connell reiterated that he hoped to 'include all – Protestant, Presbyterian and Catholic'.[11] These objectives were reflected in the references to shared aspects of Irish tradition and history which were apparent in the Repeal meetings. The endeavour to rally extensive Protestant support was unsuccessful, but some prominent individual non-Catholics became enthusiastic activists, notably William Smith

O'Brien and Thomas Davis, leader of a group of men centred on *The Nation* newspaper who became known as Young Ireland.

Davis preached a nationalism which was noticeably different in emphasis from that of O'Connell. Background and conviction combined to cause him to search for a way of expressing Irishness that could overcome the sectarian divide. He saw a nation as 'a spiritual essence' with a unique character, formed by its literature, history and language. All Irishmen, whether Protestant or Catholic, had an underlying unity in their shared nationality; even immigrants and colonizers had been quickly assimilated into this. Patrick Pearse, one of the leaders of the Easter Rising of 1916, was to view Davis as a key figure in giving Irish nationalism a spiritual, quasi-religious dimension. Davis and Young Ireland did not reject or seek to supersede conventional religion, but they did hold that, given the circumstances of Ireland, the influence of the churches should be confined to the private sphere and that nationalist politics should derive its legitimacy rather from the nation's cultural identity, around which all true Irishmen could unite. This standpoint led to tensions within the Repeal movement in 1844 and 1845 as the Young Irelanders and others urged against identification with the specific concerns and priorities of the Roman Catholic Church, disputes which contributed to an outright breach in 1846.

The divergence between O'Connell and Davis has been seen as a matter of principle as to whether Irish nationalism should be Catholic or secular, but, given the manner in which the Liberator himself was prepared to pay more than lip-service to his desire to involve Protestants, it would be better characterized as a tension between ideology and practice. In the circumstances of the 1840s the Roman Catholic Church was an indispensable partner in the achievement of the large-scale committed mobilization of public opinion which O'Connell sought. There was a price to be paid for this, but it was one which O'Connell, whose personal religious commitment here reinforced his sense of political practicalities, was ultimately willing to pay. Davis's 'spiritual essence' was something too rarefied to engage mass emotions if it was detached from Catholicism. Even among the Dublin middle class, relatively well-educated and independent of clerical influence, the cause of Ireland was not readily distinguished from the cause of Catholicism.[12]

The events of the next few years were, if anything, to reinforce that identification. In the spring of 1847, O'Connell, realizing that he was dying, set out for Rome where he wished to spend his last days, but died at Genoa some hundreds of miles short of his destination. His body was returned to Ireland, to lie at Glasnevin cemetery in Dublin, but his heart was taken on to Rome. The symbolism of this did not go unnoticed at home, where many thousands of his compatriots were also dying in the massive disaster of the great famine. During the subsequent generation the cause of Irish political nationalism did not sustain its momentum but, as was noted in previous chapters, the famine was followed by a noticeable strengthening in the influence of official Catholicism, led by Archbishop Paul Cullen. He believed that 'It is our duty and interest . . . to walk in the footsteps of the great liberator [O'Connell]',[13] but he evidently perceived these as leading in a direction where no conscientious Protestant could follow.

Nevertheless the writers of the numerous ballads which appeared lamenting the death of O'Connell showed a less specific kind of religion than that apparent in the lines on Chalmers quoted above. Christian, and indeed Roman Catholic, motifs were prominent, but these were applied to the identification of Ireland and its perceived destiny:

> To Mullahmast [sic] and likewise Tara,
> As a modern Moses he led us you see
> Though pursued by proud haughty Pharoh [sic],
> In the land of promise he left us free
> A shout is gone forth from Derry to Dingle,
> Along the Boyne and the Liffey Nore,
> And all repeat in mournful accent,
> Our noble leader, brave Dan's no more.[14]

In that spring of 1847 as O'Connell was setting out on his last journey to Italy, three English lawyers were nearing the end of some six months of energetic travelling around every parish in Wales. They had been appointed in response to a motion in the House of Commons to inquire 'into the state of education in the principality of Wales, especially into the means afforded to the labouring classes of acquiring a knowledge of the English language'. In their copiously documented reports the commissioners painted a picture of educational standards in day schools which fell a long way short of satisfactory: teachers were untrained and often incompetent; physical conditions were crowded and unpleasant; and the children were woefully ignorant. The day schools suffered further from being generally conducted in English even in areas where the population was entirely Welsh-speaking, with no attempt at interpretation, or teaching in the English language itself. On the other hand there were numerous Welsh-speaking Sunday Schools, particularly those associated with the Nonconformist chapels, which were, on their own terms, much more successful. Pupils of all ages learnt to read, gained considerable religious knowledge, and benefited from genuine mental stimulus and participation in a well-structured organization.[15] The interaction of language and religion meant, however, that people whose only education came from these institutions were effectively isolated from external cultural influences:

> The language cultivated in the Sunday-schools is Welsh: the subjects of instruction are exclusively religious; consequently the religious vocabulary of the Welsh language has been enlarged, strengthened, and rendered capable of expressing every shade of idea, and the great mass of the poorer classes have been trained from their childhood to its use. On the other hand, the Sunday-schools, being religious instruments, have never professed a wider range. They have enriched the theological vocabulary, and made the peasantry expert in handling that branch of the Welsh language, but its resources in every other branch remain obsolete and meagre, and even of these the people are left in ignorance.

Out of a sample of 405 Welsh books examined, 309 were found to relate to religion or poetry. Moreover as the religious culture was exclusively proletarian it was no check to the 'social defects to which they are habituated'.[16] In particular it was alleged that religion itself could even promote a cloak for sexual irregularity: according to one witness at Builth, 'evening services are quitted by the younger people in a riotous manner, and much immorality then occurs'.[17] One of the commissioners summarized his evidence with the following sweeping judgements:

> Poetical and enthusiastic warmth of religious feeling, careful attendance upon religious services, zealous interest in religious knowledge, and comparative absence of crime, are found side by side with the most unreasoning prejudices or impulses; an utter want of method in thinking and acting; and (what is far worse), with a wide-spread disregard of temperance, wherever there are the means of excess, of chastity, of veracity, and of fair dealing.[18]

The reports of the commissioners were published as Parliamentary blue books in the summer of 1847 and stirred a storm of protest in Wales. The implications that the language and religion of many Welsh people were a serious obstacle to their cultural, economic and social advance was bad enough; but the suggestion that both were linked to serious moral deficiencies was felt to be outrageous. Pamphleteers of various backgrounds attacked the commissioners and their informants for adopting defective methods of enquiry and indulging in outright fabrication. It was claimed that the generalized conclusions drawn in the reports built far too much on isolated pieces of evidence. The controversy also figured prominently in the Welsh and English press. In an emotive analogy, which became part of the mental furniture of all Welsh people, the affair was labelled 'the treason of the Blue Books' recalling a legendary incident in the fifth century 'the treason of the Long Knives', when the Saxon chieftain Hengist had invited all the British nobles to a banquet and then ordered his men to murder their guests. Following this massacre the Britons had been driven westwards into the mountains of Wales.[19]

The affair proved to be an important catalyst in the development of Welsh national consciousness, and particularly in its interaction with religion. Beneath the layers of prejudice and incomprehension evident in the blue books, the commissioners were accurate in their perception that a distinctively Welsh language and culture had become intimately bound up with the religious life of the Nonconformist chapels in the principality. Although Nonconformity was strong all over Wales, it was especially important in the newly industrialized areas of the south as a basis for social cohesion and community identity. It is true that the commissioners failed to appreciate that this particular variety of Welshness was only one strand, albeit an increasingly important one, in a wider stirring of national consciousness which had been under way since the mid-eighteenth century. Aspects of this movement included the restoration of the *eisteddfod* festivals associated with the flowering of music and poetry; the investigation of the Welsh past in a manner which was no less influential for being informed as much by legend and sheer invention as by serious scholarship; and the systematic study of the language. There was initially little linkage with Nonconformity: many of the early protagonists of cultural renaissance were Anglicans who were obviously unlikely to see religion as a feature of Welsh distinctiveness, while others, such as the bard Iolo Morganwy (Edward Williams) devised their own diffuse spirituality from a combination of Unitarianism, nature-worship and neo-Druidism.[20]

The treason of the Blue Books, however, came at a time when the Nonconformist impact on Welsh society was reaching its greatest extent and served, albeit in a negative fashion, to confirm and highlight its importance. Although some of the most vigorous critics of the commissioners, notably Henry Cotton, the Dean of Bangor, were Anglicans,[21] 1847 marked the beginning of a process whereby the mainstream of Welsh culture was increasingly perceived as bound up with Nonconformity and the Church of England accordingly attacked as an alien intrusion. The consequence was that Welsh national concerns became closely associated with specifically religious matters, particularly the long-running campaign for disestablishment of the Church of England in Wales.

The incidents discussed in this section raise questions about the character of religious life in Scotland, Ireland and Wales which will be further explored in subsequent chapters. In the meantime they serve to indicate the importance of the churches as a focus for national identity and aspirations in all three countries. There were of course other influences at work, notably the various forms of assertion of national culture associated with Young Ireland and Iolo Morganwy and his contemporaries. These had their parallel in the Scotland of the early nineteenth century in the novels of Sir Walter Scott and the romanticization of – largely invented – Highland tradition. Nevertheless the 1840s were a decisive decade in demonstrating that these cultural currents at present could not match organized religion in its capacity to stir popular opinion. In Scotland an essentially ecclesiastical event was a major focus of public interest; in Ireland the Roman Catholic Church was an indispensable agent of political mobilization; and in Wales the chapels decisively established a position as a central bastion of its language, traditions and aspirations. These achievements on the part of the churches were a testimony to the strength of the forces of evangelicalism and Catholicism discussed in Chapter 2. Certainly compromises and accommodations had been made, but the full significance of these was only to become apparent over the course of the ensuing century, and for the moment it seemed that, at least in a qualified sense, 'holy nations' had indeed emerged. This does not mean that everyone actively participated in religious observance, let alone that they subscribed to the full fabric of Christian belief preached by clergy and ministers. It does imply that if people thought of their nation and sought, with whatever degree of articulateness, to perceive its identity and character, it was the language and institutions of its Christianity which usually came most readily to mind. How then can this analysis be related to the situation of England and to the wider problem of defining and sustaining identity in the multi-national British state?

2. PROTESTANTISM, ENGLAND AND BRITAIN

On 5 November 1850 the traditional Guy Fawkes celebrations on the Cathedral Green at Exeter were particularly elaborate, colourful and vigorous. The festivities were stimulated by reaction to the announcement a few weeks earlier that Pope Pius IX had created a hierarchy of Roman Catholic bishops for England and Wales and assigned to them titles derived from particular towns and cities.[22] The procession in Exeter was headed by 'forty begging bare-headed friars' who were followed by effigies of the Inquisitor General, the Pope, the newly-created Roman Catholic Archbishop of Westminster, Cardinal Wiseman, and his fellow bishops. At the rear came 'the true and faithful citizens of Exeter – giving expression to the religious and loyal feeling of their hearts by shouting "The Protestant Church of England for ever! Down with the Pope and Papacy! The Queen Supreme!"' The effigies were then burnt outside the cathedral, 'with all the indignity heaped upon them which their late daring and impudent, but . . . contemptible usurpation of power over the British people deserves'. The band played 'God save the Queen' and the people sang 'Frustrate their Popish tricks, Confound their politics, God save the Queen'.[23]

This demonstration represented just one dimension of a massive storm of protest which swept the country in response to the perceived 'papal aggression'. Guy Fawkes celebrations were a focus for local feeling in a number of other centres and there were also instances when Protestant demonstrations, on this and other occasions, led to violence and sectarian clashes with Catholics. At a more decorous level numerous clergy preached sermons attacking the Pope and all his works; and a wave of public meetings adopted petitions to Parliament demanding legislative action against the new bishops. The whole atmosphere was further substantially influenced by a letter from the Prime Minister, Lord John Russell, to the Bishop of Durham which attacked the Pope's measures and was published in *The Times* on 7 November 1850. Russell described the new Roman Catholic hierarchy as:

> a pretension of supremacy over the realm of England, and a claim to sole and undivided sway, which is inconsistent with the Queen's supremacy, with the rights of our bishops and clergy, and with the spiritual independence of the nation, as asserted even in Roman Catholic times.[24]

Early in 1851 the government introduced legislation, the Ecclesiastical Titles Bill, to render the new episcopal titles illegal, and the subsequent political wranglings and manoeuvres were to consume a substantial proportion of the Parliamentary session.

What lay behind all this? In part the furore can be viewed as a dramatic late manifestation of the strong tradition of anti-Catholicism in

British culture which can be traced back to the Reformation. In conjunction with this there were much more immediate causes. In announcing the new hierarchy to English Roman Catholics, Cardinal Wiseman had used inadvisedly grandiloquent language, writing of the restoration of 'Catholic England' to 'its orbit in the ecclesiastical firmament' and of his own jurisdiction over the counties of south-east England without making it clear that it extended only to Roman Catholics.[25] Matters were further influenced by the Prime Minister's intervention in the affair. Moreover in the recent past questions concerning Roman Catholicism had been prominent on the political agenda: in 1845 Sir Robert Peel's attempt to take some of the steam out of the pressure for Repeal in Ireland by improving state provision for the Roman Catholic college at Maynooth had aroused major protest; there was continuing concern in the late 1840s over the activities of Irish priests; and there were abortive but controversial attempts to establish diplomatic relations with the papacy and to endow the Roman Catholic Church in Ireland from public funds. Meanwhile, swelled by the influx of immigrants from an Ireland in the grip of famine, the Roman Catholic Church in England, Scotland and Wales appeared to be growing fast and presenting an increasingly serious challenge to Protestantism, especially in north-west England and south-west Scotland. The rivalry was one which had social and cultural as well as ecclesiastical dimensions. At the same time concern was growing regarding the impact of the Oxford Movement in stirring a Romeward tendency within the Church of England, as variously manifested in the conversion of John Henry Newman to Roman Catholicism in 1845 and the introduction of allegedly ritualistic practices in some churches. 'Renegade members of the Church of England' appeared in the Exeter procession following the friars and Catholic bishops and the crowd also shouted 'No Puseyism![26] No traitors within the Church!' The issue also loomed large in Russell's preoccupations: in the Durham letter he attacked 'clergymen of our own Church' who 'have been most forward in leading their flocks "step by step to the very verge of the precipice".'[27]

The whole affair occurred a few months before the Great Exhibition and represented a very different but complementary image of Britain at mid-century. It indicated that at the very time when that celebration of national technological achievement was in preparation, the links between religious and patriotic consciousness were also strong. The Pope, Wiseman and their supporters seemed for a few months to present a greater threat to national integrity than anyone since Napoleon. Religious belief and institutions, whether a generalized Protestantism or a specific allegiance to the Church of England, were an essential part of people's perception of what gave the nation its identity and character and hence a challenge to their religion seemed to be a challenge to their nationhood. Moreover in such an environment the 'Puseyites', internal critics who sought a redefinition of the Church of England, appeared to be traitors in a political as well as a religious sense. Here were many aspects of a nationalist frame of mind, but closely bound up with commitment to religious institutions. On this occasion too a religious issue was serving to emphasize the common ground of identity between the component nations of Britain. Even though the new hierarchy did not extend north of the Border there was extensive protest in Scotland: the commission of the General Assembly of the Free Church judged the Pope's actions as 'well fitted to awaken the alarm of all sound Protestants and patriots'.[28] In Wales too there were numerous statements of indignation, although a public meeting at Swansea, while 'expressing its hearty and unwavering attachment to the Protestant religion' also deprecated 'any attempt to repress the perfect and proper exercise of religious opinion by the secular arm'.[29] Ulster Presbyterians also added their voices to the chorus.[30] Although a sense of Nonconformist or Presbyterian distinctiveness was by no means overcome by a feeling of 'British' Protestant identity, the countervailing force was still a significant one.

On the other hand the reaffirmation of Protestantism as being of the essence of nationhood in Britain, threw into sharp relief the position of Roman Catholics in the United Kingdom. In relation to Ireland, it reinforced the identification between Roman Catholicism and nationalism, as expressed politically in the strenuous opposition to the Ecclesiastical Titles Bill maintained by a group of Irish MPs in 1851. This laid the basis for the Independent Irish Party of the 1850s. The prospects for non-sectarian politics in Ireland were further weakened by the consolidation of Cullen's reforms of the Catholic Church in parallel with a re-emergence of militant Protestantism, itself fuelled in part by the 'papal aggression' affair. The position of Roman Catholics in Britain was more ambivalent. Although some identified with the Irish, others were certainly not prepared to accept the premise that Roman Catholicism was in fundamental conflict with patriotism. Part of the offensiveness of Wiseman's announcement of the new hierarchy in the eyes of Protestants lay precisely in this point: the Cardinal referred to 'Your beloved country' and presented current developments as the fulfilment of its religious destiny and an indicator of the virtues of English saints and martyrs.[31] Similarly in his sermon on 'The Second Spring', preached to the assembled

Roman Catholic bishops in 1852, J. H. Newman presented the restoration of the hierarchy as a resurgence in the *English* Church. He dwelt on the glories of the medieval Church: 'Mixed up with the civil institutions, with kings and nobles, with the people, found in every village and in every town – it seemed destined to stand, so long as England stood, and to outlast, it might be, England's greatness'. [32] Likewise, the much-derided 'Puseyites' in no way accepted the premise that they were undermining the religious identity of their country; rather they regarded the promotion of Anglo-Catholicism as an upholding of the essential spiritual character and heritage of the nation.

The creation of the Roman Catholic hierarchy and the responses to it thus illustrate graphically the manner in which in the mid-nineteenth century an issue that seemed essentially concerned with the structures of institutional religion could stir a much broader resonance in the public mind. Ecclesiastical organization was, on this occasion at least, an important focus for patriotism. Eighteen months or so later, in the autumn of 1852, the death and funeral of the Duke of Wellington served to indicate that the converse relationship between religion and patriotism was also strong, as an essentially national occasion readily acquired religious dimensions on a variety of different levels.

The victor of Waterloo, who had also been Prime Minister from 1828 to 1830 and was a controversial political figure during the 1830s, lived long enough for the memory of his military achievements and his dignity as an elder statesman to obscure many of the antagonisms stirred by his intervening career. Although over eighty, he had continued to be an active public figure and accordingly his sudden death from a stroke on 14 September 1852 took the world by surprise. During the next two months countless eulogies and tributes were published, both separately and in the newspapers, and numerous clergy took the Duke and his death as a theme for a sermon. Mourning culminated in a massive procession through London in front of vast crowds and a funeral at St Paul's Cathedral on 18 November, arguably the most spectacular state occasion in Britain between the coronation of George IV in 1821 and the golden jubilee of Queen Victoria in 1887. On the same day processions, church services and other commemorations took place in towns and cities all over England and Wales, although recognition of the occasion in Scotland and Ireland was more limited. In the course of this elaborate apotheosis, the Duke was venerated, not only for the achievements of his undeniably remarkable career, but as a kind of departed ideal of national character; as Tennyson put it, 'The last great Englishman is low'. [33]

115

In what senses can this process of mourning and commemoration be viewed as religious? It will be helpful here to recall again the conceptualization of different ways of being religious which was set out in Chapter 1. In the hands of clergy the Duke's death was readily seen as having defined institutional and theological significance within an official church framework. Anglican parsons extolled the deceased as a faithful son of the Church of England, upholding it in his personal life by regular attendance at public worship, and in public life by staunch resistance to the demands of the dissenters. Others drew from his life, particularly his integrity and devotion to duty, role models for the Christian, and also dwelt on the suddenness of his death as grounds for continual spiritual preparedness. These were sentiments in which Nonconformists too could readily join.[34] Church services to commemorate the Duke also served to uphold a general 'Christianity' rather than specific Anglican or denominational concerns. Thus at Leeds Parish Church, Nonconformist town councillors listened to the vicar, Walter Farquhar Hook, preach a sermon in which he tactfully dwelt on the common ground, discussing Christian patriotism, which he defined as 'the preference of our own country to any other in the world, and a desire to promote its honour as well as its welfare'. He held that this was a sentiment manifested by Jesus himself in his lament over Jerusalem, as recorded in the New Testament.[35]

There was also in the reactions of observers evidence of a generalized religiousness which displayed supernatural and spiritual reference outside the framework of Christian orthodoxy. Two quotations will serve to illustrate the point. The first comes from the closing section of Tennyson's 'Ode on the Death of the Duke of Wellington':

> For though the Giant Ages heave the hill
> And break the shore, and ever more
> Make and break, and work their will;
> Though world on world in myriad myriads roll
> Round us, each with different powers,
> And other forms of life than ours,
> What know we greater than the soul?
> On God and Godlike men we build our trust.[36]

Such language, which accorded an eternal significance to the Duke's passing, was not a monopoly of poets. In a manuscript account of the funeral Miss Napier, daughter of a general who took part in the procession, showed a sharp awareness of the frustrations and disappointments experienced by spectators. Nevertheless she rejected criticism of the crowd as being 'there but to make holiday and stare'. She concluded:

> Doubtless, as we did ourselves, they felt for a portion of the time the distraction of the surrounding circumstances; but if one nature be common to us all, and all poetic faith be not in vain; if reverence for greatness gone have any power upon the soul, who shall dare to affirm that any heart there was not for some short time at least stirred by emotion deeper than usual, and uplifted to higher thoughts.[37]

The tone of these observations indicates that more cynical evaluations of the mood of the crowd were also being made, but press reports testified to the generally sober and reverent mood of the spectators both in London and elsewhere.

In the language of Tennyson and Miss Napier we have moved a long way from the precise doctrinal teaching presented in sermons. We see rather the influence of Romanticism as mediated particularly through Thomas Carlyle and his concept of the hero, as readily applied to Wellington. Other aspects of the ceremonial displayed a symbolism which owed more to pagan classicism than to Christianity. For the Duke's lying-in-state, the hall of Chelsea hospital was fitted out in black with military and heraldic images surrounding the coffin; the funeral car on which the body was carried in the procession similarly lacked any specifically Christian reference other than the words 'Blessed are the dead that die in the Lord' embroidered on the pall. It was decorated rather with trophies of arms, Victories and ducal coronets.[38] The monument to Wellington eventually erected in the nave of St Paul's was, despite its ecclesiastical location, designed in a similar vein: an equestrian statue of the duke stands on a triumphal arch, which is flanked by figures of Valour, Cowardice, Truth and Falsehood. Within the arch the duke's effigy lies on a sarcophagus surmounting a plinth ornamented with military trophies.[39]

Contemporaries were conscious of the ambivalences of the ceremonial and there were attacks on it in the Christian press. The lying-in-state in particular was charged with giving unseemly glorification to death.[40] Hook, however, in his sermon in Leeds, did not share this concern:

> An English heart can have no sympathy with the minute critics, who with foreign predilections unable to rise to a noble thought, or to throw their souls into a great national feeling, are carping at the ceremonial of the last few days [the lying-in-state] because

forsooth it has not assumed a religious character to which it made no pretension. The solemnities of this day [the funeral] are the religious solemnities; when the nation determined that the dead should lie in state, it was so determined in order that a national should precede the religious solemnity, and in such a solemnity it was fitting that not religious emblems but historical trophies should have place. And they address a sermon to the thoughtful heart in itself sufficient, and seem to say, *sic transit gloria mundi*.[41]

Hook was wanting to have it both ways: on the one hand he made a sharp distinction between the 'religious' and the 'national'; on the other, almost in the same breath he attributed to the 'national' a significance that was not only symbolic and political, but also spiritual. Such blurrings of the distinction were to become increasingly apparent in the subsequent decades.

It was in its 'national' rather than 'religious' aspects that the funeral did something to strengthen the unity of the United Kingdom. Roman Catholic Ireland which had felt itself alienated by the furore over the 'papal aggression' could now take a certain double-edged pride in the fact that Wellington was by birth an Irishman. Granted that he was a Protestant and that his only concessions to Irish political aspirations had been made under duress, the nationalist *Freeman's Journal* was still proud to point out that the London crowds 'saw in that car the bones of their greatest warrior and statesman; but they ought to have seen more – the remains of an Irishman who had won them an empire'.[42] Dublin Corporation had made a point of its anxiety to be fully represented at what it characterized as a 'National demonstration'.[43] Similarly a member of Edinburgh Town Council saw acceptance of an invitation to attend the funeral not only as a matter of respect for the deceased 'but also as a mark of honourable distinction conferred on Scotland through its Metropolitan Councillors'.[44] National dignity was served under such circumstances not in stressing one's own distinctiveness, but in ensuring proper recognition at the centre.

Considering Wellington's funeral in conjunction with the 'papal aggression' we thus gain some significant indications, both of the power of organized religion as a force for national integration at the middle of the century, and also of its limitations. Although a sense of 'common Protestantism' could obscure Anglican, Presbyterian and Nonconformist distinctions in favour of an overarching sense of 'Britishness', it accentuated differences with Roman Catholics. On a state occasion in which all parts of the United Kingdom wished to have a share, the ambiguities could be lessened by stressing the 'national' rather than 'religious' character of the commemorations, but this weakened their legitimacy in the eyes of some.

There was a curious timeliness in the date of Wellington's death, in that the early 1850s saw the establishment in France of the empire of another Napoleon and, in 1854, the 'forty years' peace' which had followed Waterloo came to an end with the entry of Britain and France into the Crimean War. This latter event provides us with a final vantage point from which to view the relationships between organized religion and forms of national consciousness at mid-century, and directs our attention to relations with the outside world.

There is a strange paradox in the manner that the Crimean War, begun with diplomatic muddle and continued with military incompetence, profoundly stirred public opinion at home, being seen as a conflict of epoch-making significance. It is true that the immediate causes of the war – squabbles between Orthodox and Roman Catholic monks over the custody of the holy places in Jerusalem and obscure frontier disputes between Turkey and Russia – did raise larger strategic questions about the balance of power in the Near and Middle East in the light of the decay of the Ottoman Empire. Nevertheless the theatre of war was a long way from home and, in contrast to the situation in the Napoleonic Wars, there was no conceivable threat of invasion. There was also considerable incongruity in the alignment of the protagonists, Britain, France and Turkey, against Russia. Some three years after the nation had professed its indignation at Roman Catholic 'aggression' and a year after it had buried with such ceremony the vanquisher of one Napoleon, it now found itself allied in war with a professed Roman Catholic power led by Napoleon III. Moreover Muslim Turkey was another strange bedfellow for Protestant Britain, and Russia was an unfamiliar adversary.

The majority of contemporaries nevertheless saw not confusion and inconsistency, but the clash of great interests and ideals. On the political front there was a perceived confrontation between the constitutionalism of Britain and the despotism of Tsar Nicholas I. There were moral dimensions too: Russia was the aggressor, having in the autumn of 1853 invaded the Danubian principalities on the west coast of the Black Sea. Turkey was regarded as a loyal but vulnerable ally, and as it was felt that all reasonable steps had been taken to resolve the crisis by peaceful diplomatic means, the war was seen as a just and unavoidable one. In that respect the Crimean War may be seen as setting a pattern for the sequence of later conflicts in which Britain saw itself as a guardian of international morality: Turkey's plight in 1853, although less extreme, was the precursor of that of Belgium in 1914; Poland in 1939; and even of that of Kuwait in 1990. This attitude can in a sense be regarded as religious in itself, reflecting the diffused application of Christian Just War ideas and manifesting a species of ultimate concern in international relations. In 1854, moreover, it was associated with the proclamation by the clergy of an explicitly theological and spiritual basis for the war. It was suggested that Britain, victorious against all the odds in 1815, avoiding revolution in 1830 and 1848, enjoying great influence abroad and substantial prosperity at home, had become the inheritor of the special relationship with God enjoyed by Old Testament Israel and was a uniquely chosen and favoured nation. The privilege was acknowledged to be a double-edged one because, as the Bible so graphically indicated, God chastised and judged Israel for declension from his standards. Accordingly the negative aspects of national experience, notably epidemics, famines and social disorder, were viewed in this light. As sermons preached at the outbreak of war readily indicated, the conflict too was seen in this framework: it might be seen positively as the opportunity for further exercise of national mission; or negatively as a sign of God's displeasure with his chosen people whom he now wished to chastise through the suffering of the battlefield. In either case, however, it was seen as a crisis of more than human significance, in which behind the superficial incongruities and messiness a national spiritual destiny was being fulfilled.[45]

The extent of public support for the day of 'Solemn Fast, Humiliation and Prayer' held on 26 April 1854 indicates that the attribution of a religious context to events was not a mere conceit of clergymen. In proclaiming the fast the government had been responding to public opinion in the face of the Queen's personal reservations and, on the day itself, both churches and Nonconformist chapels were crowded. A second fast, in March 1855, was less universally supported, but as the war continued other linkages between Christianity and patriotism were made.[46] For example, the Revd George Bull, a popular veteran of campaigns for factory reform gave a lecture on 'Home and How to Make it Happy' in aid of the families of the troops. He presented his version of the upholding of Christian values in family life as the basis of the nation's prosperity and security. He summed up his sentiments in verse:

> The Home of Affection, of Order and Peace,
>   Where Religion and Loyalty be;
> The Home of the Faithful – the Temple of God –
>   Such Homes of old England for me!

Moreover there were signs that soldiering itself was coming to be perceived as a religious vocation.[47] In December 1855 the evangelical writer Catherine Marsh published *Memorials of Captain Hedley Vicars, Ninety-seventh Regiment*, the biography of a friend who had been killed in action in the Crimea some months before. Vicars was an evangelical and the book, which enjoyed an extensive sale, explicitly set out to demonstrate that a good officer could also be a good Christian. It was a key influence in promoting a shift in the image of the soldier from the rough fighting-man of Wellington's day to the morally upright crusader of the later Victorian period. Furthermore, according to Marsh, as Vicars died, heroically, cleanly and almost painlessly, 'a welcome from the armies of the sky sounded in his ears'.[48] For the author he was being rewarded by his God for his faithful Christian virtues, but for many of her readers the ambiguity between a religious martyrdom and self-sacrifice for his country may well have been unresolved. It is perhaps significant in this connection that in the aftermath of the Crimean War – unlike the Napoleonic Wars – a few memorials were erected to the mass of the fallen, rather than merely to the leaders. Examples survive at the bottom of Regent Street in London and in the Botanical Gardens in Sheffield. Herein can be seen the beginnings of the trend which was to culminate in the much more numerous and often religiously explicit memorials to the dead of the First World War.

In moving from an Edinburgh church to a Crimean battlefield we have come a long way, contextually as well as geographically, although chronologically only twelve years separated Hedley Vicars's death from the Disruption of the Church of Scotland. All these events, however, point towards a single broad conclusion: that at the middle of the nineteenth century religion was taking a central role in the development and articulation of national consciousness in the British Isles. This applies equally whether we are concerned with the assertion of over-arching 'British' identity; with the awareness of the Scots, Welsh and Irish of their own distinctiveness; or with the attitude of the whole towards continental Europe and the rest of the world. Thus in this connection it seems appropriate to view these years as a 'high tide of faith'.

This judgement, though, needs at once to be qualified in three respects. First, the metaphor has been chosen advisedly: a tide that has risen will also equally inexorably fall, although no prior assumptions should be made about the speed, nature and extent of the ebb nor about the shape of the sandbanks after the water has receded. Second, behind the prominence of religion in these years lay a shifting pattern of influences of kaleidoscopic complexity: change the pieces or the field of vision a little and forces that seemed to be strengthening the coherence of the United Kingdom now seemed to be pulling it apart; or movements and groups of people that had drawn heavily on religious inspiration now appeared to be operating in a much more secular framework. Third, the power of religion was founded not only on its manifestations in narrowly defined forms directly controlled by the churches, but also on a wider structure of unofficial and quasi-religion. If the Tara Hill meeting and Wellington's funeral were religious events, they were not so in a manner churchmen could view with unqualified enthusiasm.

The complex nature of the interaction between religion and nationhood in the mid-nineteenth century, as discussed in this chapter, should therefore be viewed in the context suggested by the examination of official and unofficial religion in Chapters 3 and 4. At the very time that the Census of Religious Worship of 1851 was pointing up the substantial but far from universal extent of attendance at organized church services, the events discussed above indicated the potential for national consciousness to feed not only on institutional religion but also on forms of more diffuse religious sentiment. We shall now turn to examine the various ways in which such linkages developed during the subsequent decades.

6

THINE IS THE KINGDOM?

Politics, community and the monarchy

Many threads can be discerned running through the lively politics of the United Kingdom and Ireland between the mid-nineteenth century and the Second World War. There was the endeavour to come to terms with the economic and social transformations consequent upon industrialization and urbanization; and the related question of the balance of political influence between social groups and classes, reflected in the nineteenth century in debates over the reform of the Parliamentary franchise, and in the twentieth century in the growing political influence of the labour movement. A further interconnected problem was the role of the state, as the characteristic Victorian preference for limited activity, minimal intervention and fiscal restraint gradually gave way to more expansionist visions of welfare provision, closer regulation and higher taxation. Such domestic issues, moreover, were discussed against the backdrop of sometimes intense engagement with the international scene, the responsibilities of Britain as an imperial power and its interests as a European one.

Until recent years historians have tended to treat religion as very much a second-order political question. Similarly, although the prominence of 'The Irish Question' at certain junctures – notably the mid-1880s and 1910–14 – could not be denied, the wider pattern of development of nationalist politics in these islands has received relatively little attention. There is nevertheless an obvious danger that efforts to redress this balance, such as the present book, will produce their own converse distortions. Accordingly the reader who seeks a rounded view of British and Irish politics will need to weigh the discussion that follows against the emphasis suggested by other writers with more secular preoccupations. The hypothesis to be developed in this chapter is not that politics can be fully understood with reference only to religion: such a claim would be self-evidently absurd. The argument is rather that religion, especially when broadly defined, did have very noticeable influence on both the substance and the style of politics, an influence that was at its most significant when it was linked to the forces of national self-assertion.

There is no space in a single chapter to consider all aspects of the relationship between religion, politics and nationality during the period, and attention will accordingly be focused on the fifty years between 1870 and 1920 which were both particularly rich in such interrelationships, and especially formative in the emergence of modern political structures. The chapter will be divided into four sections. In the first the framework for subsequent discussion will be set by an outline of some of the key issues and developments relating to the constitutional position of religion which will serve to indicate the manner in which it shaped political life. In the second part of the chapter we shall consider further how, at both a local and a national level, religious alignments and sentiments contributed substantially to the definition and consolidation of political loyalties. In the third section the distinctive experiences of Wales, Scotland and Ireland will be examined, and the general interconnections between religion, politics and nationalism further explored. Finally, we shall examine the role of the ritual and ceremonial centred on the monarchy – a different but influential kind of politics – in providing a support for British identity and social integration in the face of the various centrifugal pressures under discussion.

1. THE FRAMEWORK OF POLITICAL CONFLICT

The starting point for the consideration of religion in politics is the position of Established (or state) Churches. At the beginning of the period these existed in all parts of the United Kingdom, although the Church of Ireland was to be disestablished in 1871 and the Church in Wales in 1920. However, the Church of England and the Church of Scotland remain established, technically at least, in the late twentieth century. They have a primacy of prestige, expressed particularly in national and local ceremonial links, and endorsed by the continuing link with the Crown. They serve as a symbolic indication that the state itself is in some limited sense Christian, rather than generally religious or wholly secular. There are further practical implications, notably in the appointment of Church of England bishops by the Crown on the recommendation of the Prime Minister, and the continuing presence of bishops in the House of Lords. There is a requirement for Parliamentary approval of certain measures relating to the internal affairs of the

Church of England, but not the Church of Scotland. In general this procedure operates as a constitutional formality, but still one with potential for controversy, as was well illustrated as late as 1928, when Parliament rejected the revised Prayer Book passed by the Church Assembly.

Nevertheless by the middle of the twentieth century the implications of Establishment had become a political by-way, an issue that aroused occasional discussion and controversy, but was hardly the staple of regular Parliamentary life. The modern reader accordingly needs to make a substantial jump of the imagination to appreciate the intense debate and ideological engagement that during the earlier part of our period was focused on the relationship between religion and the state. Something of the strength of the commitments involved has already been indicated by our discussion of the Scottish Disruption in the previous chapter. The attitudes of mind can be further illustrated by three quotations, the first from the initial statement of the British Anti-State-Church Association formed in 1844 to campaign against 'State interference' in religion:

> in matters of religion man is responsible to God alone . . . all legislation by secular governments is an encroachment upon the rights of man, and an invasion of the prerogatives of God; and . . . the application by law of the resources of the State to the maintenance of any form or forms of religious worship and instruction is contrary to reason, hostile to liberty, and directly opposed to the genius of Christianity.[1]

Historically, Nonconformity had defined itself in its resistance to state control of religion. The resistance was now being carried into the outright voluntaryist counter-attack on the Established Church's fundamental right to exist. For the advocates of Establishment, on the other hand, the wider interests and character of religion were equally bound up with the maintenance of existing ties between Church and state. The Earl of Selborne, a former Lord Chancellor, wrote in 1886:

> A nation, into whose organic life the public recognition of Christianity had entered during all the ages of its existence, could not efface from its institutions all outward and visible signs of that recognition, without practically, and to a great extent, exulting secularism, to the disparagement of religion.[2]

For others the commitment was more nationalistic and political than explicitly Christian, but none the less powerful. Disraeli said in 1864:

Broadly and deeply planted in the land, mixed up with all our manners and customs, one of the main guarantees of our local government, and therefore one of the prime securities of our common liberties, the Church of England is part of our history, part of our life, part of England itself.[3]

Taken together assertions of this kind help one to begin to understand why seemingly dry and technical questions about the constitutional status of religion could stir such strong commitments. For the protagonists the issues touched at the very heart of how they understood and practised their religion and maintained their sense of communal and national identity. When disestablishment came to Ireland in 1871 something of the consequent sense of trauma and far-reaching loss was captured by the hymn-writer Mrs C. F. Alexander whose husband was Bishop of Derry:

> Look down, Lord of heaven, on our desolation!
> Fallen, fallen, fallen is now our Country's crown,
> Dimly dawns the New Year on a churchless nation,
> Ammon and Amalek tread our borders down.[4]

Behind such emotive language the practical importance of Establishment was still considerable in the mid-nineteenth century and afterwards. It is true that the repeal of the Test and Corporation Acts in 1828 and Catholic Emancipation in 1829 were a significant step towards constitutional pluralism,[5] and that the reforms of the 1830s had set limits to the political and social power of the Established Churches. However, very significant privileges remained in three main areas.

First, in education, all state grants in Britain were until the 1870s channelled through the churches. Although these funds were also available to Nonconformists and (from 1847) to Roman Catholics, the system in effect gave the most to those who had the most already and, in England at least, this worked to the advantage of the Established Church. The contentiousness of educational issues was well illustrated at the opening of our period in 1843 when a scheme for the education of children in the factories was withdrawn as a result of Nonconformist hostility to the undue influence which it allegedly gave to the Church of England. The Act of 1870 for England and Wales, passed by Gladstone's Liberal government, weakened the position of the Church of England as the Board Schools created as a result of the measure could only offer 'nondenominational' education. The Education (Scotland) Act of 1872 in principle transferred control of schools from the Church of Scotland to popularly elected bodies, but in practice the influence of the Kirk continued to be strong.[6] Meanwhile south of the Border, in 1902 a Conservative administration did much to restore the influence of the Church by permitting rate support to be given to denominational schools, among which those of the Church of England were much the most numerous. As we noted in Chapter 4, education was seen by the churches as a central vehicle for promoting their cause and the 1902 Education Act accordingly stirred intense opposition among Nonconformists. Not only was its practical effect perceived to be the dissemination among children of unwelcome religious teaching, but it was seen as a significant symbolic check to the increasing status of Nonconformity and its growing influence in the structures of local power. Resentment was expressed in the 'passive resistance' of those who refused to pay the objectionable portion of the rates, and more generally in a surge of support for the Liberal opposition which contributed to its election victory in 1906.

At university level too the Church of England had initially maintained an effective monopoly of the ancient institutions outside Scotland. Non-Anglicans could not be admitted to Oxford at all, and could not take degrees at Cambridge. Trinity College, Dublin, was in theory open to all, but fellowships and scholarships were restricted to members of the Established Church and the atmosphere accordingly was repugnant to Roman Catholics and Presbyterians. The Scottish universities had always been more open, and legal restrictions in England and Ireland were relaxed between the 1850s and the 1870s. Nevertheless the sense of recent exclusion and disadvantage was still very tangible in the first half of our period. In Ireland, moreover, even after disestablishment, Trinity College remained in practice a bastion of Protestantism, and the lack of adequate higher education for Roman Catholics was a recurrent source of political controversy. An unsuccessful attempt to resolve this problem contributed to the downfall of Gladstone's ministry in 1873.[7]

Second, the Established Churches, directly or indirectly, made financial demands on much of the population. This was likely to stir resentment in times of economic hardship, quite apart from the conscientious objections of Nonconformists and Roman Catholics. Church rates, the charge levied by a parish for the upkeep of its church, had been abolished in Ireland in 1833 but were a considerable bone of contention in England and Wales until legislation in 1868 deprived them of compulsory force. Tithes, the traditional 'tenth' of agricultural produce, continued to be a source of dispute. Legislation in the 1830s had commuted the charge to a levy on agricultural rents, usually payable by the landlord in Ireland and the tenant in England and Wales. In

Ireland the tithes, in this modified form, survived disestablishment, but were subsequently paid to the state rather than the Church, thus ending their significance as a religious issue. In England, and Wales in particular, tithes continued to be a substantial source of grievance and led in the 1880s to vigorous demonstrations, refusals to pay and distraint of goods. In Wales, fuelled by economic depression, religious conflict and rising national consciousness were feeding off each other. The sting was taken out of the dispute by further legislation in 1891, which transferred responsibility for payment of the charge to the landlords, who were predominantly Anglican. However, this was still an indirect burden on tenant farmers, whose rents were increased, and resentment continued until the Tithe Act of 1936 abolished the charge altogether. In Scotland the financial structure for support of the Established Church was a different one. In rural areas resources were provided from 'teinds', levied like tithes on agricultural produce and rent, and in some towns there were local taxes from the proceeds of which councils paid the clergy. Both kinds of levy continued to be sources of discontent in our period, and teinds continued until they were commuted for a fixed payment in 1925.

Third, a less tangible but crucially important aspect of the position of the Church of England in particular was the manner in which it was intertwined with the structures of social and political power at a range of different levels. At the top of the hierarchy explicitly political action by bishops had by the Victorian era become less common and acceptable than it had been in the eighteenth century. Nevertheless there were still links with the past such as Henry Phillpotts, the staunchly Tory Bishop of Exeter, who lived until 1869. Prime ministers still took political loyalties into account in making appointments to the Bench and, even in the early twentieth century, Randall Davidson, as Archbishop of Canterbury, was able to exercise a significant influence in matters of state, extending beyond the strictly ecclesiastical. Bishops, in virtue of their position, were important local figures in their dioceses and cathedral cities, and, when they exerted themselves, could readily have an influence. During the later part of the nineteenth century some, such as Fraser at Manchester and Westcott at Durham, were ready to associate themselves with more radical causes, a tendency developed further by William Temple at Manchester, York and Canterbury, and Bell at Chichester in the second quarter of the twentieth century. By contrast, in the First World War Winnington-Ingram of London proved an uncritical and influential supporter of the nation's involvement in the conflict.

At the grass roots, parsons, although no longer a mainstay of local government, could still play an influential role in affairs, especially when they had the social status and economic resources to give weight to their interventions. They also had links with the wider structures of power, particularly in the countryside, where landlords, under the system of lay patronage, frequently appointed the clergy on their estates. Lay patronage continued in England throughout the period, but was abolished in Ireland and Wales as part of disestablishment, and in Scotland by the Patronage Act of 1874.

One can of course cite religious figures outside the Church of England who similarly had a wider social and political influence: for example, the Roman Catholics John MacHale in Ireland and Henry Manning in England; and Nonconformists such as the Baptist John Clifford and the Methodist Hugh Price Hughes. Nevertheless the prestige of such men tended to be more limited outside their own communities and it was often to a significant degree achieved, in a negative sense, with reference to the Established Church which they attacked as an unjustly privileged institution.

The widespread powers of the Established Churches touched numerous areas of life. They were at the centre of extensive political debate and did much to define and reinforce party alignments, with the Conservatives generally the defenders of the Establishment and the Liberals pressing for the reduction of its privileges or even for disestablishment. We shall explore this point in more detail in the next section, but it remains to note here the main phases in the changing position of religious Establishments. First there was from the late 1820s to the early 1840s a period of reform in which Roman Catholics were admitted to Parliament, the Church of England modestly reorganized, the Church of Ireland substantially reduced in scale, and the Church of Scotland greatly weakened by the Disruption. Second, there was a generation which, despite considerable Nonconformist militancy, saw relatively little further change. Third, between 1868 and 1874 there was a period of renewed reform, with the abolition of compulsory church rates in England, the disestablishment of the Church of Ireland, the Education Acts of 1870 and 1872, and, in Scotland, the abolition of patronage which removed one of the major grievances that had precipitated the Disruption in 1843. Fourth, between the mid-1870s and the eve of the First World War there was another period of stability. Indeed, with Conservative governments in power for much of the time, it can even be argued that the position of the surviving Established Churches grew stronger: new dioceses were set up; the campaign for disestablishment was fought off in England and Scotland and stalemated in Wales; and the 1902 Education Act was perceived as a substantial extension of Anglican power. Finally, between 1912 and 1936 there was another period of the removal of privileges, disestablishment in Wales, commutation of teinds and the abolition of tithes. By the 1920s, and certainly by the Second World War, there remained insufficient practical grievances for the Establishment question to focus political engagement in the manner that it had done in the Victorian era.

2. RELIGION AND POLITICAL LOYALTY

The old adage that the Church of England was 'the Tory party at prayer' should not be accepted without a measure of qualification, but does contain a substantial element of truth. The Church itself consistently perceived the Conservatives as more likely to be sympathetic to their interests than were their opponents. Thus, for example, the Church Defence Institution, a pressure group which campaigned against disestablishment between the late 1850s and the 1890s operated in effect to muster support for the Conservatives. The compliment was returned by Tories who, whether or not personally pious, saw the Church as an essential part of that existing constitutional and social hierarchy which they wished to preserve, an attitude encapsulated in the quotation from Disraeli given above. North of the Border, a broad sympathy between the Conservative Party and the Church of Scotland can be discerned, although here the overwhelming strength of the Liberals suggested that in practice the electoral loyalties of the kirk's supporters were more divided.

Such relationships did not necessarily mean that the Conservatives did everything that the Church wanted: indeed they claimed the privilege and concern of friendship to carry out pressing reforms in order to preserve the essential structure, sometimes in face of the unease of substantial numbers of clergy. The process of church reform had been initiated by Sir Robert Peel's government in 1835 and later Conservative administrations concurred in the church rates measure of 1868 and enacted the Patronage Act of 1874 and the Tithe Act of 1891. They were secure in the knowledge that more die-hard defenders of the status quo might at the time be vocal critics of compromise, but when it came to the realities of the next election they would have nowhere else to go.

On the other side of the House of Commons the loose alignment of Whigs and Radicals which came together in the 1860s to form the Liberal Party was in varying degrees committed to the reform or even to the abolition of religious Establishments. It is important to emphasize the diversity of shades of opinion. At the moderate end the Whigs were essentially conservative in their general political outlook, anxious to maintain the Church but also wanting to reduce its political and institutional independence and to reform it to adapt to an increasingly pluralistic society. Indeed some of them wanted to 'level up' other religious groups to a degree of parity with the Establishment through concurrent endowment by the state, an idea widely discussed at the time of Irish disestablishment. They would have agreed with Disraeli that religion was part of the necessary cement of the social order, but differed from him in believing that this role would best be performed by a substantial reorganization of the connection between the state and the Church. Their view was an emphatically Erastian one: in other words, that all religion should as far as possible be linked to the state in order that it could be most effectively controlled.

On the other hand the substantial body of Nonconformist supporters of the Whigs and Liberals wanted to 'level down' the Church of England rather than to give state support to other groups. They did not want government money for themselves, and they were appalled at the idea that it might be given to the Roman Catholics. These too valued their independence too much to want money from the state. Accordingly a long campaign was waged against the privileges of the Church of England, spearheaded by the Anti-State-Church Association. In 1853 this changed its name to the Liberation Society and became a major force in the Liberalism of the second half of the nineteenth century.[8] Initially, when official Liberal Party organization had not developed very far, this well-developed and vociferous pressure group had considerable importance in co-ordinating electoral support. From the 1870s and 1880s the attack on the Establishment broadened into the wider phenomenon of the so-called 'Nonconformist conscience', a loose alignment between the Free Churches and the Liberal Party on a range of religious and moral concerns. The link was cemented by the leadership of William Ewart Gladstone. Despite his own High Church Anglicanism the 'Grand Old Man' was at one with Nonconformists in his desire for religious freedom and moral probity in public life. Above all, a Baptist minister who heard him speak in 1877 'recognized him as devoted lover of our Lord'. Especially in the Midlothian campaign of

1879, Gladstone's political progress could assume something of the fervour and spiritual intensity of a revivalist crusade.[9]

The late Victorian Liberal Party contained a variety of other strands of opinion, including secularly minded Radicals who might share the Nonconformist desire for an end to Anglican privileges, but from very different motives and presuppositions. United action on religious matters was based on negatives, antagonism to the Church as it stood, rather than a positive agreed programme as to what, if anything, should replace it. Hence, particularly when Liberal governments were in power, underlying disagreements on religious policy could also be a source of disunity. This was evident, for example, in Gladstone's first ministry between 1868 and 1874 which, after achieving considerable reforms, became bogged down in internal disagreement. Much later, the Liberal governments after 1906 attempted to discharge their political debt to the Nonconformists with educational reforms, but lacked the political will to persist with them in the face of the opposition of the Church and the House of Lords.

The relationship between religion and politics at the local level needs to be understood in the context of the changes in the nature of the electoral system which occurred during the period. Under the 1832 Reform Act the franchise was limited by a property qualification, but in 1867 this was changed to give the vote to male householders in the boroughs, and the 1884 Reform Act extended this to the counties as well.[10] However, in effect this still fell far short of manhood suffrage: when one takes into account men who were not householders, and the difficulties of registration which particularly disadvantaged people who moved frequently, it has been estimated that in 1911 only 59 per cent of the adult male population had the vote.[11] Of course no women at all had the Parliamentary franchise until 1918, and they did not obtain equality with men until 1928. Two further important changes were the Ballot Act of 1872 which replaced the previous system of open public voting with the secret ballot, and the redistribution of seats in 1884–5 in which relatively small single-member constituencies replaced large two- or three-member constituencies which had covered a whole large town or small county, or a substantial part of a large county.

Much of our period thus corresponds to a phase of transition between the small-scale politics of the Georgian era, controlled in large measure by the landed magnates, and the mass democracy of the mid-twentieth century: this was accompanied by a change of emphasis from local to national concerns and the increasing power and sophistication of party structures. Between 1867 and 1918 the electorate was large enough and independent enough for the impact of personal influence and coercion to be much attenuated; but small enough and coherent enough for a strong sense of engagement to be maintained by voters, whose political loyalties were likely to be most intense when they were reinforced by the wider social and cultural structures in which they lived. This period also corresponded, as we have seen in previous chapters, to the institutional highwater mark of official religion, which had a particularly crucial impact on those groups of the lower middle class and upper working class enfranchised in 1867 and 1885.[12] Under these circumstances religious ties assumed for a few decades considerable electoral significance. In further substantiating and developing this point the component parts of the United Kingdom need to be considered separately. The remainder of this section will be concerned with England and in the final part of the chapter we shall turn our attention to Wales, Scotland and Ireland.

The influence of religion on English politics needs to be understood as operating on a number of different levels. Its most obvious manifestation was in the electoral activity of Anglican clergy, Nonconformist ministers and other people in official positions, such as Sunday School teachers and chapel deacons. It was reported that on the Conservative side in North Norfolk in 1868, 'the parson of the parish, naturally enough, thinking the Church was in danger, and the squire . . . were acting in each particular parish as a sort of committee'.[13] On the other side of the political fence, local Free Church councils often mobilized their supporters to vote for the Liberal candidate, notably in the 1906 general election. Roman Catholic clergy also intervened in elections, particularly in the early twentieth century, although their influence was politically divided, some favouring the Conservatives because of their education policy; others the Liberals because of sympathy for Home Rule in Ireland.[14] One could multiply such instances of explicit political campaigning during the period between the 1867 Reform Act and the First World War, although assessments of their importance need to be balanced by an awareness of the other religious leaders who held back from such activity, or simply lacked the requisite energy and organizational ability.[15]

The underlying significance of religion lay, however, in the importance of church and chapel in defining the outlook of local communities, which then tended to act as a unit in expressing their political loyalties. Where sectarian identities – as discussed in Chapter 4 – were strong this could lead to very pronounced polarization. Such loyalties were an important influence on the electoral behaviour even of those who were not regular attenders at religious worship. In a sample derived from oral evidence and relating to the thirty years or so before the First World War, 67 per cent of churchgoers, but only 16 per cent of chapel-goers voted Conservative. It is possible to ascertain the broad denominational loyalty of many non-churchgoers from information on the Sunday Schools attended by their children. It emerges that 64 per cent of non-churchgoers with children at Anglican Sunday Schools voted Conservative; but only 25 per cent of those with children at Nonconformist Sunday Schools.[16] Although the connection between religious and political loyalty was not a universal one it was clearly widely influential. Sunday Schools indeed played an important part in defining and maintaining such identities through their regular marches, other meetings and demonstrations.

Unofficial religious attitudes also impinged on political life in ways which reflected the more diffuse influence of the churches, but lay outside their direct control. The Church of England and the Conservative Party were sometimes the beneficiaries of popular patriotic sentiment in which the Church was presented as an institution which was genuinely 'of the people' and a focus for national loyalty. Such linkages had their roots in a radical Tory tradition which went back to the 1830s, and beyond, to the popular grass roots political opposition used by eighteenth-century Tories as they linked together the causes of Church and King. In the second half of the nineteenth century such attitudes could derive renewed stimulus from the activities of occasional populist parsons and from antipathy to the perceived ethos of Nonconformity. Its social and moral discipline was felt to be oppressive, above all when manifested in the crusading zeal of the temperance movement, which directly confronted a major aspect of working-class leisure activity.[17]

Strong political commitments were also associated with the militant Protestantism possessed in good measure by a substantial proportion of the electorate. Among some committed Nonconformists theological antipathy to Roman Catholicism contributed to disillusionment with Gladstone after his espousal in 1886 of Home Rule for Ireland, thus strengthening the Liberal Unionists who split with him over the issue and ultimately merged into the Conservative Party. At a less sophisticated theological level in areas of widespread Irish Catholic settlement, above all in Lancashire, Protestant sectarian loyalties were channelled to the support of the Conservative party through the agency of agitators such as William Murphy, who was active in the later 1860s, and the

Orange Order which, having been proscribed in 1836, revived in Lancashire between the 1850s and 1870s.[18]

Popular Toryism was given broader institutional development by the Primrose League, founded in 1883. The League took its name from Disraeli's supposedly favourite flowers and was steeped in an elaborate structure of hierarchy and romantic titles. It provided a regular pattern of entertainment to sugar the pill of explicitly political activities. Branches (known as 'habitations') were widespread during the last two decades of the nineteenth century and it proved a very effective basis for Conservative electoral success. It was active throughout Britain in the late Victorian and Edwardian years, although it proved to be rather less successful in Scotland than in England and Wales. The character of the creed which it represented is well illustrated by the declaration required from new members, who could not be atheists or 'enemies of the British Empire': 'I declare, on my honour and faith, that I will devote my best ability to the maintenance of Religion, of the Estates of the Realm, and of the unity of the British Empire under our Sovereign'. The 'Religion' in question was of a generalized kind, with only diffuse affinities to official religion and containing significant elements of unofficial and quasi-religion. Membership was open to Jews as well as Roman Catholics, Nonconformists and, of course, Anglicans; the ideological place of religion was inextricably bound up with other ultimate concerns, the Crown, the Empire and the 'Estates of the Realm' and the whole sustained by an elaborate system of symbolic meaning. The League avoided any specific commitment to the Church of England, standing aloof from current controversies over the Establishment with a view to recruiting non-Anglicans to Conservatism. The measure of its success with Nonconformists is unclear, but Roman Catholics were certainly attracted to a significant extent. An interesting feature of the League's membership was the extensive and active support that it received from women, who were often, it would appear, moving into politics on the basis of experience gained in religious or philanthropic activity.[19]

In parallel fashion popular Liberalism drew on important cultural currents which can be traced back to the legacy of the Puritanism of the seventeenth century as well as to the more immediate impact of Nonconformity. John Bunyan's *Pilgrim's Progress* carried the message not only of Christian perseverance but also of dignity in the face of oppression, and continued to enjoy great popularity in the nineteenth century.[20] The British Library catalogue lists thirty-four editions and reprints between 1840 and 1859; fifty-eight between 1860 and 1879; thirty-three between 1880 and 1899 and thirty-four between 1900 and

1914.[21] The strong sense of self-worth and eternal destiny that was the legacy of evangelical conversion experiences could empower political action even if its spiritual intensity faded, while an acquaintance with biblical calls for justice and for the building of the Kingdom of God was present in the consciousness even of some of the less outwardly pious of liberal supporters.[22] Such convictions were focused by veneration for Gladstone himself, placed on a pedestal at the centre of a powerful personality cult which, as the letters sent to Mrs Gladstone on his death amply testify, attracted a wide variety of devotees, as diverse in their religious outlooks as in their social backgrounds. One example from a Staffordshire woman, indicates how Gladstone's leadership could imbue politics with intense moral fervour even when specific religious language was lacking:

> Mr Gladstone has been my hero and my ideal since childhood and all through my girlhood I have held him the greatest and best on earth. His name shall ever live in our family as a synonym of all that is good and all that true noble [sic]. When I think of him I wish to do something worthy of him for his sake.[23]

As political movements developed their own dynamic they continued to appropriate religious language but to utilize and interpret it on terms increasingly detached from the structures of official religion. 'The Nonconformist conscience' was losing some of its spiritual intensity and direct relationship to the grass roots and becoming more of a loose umbrella of moral concerns. Meanwhile the two most prominent Liberal leaders of the generation succeeding Gladstone, Asquith and Lloyd George, lacked his intensity of Christian conviction, but came from Nonconformist backgrounds and derived personal satisfaction and political profit from the external manifestation of affinity with the chapels.[24]

A similar tendency to a shift in the character of religious language was also evident in the development of radical and working-class politics, although here, initially at least, there was not so much a dilution of Christianity as an endeavour to reorientate it. During the Chartist unrest of the 1830s and 1840s there had been occasions when the protesters seemed to be presenting an alternative Christianity, occupying churches, quoting the Bible against the clergy and the authorities and claiming that Jesus Christ was the 'first Chartist'.[25] Chartism also stirred the earliest 'Christian Socialists', led by Frederick Denison Maurice, a theologian; Charles Kingsley, a clergyman and novelist; and John Malcolm Ludlow, a lawyer. In 1848 against the backdrop of revolution in Europe and unsuccessful resurgence of Chartism at home, members of this group began to proclaim their concern for the poor and their sense of the injustice of contemporary social structures. In 1851 Kingsley explicitly linked Christianity and radical social change in a patriotic framework:

> the will of God is, good news to the poor, deliverance to the broken-hearted, light to the ignorant, liberty to the crushed, and to the degraded masses the acceptable year of the Lord – a share and a stake, for them and for their children after them, in the soil, the wealth, the civilization and the government of this English land.[26]

The initial group of Christian Socialists lost momentum by the mid-1850s, but the movement revived in the last quarter of the century, with the emergence of the Guild of St Matthew, and the Christian Social Union, a much larger but more moderate body founded in 1889. At the same period as these groups emerged in the Church of England significant pressure began to develop within Nonconformity towards a greater engagement with social problems. This manifested itself not only in the strong linkage between evangelism and social concern developed by the Salvation Army, but also in the activities of men within the existing denominations, such as Hugh Price Hughes (Wesleyan), John Clifford (Baptist) and Andrew Mearns (Congregationalist). The latter's *Bitter Cry of Outcast London* published in 1883 was a damning indictment of conditions in the slums of the capital and a call for action by the state and voluntary agencies to relieve the situation.

Nevertheless, although some individual clergy and denominational leaders were prepared to associate themselves with the labour movement and to espouse what became known as 'the social gospel',[27] in general the importance of such official Christian activity lay more in reducing the antipathy of the churches themselves towards Socialism than in directly stimulating working-class political activity. Nevertheless there are still good grounds for arguing that in an indirect and unofficial sense religion contributed substantially to the prehistory and early development of the labour and socialist movements. Four points will be made here.

First, institutional religious activity was an important training ground for subsequent political or trade union activity. Sunday School children were required to participate in annual anniversary celebrations which often involved recitation. Methodist lay preachers gained more sustained experience in public speaking, and, as a young man, the Anglican

George Lansbury began to cut his controversial teeth by debating the question 'Should the Papacy be tolerated?' in the Whitechapel Church Young Men's Association.[28] Moreover the range of ancillary activities associated with late Victorian chapels provided an opportunity for the acquisition of organizational skills. A further linkage is suggested by the over-representation of Jews in the Social Democratic Federation: training in religious dogma provided them with mental abilities that made them adept at assimilating and developing socialist theory.[29] There is some evidence, however, that although labour leaders had frequently been associated with Nonconformist chapels, they were not normally the leading figures in them, which would imply that political activity engaged the frustrated ambitions of those whose abilities had not been fully utilized in the religious sphere. Subsequently such people were prone to move away from active religious involvement although their early training was likely to continue to influence their outlook.[30]

Second, the development of zeal against social injustice can be seen as a product of the diffusive Christianity which, as we saw in Chapter 4, was widespread among the late Victorian and Edwardian working classes. A framework of belief that was practical rather than theological and placed particular emphasis on community, good-neighbourliness and the prospect of ultimate compensation for suffering and injustice was fertile soil for ethical socialism.[31] The prospect of recompense only needed to be regarded as this-worldly rather that other-worldly for fatalist resignation to be transmuted into a crusade for social reform. Such a shift of attitudes was evident both among the rank and file and in the leadership: in 1926, the Conservative Prime Minister Stanley Baldwin observed of the House of Commons at that time: 'I find there especially among the Labour Party, many men who fifty years ago would inevitably have gone into the Christian ministry'. They possessed a deep zeal for social justice and, Baldwin suggested, a political career was indeed really a kind of ministry.[32]

Third, there were many respects in which working-class movements in the three decades before the First World War assumed religious forms of organization and activity. This was manifested most strikingly in the 1880s and 1890s in John Trevor's Labour Church movement. The recommended order for its meetings included hymns, prayers, choral music, a reading, an address and even a benediction. In practice this sequence was simplified, but there was still singing as well as talks and readings and the atmosphere must have been similar in many respects to that of Nonconformist worship. More broadly, religious idioms of 'conversion' and 'preaching' were prominent, churches were sometimes used for meetings, and ritual and music were used to consolidate morale.[33] George Lansbury recalled branch meetings of the Social Democratic Federation in Bow and Bromley in the early 1890s which, he wrote, 'were like revivalist gatherings'.[34] The Welsh socialist leader Mabon (William Abraham) would sing hymns in order to defuse any tense moments at meetings.[35] In 1923 a Conservative spectator at a Labour victory celebration was struck by the religious tone of the proceedings: 'It struck no note of revolution but rather of respectable middle class nonconformity. They sang hymns between the speeches, which were all about God'.[36]

Fourth, due weight should be given to those socialist writers and speakers who explicitly referred to their beliefs as religious. William Morris wrote in 1883: 'Nothing can argue me out of this feeling which I say plainly is a matter of religion to me: the contrasts of rich and poor are unendurable and ought not to be endured by either rich or poor'. In 1897 Robert Blatchford stressed that the labour movement was part of a new ethical and spiritual order 'to which it is affectation, if not folly, to refuse the name of Religion'.[37] In 1928 Lansbury was still expounding his socialism in language that included numerous references to God.[38]

Nothing said above is intended to gainsay the other more secular strands in the early history of socialism and the labour movement; nor the extent to which even their more religious aspects were associated with a repudiation of existing institutional Christianity. William Morris's call for 'single-hearted devotion to the religion of Socialism' must not be separated from his declaration that this was 'the only religion which the Socialist League professes'.[39] Nevertheless there was a strong parallel to the contemporary use of Religion (with a capital 'R') by the Primrose League; a similar, indeed more intense, profession of ultimate concern and a comparable ability to draw upon and develop the attitudes of unofficial and quasi-religion.

There are good grounds for seeing the years from 1910 to 1923 as a watershed between the religious politics of the nineteenth century and the class politics of the more recent past. This change was associated particularly with the ending of religious issues as a major focus for Parliamentary debate and the collapse of the Liberal Party, the traditional political power-base of Nonconformity. Nevertheless the continuities were also significant. The case for this does not rest only on the localized survival of religious loyalties in electoral politics; nor merely on the occasions when religion did still find a place at the centre of political debate, as in connection with the 1928 Prayer Book and the 1944 Education Act. The key point is rather that both the great parties which were to dominate twentieth-century politics during their formative years in the late Victorian era drew in significant ways upon popular religious consciousness. This legacy certainly became more diluted as time went on but it was never repudiated.

3. NATIONALISM AND RELIGION

The respective experiences of Wales, Scotland and Ireland between 1850 and the Second World War provide contrasting patterns in the development of political nationalism. Scotland for much of this period lacked any effective nationalist movement; at the other extreme in 1921 the twenty-six counties of southern Ireland achieved virtual independence with the formation of the Irish Free State. Wales was in something of an intermediate position: during the half century before the First World War its concerns were vigorously advocated in Parliament, but the outcome was a qualified recognition of the distinctive nature of the principality within the British state, comparable to the pre-existing status of Scotland, rather than any trend to separation as occurred in Ireland. In this section the varied political fortunes of the three countries will be related to the nature of their religion.

As we saw in the previous chapter, a gradual awakening of Welsh national consciousness had been given focus and impetus by the Blue Books controversy of 1847. Nonconformity had also begun to assume political significance; for example, in local disputes over the building of Anglican churches. The chapels also served as important channels for the exercise of power and influence in local communities.[40] It was, however, only after the Reform Act of 1867 that their influence began to manifest itself in sustained political action on a nationwide basis. The extension of the franchise disproportionately increased the size of the electorate in Wales and greatly enhanced the political significance of the Nonconformist majority. As religious grievances were forcefully agitated it became helpful to argue for separate treatment for Wales in the light of the relatively much weaker and allegedly alien condition of the Anglican Church there. A precedent for separate legislation for Wales was set by the Sunday Closing Act of 1881, which prevented public houses from opening on the 'Sabbath', and was a triumph of Nonconformist temperance agitation. A religious impetus was also a significant factor in campaigns for improved educational provision which resulted in the formation during the 1870s and 1880s of university colleges at Aberystwyth, Bangor and Cardiff, all eventually receiving support from the state; and the passing of the Welsh Intermediate Education Act of 1889 which set up a system of secondary schools.[41]

It was in the campaign for disestablishment of the Church in Wales that national consciousness drew most strongly on the resources of Nonconformity. The enactment of disestablishment for Ireland in 1869 had been seen as a springboard for campaigns for the dissolution of connections between Church and state elsewhere. However, although Wales now seemed the most vulnerable target, there was reluctance on the part of the Liberation Society to address its situation separately from that of England. This led the Welsh disestablishment movement increasingly to diverge from its English counterpart and to argue the question on national lines. Thus in 1886 Lewis Dillwyn, arguing that 'Wales is practically a separate nationality', moved in the Commons that

> as the Church of England in Wales has failed to fulfil its professed object as a means of promoting the religious interests of the Welsh people, and ministers only to a small minority of the population, its continuance as an Established Church in the Principality is an anomaly and injustice which ought no longer to exist.[42]

On 13 September 1892 Gladstone opened a new path up Snowdon amidst a scene of considerable patriotic and religious fervour. He was preceded up the coach road by a crowd singing hymns. Speaking from a rock, the octogenarian Prime Minister expressed his delight at the sound he had just heard and declared 'If you want to know whether the Welsh are a substantive historic race, go and listen to their music'. In front of this audience he considered the disestablishment question as not needing any argument: 'I might as well', he said, 'address the top of Snowdon on the subject of disestablishment as address you about the matter'. More hymns were sung and the subsequent resolution referred to 'the struggle for religious freedom and self-government which has been waged in these glens so long and so continually'.[43] The campaign for disestablishment reached a climax after Gladstone's retirement when, in 1894 and 1895, legislation was twice brought before the Commons, only to founder in the face of the weakness of the government of the Earl of Rosebery and the known intransigence of the Conservative-dominated House of Lords.

It is true that in the 1880s and 1890s there was an alternative articulation of Welsh nationality in the shape of *Cymru Fydd* (Young Wales) which derived legitimacy from language and culture rather than directly from organized religion. This movement channelled the energies of the young Lloyd George and was active in all parts of Wales by

1891. *Cymru Fydd* supported the campaign for disestablishment, but as a means to the wider end of Home Rule for Wales rather than as the overriding single focus of Nonconformist agitation. Lloyd George wrote in 1895: 'I maintain strongly that all our demands for reform, whether in Church, Land, Education, Temperance or otherwise, ought to be concentrated in one great agitation for national self-government'.[44]

Nevertheless religion was, in the medium term at least, to provide a more secure basis for the promotion of Welsh concerns. *Cymru Fydd* collapsed as a viable political force in 1896, but the energies of Nonconformity were revitalized by the particularly intense hostility which the 1902 Education Act stirred in Wales, and by the Revival of 1904–5. The result in the 1906 General Election was the failure of the Unionists to return a single MP from Wales. Nevertheless the achievement of disestablishment had to await the implementation of the 1911 Parliament Act which made it possible to override the continued opposition of the Lords. It was then further delayed by the First World War.

By the time the final Welsh disestablishment measure reached the statute book in 1919 the political and religious landscape which had produced it was undergoing substantial change. Following its brief Edwardian Indian Summer, Nonconformity was now in noticeable decline, while the Labour Party with its appeal to social rather than nationalist and religious concerns was rapidly gaining ground in the principality. The effect was the political marginalization of Welsh nationalism for half a century after disestablishment. A new party, *Plaid Cymru*, founded in 1925, sought consciously to distance itself from older traditions, but in reality came still to draw on the cultural links between Nonconformity and Welsh identity.[45] However, these were now a declining political asset and it was only at a much later date and under very different circumstances that *Plaid Cymru* gained its first Parliamentary seat with the return of Gwynfor Evans at the Carmarthen by-election of July 1966.

The case of Scotland was significantly different from that of Wales. Its distinctness from England had always been acknowledged in legislation and separate legal, educational and religious institutions had maintained a continuous history. Thus nationalist movements started from a more advanced position: there was much less initial need to campaign to justify claims to separate nationality, as the advocates of Welsh disestablishment were doing. Also Scotland in general lacked issues comparable to Welsh disestablishment and education with their capacity to produce a mutually reinforcing alignment of religious and nationalist concerns.

This last statement must be qualified to some extent by recognition of the position of the Free Church in the mid-nineteenth century. In the light of the patriotic undertones of the Disruption, it is probably no coincidence that when an embryonic nationalist movement emerged in the 1850s, two of its leading figures, James Begg and Hugh Miller, were prominent Free Churchmen. Miller used the leading Free Church newspaper *The Witness*, of which he was editor, as a platform for stating national grievances against the English, while Begg saw the Disruption as a basis for launching a movement of Scottish spiritual, cultural and social regeneration.[46] Later the Patronage Act of 1874 aroused considerable hostility from the Free Church because it was seen as a cynical attempt imposed by Westminster to strengthen the public standing of the Church of Scotland, and during the subsequent twenty years disestablishment was widely urged on 'national' grounds. More broadly, during the two generations following the Disruption both the Church of Scotland and the Free Church sought to legitimate their position against the other by appeals to patriotism and historic Scottish religious identity.[47]

However, the Free Church was not in a position to be a rallying point comparable to Welsh Nonconformity. Despite the panegyrics to Thomas Chalmers's religion and patriotism that were penned at the time of his death in 1847, the memory of the great Free Church leader rapidly faded: it is significant that a monument to him in Edinburgh was not erected until 1878, and then in a spirit more of duty than of enthusiasm.[48] Moreover the spiritual heirs of James Begg, whose strongly Calvinist social vision rendered him more Chalmersian than Chalmers, were eventually to be found not in any recognizably nationalist movement but rather in the Highland austerity of the Free Presbyterians and the 'Wee Frees', small denominations which separated from the majority in 1892 and 1900 respectively. For its part, early Scottish nationalism, as manifested in the National Association for the Vindication of Scottish Rights of 1853–4 and the campaign of 1856–69 to erect the Wallace Monument outside Stirling, reflected inspiration from Romanticism and antiquarianism as much as from organized religion.[49]

The lack of a strong link with religion helps to explain the relatively limited impact of nationalism in Victorian Scotland, when this is compared with its Welsh and Irish counterparts. A Scottish Home Rule Association did come into being in the 1880s and enjoyed some impact on the Liberal Party, but its ambitions did not come into the frame of practical politics. In the meantime the political impact of religion in Scotland was as much sectarian as nationalist in character. In Glasgow in particular the influence of the Orange Order and other Protestant organizations channelled some popular anti-Catholicism into support for the Unionist (Conservative) Party and a sense of 'British' as much as 'Scottish' identity in the face of Home Rule in Ireland. At the same time, as in Wales, the Labour Party was increasingly attractive to the working classes.[50] During the interwar period specifically Protestant parties proved to be vigorous if localized rivals of the nationalists for the support of those disillusioned with mainstream politics. The Presbyterian churches reinforced this tendency by campaigning against Roman Catholic immigrants as antithetical to Scottish identity.[51] It was true that in 1934 the Scottish National Party, which had been founded in 1928, had a membership of over 10,000, but at around the same time Protestant Action had 8,000 members in Edinburgh alone.[52]

During the first half of the twentieth century the progress of reunion among the Presbyterian Churches meant that the Church of Scotland now emerged as a focus for national consensus rather than a bone of contention. In 1949 the self-styled 'Scottish National Assembly' launched a campaign for a Scottish Parliament by means of a Covenant eventually signed by 2 million people, a significant latter-day reference to the Presbyterian Covenants of the sixteenth and seventeenth centuries. A leading churchman contended:

> The Church is perhaps the greatest remaining depository of our Scottish national sentiment and self-consciousness and the true symbol of the national character and temperament . . . only a rediscovery of our Christian heritage, values and convictions will provide the necessary inspiration and dynamic for a revival of the Scottish nation in the widest sense of the word.[53]

Admittedly in the lukewarm spiritual climate of the mid-twentieth century this was stronger on pious aspiration than objective insight. Nevertheless, as we saw in Chapter 3, the Church at this time still enjoyed the specific adherence of a quarter of the population, and its influence should not be underestimated. It served as a basis for the firm but moderate assertion of distinctive Scottish identity within the United Kingdom and a check until the 1960s to the emergence of full-blown nationalism.

Before turning to consider the case of Ireland it will be helpful to underline the contrasts and similarities between Wales and Scotland. In Wales the alignment of religious and national issues was underpinned by the vigorous culture of Nonconformity and produced between the 1867 Reform Act and the First World War a strong nationalist movement with ideology and aspirations permeated by the concerns of organized religion. In Scotland, on the other hand, there was relatively little alignment and mutual reinforcement, and nationalism was less religious, intense and effective. Moreover, in both countries, religious influences could work against separatist nationalism as well as in favour of it. A sense of common Protestantism and of shared responsibility for mission to an overseas empire did much, especially in Scotland, to keep alive an overarching consciousness of British identity. This point will be explored further in subsequent chapters.[54]

On a superficial reading the history of Ireland in the nineteenth and twentieth centuries can be presented to a large extent in religious terms with Roman Catholicism serving as the foundation of nationalist politics and Protestantism seen as synonymous with British imperialism. Thus the national cause is equated with the religious one, and the gradual institutional retreat of the Church of Ireland presented as a sign of national progress. The late nineteenth-century campaign for Home Rule is seen as the next stage in a process which had begun with the reform of the Church of Ireland in 1833 and its disestablishment in 1871. Hence the eventual partition of the island, which took place in 1921, is perceived as inevitable because of the fundamentally irreconcilable nature of Catholic and Protestant national aspirations.

This is history with a very broad brush, but it contains an element of truth. Moreover it was influential at the time in shaping popular perceptions of events, and has been important in the recent past in legitimating entrenched positions in the politics of Northern Ireland. However, there are also significant respects in which this kind of interpretation distorts Irish history through the prism of hindsight. It ignores the substantial complexities and cross-currents that existed for much of the nineteenth century, despite the undeniably polarized nature of the Protestant and Roman Catholic communities. Three particular points need to be made here.

First, Irish resentment against British rule encompassed grievances which went well outside the specifically religious. As we have seen in previous chapters, opposition to the Union was couched in political and cultural as well as religious terms. Whereas disestablishment in Wales was associated with a medium-term cessation of nationalist agitation, there was no such sequel to disestablishment in Ireland. On the contrary, the 1880s saw the most vigorous phase of political agitation for Home Rule since the death of O'Connell, under the leadership of

Charles Stewart Parnell. The campaign for constitutional change then had its popular base not so much in religious grievances as in agrarian agitation for land reform and fair rents.

Second, Protestantism in Ireland cannot be crudely equated with resistance to nationalist demands. For one thing it was by no means a united block: although common suspicion of Roman Catholicism could cause Anglicans, Presbyterians and other groups to work together, very real differences remained between them. Moreover until well into the nineteenth century Protestants were not necessarily automatically prepared to accept their minority status as permanent. Movements such as the Irish Church Missions to Roman Catholics, at its height during the decade after the famine, reflected a vision of an Ireland of the future reforging its national identity on the basis of the triumph of Protestantism. The unrealistic nature of such aspirations did not prevent them from being held, at least until disestablishment served to underline the cold realities of the Protestant situation.[55] Even thereafter the fluidity of attitudes in the 1870s and 1880s is indicated by the fact that both Isaac Butt, first leader of the Home Rule League, and Parnell, his successor, were nominal Protestants whose nationalism was conceived in essentially secular terms. At a still later date Protestants such as Douglas Hyde, eventually in 1938 to become President of Eire, took a leading role in efforts to revive Gaelic language and culture through the Gaelic League founded in 1893.[56]

Third, and conversely, there were considerable ambivalences in the relationship between nationalism and the Roman Catholic Church. Numerous clergy continued to be politically active during the second half of the nineteenth century, but, after the death of O'Connell, their involvement lacked overall coherence and was regarded with caution by most of the hierarchy.[57] It was not that Cullen and his fellow bishops opposed political activity in principle, but they were normally prepared to sanction it only when it was directed to specifically religious ends. In 1864 the National Association was organized under the close control of the Church primarily to campaign for disestablishment and improved provision for Roman Catholic education. It failed to galvanize public opinion. The observation of *The Times*, made in relation to the Repeal movement in 1843 and noted in the previous chapter, thus remained very true: the priests had to be prepared to follow the popular mood as well as to direct it if they were to maintain their influence. Moreover, if constitutional nationalist political activity was regarded with caution, the path of violent revolution pursued by the Irish Republican Brotherhood (Fenians) in the 1860s, was met with widespread clerical denunciation.[58] Clergy were concerned to preserve the moral integrity of the nationalist cause, as Charles Stewart Parnell was to find in 1890–1 when the revelation of his adulterous affair with Kitty O'Shea turned the majority of Roman Catholic priests firmly against his continued leadership of the Parliamentary Home Rule party.

It is, then, unhistorical to see independence and partition as the inevitable political result of Ireland's religious divisions. Indeed during the later Victorian period disestablishment and land reform removed the most serious practical grievances against British rule. It is not inconceivable that, had the limited self-government proposed in Gladstone's unsuccessful Home Rule Bill of 1886 been conceded at that point, subsequent events would have been very different. Thus although the experience of Ireland in the nineteenth century showed the force of official religion as a foundation for nationalism, it also, as in Wales and Scotland, revealed its limitations when the nationalist agenda moved beyond specifically ecclesiastical issues.

Nevertheless by 1914 the forces of Catholic nationalism and Protestant Unionism seemed to be firmly set on a collision course and in 1921 the division of Ireland with the virtually complete independence of the south was to be agreed. A major factor in bringing about this outcome was the trend before and during the First World War for both official and quasi-religion to assume greater importance in defining the identity and ideology of both sides, and thus raising the struggle to a clash of ultimate concerns in which neither side could contemplate compromise.

Protestants in Ulster, especially Presbyterians, had always had a sense of strong distinctiveness from the rest of Ireland, but events in the second half of the nineteenth century served to render this still more pronounced. The Revival of 1859 and the later visits of the evangelists Moody and Sankey kept evangelical fervour and associated intense anti-Catholicism very much alive. Roman Catholic migration to Belfast and Derry brought sectarian rivalries on to the streets of the province's major towns. Meanwhile disestablishment removed a major bone of contention between the Church of Ireland and Presbyterians, and opened the door to more effective united action. The catalyst for this came with the first Home Rule Bill of 1886 which excited the strong opposition, often couched in theologically anti-Catholic terms, of all the major Protestant churches. There was accordingly a convergence between official religion and the popular sectarianism represented by the Orange Order.[59] Evangelicalism was a central influence giving coherence and legitimacy to Unionist intransigence, and it also – through links with co-religionists on the mainland – heightened a sense that Irish Protestants would find security through the association of a 'British' identity. It is true that loyalty to Gladstone and relatively liberal theological sentiments limited the extent of solidarity among English Nonconformists, but, as we noted above, the more anti-Catholic among them were liable to be drawn into the Unionist camp. In Scotland stronger religious ties with Ulster contributed to particularly widespread support for Unionism. Moreover any symptoms of lukewarmness in Britain served, it would seem, further to increase the stridency of utterances in Ulster. The small minority of Protestant Home Rulers looked increasingly isolated.[60]

During the subsequent thirty years the continued political struggle over Home Rule underlined the identification of Protestantism with the 'freedom' of Ulster. This is not to deny that there were other motivations – economic, cultural, racial – at work, but religious convictions ran deep and served as the ideological and emotional spearhead of resistance to Irish self-government. By 1912 the dependence of Asquith's Liberal government on Irish support in the Commons and the passing of the Parliament Act, enabling the opposition of the Lords to be over-ridden, meant that the enactment of Home Rule now became very probable. Nearly half-a-million Ulster Protestants showed their defiance by signing the Covenant, which had very self-conscious religious and historical reference:

> we, whose names are underwritten, men of Ulster, loyal subjects of His Gracious Majesty King George V, humbly relying on the God whom our fathers in days of stress and trial confidently trusted, do hereby pledge ourselves in solemn Covenant . . . in using all means which may be found necessary to defeat the present conspiracy to set up a Home Rule Parliament in Ireland. And in the event of such a Parliament being forced upon us we further solemnly and mutually pledge ourselves to refuse to recognize its authority. In sure confidence that God will defend the right we hereto subscribe our names. . . . God save the King.[61]

The signing of the Covenant was initiated at Belfast City Hall on 28 September 1912, following numerous church services and in an atmosphere of religious dedication. The first signatures were those of the movement's political leaders, Sir Edward Carson and the Marquess of Londonderry, but these were immediately followed by those of the moderator of the Presbyterian General Assembly and the Church of

Ireland Bishop of Down. The latter saw their stand as 'essentially religious':

> We contend for life, for civil liberty, for progress, for our rightful heritage of British citizenship. We contend for faith and the freedom of our souls. We are fighting not for ourselves alone but for the whole country for these are the things which alone can make Ireland great and happy.[62]

Meanwhile as the scope of religion was thus being broadened in Ulster something of a parallel development was occurring in the south. Cardinal Cullen died in 1878, and two of the leading Roman Catholic prelates of the next generation, Thomas William Croke, Archbishop of Cashel from 1875, and William Walsh, Archbishop of Dublin from 1885, had strong nationalist sympathies and were much more ready to countenance the political activity of the Church in spheres outside the specifically ecclesiastical. Croke's first act as Archbishop of Cashel was to preach at the celebrations of the centenary of the birth of Daniel O'Connell and during the 1880s he gave strong support to Parnell and the Land League. Croke's lead was followed by some of the lower clergy, although his activities were regarded with unease at Rome and by some of his episcopal colleagues.[63]

A movement to assert Irish Gaelic cultural identity was manifested in organizations such as the Gaelic Athletic Association (founded 1884) and the Gaelic League (founded 1893). These were initially supported by some Protestants, but when, around 1900, the Gaelic League became a mass movement, it was overwhelmingly Roman Catholic in composition. There proved to be significant ties of sympathy with the clergy who shared a sentimental attachment to Irish tradition and a belief that the language and culture would serve to insulate their flocks from the perceived moral declension of the rest of Europe.[64] A further symptom of the hierarchy's desire to reinforce the ties of Roman Catholic identity came with the decree *Ne Temere* of 1908 which forbade mixed marriages and only permitted exceptions if all the children were to be raised as Roman Catholics, an ending of earlier Irish practice whereby the sons of such unions were brought up in the father's allegiance, and the daughters in the mother's. Such developments served further to reinforce Protestant suspicions of the potential religious as well as political consequences of Home Rule. Nevertheless in the prewar period the Roman Catholic Church continued to adhere, albeit with some reservations, to the moderate constitutionalism of the Irish Parliamentary Party and there was no Catholic counterpart to the Ulster Covenant.

Unofficial interpretations of Catholicism were, however, much less restrained. The radical nationalist Patrick Pearse firmly identified the cause of Irish nationhood with the cause of Christ. He condemned the members of the Irish Parliamentary Party for their readiness to compromise, alleging that they 'have not recognized in their people the image and the likeness of God. Hence the nation to them is not holy, a thing inviolate and inviolable, a thing that a man dare not sell or dishonour on pain of eternal perdition'. For Pearse national freedom was like a 'divine religion'.[65] This view was not simply a matter of language but also one of deeply emotive action. On 24 April 1916, Easter Monday, insurgents led by Pearse, the majority in a mood of strong Catholic devotion, took control of key points in Dublin. From the steps of the General Post Office Pearse read a declaration of independence and the formation of a republic. The Easter Rising did not attract widespread support and collapsed after a week. However, Pearse and fourteen of his associates were subsequently shot by the British. Through this perceived martyrdom they achieved in death what they had failed to do in life: they focused outrage against British rule and demonstrated the moral bankruptcy of constitutional nationalism.

The majority of the Roman Catholic hierarchy now threw their previous caution to the winds and identified with the cause of revolution. In September 1917 Michael Fogarty, Bishop of Killaloe, who was subsequently to praise the 'good Christian lives' of those who belonged to Sinn Fein, delivered a panegyric on Edward Thomas O'Dwyer, the recently deceased Bishop of Limerick, dwelling upon his passionate nationalism:

> The omnipotent Hand of God has scattered in this earth some seeds that are immortal, which nothing can kill. National spirit is one of these. It grows in every land; and is cherished as sacred wherever it grows . . . 'Ireland', he [O'Dwyer] said, 'will never be content to be a province. God has made her a nation, and while grass grows and water runs, there will be men in Ireland to dare and die for her'.[66]

Pearse's ideas received even more emphatic statement from Terence MacSwiney, the Lord Mayor of Cork:

> The liberty for which we today strive is a sacred thing, inseparably entwined with that spiritual liberty for which the Saviour of man died, and which is the inspiration and foundation of all just government. Because it is sacred, and death for it is akin to the Sacrifice of Calvary, following far off but constant to that divine

example, in every generation our best and bravest have died. . . .
No lesser sacrifice would save us. Because of it our struggle is
holy.[67]

Such language indicates that Irish nationalism could now validly be
described as a quasi-religion, at the very least manifesting intense
ultimate concern, and arguably even reinterpreting on its own terms the
teaching of Catholic orthodoxy. After MacSwiney died on hunger strike
in Brixton Prison on 24 October 1920, eight bishops joined the
procession to his burial in Cork.[68]

It was true that in October 1922 the hierarchy was to show the limits
of its sympathy for republicanism by denouncing those who were
waging a civil war against the government of the newly constituted Free
State which had reached a compromise with Britain. On subsequent
occasions the bishops condemned the Irish Republican Army. Nevertheless there were individual pious Roman Catholics who found no
incompatibility between their faith and militant nationalism.[69]

From December 1921 Ireland was divided between six counties of
the province of Ulster which constituted 'Northern Ireland', still part of
the United Kingdom but with its own Parliament at Stormont; and the
twenty-six remaining counties (including the three Ulster counties of
Cavan, Donegal and Monaghan) which became the Irish Free State.
Initially the Free State remained nominally under the British Crown, but
the 1937 constitution created a presidency and in 1948 it became a
republic in name as well. In retrospect the division of Ireland is readily
perceived as a logical outcome of the polarization outlined in the
preceding pages, but at the time it was widely viewed as both unnatural
and temporary. However, the creation of two separate states, one with
an overwhelmingly Roman Catholic population, and the other with a
predominantly Protestant one, served in practice to institutionalize and
reinforce the separation.

In the south, Roman Catholic moral teaching shortly began to be
endorsed by legislation and a controversy in 1930–1 over the appointment of a Protestant as County Librarian in Mayo illustrated the
strength of the pressure towards a Roman Catholic confessional state.
The 1937 constitution recognized 'the special position of the Holy
Catholic Apostolic and Roman Church'.[70] On the other hand there are
indications that this fell short of what the Church itself wanted, and
Irish politicians were generally careful to maintain a certain distance
between Church and state, and to ensure that confessionalism did not
slide into clerical domination.[71] In the meantime, however, a quasi-
religious tone continued to be apparent in Irish political life, even if it

now lacked the intensity of the revolutionary era. This was articulated particularly by Eamon de Valera, a devout Roman Catholic and the dominant statesman of the first half-century of Irish independence. De Valera encouraged the development of a calendar of national ritual and commemoration, and in his own speeches emphasized the spiritual absolutes of Irish character. Looking back in 1966, he characterized the vision of 1918 as being that Ireland should again become 'a great intellectual and missionary centre from which would go forth the satisfying truths of Divine Revelation, as well as the fruits of the ripest secular knowledge'.[72]

In many respects the situation in the north was a parallel one, although here the relative size of the minority (more than 30 per cent Roman Catholic as opposed to less that 10 per cent Protestant in the south) gave a significantly different tone to developments. Whereas southern Protestants did not present any real threat to the constitutional order in Dublin, northern Roman Catholics were a genuine challenge to the Protestant majority. Successive Unionist governments at Stormont were fundamentally unable to contemplate the kind of compromises that might have reconciled Roman Catholics to the Northern Ireland state. Accordingly from the 1920s to the 1960s they promoted a structure of political, social and economic discrimination that kept the minority in a subordinate position. This situation received powerful legitimization from the religious life of the province. The Orange Order, whose membership probably amounted to a third of the adult male population, combined political and Protestant references in its lodge rituals and 12 July parades. Meanwhile evangelicalism of a strongly anti-Catholic cast continued vigorous: a strand of influence can be traced through from the revivalistic campaigns of William P. Nicolson in the 1920s to the meteoric ecclesiastical and political rise of Ian Paisley in the 1960s and 1970s.[73]

Since the outbreak of the 'Troubles' in 1969 much journalistic and academic ink has been expended in the endeavour to 'explain' the situation in Ireland, and in Northern Ireland in particular. A recurrent theme in such analysis has been discussion of whether the conflict is a 'genuinely' religious one or whether the labels 'Protestant' and 'Catholic' are simply a convenient shorthand for groups whose confrontation should in reality be understood in primarily secular terms.[74] In part this debate reflects the divergent presuppositions of contemporary observers, but it also mirrors the historical reality of the fusing together of the religious and the political in Ireland.

It has been argued here that this very ambiguity was a major reason for the force of both Irish nationalism and Irish religion in the twentieth century. Politicians were able to channel the commitments of official religion into an agenda and ideology that moved well beyond the specifically ecclesiastical. Herein lies the key contrast with Wales, with a political nationalism predominantly stimulated by the particular concerns of Nonconformity and losing momentum once these had been achieved; and with Scotland, with a limited nationalism unable to harness the legitimating power of religion. In other words, to apply our initial theoretical formulation, Irish nationalism and Unionism were powerful because they became religious in all senses of the word, with official religion and quasi-religion reinforcing each other; Welsh nationalism was transient because it lacked the same enduring quasi-religious elements which could protect it from the defection and decline of official religion; and Scottish nationalism was feeble because it failed to become religious in any effective sense.

4. THE MONARCHY AND NATIONAL UNITY

On 8 July 1911, following their coronation at Westminster, King George V and Queen Mary paid a ceremonial visit to Dublin, entering the city in front of cheering and hospitable crowds. They attended a service at St Patrick's Church of Ireland Cathedral and subsequently paid a visit to the Roman Catholic College at Maynooth where they were received by a party headed by Cardinal Logue and Archbishop Walsh, and a boys' choir which delivered a hearty rendering of the National Anthem. There was virtually no public sign of hostility to the royal party.[75] This event serves to check any assumption that there was an irrevocable trend towards separatism in the south of Ireland. It also provides us with an initial illustration of the use by the British state of ceremony and ritual, centred particularly on the monarchy, to cultivate a sense of a united imperial community and thus to exercise a check on contemporary pressures towards conflict on social and national lines. Ultimately in Ireland the countervailing forces were too strong, but elsewhere in the British Isles royal rituals proved to have an enduring and effective integrative effect. They are accordingly worthy of closer attention as a manifestation of religion at least in the most general sense of a 'system of symbols' and as a form of politics all the more powerful for being perceived as 'above politics'.

A further significant event of this kind was to occur just a few days later at Carnarfon Castle when the King invested his seventeen-year-old son (the future Edward VIII) as Prince of Wales. Despite the copious medieval and chivalric references of the ceremony it was in reality a completely new departure for the 'accession' of a new prince to be marked in this way. In his speech the King explicitly set the cultivation of Welsh identity in a wider British context:

> I believe that the occasion will serve a still deeper purpose in assembling in union and power around his person all the forces of Welsh national life which preserve the fame and achievements of your ancestors, and will sustain in the world of modern times the virtues of the British race and the glories of the British Empire.

Some parts of the ceremony also struck a chord with committed Welsh Christianity. The young Prince concluded his speech with the saying *'Heb Dduw, heb ddim; Duw a digon'* (Without God, without anything; God is enough) and during the subsequent interdenominational service the hymn *'Marchog, Iesu, yn llyddianus'* (Lord, ride on to triumph glorious) was sung. This had strong associations with the Revival of 1904–5.[76] The royal tour was concluded with a visit to Edinburgh where the popular reception was characterized as less 'effervescent', but no less 'sincere'. *The Times* judged that 'Each demonstration has struck the same note of universal love and loyalty, different only in the temperament, not in the temper of the different nationalities which took a common and equal part in it'.[77]

The trend to more self-conscious and calculated royal ceremonial which reached its culmination in the years immediately before the First World War can be traced back to the aftermath of an incident in December 1871 when the then Prince of Wales (later Edward VII) almost died of typhoid. Before that date the rituals associated with the monarchy, although sometimes elaborate and expensive, most spectacularly so in the coronation of George IV in 1821, tended to be poorly managed and had often lacked popular appeal.[78] The funeral of the Duke of Wellington, discussed in Chapter 5, represented something of a new departure in the nature of great state occasions, but is also notable for the manner in which its magnificence completely overshadowed the coronations, royal funerals and marriages of the middle decades of the nineteenth century. Following the Prince Consort's death in 1861 the Queen severely restricted her public appearances, but in 1871–2, against a background of radical and republican criticism of the monarchy, Gladstone persuaded her to mark the Prince of Wales's recovery by a service of thanksgiving at St Paul's. The careful attention of the government to the details of the ceremony suggests a keen awareness of its political and social significance. Correspondence between sovereign and premier also illustrates interestingly divergent perceptions of religion. Victoria thought that 'no religious act ought ever to be allied with pomp and show' but Gladstone saw such display as essential in order to elicit the desired popular religious engagement. In the event the procession and service on 27 February 1872 was to be a great success and reinforced the public enthusiasm for the monarchy stirred by the Prince of Wales's illness.[79]

There was no immediate opportunity to repeat this kind of ceremonial, but in 1887 the fiftieth anniversary of Victoria's accession was marked by the grand pageantry of the golden jubilee, with a service at Westminster Abbey providing the centrepiece. There was extensive evidence of great public reverence and enthusiasm. During the next twenty-five years the chances of the royal life-cycle produced a rich range of occasions which traversed the full range of human experience and emotion: in 1892 the untimely death of the Duke of Clarence, elder son of the Prince of Wales and second in line to the throne; in 1893 the marriage of Princess May of Teck to the future George V; the diamond jubilee of Victoria in 1897 and her death and funeral in 1901; the coronation of Edward VII in 1902; his death and funeral in 1910; and the coronation of George V in 1911. Participation in these events was not restricted to the relatively limited numbers of people who could watch ceremonies at London and Windsor: churches throughout the land held services at the same time as the central ones while processions were organized in most towns attracting large crowds. In those days before radio and television, attendance at such local commemorations was the best means of gaining a sense of involvement in the event itself. Newspaper reports indicate that churches were generally very crowded, with much larger congregations than on a normal Sunday.[80]

Assessments of the real extent and significance of public enthusiasm for such events is difficult, as is indicated by juxtaposing two quotations from the diary of Edward White Benson, Archbishop of Canterbury at the time of Victoria's golden jubilee. On 14 May 1887 he wrote of the cheering crowds that received the queen on a visit to the East End:

> the thought of communism, or socialism, or unbelief having hold on these people *seems* ridiculous in sight of this enthusiasm. . . . That the Church too was not valued and even loved could never have entered the mind. . . . They are not a church-going race – but less a chapel-going one. But there is a solemn quiet sense of religion for all that in their sayings and doings.

On the other hand on 13 July the Archbishop noted reports from a Scripture woman of popular attitudes in Lambeth: 'the mass of the people are intensely radical – and never so much so as in *the last eighteen months*. The Queen and Monarchy are constantly discussed and disparaged'.[81] One could speculate that attitudes in south London differed from those in east London, and that the golden jubilee itself marked an important stage in the transition between earlier nineteenth-century criticism of the monarchy and twentieth-century adulation. Nevertheless we need to be alive to the possibility that the very people who cheered the Queen and impressed Benson with their broadly 'religious' demeanour could in a different context display much more critical attitudes. The reflection that within five years of George V's visit to Ireland the streets of Dublin were to echo to the sounds of rebellion presents the same issue in particularly stark form.

However, while one should not take claims of universal consensus at face value, tensions and signs of dissent should not assume disproportionate significance. The strength of British state ceremonial lay in its capacity to absorb some social, political and national conflicts through its capacity for malleable interpretation. This process is well illustrated in the concept of jubilee itself, originally derived from the Old Testament in which it referred to a redistribution of land at the end of a fifty-year period so as to preclude long-term accumulations by the wealthy.[82] In the late eighteenth and early nineteenth century the concept had accordingly been popular among social and political radicals and in his famous sermon of 1851 Charles Kingsley still used the word in this traditional sense.[83] The use of the jubilee to mark the fiftieth anniversary of the sovereign's accession had had its precedent from the reign of George III, but the celebrations of 1887 still represented a bold appropriation of the language of popular protest, originating in a religious context. In this respect they were illustrative of a broader trend, a shift during the nineteenth century in the primary locus of patriotic rhetoric from political radicalism to the conservative establishment.[84] In a parallel development we have seen how, by 1911, royal ceremonial was serving as a channel for the expression of Welsh, Scottish and Irish national aspirations within the framework of the United Kingdom.

After the First World War the pattern of royal ceremonial was fully established, and was maintained by means of the marriages of the children and grandchildren of George V, the silver jubilee of 1935 and the coronations of George VI in 1937 and of Elizabeth II in 1953. Especially now that the independence of the south of Ireland had been conceded, there was even less evidence of explicit dissent from the perceived national consensus than in the late nineteenth century, although incidents such as the theft of the Stone of Scone from Westminster Abbey in 1950 and the resentment of Roman Catholics in Northern Ireland at the coronation celebrations in 1953, pointed to the continuing existence of alternative positions.

The popularity of state ceremonial should not be seen as a reflection of crude social control by an élite imposing its values on the masses, much less as the expression of some universal monochrome national consensus. Rather jubilees, coronations and the like were successful because of their capacity to be 'all things to all men' and women. On the political front they gave the powerful an opportunity to revel in the perceived magnitude of national dignity and achievement and the powerless the means to feel enlarged by participating on their own terms in a greater whole.[85] Gender politics are also relevant here: as long as Victoria lived women were able to identify with the veneration accorded to a member of their sex, and even after 1901 successive queens consort gave prominence to the female aspect of the monarchy.[86] For the monarchy itself this was seen as a kind of glorious apotheosis: a display of the outward trappings of power which was now acceptable in a way it had not been when symbol had been supported by the exercise of real political force. However, this very retreat from the arena of combat opened up fresh channels of influence. It is by no means obvious that George V and George VI, with their capacity to encapsulate and foster strong traits in the national self-image, had less impact on the lives of their subjects than the unpopular and politically active George IV had done a century before.

There were significant connections and parallels between the political status of the monarchy and that of religion. Royal ceremonial itself was malleable in religious terms just as it was flexible politically: in the eye and heart of the beholder it could be either a solemn Christian observance, an affirmation of general religiosity or a quasi-religious celebration of the perceived solidarity of the national community. Meanwhile organized religion at a somewhat later date than the monarchy, in general ceased in Britain to be a central focus of political confrontation and became rather part of a diffuse framework of shared assumptions, fluid enough to accommodate differences between Scots, Welsh and English,[87] as well as between Liberal, Tory and – with some qualifications – Labour. When Disraeli and Gladstone in the 1860s and 1870s spoke of religion they were mobilizing their forces against each other; when Lloyd George and Baldwin did so in the 1910s and 1920s they were, increasingly, affirming their common ground.

The importance of the interconnected impulses of religion and of devotion to the monarchy in the maintenance of the political unity of the United Kingdom in the twentieth century are pointed up by the contrasting experience of Ireland. Here the Roman Catholicism and eventual republicanism of the south were of considerable importance in bringing about complete separation. In Ireland as a whole the continuing potent mixture of religion and politics absolutized the struggle and rendered its resolution a distant prospect. In Britain, on the other hand, the impulses that contributed to national coherence were well indicated by the *Spectator* in its comments on Queen Victoria's death in 1901. The magazine noted an antagonism between Britain and the Roman Catholic Church and went on to observe how the reign had seen a shift from tepid loyalty to deep affection for the sovereign. It then implicitly linked these two points with the suggestion that Victoria's popularity rested in her affinity for the Puritan values of her people, 'the love of purity itself, the loyalty to truth, the steadfast adherence to duty, and the conscious dependence on God'.[88] Such non-specific Protestantism might be applied and interpreted in very different ways in the various parts of the United Kingdom but it still served as a common point of reference.

7

THE REAL FREE CHURCH?

Culture and belief

In the year 1854 two very different works of religious art were first exhibited. John Martin (1789–1854), who painted and engraved visions of fantastic imagination to illustrate editions of the Bible and Milton's *Paradise Lost*, closed his career with a trilogy of massive paintings of the Apocalypse (now in the Tate Gallery). They attracted large crowds. Such images of divine judgement were taken seriously by a public that a few years earlier had shown comparable interest in the 'Apocalyptic Sketches', lectures on prophecy by a Presbyterian divine John Cumming.[1] In the same year one of the early works of a much younger artist, *The Light of the World* (now at Keble College, Oxford) by William Holman Hunt (1827–1910) was exhibited at the Royal Academy and initially provoked hostile and dismissive comments. The contrast with Martin's work could not be more remarkable; the one cosmic, awesome and hostile, the other human in scale, serene and gentle in its setting, even if it carried an underlying disquieting spiritual message. The subsequent history of the paintings contrasted equally dramatically: while Martin's reputation quickly evaporated, and his apocalyptic pictures were to be sold in 1935 for the derisory sum of seven pounds, Hunt's painting was to become one of the most familiar and widely reproduced images in the history of art.[2] In the opening years of the twentieth century the aged artist (probably with substantial assistance) painted another copy of the picture (now in St Paul's Cathedral), which was exhibited to large crowds in numerous parts of the Empire. For Hunt this was a realization of the religious, moral and patriotic purposes that he aimed to fulfil through art: 'in love of guileless beauty, to lead man to distinguish between that which, being clean in spirit, is productive of virtue, and that which is flaunting and meretricious and productive of ruin to a nation'.[3]

Plate 1   The Great Day of His Wrath, engraving after the painting by John Martin (1854)
Source: The British Museum

Plate 2   *The Light of the World*, engraving by W. Ridgeway (1863)
after the painting by William Holman Hunt (1854)
Source: The British Museum

The histories of these two paintings hint at some of the issues that will concern us in the ensuing analysis of relationships between religion, culture and national consciousness. We shall begin with an outline of changes in theological ideas in the later nineteenth century, which provides a necessary context for the subsequent discussion, and will indicate how increasing theological fluidity was linked to a developing nationalism. In the subsequent sections the changing position of religion in relation to wider national cultures will be explored.

1. THE DIVERSIFICATION OF THEOLOGY[4]

In the following brief survey we shall consider first the broadening of theological thought within the churches, before turning, to examine the development of more radical ideas that implied complete rejection or reinterpretation of orthodox Christianity.

The second quarter of the nineteenth century had seen a laying of intellectual foundations for the acceptance of increased theological diversity in the Church of England and elsewhere, in part derived from the latitudinarian ideas of the seventeenth and eighteenth centuries, in part from the more immediate influence of thinkers such as Samuel Taylor Coleridge and Thomas Arnold. In his posthumously published *Confessions of An Inquiring Spirit* (1840) Coleridge showed himself a pioneer of more liberal attitudes to the Bible, eschewing literalism in favour of historical sensitivity and openness to the living inspiration of the Holy Spirit in the experience of the reader. In Arnold's mind a liberal conception of Anglicanism was linked to an intense sense of the religious identity of the nation, and this viewpoint was restated by various churchmen in the decades after his death in 1842. F. D. Maurice argued theologically for a comprehensive Church and saw consciousness of national identity (but not exclusive nationalism) as a valuable reinforcement of faith in God. Englishmen, he held, were entitled to speak of their nation as holy 'in virtue of God's calling'.[5] A similar vision was applied to Wales by Rowland Williams in 1847:

> If, instead of bending all your efforts in a single direction, you endeavour to enter broadly into the spirit of our National Church . . . if . . . you try to make men Christians as much as churchmen, and if at the same time you spread information which may prepare the soil for the seed of the Church's doctrine, and smother by a more wholesome growth the tares of irregular teachers, it is in your power to do our mountain-land and her primitive Church the greatest service they have received for centuries.[6]

Charles Kingsley, through his stirring sermons, novels and poetry, linked an expansive Christianity with a fervent patriotism and became greatly revered by a wide cross-section of society. A further important contributor to this tradition was Arthur Penrhyn Stanley (1815–81), Arnold's biographer and Kingsley's colleague, who became Dean of Westminster in 1864 and sought to make the Abbey a focus for a wide range of religious opinion.

Nevertheless, many others continued to see the precise definition of Christian teaching to be a matter of supreme importance. The rivalry between evangelicalism and Catholicism generated competing conceptions of the nation's relationship to God. For Roman Catholics the expectation of the conversion of England was a promise of a restored destiny as part of the Church universal. For evangelicals, on the other hand, the British nation was defined by its Protestantism. They conceived of a religious unity encompassing Scotland and Wales as well as England, and, despite Roman Catholic Emancipation, Ireland's ultimate destiny was still felt to be conversion to the creed of the rest of the Greater Britain. The nation was held to be specially favoured by the Almighty in virtue of its adherence to Protestant truth: continuing faithfulness to Protestantism would bring great rewards, but falling away from it could provoke the just punishment of an outraged God.[7]

Struggles over doctrine could be intense. For example, in 1845 William George Ward, an Anglican clergyman, was degraded from his degrees at Oxford University for writing a book idealizing the Church of Rome; in 1853 F. D. Maurice was dismissed from his professorship at King's College, London, for allegedly denying the doctrine of eternal punishment. It was an era in which full-blooded and specific belief was still expected from those in positions of ecclesiastical and educational leadership, implying, for example, acceptance of the Bible as literally true, and the conviction that hell was a real and dreadful place.

The Church of England, with its increasing internal diversity, was a microcosm and a focus for wide disputes, notably the case of Gorham versus the Bishop of Exeter. This *cause célèbre* began in 1847 when the Bishop of Exeter, Henry Phillpotts, refused to institute George Cornelius Gorham, an evangelical, to the living of Brampford Speke, on the grounds that his doctrine was unsound. In March 1850 the judicial committee of the Privy Council, reversing the decision of a lower court, found in Gorham's favour. The decision was greeted with great relief by evangelicals who feared that they might have to leave the Church of England if it went against them, but with alarm and despondency by those with Catholic sympathies, such as Henry Manning, who shortly afterwards became a Roman Catholic, and William Gladstone who felt that 'at present it is all dark or only twilight which rests upon our future'.[8] According to Disraeli, not normally himself the most engaged observer of church events, the affair 'pervades all classes – literally from the palace to the cottage'.[9]

The doctrinal point at issue seems to many late twentieth-century eyes to be a remarkably small and obscure nut to provoke the application of such substantial legal and polemical sledgehammers. Did the baptism of an infant automatically render it spiritually regenerate (Phillpotts's position) or was this regeneration sometimes conditional on the child's subsequent acceptance of saving grace (Gorham's position)? Both parties were agreed on the validity of infant baptism, and on the importance of right reception when an adult was baptized. In a later age when theological controversy centres around issues such as the authority and accuracy of the Bible, the Virgin Birth, Incarnation and Resurrection of Christ, and even the very existence of a transcendent God, it is hard to appreciate why such relatively minor differences over the significance of a particular sacrament should provoke such passionate engagement.

The explanation lies in the manner in which the particular doctrine at stake was seen as the touchstone of wider questions about the means of salvation and the whole nature of the Church of England, whether it was a Catholic (but not Roman Catholic) body in which the sacraments were the principal channel of grace, or a Protestant, evangelical one in which the emphasis was placed rather on the individual's spiritual response to God in conversion. However, the court did not resolve this matter but left it controversially ambiguous. In rejecting Phillpotts's claim that Gorham taught unsound doctrine, there was no condemnation of the opposing position: both views were, in effect held to be admissible Anglican doctrine. This indicated that it was unlikely that any of the competing factions in the Church would be able to find unassailable legal grounds for excluding its opponents. The Gorham Case was thus an important watershed between an era in which at least lip-service had been paid to the idea that there was a single definable religious 'truth' which could be upheld by the Established Church, and a growing recognition that the Church of England was a capacious umbrella under which adherents of a diverse range of views could shelter.

The trend to less dogmatic and defined theology was fuelled by the appearance in 1860 of the work of seven Anglican writers in *Essays and Reviews*, a bland title for a book which came to be seen by many as subversive of essential Christian doctrine. However, the essayists, who included a future Archbishop of Canterbury, Frederick Temple (1821–1902), saw themselves not as undermining Christianity but as defending it and redefining it. The main thrust of the contributions was a call for a more critical and scholarly approach to the interpretation of the Bible. Benjamin Jowett (1817–93), later Master of Balliol College, Oxford, called for Scripture to be interpreted 'like any other book' and other contributors explored some of the consequences that followed from a more critical attitude to the Bible: for example, Baden Powell (1796–1860), professor of geometry at Oxford and father of the founder of the Scout movement, maintained that the spheres of science and religion had to be distinguished, and questioned the validity of belief in miracles.

The essay on the national Church by Henry Bristow Wilson (1803–88), vicar of Great Staughton, Huntingdonshire, was one of the most controversial pieces in the volume. Wilson's offence in his essay was to argue that statements of religious dogma should no longer be fixed, in order that the Church of England could be as diverse and comprehensive as possible. He looked for a national Church which would correspond to the national character: accordingly 'the freedom of opinion which belongs to the English citizen should be conceded to the English churchman'. It was, Wilson thought, 'a strange ignoring of the constitution of human minds, to expect all ministers . . . to be of the same opinion in theoreticals'.[10] He had thus developed the position advanced by Thomas Arnold three decades before, in which theological diversity and imprecision were accepted as a necessary price for restoring the Church of England to genuinely national acceptance.

Wilson's work was significant in that it pointed the way towards that very increase in the theological diversity acceptable within the Church of England which was to be the outome of the controversy. There was an attempt to prosecute two of the authors, but the outcome was even more ambiguous than in the Gorham Case. There were various demonstrations of clerical disapproval, but these failed to attract the active support of more than substantial minorities. It thus seemed that although many still adhered to conservative positions, there was also extensive sympathy for the essayists, or at least a passive readiness to allow their views to continue to be represented within the Church of England. Increasing flexibility was endorsed by the passing of the Clerical Subscription Act of 1865, which relieved clergy of the requirement to give specific and unreserved assent to the Thirty-nine Articles and the Prayer Book. In 1869 one of the contributors to *Essays and Reviews*, Frederick Temple, was appointed to succeed Henry Phillpotts as Bishop of Exeter.

Similar trends were evident in other major Protestant denominations. The very burgeoning of Nonconformity greatly broadened the range of religious options and, for the uncommitted, underlined the problematic nature of claims to universal and absolute truth by a single body.[11] The Congregationalists were divided in the mid-1850s by controversy over a collection of religious poems by Thomas Lynch entitled *The Rivulet*, which were alleged to be unorthodox, and by argument over the moderately critical view of the Bible expressed by Samuel Davidson, a lecturer at the Lancashire Independent College where ministers were trained. This latter affair ended with Davidson's resignation, but he had had a significant degree of support. During the 1860s and 1870s, under the influence of the 'new evangelicalism' of Robert William Dale, the traditional exclusive preoccupation with personal salvation was eroded in favour of the theological rationalization of more active participation in national life. Tensions within Congregationalism came to a head as a result of the liberal theological statements made at a conference in Leicester in 1877. Conservative positions were reaffirmed in a resolution of the Congregational Union in 1878, but this did not halt the gradual advance of liberalism.[12] Among Baptists the process was slower, but when controversy did arise in the 1880s over the charges of the famous preacher Charles Haddon Spurgeon that his contemporaries were 'downgrading' Christian truth, it ended with Spurgeon himself resigning from the Baptist Union because he considered its position not sufficiently exclusively conservative.

The Scottish Presbyterian churches experienced a similar trend. During the third quarter of the century all the major groups became increasingly flexible in the interpretation and application of the Westminster Confession of 1642, the original Calvinist foundational statement. This was comparable to the increasing latitude in the interpretation of the Book of Common Prayer and the Thirty-nine Articles which was developing in the Church of England at the same time. Debate over approaches to the Bible reached a climax between 1876 and 1881 with the case of William Robertson Smith, a professor at the Free Church College in Aberdeen, whose calls for a historical and critical approach to Scripture were attacked by other members of his denomination. The case ended in 1881 with Robertson Smith's dismissal from his chair, but as in the cases of the writers of *Essays and Reviews* and of Samuel Davidson in England, it was clear that he received considerable support and passive sympathy. In the Free Church too, as among the Baptist Churches in England, it was ultimately the conservatives who felt themselves marginalized. This feeling lay behind the splits of 1892 and 1900, which resulted respectively in the Free Presbyterian Church and the continuing Free Church of Scotland.[13]

It is important to emphasize that the trend towards theological diversity was already under way independently of the issues raised by the publication of Charles Darwin's *Origin of Species* in 1859. Indeed responses to the theory of evolution by natural selection reflected a wide range of pre-existing perspectives. Certainly some saw Darwin's theory as fundamentally at variance with Christian belief and vigorously denounced it, but others believed that a modified version of the evolutionary hypothesis could be reconciled with Christianity. Others again hailed Darwinian ideas as testimony to the continual creative intervention of God in the world, through the ongoing process of evolution. Darwin himself had written of the 'impossibility of conceiving that this great and wondrous universe arose through chance'. Charles Kingsley revelled in the way that the great scientist's work forced a stark choice 'between the absolute empire of accident, and a living, immanent, ever-working God', and had no hesitation in declaring his own conviction in the reality of the latter.[14]

The occasional religious language to be found in Darwin's writings could readily be dismissed as convention, as his intellectual development certainly led his personal convictions away from traditional Christianity towards agnosticism if not atheism. Nevertheless Darwin's readiness to respect convention, not only in his writings but in his support for his local parish church, was in itself profoundly significant. Not for him was the radical defiance of the organized secularist movement. Rather his career seemed to point the way to the further extension of the range of belief possible within the capacious institutional limits of the Church of England, which on his death in 1882 ultimately accorded him the posthumous sanction of burial in Westminster Abbey. In his sermon at the funeral Harvey Goodwin, the Bishop of Carlisle, contrasted the manner in which in Britain an accommodation between science and religion was possible, with the situation prevailing in France where an entrenched anti-clericalism was reflected in scientific attitudes.[15]

Acceptance, or at least toleration, of Darwin was perhaps the most telling indication of the advance across the Protestant churches of a softer and less dogmatic theology. Its adherents did not regard the Bible as literally the word of God in every detail, but still saw it as a key source of revelation when interpreted in a critical and historically aware fashion. They were prone to modify the traditional doctrine of hell, considering that the fate of the unrepentant would be annihilation or conditional immortality rather than eternal punishment, or even that God might ultimately save all humankind. They also moved away from a stark interpretation of the doctrine of atonement, that Christ died on the Cross to propitiate the righteous anger of God at the accumulated sins of the world, and increasingly emphasized the incarnation of Christ, God made flesh as a source of dignity, inspiration and comfort for struggling humanity. It followed that sin and judgement receded from view. An important Anglican statement of this theological outlook came in 1890 with the publication of a volume of studies under the title of *Lux Mundi*.[16] The book was edited by Charles Gore (1853–1932), Principal of Pusey House, which had been set up to maintain the legacy of the Oxford Movement, and was thus an indication that even the Catholic wing of the Church was by no means impervious to more liberal theological ideas.

In the meantime such views were being mediated to the laity through lives of Jesus such as that by the Frenchman Ernest Renan, which appeared in England in 1863, and *Ecce Homo* (*Behold the Man*), written by the historian John Robert Seeley (1834–95) and published anonymously in 1865. Both books showed Jesus in a very human light and, while churchmen argued about their orthodoxy, they clearly met a popular demand. Such lay interest was satisfied further in F. W. Farrar's *Life of Christ* of 1874, and a host of subsequent imitations. Their collective tendency was to promote a soft and somewhat sentimentalized religion, such as that conveyed by one of Farrar's own hymns:

> And the shepherds came to the manger,
> And gazed on the Holy Child;
> And calmly o'er that rude cradle
> The virgin mother smiled;
> And the sky, in the starlit silence,
> Seemed full of the angel lay, –
> 'To you in the city of David
> A Saviour is born to-day.'[17]

Around the turn of the century there was further influential advocacy of the positive value of theological ambiguity in enhancing the comprehensiveness of the Established Church, notably from Mandell Creighton (1843–1901), Bishop of Peterborough and then of London. He believed passionately in comprehension rather than uniformity, saw the Church of England as closely identified with the life of the nation and carried this to the extent of owning himself 'an Englishman first and a Churchman afterwards'. Brooke Foss Westcott (1825–1901), Bishop of Durham, had an almost equally strong sense of the role of the 'National Church [which] brings all the great crises of national life into connection with the unseen and the eternal'. Herbert Hensley Henson (1863–1947) carried the tradition of forceful advocacy of a comprehensive national Church well into the first half of the twentieth century. He held that the various denominations must accept each other as fully Christian. Like Frederick Temple before him Henson found that his allegedly heterodox theology stirred controversy when he was nominated to be a bishop (of Hereford) in December 1917, but also like Temple he weathered the storm and enjoyed further preferment, in his case as Bishop of Durham from 1920 to 1939.[18]

The early twentieth century saw further development in the liberalism of the later Victorian years, institutionalized in The Churchman's Union for the Advancement of Liberal Religious Thought, founded in 1898, and the journal *The Modern Churchman,* started in 1911. In 1912 a group of young Oxford churchmen published *Foundations: A Statement of Christian Belief in Terms of Modern Thought,* which included an essay in which B. H. Streeter questioned the concept of a 'physical' resurrection.[19] The Anglican 'modernists', whose leading figures included Henry Major (1871–1961) and Hastings Rashdall (1858–1924), sought to reduce Christian dogma to an essential minimum, accepting the full import of biblical criticism and rejecting the miraculous.[20] Such ideas were not new to their advocates, but when aired at a conference in Cambridge in 1921 they provoked reactions such as that of a writer in the *Sunday Pictorial:*

'There are some of us still left who believe in the divinity of Christ, and who totally fail to understand how men who believe the contrary can honestly occupy the pulpits of our State churches and take money for teaching people to deride the ancient faith'.[21]

The Archbishop of Canterbury, Randall Davidson, was more equivocal, cautioning against over-reaction, and upholding the cause of free inquiry. Meanwhile William Temple, then Bishop of Manchester, later Archbishop of York and Canterbury, while regretting the movement's more iconoclastic tendencies, affirmed his openness to contemporary intellectual trends.[22] It was a revealing indication of the changing mind of the Church that the erstwhile editor of *Lux Mundi,* Charles Gore, became successively Bishop of Worcester, Birmingham and Oxford and by his old age in the 1920s was to appear as a pillar of theological conservatism. Henson too had reservations about postwar trends: in 1933 he noted how modernist language was leading to a doctrinal vagueness in which the Church was too readily identified with the nation, a tendency whose dangers were graphically illustrated by contemporary events in Germany. By the 1930s, concerned particularly by the influence of Parliament over the Church's affairs evident in the Prayer Book controversy of 1928, Henson strikingly reversed his earlier views and became an advocate of disestablishment.[23]

Even evangelicalism swayed in the wind of liberalism: a collection of essays was published in 1923 under the title of *Liberal Evangelicalism*, a term defined as implying a desire to link the heritage of the Evangelical Revival with the environment of 'the modern world, with its historical method, its philosophy of personality, and its scientific view of the universe'.[24] Similar tendencies were apparent outside the Church of England among the traditionally evangelical Nonconformist denominations. The 'New Theology' of the Congregationalist R. J. Campbell, with its radical identification of deity and humanity, had excited considerable controversy in the Edwardian years. More moderate, but more indicative of trends in the mainstream of evangelicalism, was the readiness of the Methodist professor George Jackson to argue for the acceptance of biblical criticism, and the election in 1923 of T. R. Glover, who had comparable views, to be Vice-President of the Baptist Union.[25]

Nevertheless the understandable tendency of intellectual historians to concentrate on the innovative and the fashionable can lead to underestimation of the extent of continuing conservatism, of which the Roman Catholic Church was the most conspicuous and coherent example. It was not that there were no progressive thinkers within its fold, but rather that attempts to question orthodoxy were firmly and successfully resisted. Furthermore the international character of the Church rendered it relatively resistant to the pressure to assume a national comprehensiveness. During the 1850s and 1860s the Liberal Catholic movement, in which Sir John (later Lord) Acton was the most prominent English figure, sought to strengthen intellectual activity in the Church and proved receptive to new ideas on biblical criticism and science. However, in 1864 Pope Pius IX published the Syllabus of Errors which was viewed as an emphatic rejection of modern currents of thought, an impression reinforced by the decrees of the Vatican Council in 1870. These measures meant the end of the mid-Victorian movement, but at the close of the century the Englishman St George Jackson Mivart and the Irishman George Tyrrell sought to revise traditional teaching on matters such as biblical criticism, hell and eternal punishment. But unlike their Anglican counterparts these men continued dangerously isolated, could gain no ecclesiastical sanction whatsoever for their views, and died excommunicate. The Roman Catholic Church was to continue until well into the twentieth century to be a bastion of conservative theology, nowhere more so than in Ireland where strong influence over the educational system could nip dissent in the bud. As late as 1961 Archbishop McQuaid of Dublin rejected the notion 'that a university is a school in which youth is expected to think for itself'.[26]

On the Protestant side conservative views still had prominent advocates, notably John Charles Ryle, Bishop of Liverpool from 1880 to 1900, and Edmund Knox, Bishop of Manchester from 1903 to 1921. Bishops with such opinions were admittedly few in number, but they were representative of a more extensive strand of opinion among both clergy and laity which was firm in its opposition both to the rationalism of biblical criticism and the ritualism of the Anglo-Catholics. It was often the latter that stirred the most vigorous reactions. The 1870s and 1880s saw a succession of prosecutions instigated by evangelicals culminating in the case of the Bishop of Lincoln, Edward King, which dragged on from 1888 to 1892. Such controversies had their Scottish counterpart in hostility to increasingly elaborate worship in Presbyterian churches and concern about the resurgence of Episcopalianism. Militant anti-Popery was promulgated north of the Border by men such as Jacob Primmer, for whom, like his English contemporary John Kensit, the political and spiritual security and unity of Britain continued to be dependent on its emphatic antagonism to Rome.[27] Later, in the 1920s, the liberalizing trends in evangelicalism provoked a backlash from those who felt that the essentials of the faith were being betrayed, although fundamentalism in the American sense failed to gain much headway in Britain. During the 1930s neo-conservative theological influences from abroad, notably those of Reinhold Niebuhr and Karl Barth, began to give a renewed intellectual credibility to more traditional Protestant positions.[28]

Such conservative survival and regrouping means that it is unsatisfactory to interpret theological trends between the mid-nineteenth century and the mid-twentieth as a straightforward process of liberal advance. It is more accurate to think in terms of diversification: liberal views certainly gained ground, but co-existed not only with traditionally conservative positions, both evangelical and Catholic, but also with various endeavours to find a middle path, notably 'liberal evangelicalism' and Gore's brand of Anglo-Catholicism. The picture was at times a bewilderingly complex one because of the manner in which the divisions of Protestant and Catholic cut across those of modernism and traditionalism. In the context of the wider argument of this book it is noteworthy both that such confusion served to blur the boundaries of official religion, and that attempts to develop an inclusive concept of religion were often linked, especially in the Church of England, to a strong sense of the role of the Church in national life.

When the field of view is widened to include alternatives to Christianity which might collectively be characterized as the unofficial and quasi-religions of intellectuals, these trends are further illustrated. Mid-nineteenth-century critics of orthodoxy included Thomas Carlyle (1795–1881), who linked the pantheism of German Romanticism to the Calvinism of his own Scottish ancestors. He believed God to be an immanent and potent spirit working through nature and, above all, in man. George Eliot (1819–80, born Mary Ann Evans) rejected the evangelicalism of her youth in favour of intense advocacy of a 'religion of humanity' in which God and immortality were inconceivable, but duty to one's fellow human beings was of overriding importance. Her views were first forcefully stated in a devastating attack published in 1855 on the Scottish evangelical preacher Dr Cumming, and further developed through the medium of her novels. For Eliot as for Carlyle, rejection of conventional belief was associated with a zealous search for a replacement. A similar, if less pronounced, tendency was even evident in the philosopher John Stuart Mill (1806–73) who, despite a deliberately non-religious upbringing, still found himself groping in later life towards some kind of theistic understanding of the world.[29]

Others developed new forms of belief which remained decidedly supernaturalist. In the 1850s spiritualism began to gain some ground, as a creed that offered verification of the immortality of the soul through direct contact with the dead, but implied a rejection of traditional Christian concepts of heaven, hell and judgement. It was to enjoy a considerable vogue around the time of the First World War. Meanwhile in the 1870s the Theosophical Society was formed to develop and promulgate occult spiritual insights derived initially from ancient Egypt and Greece, and subsequently also from contemporary Hindu revivalism. This decade also saw, in 1875, the publication in America of Mary Baker Eddy's *Science and Health and Key to the Scriptures*, which was to become the foundational text of Christian Science on both sides of the Atlantic.[30]

Others had no such new religious options to propose but still found themselves questioning traditional Christianity, often because they found its claims incredible or its teaching immoral. This could mean, in the short term at least, the sacrifice of position and aspirations. James Anthony Froude was a deacon in the Church of England and a fellow of

Exeter College, Oxford, when in 1849 he published his autobiographical novel of doubt and credulity *The Nemesis of Faith*. He was obliged to resign his fellowship. Similarly, in 1864, Leslie Stephen, a priest and fellow of Trinity Hall, Cambridge, was also driven to resignation by a sense that his Christianity lacked 'fundamental conviction'. For these two earnest mid-Victorians there was no reconciling doubt with remaining an Anglican clergyman, but by the end of the century more flexible attitudes were reflecting the Church's aspirations to comprehensiveness.[31]

Running through all these varieties of alternative belief, spiritual experimentation, and agonized doubting was an underlying religiosity. Men and women might reject the teaching of a specific Church or even Christianity as a whole, but they remained desperately concerned to find some kind of religion or, at least, 'ultimate concern' to give meaning and coherence to their own lives and to the society and culture in which they lived. In 1904 G. K. Chesterton looked back on the cultural atmosphere of the third quarter of the nineteenth century:

> It is difficult to know whether it should be called doubt or faith. For if, on the one hand, real faith would have been more confident, real doubt, on the other hand would have been more indifferent. . . . Men were, in the main, agnostics: they said, 'We do not know'; but not one of them ever ventured to say, 'We do not care'.[32]

Implicit in Chesterton's observation, of course, is the feeling that by the Edwardian years agnosticism had become more complacent and less agonized. Whereas in the late Victorian period outright critics of Christianity, such as the poet Algernon Charles Swinburne, still appeared to be the intellectual rebels; during the first quarter of the twentieth century agnosticism became increasingly the consensus of the cultural élite.

Nevertheless, a considerable ideological and cultural deposit was left by those who strove to develop alternative frameworks of belief. In particular there were notable instances in which the redefinition of religion was associated with the strong assertion of nationhood. Matthew Arnold (1822–88), son of Thomas, differed from his father in developing an underlying scepticism towards traditional Christian dogma: for him God was not a literal personage, but rather 'the power that makes for . . . righteousness'.[33] On the other hand Matthew did inherit his father's earnest zeal for a religion woven into national life by

173

the agency of an Established Church. Thus Arnold sought in approaching the Bible as a literary critic to uphold its moral and spiritual
standing, while rejecting its accounts of the miraculous and dismissing
the 'bibliolatry' of those who saw it as completely accurate divine
revelation. The Church of England too was of great importance as an
institution. It was

> a great national society for the promotion of what is commonly
> called *goodness,* and for promoting it through the most effectual
> means possible, the only means which are really and truly effectual
> for the object: through the means of the Christian religion and the
> Bible.[34]

To this end Arnold wished to maintain and extend the comprehensiveness of the Church of England, a concern strongly evident in *Culture
and Anarchy* (1869), a work replete with religious allusion. He criticized
Nonconformists for their 'provinciality' and isolation from the main
currents of national life and upheld Establishments as the institutional
foundation of spiritual elevation and cultural enrichment. To this end he
advocated the establishing 'in Ireland the Roman Catholic and the
Presbyterian Churches along with the Anglican Church; and, in England, a Presbyterian or Congregational Church of like rank and *status*
with our Episcopalian one'.[35]

A closely related framework of ideas is apparent in the work of J. R.
Seeley, the author of *Ecce Homo.* Seeley's intellectual development, like
that of Matthew Arnold, well illustrates generational change, as his
father Robert Benton Seeley (1798–1866) was a leading evangelical
writer and publisher. The younger Seeley, who moved through liberal
Anglicanism to a more or less explicit rejection of revealed religion, held
that the scope of religion is 'much more national and political, much less
personal, than is commonly supposed'. Its great function had been 'the
founding and sustaining of states'. Religion was founded on morality
(rather than the other way round), and morality in turn should be taught
primarily through the study of national history rather than with reference to the Bible. These ideas were worked out in Seeley's *Life and
Times of Stein, or Germany and Prussia in the Napoleonic Age* (1878)
and applied to his own country in the enormously successful *Expansion
of England* (1883), a confident exposition of the nation's imperial
destiny.[36]

The quasi-religious development from the liberal Anglican tradition
exemplified by Matthew Arnold and J. R. Seeley was explicitly but
unselfconsciously English rather than British. Thomas Arnold had

spoken triumphalistically of 'this great English nation', and his son, while admittedly recognizing the distinctive character of Ireland, could still advocate a Presbyterian establishment in England without mentioning that one already existed in Scotland. Seeley indicated that England was something more than the geographical area south of the Tweed. 'By England', he wrote, 'I mean solely the state or political community which has its seat in England', an entity which also governed the rest of Britain and Ireland.[37] This emphasis reflected Seeley's perception of the realities of power and institutional structures, including the pre-eminence of the Church of England as the religious expression of nationhood.

This broadly Anglican and English construction of the nation existed, as has been indicated above, alongside a Protestant and British one.[38] While the latter served to counterbalance centrifugal tendencies in Nonconformity and Presbyterianism, even while it pointed up the division with Irish Catholicism, the former provided a point of contact for English Catholics, both Anglican and Roman, in the affirmation of their own essential patriotism. There was a thread here which, as we shall see, ran through from the rhetoric of Victorian converts to Rome, such as J. H. Newman and F. W. Faber, to the 'Englishness' of Edward Elgar's music and the writings of G. K. Chesterton. The increasingly diverse theological ideas of the later nineteenth century, conservative as well as liberal, thus proved to be fertile soil for the development of divergent but ultimately complementary perceptions of nationhood.

2. THE ARTS AND RELIGION IN THE LATER NINETEENTH CENTURY

The foregoing discussion of the growth of theological diversity and the diminishing influence of rigid dogma provides the background for our examination of the relationship of religion to the arts in the same period. It will be argued that the advance of doctrinal latitude and imprecision was accompanied by a corresponding increase in ambiguity as to whether and in what way art was or was not religious. In a closely related process a variety of forms of cultural expression became imbued with a quasi-religious nationalist fervour. It must be stressed at the outset that the current survey is designed to be illustrative rather than comprehensive: full coverage of the developments outlined here would require a book in its own right.

The mid-nineteenth century starting point for our analysis is found in the use of the arts as channels for upholding official Christianity. Roman

Catholics and Anglo-Catholics saw particular significance in architecture and music as vehicles for the support and development of Christian worship. Evangelicals looked particularly to literature, as a natural extension of their own consciousness of being a people of the book, drawing inspiration and authority from the study of the Scriptures. However, competition and mutual influence led all groups to diversify the range of cultural tools which they employed.

The Gothic Revival in architecture initially reflected the antiquarian experimentation of the builders of houses such as Horace Walpole's Strawberry Hill. But by the early nineteenth century Gothicism was becoming linked to a more visionary, Romantic and, arguably, quasi-religious fascination with the ideals of the Middle Ages. It was in this context that, during the 1830s and 1840s, official religious aspirations came for a time to dominate the development of architecture. There was an increasing aversion among religious reformers to the church furnishings inherited from the eighteenth century. Box pews, rented by those who could afford to do so, covered the floor space, giving churches a cluttered appearance and relegating the poor to ignominious corners. Triple-decker pulpits were the most conspicuous objects, in a manner disconcerting to Catholic churchmen wanting to focus worship towards the celebration of the Eucharist at the altar. A wider ideological framework for such changes was articulated by Augustus Welby Pugin (1812–52), a convert to Roman Catholicism, who argued for a much more rigorous and 'correct' style of Gothic architecture than previously had been practised. He saw the condition of architecture as intimately linked to the moral and spiritual condition of society, and maintained that the building of accurately recreated Gothic churches was an essential part of the restoration of a Catholic culture. The Anglican Cambridge Camden Society, founded in 1839, sought to promote the building and restoration of churches in a manner consistent with the liturgical and theological teachings of the Catholic revival in the Church of England. The impact of the movement set in motion by Pugin and the Camden Society, when mediated and developed by, in particular, William Butterfield (1814–1900), George Gilbert Scott (1811–78), and the latter's assistants, pupils and family, altered the face of Britain in a way that only energetic architects and their patrons could. It was their good fortune that the rapid expansion of towns in the nineteenth century reinforced ecclesiastical trends in providing them with ample opportunities for building, altering and restoring churches in their preferred styles.

In a similar manner the early Victorian period saw energetic endeavours to transform church music. This was a reaction to the perceived dreariness and indecorum of public worship in the Georgian era. The impulse to reform at first owed something to evangelicals, concerned for good order in the conduct of public worship and anxious to promote the participation of the whole congregation in a manner which would enable them to express genuine religious feeling.[39] In the Church of England, however, the initiative was increasingly gained by high churchmen, concerned to cultivate the 'beauty of holiness' through high standards of choral music expressing the sacramental dignity of the Church. Important pioneers included Samuel Sebastian Welsey (1811–76), a composer and organist successively of Hereford, Exeter, Winchester and Gloucester Cathedrals and of Leeds Parish Church. The process of reform reached its culmination in the partnership in the 1870s and 1880s at St Paul's Cathedral, as organist and dean respectively, of John Stainer (1840–1901) and Richard William Church (1815–90), an adherent of the Oxford Movement.

Meanwhile, from the 1840s, choral aspirations and knowledge were being diffused into the parishes particularly through the work of Thomas Helmore (1811–90) with trainee teachers at St Mark's College, Chelsea.[40] Not without some conflict, the advocates of choral worship in the Church of England achieved during the mid-nineteenth century an ascendancy over older styles of music. Organs replaced instrumental music; surpliced choirs in the chancel superseded singers in the gallery. This can be seen as part of the wider process described in Chapter 4 whereby former varieties of unofficial religion were being eroded and ecclesiastical authority trying, with ambivalent effect, to recast popular religious consciousness into a new mould.

Hymns played an important role in this process. The Evangelical Revival greatly enriched the repertoire, and following initial reservations – for example, the use of hymns in the Church of England was of uncertain legality until 1822[41] – most denominations came to accord them a central place in worship. There was stronger resistance in the Scottish Presbyterian Churches than there was south of the Border, but even there hymns and the organs which accompanied them were being widely adopted in the Lowlands by the 1870s.[42] The fashion, moreover, extended to Catholics, both Anglican and Roman. John Keble's *Christian Year* (1827), a collection of verses for every Sunday and feast day in the Anglican calendar, was popular not only as an aid to private devotion, but as a source of hymns, notably 'Sun of my soul' and 'New every morning'. Likewise, when appropriate music had been written, the poetry of the Anglican converts to Rome, John Henry Newman and Frederick William Faber, provided the text of several well-known hymns. In 1861 *Hymns Ancient and Modern* was published, predominantly reflecting Tractarian loyalties, and including many translations of ancient Christian hymns made by John Mason Neale. Despite the suspicions of evangelicals, within a generation it had established itself as the most widely used Anglican hymnal.

The growing popularity of hymns rendered them an important point of contact between official Christianity and popular culture. During the later decades of the century the softening of dogma was reflected in the increasing prominence of hymns which expressed a self-centred and sentimental piety. Wesley's 'Jesu, Lover of my soul' became much more popular than his 'O for a thousand tongues to sing'.[43] As the celebration of Christmas became more widespread and elaborate in the mid-Victorian period new carols such as 'Once in royal David's city' (1848) and 'In the bleak mid-winter' (1872) rapidly became part of the cultural fabric of the season.[44] At the same time a more vigorously activist spirit was expressed in hymns such as 'Fight the good fight', written in 1863, and 'Onward Christian soldiers' (1864), and in the straightforward language and tunes associated with the Sankey and Moody campaigns of the 1870s. A combination of a good tune and accessible words could give a hymn a lasting place in the consciousness even of the non-churchgoer. 'Abide with me' was sung at the FA Cup Final from 1927 and perceived as taking 'many back to their early years and it may be a long broken link with spiritual things'.[45]

Meanwhile novels also served as important channels for spreading doctrinal and moral teachings, and reinforcing the convictions of the faithful. The pattern had been set in the 1790s and early 1800s by Hannah More, who wrote 'Cheap Repository Tracts' aimed to edify a lower-class readership and a novel with a spiritual message, *Coelebs in Search of a Wife*, which was published in 1809. Her works were widely circulated and were emulated by other evangelical women such as Charlotte Elizabeth Tonna (1790–1846) and Mary Martha Sherwood (1775–1851), who were at the height of their popularity at the opening of our period. The work of such novelists is almost entirely unknown to modern readers, a consequence of the fall from fashion of the intensely moral and didactic tone which they represented.[46] The fundamental purpose was not to entertain but to edify: Christian virtue receives its reward, either in a happy ending in this world, or in a serene death-bed as a prelude to salvation in the next; sin is punished, and, above all, repentance and conversion are sought.

During the second half of the century the tradition of evangelical novel-writing was maintained by authors such as Catherine Marsh and Emma Warboise,[47] while at the same time the genre was adopted by writers from other strands of Christianity. Charlotte Mary Yonge (1823–1901) was a prolific writer of novels reflecting an Anglo-Catholic standpoint. She regarded herself 'as a sort of instrument for popularising Church Views' and in her most successful novel *The Heir of Redclyffe* (1853) brought Romanticism into the service of Christian morality.[48] Liberal Anglicans, notably F. W. Farrar, Charles Kingsley and Thomas Hughes, also produced novels designed for the edification of their readers. Farrar became a bestselling author in 1858 with *Eric; or Little by Little*, a fictional account of the moral decline and subsequent repentance of a school boy. The novels of Hughes and Kingsley, also written with a strong religious purpose, but with a less introspective morality, enjoyed a more enduring reputation. In *Tom Brown's Schooldays* (1857) and its sequel *Tom Brown at Oxford* (1861) Hughes chronicled the youth of a hero who was honest and upright rather than intensely spiritual; athletic and courageous rather than particularly intellectual. The dominant ethos was characterized as 'muscular Christianity'.[49] Kingsley's novels, including *Alton Locke* (1850), *Hypatia* (1853), *Westward Ho!* (1855) and *The Water Babies* (1863), developed some of the wider ramifications of such ideals, relating them to crusades for social improvement and against corrupt religion. His work was permeated by a strong patriotism with racialist undertones. A further contrasting manifestation of liberal Christianity appeared in the work of George MacDonald (1824–1905), a Scot and former Congregationalist minister who had been obliged to resign after charges of heresy. He came to see the novel as a substitute for the pulpit and wrote 'theological romances' in which his characters struggle with moral and spiritual dilemmas and the incarnate Christ charges every detail of life with significance.[50] Many of his works were set in his native Scotland, but in *The Princess and the Goblin* (1872) and *The Princess and Curdie* (1883) he moved into fantasy, exploring the interpenetration of the natural and the supernatural through the encounters of his human characters with fairies. G. K. Chesterton considered that MacDonald provided everyone with 'the end of an elfin thread that must at last lead them to Paradise'.[51]

An artistic parallel to MacDonald's novels is found in the paintings of the Pre-Raphaelites, mystical, realist and heavily encumbered with symbolism. The Pre-Raphaelite Brotherhood had been formed in the summer of 1848 with the object of producing art with inner meaning which genuinely reflected nature and was inspired particularly by the paintings of the late Middle Ages. Many of their subjects were historical, literary or mythological in nature, but, particularly in the early years of the movement, specifically religious themes were also chosen. *Christ in the House of his Parents* (1849–50) by John Everett Millais (1829–96) symbolized Tractarian ideas of the eucharist and baptism and the interrelationship between the material and spiritual worlds. In the year after he first exhibited *The Light of the World* Holman Hunt painted *The Scapegoat* beside the Dead Sea. The picture shows a shambling goat in an arid landscape and was intended to symbolize the Jewish ritual of atonement, itself a prefiguration of the crucifixion of Christ. Such relatively obscure theological allusions were lost on the majority of those who saw the pictures, but they still took away vivid religious images.[52] Moreover, although *The Light of the World* showed Christ in a somewhat mysterious spiritualized light, Hunt later declared a purpose of removing 'sacerdotal gloss' from perceptions of his life. This human image was expressed in his own later works such as *The Shadow of Death* (1869) and other Pre-Raphaelite paintings including Ford Madox Brown's *Jesus Washing Peter's Feet* (1852). Such pictures reinforced the outlook derived from the lives of Jesus by Renan, Seeley, Farrar and others, and more generally served to present his life on earth as an archetype of the 'muscular Christianity' of Hughes and Kingsley.[53] The imagery of the *Light of the World* was even carried into hymns, notably in the following lines by Bishop Walsham How:

> O Jesus, Thou art standing
> Outside the fast-closed door,
> In lowly patience waiting
> To pass the threshold o'er:
> Shame on us, Christian brethren,
> His name and sign who bear,
> O shame, thrice shame upon us,
> To keep Him standing there![54]

It is a revealing irony that the work of Holman Hunt, a non-churchgoer, should have inspired an Anglican bishop in this way. It illustrates the other side of the relationship between official religion and culture; how even as churchmen and women sought to use architecture, novels, music and art as a means of communicating their teaching, official Christianity was itself being moulded by developments in the surrounding culture. Another illustration of this process is provided by the development of church music in the mid-Victorian period, as the endeavour to improve standards led to the imitation of secular styles. The result was an orientation to 'performance' and dramatic effect which was in uneasy tension with the traditions of liturgical music.[55]

Religious art had, moreover, a dynamic of its own which could not be contained within the straitjacket of didacticism and conventional spiritual edification. This is well illustrated by an incident in the early 1850s, when Holman Hunt was beginning work on *The Light of the World*. He was congratulated by Dante Gabriel Rossetti on his choice of subject. Rossetti said that he had himself read the whole of the New Testament through 'in the hope of finding some hitherto untreated circumstances suitable for painting'. The tone of this comment together with the manner in which Rossetti soon tired of Christian subjects, indicate that for him, their attraction stemmed essentially from their aesthetic possibilities rather than from any conscious desire to direct his art to official religious purposes. Others still found a deep appeal in Christian art, but not for orthodox religious reasons. At the end of the century Edward Burne-Jones, one of the last of the Pre-Raphaelite circle, dismissed the Church of England as an institution, but praised Christianity as a cultural force:

> I love Christmas Carol Christianity, I couldn't do without Medieval Christianity. The central idea of it and all it has gathered to itself made the Europe that I exist in. The enthusiasm and devotion and the art, the humanity and Romance, the self denial and splendid achievement that the human race can never be deprived of, except by a cataclysm that would all but destroy man himself, all belong to it.[56]

There was nothing shallow about the artistic motivation of Rossetti or Burne-Jones or Morris, but rather a reflection of the decisive critical influence of John Ruskin (1819–1900). The child of evangelical parents, Ruskin eventually rejected the dogmas of his youth, but retained a profound knowledge of the Bible and a deep sense of the interconnected nature of art, morality and social conditions. In the early 1840s he had written: 'You say that infinity of conception ought to belong only to religion. Granted. But what object or sensation in earth or heaven has not religion in it – that is, has not something to do with God and therefore with both infinity and mystery?'[57] This was the spirit in which Ruskin produced during the next two decades his seminal works of art criticism, *Modern Painters* (1843–60), *Seven Lamps of Architecture* (1849) and *The Stones of Venice* (1851–3). He was passionately moved by the beauty of Gothic art and saw it as a reflection of spiritual and social conditions much superior to those of the contemporary world. It was this aesthetic sensibility which led Ruskin to praise the Pre-Raphaelites and thus to establish their reputation, while they for their part found in his work a source of great inspiration. Viewed as a whole their art expressed the way in which Christianity appealed to the mature Ruskin not as objective dogma, but as part of the cultural framework of an ideal society.

Ruskin's influence was also important in widening the appeal of the Gothic Revival. His Protestant sensibilities had initially caused him to be suspicious of the Catholic religious agenda that had come to be associated with it. By 1855, however, his aesthetic convictions had triumphed over his declining religious preferences and he endorsed the use of Gothic styles. This helped to encourage the use of Gothic in religious buildings of all traditions, as well as in secular architecture.[58] It became a badge for Anglicans of all varieties, with its attraction reinforced by patriotic sentiment.[59] In spite, or perhaps because of this, some of the most impressive buildings to use the style were constructed on the periphery of England, or outside it altogether, as in Truro Cathedral in Cornwall (1880–1910), the restoration of Llandaff Cathedral near Cardiff, and St Finn Barr's Cathedral at Cork (1865–76). In such buildings an Anglican Church all too conscious of its vulnerability was seeking to assert grandeur and solidity. In Scotland too the growing pretensions of the Episcopal Church and its increasing identification with the post-Oxford Movement Church of England was reflected in the construction of Gothic cathedrals at Perth, Inverness, Glasgow and Edinburgh.

Non-Anglican Protestants also shared in this enthusiasm. Mill Hill Unitarian Chapel in Leeds (1847–8) was an example of a building by a prosperous and powerful Nonconformist group showing a desire to emulate the Church of England.[60] Although some Nonconformist congregations continued to build in classical styles in the second half of the century, Gothic became increasingly attractive as a status symbol. The style was now freely adapted to Nonconformist traditions and functional needs in a manner which showed that the specific original ideals of Pugin and the Camden Society had been left far behind.[61] Scottish Presbyterians were perhaps a little slower to follow suit, but from the middle of the century the rebuilding of Old Greyfriars in Edinburgh and the restoration of St Giles and Glasgow cathedrals began to set precedents.[62] The last quarter of the century saw the erection of impressive neo-Gothic buildings such as Mayfield Free Church (1876) in Edinburgh, and the Barony Church in Glasgow

Plate 3   St Mary's Episcopal Cathedral, Edinburgh, designed by Sir George Gilbert Scott and built 1874–1917

(1886–90). The latter was erected during the ministry of John Marshall Lang, a leading protagonist of more elaborate styles of worship in the Church of Scotland, and father of a future Archbishop of Canterbury.[63]

The most significant exception to the ecclesiastical popularity of Gothic was that of the Roman Catholic Church, ironic in view of the importance of the advocacy of Pugin in the early stages of the revival of the style. However, 'no prophet is acceptable in his own country' and, although Pugin was employed as architect for some Catholic buildings, such as St Giles's, Cheadle, St Chad's Cathedral in Birmingham and St Patrick's College at Maynooth in County Kildare, this was controversial. There was a strong continuing preference for Renaissance or Baroque styles among those who sought to reassert solidarity with Rome, which was manifested, for example, in the Brompton Oratory (1880–4). When Westminster Cathedral was built (1895–1902) the neutral Byzantine style was chosen in order to avoid apparent partisanship.

In the meantime the fashion for Gothic had spread to secular buildings. Although its ascendancy was never complete, it became the characteristic style of public buildings in the later nineteenth century, in edifices as diverse as the University Museum at Oxford (1855–60), St Pancras Station (1868–74) and Manchester Town Hall (1868–77). However, it proved difficult for the style to outgrow its strong ecclesiastical associations. John Betjeman commented on the cathedral-like atmosphere of the Law Courts in the Strand (1874–82); Mrs Enriqueta Rylands, founder of the John Rylands Library (1890–9) in Manchester, might struggle 'to avoid anything that gives an ecclesiastical appearance to the building' but the character of the resulting structure showed her efforts to have been in vain.[64] With public buildings of this kind there was no marked division between the environment of religious worship and that of secular activity.

A similar tendency to diffusion of theological impulses was evident in the history of music. The revival of choral services initially expressed a spiritual and pastoral agenda; it later acquired its own momentum. This trend was not an unqualified blessing for those, especially evangelicals, who had looked more for the general elevation of the standard of congregational singing and devotion than for the performance of the liturgy by choirs in a manner which left congregations more observers than participants.[65] Conversely, attendance at musical performances was judged by some to be 'almost as good as going to church'.[66] Moreover the dominance of the churches in English musical life meant that they were inescapable cultural and aesthetic influences, even on those with an ambivalence towards their teaching. At a more material level they were for most musicians essential sources of patronage and income. Arthur Sullivan (1842–1900) wrote numerous hymn tunes in the 1870s, but evinced little sign of personal Christian motivation; Hubert Parry (1848–1918) composed religious music and even sang in his church choir despite agnosticism in his own beliefs.[67] Edward Elgar (1857–1934), a Roman Catholic by upbringing, started his career as organist of the chapel his family attended in Worcester, and later at the turn of the century, while his own faith became increasingly insecure, established his reputation with strongly Christian works such as *The Dream of Gerontius*, *The Apostles* and *The Kingdom*. Ernest Newman wrote of him:

> His Catholicism seemed to me to be in large part the product of the impact on him from boyhood onwards of all the magnificent art that Christian emotion has called into being throughout so many centuries. And so, when put to a sharply realistic test his religion, I think, was apt to give him scant support.[68]

The cultural and religious climate of the later nineteenth century was such that ambivalences of this kind were inevitable and widespread. As theological dogmas relaxed and doubt became intellectually respectable, it was less usual for musicians of stature to be also convinced orthodox believers. At the same time the depth of Christian reference in musical history continued to be a source of aesthetic inspiration and the breadth of conventional religiosity in society provided a source of continuing demand. This was satisfied not only in hymns, but also in oratorios, generally religious in their subject matter. These were initially at least frowned upon by the churches as degrading sacred history by making it the inspiration for entertainment rather than for worship, but for that very reason, enjoyed considerable popularity among the numerous choral societies and local festivals of later Victorian England.

In parallel fashion literature also served to give wide cultural currency to religious references, while softening their theological focus. Both Charles Dickens and Anthony Trollope were adept at satirizing the superficialities and hypocrisies of the conventionally religious, resulting in the creation of such memorable characters as Mr Chadband (*Bleak House*) and Mr Slope (*Barchester Towers*). Such use of official religion as a source of entertainment could become an end in itself, but it can be argued that, for Dickens in particular, there was a more serious underlying motive. The exposure of conventional pieties pointed the way towards more humane alternatives, genuine concern for the socially disadvantaged and a recognition of goodness and spiritual integrity wherever it was found.[69] This was a trend that achieved its fullest development in the work of George Eliot, perhaps the most successful of all novelists in her capacity to explore the influence of various forms of religious belief in shaping human personality and action. Her characters, from the tragically mundane Amos Barton (*Scenes of Clerical Life*, 1858) to the piously twisted Bulstrode (*Middlemarch*, 1871–2), subtly point up the limitations and dangers of their creeds.

Poetry too was a powerful vehicle for the expression of religious doubt and the formulation of alternatives to orthodoxy, as could be variously illustrated from the work of Alfred Tennyson, Robert Browning, Matthew Arnold and others. Indeed Tennyson's lines from *In Memoriam* (1850) have often been quoted as epitomizing the theological questionings of the second half of the nineteenth century:

> There lives more faith in honest doubt,
> Believe me, than in half the creeds.

At the same time he was hailed by others as a deeply religious poet, offering strong ethical support for Christianity, a conviction of the reality of immortality, and of the transforming power of love. Tennyson's unofficial Christianity was linked, moreover, to a deep patriotism, which was expressed in his sense of the significance of place, in his odes on great state occasions, and in his treatment of the Arthurian legend. His 'Ode on the Death of the Duke of Wellington' was later hailed as 'a true "word of God"'.[70]

A full analysis of the treatment of religion in the canon of Victorian English literature from the Brontës to Thomas Hardy, would be quite outside the scope of the present book. In the context of our general theme, however, it is important to notice the work of less remembered authors who, particularly in Scotland, did offer some alternatives to English cultural dominance. The Scottish inspiration of much of George MacDonald's work has already been noted, and a similar influence was evident in the prolific writing of his near contemporary Margaret Oliphant (1828–97). Not only did she write novels on Scottish ecclesiastical themes, but she was also a successful biographer of religious leaders, notably Edward Irving (1862) and Thomas Chalmers (1893).[71] An awareness of the place of religion in Scottish culture and social life was also very much apparent in the work of the Kailyard (kitchen-garden) School in the 1890s. The three authors bracketed together under this unflattering designation were Samuel Rutherford Crockett, John Watson (who wrote under the name 'Ian Maclaren'), both Free Church ministers, and James Matthew Barrie, a lay adherent of the same church, who was later to become a successful playwright. All three specialized in novels and short stories of Scottish rural and small town life. Barrie drew inspiration from his mother's recollections of the community of Auld Lichts (Presbyterian dissenters) in Kirriemuir (fictionalized as 'Thrums') earlier in the century; while Watson placed the Church at the centre of the intellectual and social life of his characters in 'Drumtochty' (Glen Almond).[72]

Reactions to the Kailyard were significant and revealing. On the one hand the novelists were criticized for implicit theological liberalism, as in Barrie's gentle satirizing of the narrow-mindedness of the Auld Lichts. On the other hand, though, they were charged with denying the realities of life in late Victorian Scotland; of subverting national dignity in favour of a condescending provincialism; and of obscuring the secularization consequent upon urbanization by dwelling nostalgically on rural religiosity.[73] The critical debate, which has revived at various times in the twentieth century, thus underlines the uncertain role of religion in the construction of Scottish identity, as noted in a political context in the previous chapter. At the same time the tendency for the Kailyarders to be disowned by their compatriots implies that their contribution should be set in a British as well as a Scottish context. An important factor in promoting their undeniably commercially success-ful work had been the influence of William Robertson Nicoll, himself a former minister of the Free Church, who had founded the *British Weekly* in 1886 because he 'thought that much more might be done in the way of uniting religion with literature, believing that Nonconfor-mists had too long behaved as exiles from the world of culture'.[74] It was in Nicoll's London periodical that some of Barrie's and Watson's early writings appeared and it seems that they had a ready appeal to English Nonconformists, who found Scottish sources attractive in reinforcing their own sense of British Protestant identity.[75]

Thus during the second half of the nineteenth century the seamless intermingling of religion, art and patriotism was a widespread cultural phenomenon. Charles Kingsley glorified Christian English manhood; Gothic architecture and choral evensong came to be valued as pillars of 'Englishness' even by those sceptical of Christianity. The ethos was predominantly English, although not unambiguously so as was indi-cated by the popularity of the Kailyard and by signs of cultural vitality in other parts of the United Kingdom. These included the strength of Welsh musical traditions as professionalized by Joseph Parry (1841– 1903) and the beginnings of Celtic revival in Irish art and architecture. In both these instances links with official religion were important, respectively, by providing Parry with his inspiration and subject matter in cantatas, oratorios and hymn tunes; and through the building and decoration of ecclesiastical buildings which offered opportunities for the use of historic Irish styles and motifs.[76]

Cultural activity also provided a powerful vehicle for the articulation of alternative structures of belief. George Eliot sought to enunciate a framework of humanistic religion founded on what she considered the most essential product of Christianity – love towards one's fellow human beings. She described the duty to love as 'peremptory and absolute', which suggests that it could be fairly categorized as quasi-religious ultimate concern.[77] For Matthew Arnold too the faltering of Christian orthodoxy stirred an intense searching for a replacement, which had its nostalgic metaphor in the quest of the elusive Scholar-Gipsy around the Oxford countryside:

> Thou hadst *one* aim, *one* business, *one* desire:
> Else wert thou long since number'd with the dead –
> Else hadst thou spent, like other men, thy fire.[78]

In *Culture and Anarchy* Arnold argued powerfully for the development of culture as a means to perfection, 'sweetness and light', in human society. Religion in its traditional sense stood alongside culture as a means to an end, that of 'setting ourselves to ascertain what perfection is and to make it prevail'.[79] Here was ultimate concern analogous to Eliot's overriding sense of the duty to love. The composer Hubert Parry had not been particularly impressed by *Culture and Anarchy* when he read it in his youth, but while he might lack Arnold's specific vision, he had a comparable sense of the role of the arts in extending the sphere of religion. He wrote:

> Religion includes Art as well as definite devotional exercises. . . .
> Art is a form of devotion. Everything that endeavours to beautify and make lovable the surroundings and the ideas of man is part of devotional religion. It is devotion to the most beautiful aspect of things – the things which minister to spiritual well-being, to truth.

Something of a counterpart in painting was to be found in the work of George Frederick Watts, who sought to give beauty back to the world and, stirred by patriotism, to elevate the standard of English art. For example, in his late work *Faith, Hope and Charity* (1902) Watts sought to soften and broaden the perceived belligerence of traditional Faith, by showing it being guided by Hope and Charity to 'the reviving spring of Truth'.[80]

For other writers and artists in the last quarter of the century, such terrible earnestness seemed too heavy a burden to carry and, as they loosened their moorings to official religion, they were ready to ride more freely on a tide of fantasy. Adventure stories such as those of Robert Louis Stevenson and Henry Rider Haggard enjoyed great popularity in the 1880s and 1890s, while H. G. Wells began to explore still more exotic regions of time and space. Fictional characters began to assume a 'life' of their own, as Arthur Conan Doyle found when, having tried to free himself from Sherlock Holmes by throwing him over the Reichen-bach Falls, he was obliged by the ensuing public outcry to provide him in 1894 with a somewhat contrived resurrection. In a similar confusion of fiction and real life J.M. Barrie moved from the Kailyard to the theatre, in 1904 transforming Peter Llywelyn Davies into Peter Pan and reviving the fictional Tinkerbell in response to the fantasies of a flesh-and-blood audience.[81] A similar trend was evident in painting, as artists turned to legendary and fictional subjects.[82] Also characteristic of this period was the widespread appeal of the supposed ideals of medieval chivalry as mediated through the work of Tennyson and others. This found expression, for instance, in the erection in 1903 of an equestrian statue of the Black Prince in Leeds as the centrepiece of a monumental array of the city's more recent worthies. A further development of the idea came in 1912 with the play *Where the Rainbow Ends* concerning the adventures of children with an idealized St George who concludes by introducing the singing of the National Anthem with the lines

> Rise, Youth of England, let your voices ring
> For God, for Britain, and for Britain's King![83]

These cultural trends represented the end point of religious diffusion in assorted 'systems of symbols' which in the consciousness of many tended to supersede the dogmatic structures of official Christianity. The transition occurred, in England at least, without much obvious conflict or discontinuity, which meant that people still readily thought of themselves as 'Christian', even when the nature of their belief structures had changed considerably. At first sight the kaleidoscopic mixture of ideas and convictions found in late Victorian and Edwardian culture might seem too fragmented to form any system sufficiently integrated to justify its description as 'religious'. However, the decades before the First World War revealed the potential of powerful national loyalty to weld together such apparently disparate cultural and spiritual impulses. This point can be illustrated by reference to two of the most prominent cultural figures of the early twentieth century, Edward Elgar and

Plate 4 City Square, Leeds, showing Mill Hill Unitarian Chapel (1847–8) and the statue of the Black Prince (1903)

Rudyard Kipling (1865–1936). While seldom considered together, they did in fact have much in common. They were near contemporaries; both established their careers in the 1890s, completed much of their best work before the First World War, and lived well into the interwar period. Both had an ambivalent relationship with official Christianity, but produced work with a spiritual dimension which often served to support a strongly imperialist vision. Both had an intense love of the English countryside and evoked it memorably in their work.

As a child Kipling had been left by his parents at what he later called the 'House of Desolation', subjected to the care of a woman who exposed him to the full rigours of evangelicalism in its most negative form. He grew up with a hostility to formal creeds, but a fascination with questions of death, eternity and meaning. He was attracted to the occult and, as T. S. Eliot put it he 'knew something of the things which are underneath, and of the things which are beyond the frontier'.[84] In his earlier works, strongly influenced by his experience of India, his preoccupations were imperial. From 1902, however, having settled in Sussex, where

> . . . little, lost Down churches praise
> The Lord who made the hills . . .[85]

he turned to the literary exploration of the spiritual and historical character of England. In *Stalky and Co* (1899) he dwelt on the sacredly private nature of patriotic impulses; and in *Puck of Pook's Hill* (1906) he endued them with an explicitly religious force:

> Land of our Birth, we pledge to thee
> Our love and toil in years to be;
> When we are grown and take our place
> As men and women with our race.
>
> Father in Heaven Who lovest all
> Oh, help Thy children when they call;
> That they may build from age to age
> An undefiled heritage . . .
>
> Teach us Delight in simple things.
> And Mirth that has no bitter springs;
> Forgiveness free of evil done,
> And Love to all men 'neath the sun!
>
> Land of our Birth, our faith, our pride,
> For whose dear sake our fathers died;

O Motherland, we pledge to thee
Head, heart, and hand through the years to be![86]

As the penultimate stanza indicates, Kipling's nationalism was not without its gentler side, a sense that dedication to the 'Motherland' implied not only moral rectitude, but also generosity of spirit. Moreover in his 'Recessional', written at the time of the diamond jubilee of 1897, he had marked that climax of Empire with a haunting prophecy of accountability and decay:

> Far-called, our navies melt away;
>   On dune and headland sinks the fire:
> Lo, all our pomp of yesterday
>   Is one with Nineveh and Tyre!
> Judge of the Nations, spare us yet,
> Lest we forget – lest we forget![87]

Kipling himself was in little danger of forgetting, and his power and influence as an advocate of 'England' and her empire, owed much to his own capacity to build upon the religious deposit in Edwardian culture.

Elgar was closer to official religion than was Kipling, but, as we have noted, the Christian themes of his oratorios around the turn of the century obscured increasing personal uncertainties. It is therefore significant that it was in precisely these years that the explicitly patriotic themes of his other music contributed to his growing popularity. Elgar became a notable contributor to the atmosphere of great state occasions, with *The Banner of St George* and the *Imperial March* for the diamond jubilee, the *Coronation Ode* (1902), the *Coronation March* (1911) and the *Crown of India* (1912). The *Coronation Ode* for Edward VII used some of the music first composed in the previous year for the march *Pomp and Circumstance*, No. 1, for which Arthur Benson had specially written the words of 'Land of hope and glory'. This quasi-religious elevation of England's dignity and mission gained rapid and widespread success, with the song printed separately from the larger composition of which it was a part. Moreover there were occasions on which Elgar's patriotic compositions seemed directly to recall his more conventionally religious work. In *Caractacus* (1898) some of the music given to the ancient British hero recalls that given to Christ in *Lux Christi* (1896). More subtly, the First Symphony (1908), greeted with great acclaim as a sign of new stature in English music, strongly echoed the creative mood and content of *The Apostles* (1903) and *The Kingdom* (1906). It was true that Elgar's own patriotism, although deeply held, was not unmeasured, but popular responses to his music acquired a momentum of their own.[88]

If the linking of religion with the nation in the music of Elgar stemmed from the composer's own spiritual ambivalences and the pressures of his relations with his patrons and his public, no such tensions were to be found in the poetry of Rupert Brooke (1887–1915). A generation younger than Elgar and Kipling, his ties to traditional Christianity were much weaker, but, while he might be agnostic about God, he was a passionate believer in 'England'. Having landed at Plymouth in 1914 after his return from the South Seas, the mundane experience of a railway journey stirred him profoundly: 'O noble train, oh glorious and forthright and English train, I will look round me at the English faces and out at the English fields – and I will pray'. While explicit reference to an 'English heaven' was to await the outbreak of war, the idea seems implicit in the banal intensity of the closing lines of 'The Old Vicarage, Grantchester' (1912):

> Say, is there Beauty yet to find?
> And Certainty? and Quiet kind?
> Deep meadows yet, for to forget
> The lies, and truths, and pain? . . . oh! yet
> Stands the Church clock at ten to three?
> And is there honey still for tea?

The church might be comparable only to honey in Brooke's world view, but it was none the less significant for all that.[89]

The Edwardian ambiguities between worship of God and worship of the nation were nowhere better illustrated than in hymns. Whether sung in church, Sunday School, or public school, these were a potent influence in shaping consciousness, particularly that of the rising generation. It is true that Rupert Brooke did not find his way into the hymnbooks, but Rudyard Kipling did, with both 'Land of our birth' and 'Recessional'. This was symptomatic of a growing tendency towards deification of the nation in verses printed for Christian worship, such as in the following lines:

> England! where the sacred flame
> Burns before the inmost shrine
> Where these lips that love thy name
> Consecrate their hopes, and thine.
>
> . . .
> Watch beside thine arms tonight;
> Pray that God defend the right.

193

This is an extreme example, but the general tendency in the hymnbooks used in late Victorian and Edwardian Britain was to reduce the space given to hymns confined to the statement of Christian dogma, and to include rather those that dwelt on mission and service, with the national and the Christian blended together.[90] Associated with this was a confusion of England and Britain, as was well illustrated in the hymn composed by Bishop Walsham How for the diamond jubilee:

> Where England's flag flies wide unfurl'd
> All tyrant wrongs repelling,
> God made the world a better world
> For man's brief earthly dwelling.[91]

It is true that the bishop received 'showers of abuse', apparently largely from Scotland, for having written 'England' not 'Britain'. Significantly, though, it appears that the complainants were not demanding the specific recognition of Scotland and Wales, simply objecting to the 'arrogant' broad application of 'England'. Nevertheless, such expansive geography persisted, as illustrated notably in the glorification of 'England' in Hubert Parry's setting in 1918 of William Blake's 'Jerusalem', which transformed the poet's questing mysticism into a rousing patriotic statement.[92]

During the second half of the nineteenth century there were only scanty indications that Ireland was developing cultural alternatives to prevailing English and British identity that were any more vigorous than those existing in Scotland and Wales. The period before the famine of 1845–7 had seen an extensive patriotically inspired literature which culminated in the work of Young Ireland writers such as Thomas Davis and James Clarence Mangan. Although notable more for romantic nationalist fervour than for literary merit, Young Ireland still appeared in retrospect as a high point of Irish cultural achievement. The appalling tragedy of the famine scarred the national consciousness during the ensuing decades and it was not until the end of the century that Irish literature began to recover a distinctive creative vision.[93] A similar weakness was apparent in art and music: leading painters of the second half of the century were prone to work abroad and, although some evocative images of the Irish past were produced, there was little indication that a national school was emerging.[94] Similarly, one of the most distinguished Irish musicians of the later Victorian era, Charles Villiers Stanford (1852–1924), made his career in England and produced work that came to epitomize the flowering of Anglican church music.[95] We noted above the role of church buildings as a medium for the expression of Irish styles and motifs and it is true that there were some striking interrelationships between national and religious motifs. For example, the memorial to Daniel O'Connell (1869) in Glasnevin Cemetery in Dublin took the form of a round tower, recalling the early centuries of Christianity in Ireland. Nevertheless in Ireland the Celtic style did not gain general acceptance and, in significant contrast to Gothic architecture in Britain, it was very rarely used for secular buildings.[96]

Between the death of Parnell in 1891 and the ending of the Union thirty years later the increasing sectarianization of politics (described in Chapter 6) was accompanied by a similar trend in culture. Canon Patrick Augustine Sheehan (1852–1913) might deplore the maintenance of sectarian bitterness, but in practice his own novels portrayed a vision of Ireland that was exclusively Roman Catholic in character.[97] For many, Irish cultural identity came to imply a convergence between Roman Catholicism and Gaelic culture, with the use of the language promoted on religious as well as national grounds. According to Eion McNeill, one of the founders of the Gaelic League, 'When we learn to speak Irish, we soon find that it is what we may call essential Irish to acknowledge God, His presence, and His help, even in our most trivial conversation'.[98] Patrick Pearse was a devout if unorthodox Catholic and also a passionate admirer of the culture of Gaelic Ireland which he sought to celebrate in his poetry and prose. In particular he venerated the ancient hero Cuchulain whom he explicitly saw as a Christ-figure symbolizing 'the redemption of man by a sinless God'.[99] The full development of Pearse's ideas might appear embarrassing for the Church, but in light of the events of 1916 they became, as we saw in Chapter 6, part of the ideology of Irish nationalism. Moreover with the formation of the Free State in 1921 the cultural links between Gaelicism, Catholicism and nationalism received powerful institutional reinforcement. The corollary of this was that Protestant Ulster was increasingly detached from the Gaelic strand in Irish tradition and forced back on its religion as its primary source of identity. The result, in the late nineteenth and early twentieth centuries, was a cultural austerity that caused the province's more creative writers and artists to move away in search of more congenial environments. In the meantime the popular culture of Orangeism, with its rich symbolism of banners and ritual, enjoyed a period of resurgence.[100]

There were nevertheless eloquent voices that spoke up for a more inclusive sense of Irish cultural identity. An early instance of this came with Standish James O'Grady's *History of Ireland* (1878–80). In this and subsequent writings O'Grady evoked the heroic myths and deities of the pre-Christian past, thus suggesting a spiritual basis for Irish identity that transcended the divisions of contemporary Christianity.[101] From the 1890s this conception began to take much clearer shape, particularly through the work of the dramatist and poet William Butler Yeats (1865–1939) and the poet, artist and journalist George William Russell, always known as 'AE' (1867–1935). Yeats and AE, who enjoyed a close if stormy personal friendship, were both Protestants by background, but came to be profoundly influenced by the teachings of theosophy, with its aspirations to unite all religions, and its teaching of the reality of occult and mystical powers. Ultimately AE proved more interested in inner mystical experience while Yeats turned to magical practices, but both men came to relate their unconventional religion to a strong sense of the cultural and spiritual power of Ireland's pre-Christian Celtic heritage. In his writings, from 1897 onwards, AE attacked both the industrialism of England and the power of the Roman Catholic priests. He affirmed that the true national religion of Ireland was Druidism reconstructed on theosophical lines.[102] Meanwhile Yeats hoped to create an Irish Mystical Order linked to a 'Unity of Culture' in the nation. A key source for this vision was the unofficial religion of the Irish countryside: 'folklore', he wrote in 1893, 'is at once the Bible, the Thirty-nine Articles, and the Book of Common Prayer'. Yeats believed that the true Celtic nature of the Irish would find expression through intimate contact with the occult, while his dislike for official Roman Catholicism led him to ignore the reality of its influence among the peasantry.[103]

Yeats's nationalism found its most powerful expression in his short play *Cathleen ni Houlihan* (1902) in which an old woman, personifying Ireland, successfully calls upon the son of a peasant cottage to sacrifice himself for her, and through the virtue of his commitment she is transformed into a young girl. It was of this work that Yeats was to write in 1938, recalling the Easter Rising of 1916:

> Did that play of mine send out
> Certain men the English shot?

The answer to the poet's agonized and somewhat egotistical question is by no means straightforward, but it is undeniable that the play contributed to the growth of the quasi-religious tenor of Irish nationalism which found powerful expression in the sequence of events that began in April 1916.[104]

Other leading figures in the Irish literary revival at the turn of the twentieth century were also notable for their rejection of official Christianity. The dramatist John Millington Synge discarded his family's Protestant beliefs and, like Yeats, tended in his work to highlight the unofficial beliefs rather than the Roman Catholicism of Irish rural life. His *Playboy of the Western World* (1907) led to riots when it was first performed in Dublin because of public outrage at its portrayal of the peasantry of the west as something less than perfectly moral and saintly.[105] Meanwhile James Joyce forcefully distanced himself from his Roman Catholic background, regarding the Church as another imperial power which, like England, was oppressing the Irish spirit.[106] His personal spiritual struggle subsequently found expression in his novels *Stephen Hero* (1906) and *A Portrait of the Artist as a Young Man* (1914–15). The strength of official religion in Ireland was thus expressed only in a negative sense in the most distinguished literary products of the period.

The paintings of the period primarily reflected wider European movements, such as realism and impressionism, rather than specifically Irish ones.[107] Even when artists did turn to their homeland for inspiration their attitude to its religion was ambivalent. AE's paintings offered mystical and Celtic images rather than contemporary ones.[108] William Orpen's paintings of Catholic subjects, notably *The Holy Well* (1916) with its naked figures and exaggerated gestures, were satirical rather than celebratory in tone. John Lavery was more ready to be positively inspired by Irish themes, but was careful to be even-handed in his coverage of 'Protestant' and 'Catholic' subjects.[109]

There is a significant contrast to be drawn between the susceptibility of British high culture at the turn of the century to Christian influences, and the secularity and explicit alternative spiritualities apparent in the Irish literary revival. In Britain the increasing liberalism and diversity of Christian teaching meant that writers and artists could draw diffuse inspiration from it in support of a relatively unconstrained creativity. In Ireland, on the other hand, the harder edges of sectarian identity rendered such compromises difficult to sustain: culture either had to be limited within specific religious traditions or it needed more or less explicitly to reject them and find alternative sources of inspiration. When in 1912 Rudyard Kipling gave utterance to his views on the situation in Ulster the strength of his residual Protestantism was powerfully apparent:

> We asked no more than leave
> To reap where we had sown
> Through good and ill to cleave
> To our own flag and throne.

> Now England's shot and steel
> Beneath that flag must show
> How loyal hearts should kneel
> To England's oldest foe.
>
> We know the war prepared
> On every peaceful home,
> We know the hells declared
> For such as serve not Rome.[110]

On the other hand AE, himself an Ulster Protestant by background, responded to this outburst with an open letter that reflected his own desire for conciliation and for an Irish national identity that transcended sectarian ties.[111]

However, the fragility of such aspirations had already been indicated by a pivotal personal crisis in W. B. Yeats's life. From 1889 he had been passionately in love with the actress and patriot Maud Gonne, who played the title role in *Cathleen ni Houlihan*. In 1903, after repeatedly refusing Yeats's proposals, she married John MacBride, who had become a national hero by fighting against the British in the South African War. Her motivation for the marriage was more patriotic than personal,[112] and it was accompanied by a conversion to Roman Catholicism, which, as she explained in a letter to Yeats, stemmed from the same sense of 'fulfilling a destiny':

> About my change of religion I believe like you that there is one great universal truth. God that pervades everything. I believe that each religion is a different *prism* though which one looks at truth. . . .
>
> I am officially a protestant and supposed to look at it from another and much narrower one which is moreover the English one. I prefer to look at truth through the same prism as my country people – I am going to become a Catholic. It seems to me of small importance if one calls the great spirit forces the Sidhe, the Gods and the Arch Angels, the great symbols of all religions are the same –
>
> But I do feel it important *not* to belong to the Church of England.[113]

That someone so close to the leaders of the literary revival could come to feel that commitment to Ireland meant commitment to Roman Catholicism was a telling indication of the shallowness of the soil of non-sectarian culture.

As cultural and political positions in Ireland hardened during the early twentieth century they thus served to point up the conflicts between the three most prominent alignments of culture and religion in the United Kingdom that have been discerned in the preceding discussion. All in respect of their tendency to make absolute claims may fairly be described as nationalisms. First, there was the 'English' position, with roots in expansive liberal Anglicanism but moving outside the bounds of Christian orthodoxy into an intense veneration of an 'England' that was implicitly an entity transcending the geographical limits of that country. Second, there was the 'Irish' standpoint, increasingly identified with Roman Catholicism. Finally, one observes a sense of 'British' Protestant identity, more fragmented than the first two, but drawing strength from anti-Catholic evangelicalism, Presbyterianism and Nonconformity.[114]

3.   CHRISTIANITY AND TWENTIETH-CENTURY CULTURE

By the 1920s the theological teachings of the institutional churches in Britain had, as we have seen, become diverse and sometimes diffuse. The accommodation of the modernists and the entrenched resistance of the conservatives both reflected an underlying sense that the prevailing cultural and intellectual climate had now turned decisively against Christianity. No longer were literature and the arts seen as ready vehicles for spreading official religious teachings: they were liable rather to be perceived as hostile or at best neutral. Art could be accepted with confidence as 'religious' only if it had been produced by conventional believers. Church architecture generally continued to use traditional styles such as the splendidly anachronistic Gothic of the Anglican cathedrals at Liverpool and Guildford. Similarly in music the impression was, in contrast to the Victorian era, that innovation was occurring in spite of rather than because of the influence of the churches. Apart from Elgar, the leading English composers of the first half of the twentieth century were the atheist Delius and agnostic Vaughan Williams. Christians were also lukewarm towards the cinema, despite, or because of, their ready acknowledgement of its social and cultural importance.[115] The aloofness of official religion from culture was an understandable reaction to the confusion of sacred and secular that had

Plate 5   Liverpool Anglican Cathedral, designed by Sir Giles Gilbert Scott and
built 1904–78

occurred in the previous generation, but still carried with it the converse danger of ghettoization.

In 1924 Percy Dearmer (1867–1936), an Anglican clergyman, tried to swim against this tide arguing that 'Art is . . . so akin to religion that it is difficult to separate the two'. Accordingly there could be no prospect of establishing the 'Kingdom of God' on earth,

> if we allow the estrangement to continue between those who specially claim to be engaged in the work of Christ, the 'religious world', and those who alone can give fitting and adequate expression to our vision – the poets, the prose writers, the musicians and all those other masters of expression who belong to the world of art.

Dearmer has himself been accused of not practising what he preached and instances of other churchmen responding to his call were rare.[116] However, for a significant number of writers and artists the very marginalization of religion from culture presented a challenge to redress the balance. Believers and non-believers alike came to find inspiration in the Christian tradition, now that they were free to interpret it on their own terms with little reason to fear the straitjacket of ecclesiastical authority.

The ambivalent relationships between art and official religion are well illustrated by the career of Stanley Spencer (1891–1959), who drew much of the inspiration for his painting from Christian beliefs. These were expressed in a highly individual fashion, through the location of biblical events in the setting of Cookham in Berkshire, which provided a further powerful source of the artist's creativity, and one that was permeated with mystical spiritual significance. He established his reputation with *The Resurrection, Cookham* (1923–7) in which was visualized a very literal and physical re-emergence of the dead from their graves occurring in an English country churchyard. *The Times* judged it 'the most important picture painted by any English artist in the present century', and it was purchased for the Tate Gallery.[117] The theme of resurrection was to inspire further important paintings by Spencer, and in later years he also engaged in extensive artistic exploration of the life of Christ concluding with his powerful *Crucifixion* (1958) set against the background of Cookham High Street. He cherished the unrealized vision of creating a 'Church House' to contain a comprehensive statement in art of his religious convictions and personal affections.[118] However, Spencer's vision was too distinctive to be received with enthusiasm by the official churches. Particularly problematic was his insistence on relating sexuality and religion, as joint and intertwined sources of his creative energy. The sexual act was to him a sacrament, and he had no hesitation in contemplating the display in the Church House of the disquieting double nude portraits of himself with his second wife, Patricia Preece. He wanted 'to show the analogy between the Church and the prescribed nature of worship, and human love'.[119]

A similarly controversial exploration of the connections between Christianity and sexuality was apparent in the work of the sculptor Eric Gill (1882–1940). In 1913, when his work was still very little known and he had only very recently converted to Roman Catholicism, he was commissioned to carve the Stations of the Cross for Westminster Cathedral. As Gill recalled in his biography, the choice, fortunate though it was, reflected the ignorance rather than the prescience of the ecclesiastical authorities.[120] Although the simplicity and devotional power of the Westminster sculptures was much acclaimed, the blending of spirituality and sensuality in much of his other work – for example, in his pewter sculpture *Divine Lovers* (1922) – was disconcerting for official Roman Catholicism.[121] The artistic endeavour of Gill and Spencer to celebrate sexuality in a Christian framework nevertheless provides a significant counterpoint to the literary work of D. H. Lawrence, in which the elevation of the spiritual significance of sexuality was founded on a rejection of traditional Christianity.[122]

If some artistic explorations of religion were shocking to the conventional, no such reservations hampered the career of John Buchan (1875–1940), author, publisher, politician and Governor General of Canada. The son of a Free Church minister, Buchan grew up exposed to a vigorous Calvinism, the Bible and Bunyan, but also to mythology, fairy tales and an intense awareness of the countryside of his native Fife and Tweeddale. He worked with Lord Milner in the reconstruction of South Africa after the Boer War, acquiring a 'nearly religious enthusiasm' for Empire; and from 1910 began to establish his reputation as a writer of thrillers.[123] Christianity was part of the moral framework of these novels, evident, for instance, in the strong recurrent sense of the reality of evil, in the robust spiritual integrity of heroes such as David Crawfurd in *Prester John* (1910) and Peter Pienaar in *Greenmantle* (1916), and in the Bunyanesque allusions of *Mr Standfast* (1919).[124]

Buchan has thus understandably been seen as one of the last Victorians, a late development of the 'muscular Christian' tradition derived from Kingsley and Hughes.[125] But this is to oversimplify: another and more complex side of his religion emerges from his serious novels, notably *Witch Wood* (1927), which explores the spiritual conflicts of seventeenth-century Scotland, and *The Blanket of the Dark* (1931), set in the reign of Henry VIII. In *A Prince of the Captivity* (1933) Buchan attempted a statement on the political, social and moral dilemmas of his own time.[126] In his autobiography, written under the shadow of the Second World War, he acknowledged that Christianity was under attack, but still could strike a note of optimism:

> in the world as we know it I believe that civilization must have a Christian basis, and must ultimately rest on the Christian faith . . . I believe . . . that the challenge with which we are now faced may restore to us that manly humility which alone gives power. It may bring us back to God. In that case our victory is assured. The Faith is an anvil which has worn out many hammers.[127]

In his last novel, *Sick Heart River* (1941), Buchan further explored spiritual themes through Sir Edward Leithen's search for death and salvation in the wastes of the Canadian Arctic.[128]

Thus in the last fifteen years of his life Buchan was moving towards a more explicit and sustained avowal of religious concerns. By 1940 the confident imperial vision of his early South African days had faded in favour of a Christian concept of world order. At the same time he also became more conscious of the religious identity of his native Scotland. When the churches were reunited in 1929 he articulated a quasi-Arnoldian vision of their relationship to the nation:

> It is a solemn moment when we watch the beginning of a thing fraught with such tremendous possibilities. It carries with it the destiny of future generations of our countrymen, and of that beloved and ancient and mystical thing, our Scottish fatherland.[129]

He subsequently relished his role as Lord High Commissioner to the General Assembly in 1933 and 1934.[130] In 1930 he published a short history of *The Kirk in Scotland* in which he celebrated the role of the Church in the life of the nation. Thomas Chalmers was to him not only 'the supreme religious genius of modern Scotland' but also 'a true national leader, who lifted his countrymen to a higher spiritual level'. Buchan held that 'the history of Scotland is largely the history of her Church' and visualized a pageant of its heroes stretching back until 'against a Hebridean sky we can discern him (St Columba) who was called the Dove and was both priest and prince'.[131] Nevertheless in political terms Buchan held firmly to the value of the Union with England and his Scottish patriotism was ultimately set in the framework of that wider British Protestant imperial nationalism which had led his father to repudiate the Liberals after General Gordon had died at Khartoum and Gladstone had adopted Home Rule for Ireland. The nature of his sense of identity was perfectly expressed by his choice of title when elevated to the peerage in 1935: as Baron Tweedsmuir of Elsfield he linked together the Scottish Borders of his childhood with the Oxfordshire countryside of his later life.[132]

While Buchan provided a personal link between the self-assurance of Victorian Christianity and the mid-twentieth-century search for a recovery of spiritual values, his near contemporary G. K. Chesterton (1874–1936) developed a religion that owed little to his upbringing, but rather implied a rejection of it. 'My father', he wrote in 1922,

> is the very best man I ever knew of that generation that never understood the new need for a spiritual authority; and lives almost perfectly by the sort of religion men had when rationalism was rational. I think he was subconsciously prepared for the next generation having less theology than he has; and is rather puzzled at its having more.[133]

Chesterton's acquisition of 'more' theology was a gradual process, starting with a youthful interest in spiritualism and occult, from which he moved around the turn of the century to essentially orthodox Christianity of an Anglo-Catholic variety. Finally, after many years of hesitation, he was received into the Roman Catholic Church in 1922. Thus the very lack at this time of sharp divisions between the orthodox and the heterodox, and the religious and the secular, assisted his steps towards official religion even while it readily led others away from it.

Chesterton was a fluent, witty, and prolific writer as journalist, novelist, poet and lay theologian. He was also an effective illustrator both of his own work and that of his close friend Hilaire Belloc, a staunch if unconventional Roman Catholic. All this gave him considerable effectiveness as an apologist for Christianity. This aspect of his career reached its peak in 1925 with *The Everlasting Man*, in which he vigorously argued that man was more than a beast and Christ more than a man. During the later years of his life the defence of the Catholic faith became one of his central concerns.

Chesterton, like Buchan, saw clear links between his Christianity and his patriotism, but, unlike him, the framework in which he operated was English, Anglican and Catholic, rather than British and Protestant. He advocated a patriotism closer to 'what a mystic might mean by the love of God' than to 'what a child might mean by the love of jam'. He had established his reputation in 1901 with an article exploring this problem, against the national background of the Boer War, and his personal move to Christianity and imminent marriage to a devout Anglo-Catholic. Chesterton distinguished an authentic patriotism 'of the head and heart of the Empire', which needed to be based on a true appreciation of English literature and history, from a nationalism that was rooted in the shallow glorification of trivial imperial successes at the periphery. He concluded in religious vein:

> We are the children of light, and it is we that sit in darkness. If we are judged, it will not be for the merely intellectual transgression of failing to appreciate other nations, but for the supreme spiritual transgression of failing to appreciate ourselves.[134]

In the 1920s Chesterton's patriotism became ever more closely integrated with his Christianity. When he visited Ireland he was by no means blind to the negative effects of religion, but did not see the answer as irreligion, but rather 'the extension of Christian charity'. Moreover Ireland appealed to him because Christianity had a social reality there in a manner that had been lost in England. His eventual conversion to Roman Catholicism related to his need for a decisive stand against the 'plutocracy and neglected populace and materialism and servile morality' of contemporary England, which he saw as ultimately deriving from the national Protestantism.[135] Chesterton's sense that true loyalty to England implied acceptance of the authority of Rome might seem paradoxical, but reflected his conviction that patriotism, however passionate, could only be genuine and defensible if it was qualified by a wider vision of humanity.

Chesterton's conversion to Christianity was echoed in the lives of two of his younger literary contemporaries, T. S. Eliot (1888–1965) and C. S. Lewis (1898–1963). Both, perhaps significantly, came as relative outsiders to English cultural and religious traditions, Eliot from America and Lewis from Belfast. Eliot began life as a Unitarian; Lewis with a childish Christianity that slid into atheism in adolescence. Both, however, became committed Anglicans, Eliot in 1926, and Lewis, after an intermediate conversion to deism, in the early 1930s.

T. S. Eliot's movement towards Anglicanism contrasted with that of both Chesterton and Lewis in as much as it followed from a rejection of middle ways between atheism and Christianity, rather than a readiness to use them as stepping-stones. He attacked the 'romanticism' of English literary tradition because of its failure to distinguish religion from anything else. Accordingly the modernism of his poetry had its counterpart in the doctrinal rigour of his Anglo-Catholicism. Eliot combined theological conservatism with a capacity for effective poetic and dramatic innovation, manifested for example, in *Murder in the Cathedral* (1935) and *Four Quartets* (1942), which by the 1940s gained him a very substantial reputation and influence.[136] He thus strikingly illustrated the compatibility of Christianity with cultural modernism.

Lewis's spiritual odyssey is of particular interest because in his response to his reading and experience as a schoolboy, student and academic, he traversed in a few short years much of the ground that has been surveyed in our account of the cultural developments of the preceding century. His initial youthful movement away from official Christianity stemmed from no sudden crisis, but a gradual encounter with the worlds of the occult and of fantasy. This blunting of 'the sharp edges of . . . belief' eventually left the fifteen-year-old Lewis with a sense that 'there was nothing to be obeyed, and nothing to be believed'. The subsequent reversal of the process was also gradual: it started with a fascination with Norse mythology as mediated through the plots of Wagner operas; and was greatly advanced by a reading of George MacDonald's *Phantastes, a faerie Romance*. Lewis's sense of indebtedness to MacDonald was particularly strong and in *The Great Divorce* (1946) he was to portray the Scottish author as his guide to heaven.[137] Finally, Chesterton's *Everlasting Man* left the struggling atheist with at least a subconscious realization that 'Christianity . . . was very sensible'.[138] Whereas Lewis, with his strong affinities to late Romanticism, was a less original writer than Eliot, with his vigorous modernism, he was more accessible to a larger audience. He accordingly became a popular and successful apologist for Christianity, notably in *The Screwtape Letters* (1942), the science fiction trilogy of the 1940s, and above all in the childish maturity of the Narnia books of the 1950s.

In both Eliot and Lewis the literary evocation of Christianity was associated with that of England. In *Four Quartets* the poet's imagination and spiritual searching takes him from the lanes of Somerset to the rocks of the Massachusetts coast, but he comes to rest in the church at Little Gidding in Huntingdonshire to kneel and reflect on prayer in a place where

> the intersection of the timeless moment
> Is England and nowhere. Never and always.[139]

In the 'Englishness' of these poems there was an echo of Kipling, whose verse Eliot was editing at the time, but with a firmer Christianity and less intense patriotism.[140] This is further illuminated by some of Eliot's prose writings. In *The Idea of A Christian Society* (1939) he pointed to the dangers of 'nationalistic Christianity' stemming from an inability 'to distinguish . . . between what is universal and what is local, accidental and erratic'. On the other hand in 1941 he wrote that patriotism was fundamentally a virtue, despite its capacity to pass into nationalism and pride and the need to balance it with other loyalties. 'It includes', he wrote,

> . . . the attachment to natural as well as to constructed surroundings, to place as well as to people, to the past as well as to the future; the attachment of a people to its own culture, and to its ability to make that specific and voluntary contribution to Christendom and to the world.[141]

For Lewis similarly the Christian and the patriotic were interlinked. In *That Hideous Strength* (1945) he seated the focus of resistance to the forces of evil in an idealized English village. In the Narnia novels the gentle topography of the imaginary country under the Christ-like care of the lion Aslan evoked that of an idealized pre-industrial England. When starker or more exotic locations were used, as in *The Voyage of the Dawn Treader* (1952) and *The Silver Chair* (1953) these were outside Narnia. In *The Horse and His Boy* (1954), as Shasta, the boy-hero, first crosses the pass into Narnia he makes sense of his adventures through an encounter with Aslan and then finds himself in a very English landscape:

> It was a green valley-land dotted with trees through which he caught the gleam of a river. . . . On the far side of the valley there were high and even rocky hills, but they were lower than the mountains he had seen yesterday.[142]

The parallel was made explicit in *The Last Battle* (1956):

> But you are now looking at the England within England, the real England just as this is the real Narnia. And in that inner England no good thing is destroyed.[143]

Meanwhile there were signs that a religious consciousness, sometimes assuming a specifically Christian form, was also a factor in the growth of alternatives to 'English' or 'British' culture during the mid-twentieth century. In Wales culture and religion were closely interwoven. There was an explicit linking of patriotism and Christianity in the work of Saunders Lewis (1893–1985), a convert to Roman Catholicism, and Gwenallt Jones (1899–1968).[144] This was all the more significant as it coincided with the decline of the relationship between religion and political nationalism which we noted in the previous chapter. In his *Buchedd Garmon (The Life of Germanus)*, a radio play written in 1936, Saunders Lewis related the survival of the British community in Wales at the collapse of the Roman Empire to its adherence to Christian orthodoxy.[145] Gwenallt too saw his country's Christianity as central to its identity, addressing Wales as follows:

> God chose you for his handmaiden
> And called on you for witness;
> And he inscribed the Covenant
> On your doors and your doorposts.[146]

Gwenallt linked his Christianity and his socialism together, associating them respectively with rural Wales and the aspirations of the industrial workers:

> Farm and Furnace march together
> The humanity of the pit, the godliness of the country,
> Tawe and Tywi, Canaan and Wales, Earth and Heaven.[147]

In the work of Dylan Thomas (1914–53), attitudes to religion, as indeed to Wales, were more ambivalent: there is a widespread view that 'his concern is analogy rather than the central substance of religion'.[148] On the other hand Thomas himself described his work as 'written for the love of Man and in praise of God' and some of his poetry carried a rich biblical resonance.[149]

   In relation to Scotland a similar uncertainty over the significance of religious allusions arises from consideration of the poetry of 'Hugh MacDiarmid' (Christopher Murray Grieve 1892–1978). Grieve professed to be an atheist, but as MacDiarmid he loaded his Scots epic poem 'A Drunk Man Looks at the Thistle' (1926) with extensive Christian references. The drunk man was a trenchant critic of official Christianity:

> (The Kirk in Scotland still I cry
> Crooks* whaur it canna crucify!) (l. 1663–4)

His vision for the regeneration of the Scottish soul ultimately transcended Christianity, as he sought 'a greater Christ, a greater Burns' (l. 117). However, MacDiarmid's poetic imagination clearly owed much to the piety of his upbringing in the United Free Church.[150] As the drunk man put it:

* twists

The thocht o' Christ and Calvary
Aye liddenin'* in my heid; (l. 1221–2)[151]

Edwin Muir, another leading mid-twentieth-century Scottish poet, was also ambivalent in his attitude to his nation's religion, acknowledging himself a Christian from 1939,[152] but bitterly critical of ecclesiasticism and Calvinism. He looked back in a poem of 1943 to an idealized pre-Reformation Scotland in which he has Robert the Bruce say:

> If Christ live not, nothing is there
> For sorrow or for praise.[153]

A similar sense that Presbyterianism was an aberration from Scottish identity is apparent in the attitudes of the novelist Compton Mackenzie (1883–1972). Mackenzie became a devout Anglo-Catholic as a teenager, and converted to Roman Catholicism in 1914. During the 1920s he made a passionate rediscovery of his Scottish roots and developed a neo-Jacobite brand of nationalism, associated with virulent hostility to the Reformation and aspirations for the recovery of a Catholic and Celtic culture.[154]

It is instructive to contrast the appeal of nationalism to the Roman Catholic Mackenzie, as to Saunders Lewis in Wales, with the Protestant Buchan's sense that Scotland's place was firmly within Britain. However, although Roman Catholicism might have a certain congruence with nationalism in so far as it was perceived as un-English, it still seemed to be at odds with the cultural mainstream in Scotland and Wales themselves. In the south of Ireland, on the other hand, during the two decades following the Easter Rising of 1916, the links between Roman Catholicism and national culture were asserted ever more strongly. W. B. Yeats recognized how the martyrdom of the rebels was being celebrated in quasi-Christian terms, but also warned that

> Too long a sacrifice
> Can make a stone of the heart.[155]

While Yeats thus hinted at the dangers of dwelling on 'exceptional acts of faith or sacrifice', John Lavery in his painting *Love of Ireland* (1922) depicted the dead Michael Collins, with a crucifix lying on the Irish tricolour covering the body. This was a powerful image of the ties between Roman Catholicism and nationalism in the making of the Free State.[156] In the 1920s Yeats and AE found themselves struggling against the advance of a conservative Roman Catholic cultural ethos which

* resounding

209

proved to be a more resilient and effective focus of national identity than the fruitless attempt to revive the Gaelic language.[157] This trend found notable legislative expression in the Censorship of Publications Act of 1929, energetically opposed by both men. In 1934 Yeats's poem on 'Parnell's Funeral' well conveyed his sense of disillusionment at the manner in which an expansive non-sectarian nationalism had given way to the cultural and political divisions of contemporary Ireland:

> Had de Valera eaten Parnell's heart
> No loose-lipped demagogue had won the day
> No civil rancour torn the land apart.[158]

Such distaste for the polarized cultures of twentieth-century Ireland had its northern counterpart in the Belfast-born poet Louis MacNeice's distaste for his native province where, he wrote in 1938, 'few of the Protestants or Presbyterians can see the Cross as a cross . . . they see it shoot out rays, blossom in the Union Jack'.[159]

The continuing cultural ascendancy of official religion in post-partition Ireland, as it was perceived by writers such as Yeats and MacNeice, contrasted with the situation in Britain where the churches no longer could exercise anything approaching the same degree of influence. However, in England writers and artists committed to a religious vision often still felt themselves to be at odds with official Christianity; while spiritual expressions of Welsh and Scottish nationalism were liable to be associated with a distaste for traditional indigenous ecclesiastical institutions. It is true that in the years after the Second World War church leaders became more at ease with artistic expressions of unofficial Christianity. C. S. Lewis's work was hailed with enthusiasm. Modern art was admitted into churches, notably through the work of Walter Hussey at St Matthew's, Northampton, and at Chichester Cathedral.[160] Spencer's own paintings were exhibited at Cookham Church in 1958. The work of the sculptor Jacob Epstein also became ecclesiastically fashionable in the 1950s, most conspicuously through his *Christ in Majesty* incorporated in the postwar restoration of Llandaff Cathedral. Church architecture acquired a modernist idiom, as in the new cathedral built at Coventry after the destruction of the old one during the Second World War. Meanwhile Herbert Howells drew on the artistic inspiration of Vaughan Williams together with his own Christian convictions to produce works such as his *Hymnus Paradisi*, first performed in 1950. Benjamin Britten, the most prominent composer of the 1950s and 1960s, produced a significant body of religious music which gained wide acceptance and popularity. The singing of his

War Requiem at the consecration of the new Coventry Cathedral in 1962 has been seen as symbolic of a fresh accommodation between official Christianity and the arts.[161]

Nevertheless this trend was belated and partial. The dominant impression of the relationship between religion and the arts in the twentieth century is the paradox that at a time when official churches were numerically in retreat and culturally insecure, a significant number of writers and artists still found considerable inspiration in the Christian tradition. To the cases specifically discussed above one might add others such as W. H. Auden, John Betjemen, Edwin Lutyens, Henry Moore, Dorothy L. Sayers, Graham Sutherland, J. R. R. Tolkein, and Evelyn Waugh.[162] To say this is not to deny the extent to which by 1945 the majority of cultural activity occurred in an essentially secular context. To reverse Matthew Arnold's analogy, the shoreline of the continent of faith had now retreated to form a large island. However, it would be far too simplistic to conclude that there was a uniform secularization of culture. Whereas in the 1850s George Eliot was beginning her literary career as a subtle but compelling adversary of Christianity, in the 1950s T. S. Eliot was concluding his as an equally creative and influential advocate of it. A comparison of the life and painting of Stanley Spencer with that of Holman Hunt does not suggest that Christian art had necessarily become any less a part of mainstream culture. The 1930s were also a period in which the religious inspiration in the culture of the past came to be appreciated afresh, notably in the rediscovery of the poetry of the late Victorian Jesuit Gerard Manley Hopkins. Moreover in literature at least the imagination and breadth of vision of apologists such as Chesterton and Lewis gave their creed a credibility which, in retrospect at least, had been lacking in the narrow didacticism of the 'religious' novelists of the mid-nineteenth century. As Percy Dearmer had put it in 1924, 'Literature is . . . the real Free Church of to-day'.[163]

There was also a growing reaction in Britain against that convergence of Christianity and nationalism which had been strongest in the Edwardian period. It became increasingly common for Christian advocates to seek to define their patriotism in a more limited sense. This process was reflected in the content of hymnbooks which began to revert to more orthodox Christian themes, while expressing a patriotism couched in more humble terms, such as those set by Chesterton in 1911:

> O God of earth and altar,
>   Bow down and hear our cry,
> Our earthly rulers falter,
>   Our people drift and die;

The walls of gold entomb us,
 The swords of scorn divide,
 Take not thy thunder from us,
 But take away our pride.

The words, significantly, were generally sung to a traditional English tune arranged by Vaughan Williams, rather than to the stirring marches of earlier patriotic hymnody. Even Cecil Spring-Rice's 'I vow to thee my country' (1911–17) was in the context of its time notable not so much for the 'love that asks no questions' of the first verse, but for the explicit recognition in the second of the tension between this and the 'other country I've heard of long ago' with its 'ways of gentleness' and 'paths of peace'.[164]

Here was an appreciation of both Christianity and nationhood freed not only from the blending of the two which had characterized the recent past, but also from that sense of divinely appointed national election and mission which had been powerful in the Victorian era. The trend was of course a patchy one, especially when one moves from the ground of literary intention to that of popular reception. Elgar's *Pomp and Circumstance* with the words of 'Land of hope and glory' was to have a popularity that spanned the twentieth century and, as we shall see in the next chapter, the cult of Remembrance during and after the First World War gave a new turn to ambivalence between service to God and service to the country. Moreover despite the development of alternative national identities and nationalism ambiguities between 'England' and 'Britain' remained considerable. Nevertheless the trends indicated above still provide an indicator of more general religious and social transitions occurring in the early twentieth century. In order to explore these further we must now turn to focus on two key features of the experience of the people of these islands which have increasingly impinged on our discussion in this chapter: the possession of Empire and the experience of war.

8

ONWARD CHRISTIAN SOLDIERS?

The Empire and war

In 1864 Sabine Baring-Gould (1834–1924), while serving his first curacy in the working-class district of Horbury Brig, near Wakefield in Yorkshire, wrote the lines that were quickly to become one of the most familiar of all English hymns:

> Onward Christian soldiers,
>   Marching as to war,
> With the Cross of Jesus
>   Going on before . . .

The verses were first sung on Whit Sunday 1865 at a procession of children who had been drawn to church by Baring-Gould's energetic ministry. When the words were set to Arthur Sullivan's stirring tune 'St Gertrude', which was composed in 1871, its lasting popularity was assured.[1] A considerable number of mid- and late Victorian hymns employed such military imagery. A generation later in 1894 Arthur Campbell Ainger (1841–1919), a master at Eton College, added his contribution:

> March we forth in the strength of God with the banner of
>   Christ unfurled,
> That the light of the glorious Gospel of truth may shine
>   throughout the world.
> Fight we the fight with sorrow and sin, to set their captives free,
> That the earth may be filled with the glory of God as the waters
>   cover the sea.[2]

These two examples illustrate a powerful strand in Victorian and Edwardian religious consciousness in which the language of warfare was associated with the individual's commitment to Christ, and the world-wide proclamation of the Gospel. The purpose of this chapter is to explore the connections between such Christian missionary zeal, and British encounter with the outside world, as reflected particularly in the expansion of the Empire and the involvement of the nation in war, a process that reached its climax around 1914. In Baring-Gould's and Ainger's old age the frame of mind suggested by their hymns thus began to seem a naïve and over-optimistic one and lines written by Baring-Gould, but never sung, unwittingly prophetic

> Kingdoms, nations, empires
> In destruction rolled.[3]

Nevertheless, although the furnace of European conflict was to melt away many of the easy assumptions of the past, bonds between patriotism, imperialism and religion still continued strong in the mid-twentieth century.

At the outset it will be helpful to look back over some of the ground covered in previous chapters, in order to point up the context of the wider development of religion, politics and culture. As we saw in Chapters 3 and 4, during the later Victorian period official religion displayed tremendous energy but had mixed success in shaping the beliefs and outlook of the mass of the population. Nevertheless the substantial minority with a formal affiliation to churches and synagogues did not represent the sum of religious influence. Unofficial religion had also been reshaped during the Victorian era and had tended to become less of an alternative 'folk' tradition and more of a partial and diffuse reflection of official religion. Around the turn of the century generalized supernatural reference was widespread. Its place in the consciousness of the population, moreover, was attributable not only to the direct exertions of the churches, through agencies such as city mission societies, revivalist missions and Sunday Schools. There were also, as we saw in Chapters 6 and 7, other channels through which a religious framework for life was diffused, through the issues and machinery of politics, and through numerous varieties of cultural expression. The diversification and liberalization of theology in the second half of the century served to blur earlier distinctions between Christian orthodoxy and less specific forms of religion.

In filling out this picture further we shall first examine British perceptions of the Empire and the rest of the world, and then turn to consider the relationship between fighting for Christ and fighting for the nation.

1. THE WHITE MAN'S BURDEN?

In 1819 Reginald Heber, later Bishop of Calcutta, had given expression to the Christian obligation to spread the Gospel to the whole world:

> Can we, whose souls are lighted
>   With wisdom from on high
> Can we to men benighted
>   The lamp of life deny?
> Salvation; oh salvation!
>   The joyful sound proclaim
> Till each remotest nation
>   Has learned Messiah's name.

As the century drew to a close Rudyard Kipling set out a vision which was reminiscent of Heber's in the underlying assumption that the white man had something of overiding value to be shared with the rest of humanity. However, he moved beyond Christianity while maintaining some of its imagery and, alluding to the complaints of the Israelites in the wilderness to Moses as recounted in the Bible, displayed an awareness of the obstacles and frustrations that had to be overcome:

> Take up the White Man's burden –
>   And reap his old reward
> The blame of those ye better,
>   The hate of those ye guard -
> The cry of hosts ye humour
>   (Ah slowly!) toward the light:-
> 'Why brought ye us from bondage,
>   Our loved Egyptian night?'[4]

How was the specific endeavour of Christian missionaries related to the developing creed of imperial responsibility?

The modern British missionary movement had its origins in the great evangelical upsurge of the 1790s, which saw the foundation of key organizations such as the Baptist Missionary Society (1792), the London Missionary Society (interdenominational but increasingly Congrega-tionalist, 1795) and the Church Missionary Society (Anglican, 1799). Scottish Presbyterians were relatively slow to move, but the Edinburgh (later Scottish) Missionary Society was founded in 1796, and from the 1820s the main Protestant churches north of the Border began to engage directly in missionary endeavour.[5]

During the early nineteenth century missionary activity contributed little to the expansion of British influence in the non-European world.

215

In part this was simply because the scale of activity remained small, limited primarily to the West Indies, coastal Africa, the Pacific Islands and India. More significantly, there was tension between the overriding missionary objective of spreading the Christian Gospel and the commercial interests of other groups. Thus in the West Indies the concern of missionaries for the spiritual and social welfare of the slaves brought them into conflict with the planters. In India the East India Company, which had initially been simply a trading organization, adopted a cool attitude to missionaries who, it was feared, might destabilize native politics and culture and thus hamper commerce. With the renewal of the Company's Charter in 1813, official recognition and support was given to missions for the first time, but substantial tensions remained.[6]

During the middle decades of the nineteenth century Christian influences assumed a greater importance in forming colonial policy and attitudes, as manifested in the abolition of colonial slavery in 1833.[7] A similar tendency for Empire to become linked with religious and social reform was evident in India where in 1829 and 1830 measures were taken in response to missionary pressure to outlaw the practice of *suttee*, the burning of Hindu widows on the funeral pyres of their husbands. A decade later there was a discontinuation of the tax levied on pilgrims to support the Hindu temples at Jagannath, which in evangelical eyes were an appalling centre of idolatry.[8] During the 1840s Lord Ashley (later Earl of Shaftesbury), best known for his campaigns for factory reform, also emerged as a prominent Parliamentary advocate of Christian rectitude in imperial dealings. In 1843 he proposed a motion in the Commons against the opium trade with China, holding it to be 'utterly inconsistent with the honour and duties of a Christian kingdom'. In 1844 he called for a generous attitude to the fraternity of Indian princes known as the Ameers of Scinde, in the cause of establishing 'a really Christian empire'. Also in 1844 he was outraged by French aggression in the disputed island of Tahiti, the regeneration of which had been 'given to our people as a triumph of the Cross'. 'The missionaries made it Christian' he wrote, 'they made it English in laws and constitution.'[9]

This double-edged readiness to justify the Empire in religious terms, while at the same time questioning the actions of human governments from a Christian standpoint, well illustrates the uncertainties that existed in the middle of the century. At the same time more uncritical views of the Empire were emerging in evangelical circles. These owed something to a facility at this period in relating the cause of commerce to that of Christianity, seeing the extension of trade as offering providential channels for the spread of the Gospel. This frame of mind received a considerable boost in 1856 with the triumphant return to Britain of David Livingstone from his first great journey across Africa,[10] which had been carried out with the avowed intention of combating the slave trade and promoting legitimate commerce as well as providing an opening for missionary endeavour. During the ensuing decades Livingstone acquired the status of a national hero and Protestant saint, his reputation underscored by the famous meeting with H. M. Stanley in 1871 and his death in 1873, supposedly while in prayer, still refusing to rest from his labours. Moreover Livingstone's status as an imperial and missionary martyr was underscored by his apotheosis: the body was carried to the coast by his African companions, brought back to Britain by sea and buried after an elaborate funeral in the centre of the nave of Westminster Abbey. This posthumous glorification was the more significant in that Livingstone came from a working-class background and was a Congregationalist by religion. He was also a Scot who provided a potent link between Scottish, British and imperial identities. The message of his career seemed to be that by way of Africa and Christianity it was possible to receive the ultimate accolade of the British people, a lesson that was not lost on his countrymen and his co-religionists. The inscription on his gravestone summarized the legend woven round his name:

> Brought by faithful hands over land and sea here rests David Livingstone, missionary, traveller, philanthropist, born March 19 1813 at Blantyre, Lanarkshire, died May 1 1873 at Chitambo's Village, Ulala. For 30 years his life was spent in an universal effort to evangelize the native races, to explore the undiscovered secrets, to abolish the desolating slave trade, of Central Africa.[11]

Livingstone's endeavours to combat the slave trade in central Africa had struck a chord in the public mind that was all the stronger because it coincided in time with a growth in concern about slavery in America, stimulated by Harriet Beecher Stowe's *Uncle Tom's Cabin* (1852) and gathering momentum as the tensions across the Atlantic exploded into civil war in the 1860s. The tendency of the British to set themselves up on a moral pedestal could be irritating even to Americans who shared their abhorrence of slavery.[12] At the same time anti-slavery writing tended to perpetuate a patronizing image of the black man, possessed of human dignity certainly, but still desperately in need of outside assistance if he was to realize his full potential.[13]

As involvement in Africa and observation of America stirred feelings of national mission, events in India prompted some painful reassessment. In May 1857 native troops at Meerut near Delhi mutinied because of a dispute over the use of cartridges coated with grease made from pork (unclean to Muslims) and beef (sacred to Hindus). The rebellion spread over much of northern India and was only suppressed after over a year of vigorous fighting. While the specific cause of the mutiny was only a spark which set light to much wider tensions, it was still profoundly symbolic in pointing up a sense of confrontation between the British and indigenous Indian religions. Responses to the Indian Mutiny reflected prior standpoints. On the one hand the evangelical supporters of missions saw it as a judgement of God on previous toleration of 'idolatry' and hence argued that the response to it should be redoubled efforts to secure the conversion of Indians to Christianity.[14] On the other hand, and more influential in government circles, was the view that the Mutiny had been caused by misplaced zeal in endeavouring to westernize and Christianize India too quickly.[15]

Both these perspectives were reflected in subsequent developments. The second half of the nineteenth century saw an expansion of Christian missionary activity in India and a significant degree of success in gaining converts, especially in the south of the subcontinent and among those in the lower castes who were alienated from Hinduism.[16] Nevertheless Christians in India remained overall a small minority and they also found themselves in competition with revivalist movements among other faiths, notably the Hindu Arya Samaj and the Muslim Deobandis.[17] At the end of the century theological developments gave consistency to the position of those Christians who wished to avoid straightforward confrontation: by the Edwardian period there was widespread acceptance of the idea of 'fulfilment', that other religions would gradually evolve into acceptance of a modified but still recognizable Christianity. The ideological necessity of immediate conversion was thus reduced.[18]

Meanwhile the government pragmatically sought to avoid antagonizing Indian cultural and religious sensibilities, but in practice found an entirely secular approach difficult to maintain. For one thing this was at odds with the Christian zeal of some of its own agents, with the reality of a state-supported Anglican Church in India, and with Nonconformist and Evangelical public opinion at home.[19] For another, British anxiety to respect Indian customs implied a need to come to terms with cultures that were themselves permeated by religion or at least with ritual. Following the passage of the Royal Titles Act of 1876, which made

Queen Victoria Empress of India in nominal succession to the Mughals, the viceroy Lord Lytton organized an elaborate Imperial Assemblage outside Delhi. This was designed to give ritual expression to the British concept of a social hierarchy in India with the princes filling the role of an aristocracy, leading their people in obedience to the Crown.[20]

The precedent was followed and developed on two further occasions, in 1903 following the accession of Edward VII, and in 1911 when George V and Queen Mary were present in person. These were now fully-fledged durbars, public ceremonies of recognition. In both instances there was a tacit acceptance of the religions of India, but also, away from the central ceremony, an explicitly Christian element in the proceedings. In 1903 the various princes in their addresses made references to their own religions, notably the Muslim Begum of Bhopal who dwelt on the happy coincidence of the date with the feast of Id-ul-Fitr and gave an assurance that 'faithfulness and obedience to the ruler are strictly ordained by the [Muslim] religion'. On the following Sunday the Bishop of Calcutta conducted an open-air service which was a 'definite element in the proceedings' and attributed the religious freedom of Indians to an essentially Christian principle of government.[21] Similarly in 1911 the King-Emperor attended an interdenominational parade service at which colours were dedicated and the Bishop of Madras spoke of the vast social and spiritual responsibilities of Empire. A few days later, however, the Emperor and Empress took part in a remarkable revival of the Mughal ceremony of *darshan* in which they appeared on the balcony of the Red Fort in front of processions of the various religious communities – Christian, Hindu, Muslim and Sikh – which all offered their own prayers for the welfare of the royal couple. This affair had undoubtedly been shrewdly stage-managed and it served to indicate how the need to give visibility and legitimacy to imperial rule was productive of increasing religious ambivalences.[22]

In Africa too religion played a noticeable part in sustaining the authority of the British colonial state. Here, moreover, Christian missionaries enjoyed a greater influence than did their counterparts in India. During the later nineteenth century, notably in Bechuanaland (Botswana), Nyasaland (Malawi) and Uganda, agitation by missionaries and by Christians at home was a significant factor in leading to the extension of formal control from London.[23] Once British rule had been established, its maintenance owed something to the somewhat incongruous importation of the rituals and hierarchy of the Church of England and, above all, to the cultivation of awe for a distant monarchy presented to Africans in semi-divine terms. Thus when the Prince of

Wales visited Basutoland in 1925 missionaries were disconcerted to hear an African chief say that 'I rejoice on this day like old Simeon of the Holy Scriptures who rejoiced because he had seen the Lord Jesus before he had slept in the graves of his fathers'.[24]

In regions of extensive white settlement – Australia, Canada, New Zealand and South Africa – a relationship between Christianity and the Empire could be maintained without the need for the kind of accommodations made where different religious and cultural traditions were encountered. During the last third of the nineteenth century an increasing consciousness of this 'Greater Britain' was evident in the churches. Every ten years from 1867 onwards Anglicans held Lambeth Conferences of bishops from all over the globe and the Free Churches gradually developed similar structures of their own. In 1897, the year of Victoria's diamond jubilee, the leading Baptist minister John Clifford went on a world tour. He seemed to strike a chord with his colonial audiences when he spoke of the value of imperial unity, the brotherhood of the Anglo-Saxon race, and its great mission from God as guardian of human liberties.[25] A few years later the remarkable interest in the third version of Holman Hunt's *The Light of the World* as it was exhibited around Australia, New Zealand and South Africa served further to illustrate the close links between religious and imperial sentiments.[26] Meanwhile British Protestant settlement had its counterpart in the emigration of the Irish to escape first famine and then limited opportunities in their homeland, leading to the development of strong Roman Catholic communities in Canada, Australia and New Zealand. For them the internationalist structure of their church and continuing interest in the turbulent politics of Ireland itself provided bonds of loyalty and identity which were in potential and sometimes in actual conflict with the dominant Protestant religious ethos of the Empire.[27]

The manner in which missionary endeavour and imperialism seemed increasingly in the late nineteenth century to be feeding off each other was not usually the original intention of the missionaries. Those of their number who advocated imperialistic policies, such as John Mackenzie in Bechuanaland, did so primarily because they believed that missionary interests were best served thereby.[28] Indeed, it must be noted that the extent of missionary and Christian interest was substantially wider than the political control of the British government. An important example was the development from the 1860s of James Hudson Taylor's China Inland Mission, which proved remarkably successful in recruiting men and women to work for narrowly defined evangelistic purposes in a vast country that was hardly a conceivable target for annexation.[29] In a very different way, visions of Anglo-Saxon Christian solidarity also stretched beyond the Empire to include a strong emphasis on links with the United States.[30]

During the last quarter of the nineteenth century, as the formal Empire expanded overseas and began to legitimize itself in more religious terms, there was also a notable change in the balance of public opinion at home. In the mid-nineteenth century there was a widespread desire to keep British overseas involvements as limited as possible. The word imperialism itself had a negative image, associated with the rule of the Bonapartes in France. The strength of this view as late as the 1870s was shown in vigorous criticism of the Royal Titles Act of 1876 which made Victoria Empress of India. By the 1890s, however, the Empire had firmly gripped the public imagination as was manifested particularly in the celebration of the diamond jubilee in 1897.[31]

Nowhere was the extent of the change in opinion more evident than among the Nonconformists. Until around 1880 they had been at the forefront of calls for limiting overseas commitments, advocating peace and non-intervention, but by the late 1890s many of them had become leading advocates of Empire. The reasons for this change were various: they were stirred by the inspiration of Livingstone's career; found a further Christian imperial martyr with the death of General Gordon at Khartoum in 1885; were influenced by the advocacy of annexation by contemporary missionaries; and were challenged by humanitarian needs.[32] There was also the ambivalent impact of the course adopted by their hero Gladstone. He had opposed the allegedly vainglorious expansionism associated with the Disraeli ministry of 1874–80, but still had his own strong view of Britain's role in the world as a force for international morality, which caused him to lead a widespread campaign in protest at atrocities by Turks against the Bulgarians in 1876. This movement attracted extensive support from Nonconformists. In his Midlothian speeches in 1879 Gladstone asserted the principle of seeking to preserve the peace of the world, avoiding needless entanglements, and emphasized the universal unity of humankind in the sight of God. At the same time he refused to renounce war and proclaimed the objective of fostering the strength of the Empire. It was on this basis that as Prime Minister in 1882 he could countenance British intervention in Egypt to control anarchy, and it seems that he carried Nonconformist opinion with him.[33] Indeed in due course, when imperial activity had been extended further south into the Sudan, Gladstone was to be far more strongly criticized for not saving Gordon than for becoming involved in the first place. By the 1890s, moreover, as Gladstone aged, even within his own party there were signs of a less cautious attitude to the Empire. In the medium term perhaps Gladstone was more successful in conveying to his supporters a sense of the moral and Christian justification for foreign involvement than in communicating the sometimes subtle and idealistic qualifications which he advocated. Herein lay an important source of inspiration and legitimacy for patriotic Christians.

The idea that Britain had received the Empire as a providential gift of God for the diffusion of Christianity and civilization had a long pedigree in nineteenth-century thought, but during the last decades of Victoria's reign it was a view particularly widely held by both politicians and churchmen. Thus the Earl of Carnarvon, Secretary for the Colonies under Disraeli, spoke in 1878 of the British duty to supply 'our native fellow-subjects . . . with a system where the humblest may enjoy freedom from oppression and wrong equally with the greatest; where the light of religion and morality can penetrate into the darkest dwelling places'. In 1897 Joseph Chamberlain, while holding the same office, referred to 'the work of civilisation' as 'our national mission'.[34] For its part the influential Anglican Evangelical journal *The Churchman* published reflections on the golden jubilee of 1887, in which it was suggested that the manner in which the rapid growth of the Empire had accompanied missionary endeavour was no coincidence:

And if this view be true, it follows not only that we hold our empire as the gift of God, but that it should be conferred upon us, not through any merit of our own, but because it pleased Him to choose us as the instrument for spreading His glory among the nations. It was for this that, during the ages, His Providence moulded our composite race, and endowed it with the characteristics of enterprise, love of commerce, national persistency, capacity for rule and religious earnestness. For this in the ages before Man was, He fitted these islands by situation and products to take the lead in universal, as distinguished from European politics; and for this too, when the time was come He gave us the priceless boon of 'the everlasting Gospel'. Is not this a more ennobling source of gratification than mere gloating over our material prosperity or our advance in the manipulation of natural forces? Can any destiny be higher than to be a messenger of God's goodwill to the world, and to have the privilege. . . of lifting the heavy curse from the sons of Ham?

When Queen Victoria died one poetical tribute stated still more strongly the link between Christian virtue and imperial success:

> A Righteous Ruler! Thou, Thy throne has planted
>   Beneath the Cross, where love was crucified
> Thy prayer for grace, in deep abundance granted,
>   Hath spread Thine Empire, far as flows the tide.[35]

A similar association of ideas was apparent in the tribute to the Queen placed beside her tomb at Frogmore by her daughter-in-law Queen Alexandra, which took the form of a cross resting on a Union Jack.

By the Edwardian period some churchmen were pursuing the logic of the link between Christianity and imperialism further and arguing for the concentration of missionary effort on the Empire. It was hoped that this would awaken the Christian patriotism of those hitherto indifferent to the work of the Church abroad. The Anglo-Saxon race was called by God to fulfil its 'vocation' to preach the Gospel. The Archbishop of Canterbury, Randall Davidson, acknowledged that some still felt there was a universal call to mission outside as well as inside the Empire, but noted the concern of others 'to give a Christian meaning to the misused and tortured word "Imperialism" and to make that meaning grow and glow throughout all the dominions of the King'.[36]

As the archbishop evidently recognized, the elevated sentiments of churchmen were merely the crest of the great wave of imperial enthusiasm that swept through Britain in the late Victorian and Edwardian years. Kipling, possessed of the earnestness which evoked its more spiritual aspects, nevertheless had the insight to appreciate the earthier but not necessarily less strong emotions that were also at work:

> By the old Moulmein Pagoda, lookin' lazy at the sea,
> There's a Burma girl a-settin, and I know she thinks o' me;
> For the wind is in the palm-trees and the temple-bells they
>   say:
> 'Come you back you British soldier; come you back to
>   Mandalay.'

The ex-soldier might walk 'with fifty 'ousemaids outer Chelsea to the Strand' but he still longed for his 'neater, sweeter maiden in a cleaner, greener land'. Though he had sufficient residual Christian prejudice to despise the

> Bloomin' idol made o' mud –
> Wot they called the Great Gawd Budd,

223

he still longed to be somewhere where 'there aren't no Ten Commandments'.[37]

The nature of popular attitudes to the Empire remains a matter of considerable debate among scholars, but there is credibility in the view that many were swayed more by the appeal of the exotic and exciting as a release from humdrum lives, than by the idealistic aspiration to spread civilization and Christianity. Moreover fascination for foreign climes and cultures was juxtaposed with a raucous xenophobia in which the superiority of Britain was assumed, not argued. Such was the culture of the music hall and of important strands in the popular art and literature of the period. These attitudes manifested themselves in the celebration of the diamond jubilee in 1897 and the relief of Mafeking in 1900. If such popular imperialism could at times achieve a quasi-religious intensity, its tone and aspirations were a long way from those of official Christianity.[38]

Nevertheless there was no straightforward polarization of religious and secular motives. A substantial proportion of the literature that contributed to popular feeling for the Empire was produced by mission-ary societies and other religious organizations concerned to diffuse a moral and spiritual message. The missionary adventure story had its appeal alongside the military one, and Sunday Schools guaranteed its continuing widespread promotion.[39] School textbooks set out the course of British history with a moral conviction that 'spelled out patriotism . . . with a fervour that with some edged on the religious'.[40] During the early twentieth century the celebration of Empire Day gained increasing momentum, and at least in the eyes of its creator, the Earl of Meath, this had an essentially religious and spiritual purpose.[41]

The contention of this section is not that missionary zeal and religious earnestness were the dominant characteristic of British imperial culture, either at home or abroad. Rather it is suggested that by the close of Victoria's reign such aspirations had increasingly become merged in a wider stream of sentiment in favour of the Empire, giving it a colouring of moral and spiritual legitimacy. As Lord Hugh Cecil, son of the Marquess of Salisbury, put it, 'by making prominent to our own minds the importance of missionary work, we should to some extent sanctify the spirit of Imperialism'.[42] Imperialism thus shared in the ambiguities which, as we have noted in previous chapters, were also characteristic of the unofficial religion, politics and culture of the period. In order to understand this situation further, and to relate it to the climate in which large-scale war was initially enthusiastically welcomed in 1914, we must now turn to consider the role of religion in relation to the advance of military values in later Victorian and Edwardian society and culture.

2. THE CHURCH MILITANT AND THE CHRISTIAN ARMY

At the beginning of our period the Crimean War proved to be something of a turning point in the relationship between the churches, the army and warfare. The army of the Duke of Wellington's day, whatever its fighting capacity, was in moral terms readily accepted at the evaluation of its own leader as the 'scum of the earth'. As we saw in Chapter 5, Catherine Marsh's biography of Hedley Vicars served to challenge that assumption. Moreover, according to Marsh, there was no conflict of loyalties for the Christian soldier:

> There are those who, in the face of examples to the contrary, still maintain that entire devotion of the heart to God must withdraw a man from many of the active duties of life, and who would be prepared to concede that in making a good Christian you may spoil a good soldier. To them the subject of this memoir affords a fresh and ample refutation. . . . He lived, during months of sickness and pestilence, to commend the religion he professed to all around him – while he pursued the duties of his profession with distinguished ardour and constancy – maintaining as a Christian a high reputation for bravery among the bravest of his companions in arms, and winning on his first battle-field the blood-stained laurels so soon to be exchanged for the crown of glory that fadeth not away.[43]

Here was what became in effect a manifesto for the view that Christianity and warfare went well together. There were numerous influences which contributed to the wider acceptance of this linkage during the next half-century, some of which must now be explored.

The case of Hedley Vicars illustrates a wider tendency to find in specific military men a model for virtuous Christian life and action. There was nothing new in the veneration of heroes, but at an earlier date their lives had not been so readily cast in a Christian framework, as was apparent in the reactions of preachers to Nelson's death at Trafalgar in 1805. From the 1840s, however, there was an increasing concern to relate a man's courage and achievements in war to his inner life and spiritual destiny. So it is significant that it was only during the second half of the nineteenth century that the problem of Nelson's adulterous relationship with Lady Hamilton began to perplex and embarrass his biographers.[44] Meanwhile within a few years Hedley Vicars was over-shadowed in the Protestant military pantheon by Sir Henry Havelock who served with distinction during the suppression of the Indian Mutiny before dying at the relief of Lucknow in November 1857. Havelock was a zealous Baptist, but only in the last year of his life did he become famous as a soldier. It is the more significant therefore that he was venerated not just in the churches, but also in the public houses named after this vigorous advocate of temperance, and through the rare distinction of a statue in Trafalgar Square.[45]

The ultimate military hero, however, was not to emerge for another generation. In 1884 General Charles Gordon, a man of deep if unor-thodox Christian convictions, was sent to Khartoum with secret instructions to evacuate the Sudan in the face of the revolt led by the Mahdi, a self-appointed Muslim messiah. Instead on arrival he tried to hold on to the Nile Valley but became cut off from Egypt and surrounded by the Mahdi's forces. Troops sent to rescue him arrived just too late to prevent the Fall of Khartoum during which Gordon himself was killed on 26 January 1885. Despite the way in which Gordon's fate had to a significant extent been attributable to his own rashness and disobedience he was immediately hailed as a Christian and national hero and an example and inspiration to churches and country. Moreover, the confused accounts of the manner of his death were interpreted in a manner which served to reinforce the image of a hero and martyr. Whereas it appears most probable that he was simply shot in the confusion of the capture of the town, the myth developed that he had died in a dramatic confrontation with his Muslim attackers, 'march-ing in all the pride of faith . . . to a martyr's death' (Winston Churchill).[46]

Such admiration of particular heroes reflected a wider fascination with the code of chivalry. The Prince Consort is represented as a knight in armour on his cenotaph at Windsor Castle. Similarly, after his ill-starred grandson, the Duke of Clarence, died in 1892, a stained-glass window was installed at St Mary's Church, Sand Hutton, near York, commemorating 'a Prince greatly beloved and early mourned'. The design portrays St George clad in shining armour and sharing the features of the deceased prince.[47] Such images not only linked Chris-tianity with the monarchy, but linked both to chivalric endeavour. In 1912 male passengers went down with the Titanic as the band repor-tedly played 'Abide with me', and Scott and Oates perished in the Antarctic. The 'heroism' of such deaths were endued with a quasi-religious significance that, as in the case of Gordon, obscured the very human rashness and incompetence that had helped to bring them about.[48]

The frame of mind that gave a spiritual quality to material struggle and warfare was, as noted at the beginning of the chapter, both reflected and fostered by the language of some later Victorian hymns. The metaphor of warfare in relation to the Christian can be traced back to St Paul's Epistle to the Ephesians, but the context there was explicitly one of standing against 'the wiles of the devil'. Such was the original message of Charles Wesley's hymn 'Soldiers of Christ, arise', but from the mid-nineteenth century this appeared in hymnbooks in the severely edited form still familiar today in which the Christian's battle appeared as a much less specific and more material one. A similar message of contemporary struggle was conveyed by new hymns such as William Walsham How's 'Soldiers of the Cross, arise', written in the first year of the Crimean War, and 'For all the saints who from their labours rest'. J. B. Monsell's 'Fight the good fight' (1863) was similarly vague as to the nature of the fight in question. Such linkages acquired further force from the impact on hymnody of the American Civil War, transmitted across the Atlantic by revivalists, which stirred hymns such as Ira Sankey's 'Hold the fort, for I am coming, Jesus signals still' and Julia Ward Howe's 'Mine eyes have seen the glory of the coming of the Lord', sung to the tune of 'John Brown's body'.[49]

As Christians became soldiers it was an easy step to regard rank-and-file soldiers as well as the heroic leaders as potential or actual Christians. An early example of this tendency was given by Charles Kingsley in his *Brave Words for Brave Soldiers and Sailors* sent out to the troops before Sebastopol in the Crimea in the winter of 1855. He sought to boost their morale, assuring them that Christ's blessing was with them, as symbolized by their regimental colours. 'He who fights for Queen and country in a just cause', he wrote, 'is fighting not only in the Queen's army, but in Christ's army.'[50]

It followed that the Church as well as the army needed to take the task of recruiting its soldiers seriously. Although attempts to evangelize in the armed forces dated back to the late eighteenth century, these initially had only scant success and limited support. From the 1850s, however, the Soldiers' Friend and Army Scripture Readers' Society developed large-scale operations, distributing publications, setting up Bible classes, and employing agents to visit the troops. The Wesleyans moved into work in the army with particular enthusiasm and success. The churches were also instrumental in providing social facilities for soldiers at a period when the military authorities conspicuously failed to do so. Nevertheless the government did improve official religious provision by appointing a well-organized staff of full-time Anglican, Roman Catholic and Presbyterian chaplains. This policy formed part of a wider objective of elevating the physical, social and moral conditions of military service. [51]

Evaluation of the long-term effectiveness of such activity is difficult, but at the end of the nineteenth century it was at least possible for an army chaplain to believe that the men fully concurred in the Christianity he preached.[52] Moreover, although the provision of Presbyterian and Roman Catholic chaplains had reflected an intention to make the army Christian rather than specifically Anglican, the general trend in the religious affiliation of the men was towards the Church of England. The proportion of declared Anglicans in the army rose from 59.3 per cent in 1861 to 70.6 per cent in 1913, while that of Roman Catholics fell from 28 per cent to 14.7 per cent over the same period. The proportion of Scots and Presbyterians also declined.[53] The result was to render the army more susceptible to a Christianity couched in patriotic English terms. The linkage between commitment to God and the cause of the nation was a close and explicit one as illustrated by the address of George V to the troops in Delhi in 1911 when he presented new colours immediately after the open air durbar parade service: 'A colour is a sacred ensign, even by its inspiration . . . a rallying point in battle. It is the emblem of duty: the outward sign of your allegiance to God, your Sovereign, and Country'.[54]

If the Edwardian army had acquired a superficially greater religiosity than its early Victorian predecessor, this achievement probably owed a great deal to the education and experience of its officers and men before they enlisted, something which they shared with their civilian contemporaries. Those of the élite who spent their formative years in a public school had undoubtedly been exposed to a considerable amount of religious instruction, the character of which changed significantly during the later nineteenth century. There was a shift away from the cultivation of the ideal of manliness as promoted by Thomas Arnold and his immediate disciples, as the attainment of spiritual and intellectual maturity. Rather, from around 1860 onwards, a more athletic concept of the muscular Christian began to gain ground in the public schools, inspired in part, as we noted in the previous chapter, by the novels of Thomas Hughes and Charles Kingsley. Organized games became compulsory and the successful sportsman was likely to receive the accolades of his headmaster as well as of his schoolfellows. In schools often headed by clergy, Christian language continued much in evidence, but became associated with material rather than spiritual struggle, and with institutional ethos rather than internal conviction. On that basis it could be readily assimilated by most boys, but more as a diffuse source of nostalgia and inspiration than as a coherent theological creed.[55]

By the turn of the century, moreover, there were signs that 'muscular Christianity' was developing further into 'imperial Christianity'. Headmasters such as H. H. Almond at Loretto and H. W. Moss at Shrewsbury were firmly convinced of the divinely appointed duty of Britain to lead the world and spread the Gospel, and lost no opportunity of so instructing their pupils. Furthermore the means to this end were explicitly military, as illustrated by the formation of cadet corps at various schools between the Boer War and the First World War. Moss, one of the pioneers in this movement, readily justified it in biblical language.[56] The associations made between national pride and Christianity were testified to by the painter C. R. Nevinson recalling his education at Uppingham:

> I attended endless divine services; listened to strange sermons delivered by doctors of divinity in which Englishmen were confused with God, Nelson with Jesus Christ, Lady Hamilton with the Virgin Mary. The German Fascists . . . are fed on no greater confusion of patriotism and religion.[57]

When the result of such a combination was not cynicism it was likely to be fervent nationalism and militarism.

There were an increasing number of organizations which served to convey a Christian and militaristic ethos to those who were not members of the public-school educated élite. The trend was set by the Volunteer movement, authorized by the government in May 1859 in reaction to fear of French invasion, and intended to provide a home defence force. The formation of companies was dependent on local initiatives, and in many cases these owed much to the support of the Anglican clergy.[58] Charles Kingsley was an enthusiastic advocate, perceiving spiritual and moral as well as military and patriotic advantages, as he set out in a sermon to a Volunteer camp in 1867:

> if you learn to endure hardness . . . you will be . . . alike the soldiers of Christ, able and willing to fight in that war of which he is the Supreme Commander, and which will endure as long as there is darkness and misery upon the earth; even the battle of the living God against the basic instincts of our nature, against

ignorance and folly, against lawlessness and tyranny, against brutality and sloth. [59]

The movement also attracted the interest of evangelical philanthropists, such as John MacGregor, also promoter of the Open-Air Mission and the Shoe Black Society, and John Hope, a wealthy lawyer who had already built a vigorous teetotal and anti-Catholic organization in Edinburgh. As well as being captain of a Volunteer company, Hope also created a cadet organization for boys involved in his other societies. [60]

Another enthusiastic Scottish Volunteer, William Smith, was in 1883 to become the founder of the Boys' Brigade. Troubled by the rowdiness of his Sunday School in Glasgow he decided to combat this by using a military style of organization and discipline, targeted particularly at the thirteen to seventeen age group. The primary objective, however, remained religious, and Bible classes and worship were prominent features of the programme alongside drill, bands and annual camps. The movement grew steadily during the next thirty years, achieving a total membership of over 60,000 in 1910. Its strength lay among Presbyterians and Nonconformists, but an Anglican rival, the Church Lads Brigade, was formed in 1891 and in 1908 this had around 70,000 members. The idea was also taken up by the Jewish Lads Brigade (1895), which contributed to the integration of East End immigrants into English life; and by the relatively small-scale and short-lived Catholic Boys' Brigade. [61]

It is reasonable to question how far such organizations fulfilled the religious ends of their leaders. The Bishop of Down and Connor in 1899 told a Boys' Brigade rally that 'Christian manliness is a wonderful thing, the objection which a Boy has to religion is removed by it', but for many, one suspects, the attraction remained the 'manliness', as expressed in a sense of adventure and the opportunity to go to camp, rather than the Christianity. In 1911, moreover, the Church Lads Brigade acquired official links with the Territorial Army and, unlike the Boys' Brigade, came to subordinate religious objectives to military ones. [62] In 1908 the Boy Scout movement was set up, with much less explicitly religious objectives than the Boys' Brigade, and enjoyed rapid growth. Nevertheless here too the churches played an important organizational and enabling role. [63] What is undeniable, moreover, is that these youth organizations served in effect, if not always in intent, to blend religious, patriotic and military inspiration. The Boys' Brigade and its imitators were to prove to be particularly fertile recruiting grounds in the First World War: for example, of the fifty-nine men named on a war memorial in St Nicholas Church in Durham twenty-eight had been members of the first Durham Boys' Brigade.

Women and girls had increasing opportunities to share in parallels to this male activity. The Girls' Friendly Society, launched in 1874, was intended to associate young women together in the cause of religion, purity and the family. It had nearly 200,000 members by 1913, while the Mothers' Union, formed in 1885 to promote similar values among married women, enjoyed a correspondingly substantial degree of success.[64] Such organizations were on the face of it quite the reverse of militaristic, encouraging women to cultivate their feminine qualities, and to exert their influence in the domestic rather than the public arena. Nevertheless, by elevating ideals of patriotic Christian womanhood, they provided girls with a significant counterpoint to the military images of manhood which were influencing their brothers, ideas that could be integrated together through the fashionable code of chivalry. Moreover girls' organizations began in the early twentieth century to share something of the crusading spirit of their male counterparts. The historian of the Girls' Friendly Society could see its members in the terms of A. C. Ainger's hymn, marching forth in the strength of God, while in 1900 the Girls' Guildry was formed as an equivalent of the Boys' Brigade, even emulating its marching and military drill. The Girl Guides followed in 1910, but due to poor organization this movement was in its early years much less successful than the Boy Scouts. [65]

The Salvation Army, which took shape in the late 1870s, at first sight seems another obvious illustration of the same blending of military and Christian ideals. However, in contrast with the boys' organizations just discussed, the military styles and language were more obviously metaphorical, and the overriding aims were evangelistic and social rather than patriotic. The widespread participation of women and the rapid assumption of an international character also served to soften the impression. Indeed, the Church Army, formed in 1882 as an Anglican imitation, fairly rapidly lost much of its military ethos. What both movements indicate, however, is that in the culture of the late nineteenth century, even when the purpose was religious rather than national, military forms had considerable usefulness.[66]

The work of organizations like the Boys' Brigade was complemented by an extensive periodical and fictional literature which promulgated values of patriotic Christian manliness. A significant role was played by the *Boy's Own Paper*, started in 1879 by the Religious Tract Society, offering material on hobbies, sport and the like and coupling a strongly Christian tone with stories of intrepid adventure. By the mid-1880s it had a print run of over half a million. A similar note was struck by novels for boys, although here there was a noticeable development from the pious tone of the works of R. M. Ballantyne (1825–94) to the more robust and less introspective heroes in the books of G. A. Henty (1832–1902), tremendously popular at the turn of the century.[67] In literature as in youth organizations a complementary role for women was also defined. The *Girl's Own Paper* began publication in 1880, while novels designed for a female readership depicted women as sympathetic observers and supporters of the exploits of their menfolk. They also served as reminders of spiritual convictions and values should the muscularity of a male hero run the risk of wholly superseding his Christianity.[68]

By such means the influence of militaristic forms of Christian manliness were diffused to an extensive proportion of the population, certainly far beyond the public schools with which their exposition has been primarily associated. Indeed there is some evidence that in Edwardian Britain working- and middle-class schoolchildren were exposed to even more vigorous and less religiously nuanced militarism and patriotism than their upper-class counterparts. Nevertheless there is uncertainty regarding how far such ideas penetrated into the working classes. The hundreds of thousands who joined youth organizations and read literature with a Christian militaristic tone need to be set against the millions who did not. On the other hand in the Boer War the extent of military recruitment and the signs of popular enthusiasm at home, most notably on Mafeking Night, 19 May 1900, indicated an at least temporary engagement in patriotic imperial ventures. The factors contributing to popular jingoism at this period were various, but it is noteworthy that in his contemporary analysis J. A. Hobson gave significant attention to what he called 'Christianity in khaki'.[69]

Charles Kingsley's utterances at the time of the Crimean War serve as a reminder that there was nothing new about clergy who wholeheartedly saw the cause of God as being served by military conflict:

> For the Lord Jesus Christ is not only the *Prince of Peace*; he is the *Prince of War* too. He is the Lord of Hosts, the God of armies; and whoever fights in a just war, against tyrants and oppressors, he is fighting on Christ's side, and Christ is fighting on his side; Christ is his Captain and his leader, and he can be in no better service.[70]

This was, however, but one extreme of a spectrum of views apparent in the British Protestant churches in the 1850s, which stretched in the other direction to the advocacy of pacifist non-resistance. Particularly among evangelical Anglicans and Nonconformists, responses to war were rooted in an apocalyptic and millennial frame of mind in which events were regarded as the working out of fundamental divine purposes. Radically opposed perceptions were possible according to how the divine will was perceived. On the one hand were those who anticipated the dawning of an age of universal peace without intervening cataclysm, and accordingly sought to hasten its advent through the efforts of the pacifist Peace Society. On the other, and more numerous, were views of war as an instrument of God's judgement. These were of two kinds: either the Almighty was employing Britain as an agent in the divine purpose, or, less optimistically, using war to chasten the British nation itself. In the former case war could be waged with conviction; in the latter it must spur spiritual self-examination.[71]

During the ensuing half century millennialist preoccupation declined and the more negative and cautious theological responses to war correspondingly lost ground. However, the idea of the nation at war as an instrument in God's purposes retained a strong appeal in an era of strong patriotism and imperialism, especially when the starker ideas of divine judgement and accountability with which it had been associated passed from fashion. Meanwhile among those Nonconformists with pacifist tendencies, the Gladstonian vision of Britain's role as a guardian of international morality came to supersede readiness to advocate peace at almost any price.[72] At the same time Nonconformists were influenced by the wider trend to militarism, as was demonstrated by their support for the Boys' Brigade. Thus in the Boer War, while there was a vocal minority of Christian leaders who opposed the war, such opposition was not usually rooted in any general pacifism, but rather reflected a feeling that the British cause was not a just one. John Clifford, despite his Christian imperialist ideas, was one of the most prominent advocates of such a view. This was shared by the chairman of a meeting of Congregationalists in October 1901:

> Through history God was on the side of the small peoples and might there not be some great store of service to come to the world in the future through the despised Boer of the Transvaal? It was the passion of freedom in them which made them want to do justice to men who were fighting for freedom.[73]

This outlook, though, came in 1914 to be a basis for war rather than peace: no longer was it Britain which was threatening the freedom of small nations, but Austria and Germany in their respective attacks on Serbia and Belgium. The sense that there was an overwhelming moral case for British involvement was a factor of considerable importance in uniting Christian opinion behind the war. Thus, while Clifford might deplore the flawed attitudes and diplomacy that had contributed to the outbreak of war, he saw the conflict itself in black and white terms:

> The battle now proceeding is a battle of principles, central and fundamental to man's existence, development, progress and well-being in all the coming ages. It is a battle of moral ideals and ideas against immoral; of spiritual forces against material.[74]

Even the chairman of the Peace Society supported British involvement in the war.[75]

The readiness of Nonconformists to go to war in 1914 was but the final link in the chain of Christian readiness to foster militaristic values and to countenance armed conflict that had been gathering strength during the preceding decades. It was, furthermore, a vision that promoted warfare in an imperial context which subsumed for a time the smaller scale conflicts of religion and nationality within the British Isles. In Ireland by 1914 prominent voices in both the Protestant and Catholic communities were presenting their confrontation as a 'fight' and Patrick Pearse in particular hailed bloodshed as 'a cleansing and sanctifying thing'.[76] When war broke out on the continent, however, most readily suspended their own quarrel for the present and committed themselves to the Allied cause. Only 11,000 men out of the 180,000-strong Irish Volunteers, a paramilitary force formed in 1913 to stiffen the campaign for Home Rule, refused to support the war.[77] Irish sympathies were stirred particularly by the plight of Belgium – another small nation – a factor that was also apparent in Scotland and Wales. Walter Mursell, minister of the Coats Memorial Baptist Church in Paisley declared in a sermon in November 1914:

> That one word 'Belgium' – is enough to justify our entry into this war, enough to rouse the chivalry of our people, enough to determine us to fight to such a finish that tyranny will never be able to create or to grasp such an opportunity again.

Belgium, he suggested, was Christ in modern form.[78] Similarly extravagant language was used by George Adam Smith, Principal of Aberdeen University, who equated the war with a sacrament 'in the full sense of that name as we Scots have been brought up to understand it'.[79] Meanwhile in Wales many Nonconformist ministers were second to none in their support for British involvement, an enthusiasm that was catalysed through the leadership of Lloyd George.[80] One versifier in lines that might seem grossly insensitive in their 'English' assumptions summed up this perceived unity that transcended distinctions of nationality and class:

> Sons of Shannon, Tamar, Trent,
> Men of the Lothians, Men of Kent
> Essex, Wessex, shire and shire,
> Mates of the net, the mine, the fire,
> Lads of desk and wheel and loom,
> Noble and trader, squire and groom,
> Come where the bugles of England play. . .[81]

Just as the distinction between 'England' and 'Britain' was very blurred, it was difficult to discern where religious motivation ended and secular began. The Bishop of London, Arthur Winnington-Ingram, revelled in appearing in uniform as an army chaplain and his sermons and speeches were a rousing and effective contribution to Lord Kitchener's recruiting effort. He claimed that, 'Love of our Country is implanted in us by God, and if we look at our duty to our Country as duty to God we put it on the very highest ground.[82] Meanwhile, in order to express his feelings on the outbreak of war, Rupert Brooke was moved to invoke the deity he barely believed in:

> Now God be thanked Who has matched us with His hour,
> And caught our youth, and wakened us from sleeping.[83]

Such utterances characterize a frame of mind prominent in 1914, one that was not merely a sudden response to the European crisis, but a culmination of the interpenetration of religion, patriotism and militarism during the preceding decades. The outbreak of war was accompanied by a striking, if short-lived, increase in churchgoing, but this did not imply straightforward assent to official Christian teachings. It was observed that 'The religion of 90 per cent of the men at the front is not distinctively Christian, but a religion of patriotism and valour, tinged with chivalry, and at best merely coloured with sentiment and emotion borrowed from Christianity'.[84]

The role of Christian militarism and imperialism in contributing to a state of mind in which world war could obtain such general acceptance in 1914 has to be viewed in conjunction with other cultural and political forces which cannot be considered in detail here. These included the working out of 'social Darwinist' ideas, that among races and nations of human beings as among species of animals only the fittest would survive, and that conflict was accordingly inevitable. Specific consciousness of rivalry with Germany was manifested in popular support for the naval arms race and in the growth of the National Service League in the decade before the war.[85] In art the work and philosophy of the futurists and vorticists suggested a positive acceptance of violence. In part organized religion was simply reflecting society as a whole, but through the channels outlined above it was also having a formative influence. The effect was to produce a nationalism of the quasi-religious kind that we defined in Chapter 1, making ultimate spiritual claims for the British nation.

This analysis must be set in the wider context of the place of religion in society on the eve of the First World War. To the extent that the movements described were part and parcel of official religion, their full impact was limited primarily to those social groups who were regular participants in institutional religious life. Certainly there is evidence that the Boys' Brigade and similar bodies could provoke antagonism rather than enthusiasm in working-class districts.[86] However, the channels of contact with unofficial religion discussed in Chapter 4 point to the probability of an influence, albeit much more diffuse, even on working-class non-churchgoers. The xenophobic strain in popular culture, also notably fostered by music halls, was potentially receptive soil for ideological linking of the cause of the nation with the dignity of a moral and religious crusade. This was likely to be mediated in particular through hymns, day and Sunday School education and the work of the churches in the armed forces. The predominance of the national rather than the Christian is consistent with the pattern of selective assimilation evident in other aspects of unofficial religion. Meanwhile the ambivalent place of religion in élite culture, as described in Chapter 7, meant that here too it was readily possible to imbibe a heady sense of fighting for absolute values without being really sure what these were. Such was the climate in which David Lloyd George could draw on his Nonconformist heritage and capture the mood of the people by pointing them in biblically resonant language to 'the everlasting things that matter for a nation – the high peaks we had forgotten, of Honour, Duty, Patriotism, and, clad in glittering white, the great pinnacle of Sacrifice, pointing like a rugged finger to Heaven'.[87]

3.   THE GREAT WAR AND AFTER

The impact of the two world wars of the twentieth century on the life of state and society can usefully be compared with the effect of a serious illness on the life of an individual. For some prewar political and social systems, notably Tsarist Russia and Habsburg Austria, the comparison of terminal illness is appropriate. In the British case, the experience was analogous rather to a patient who suffers from a prolonged and life-threatening disease, but ultimately recovers after surgery, although with the sense that life will never be quite the same again. During the period of sickness previous occupations have had to be put aside, while priorities and values are tested as never before. Previous experience of illness and endeavours to stay healthy prove a psychological handicap, because they arouse unrealistic expectations. To conclude the analogy, British society during the war, and religious organizations in particular evoke the image of a fitness and health-food fanatic who, after a long period of life afflicted by nothing worse than colds and migraines, has to face up to the awareness that he has a disabling cancer.

As war became the overwhelming and inescapable background to existence, there were significant respects in which religious life continued uninterrupted. The regular round of Sunday services was maintained in churches and chapels as it always had been; associated organizations continued in being. After the initial spiritual excitement of 1914, participation and membership tended to decline somewhat, but not catastrophically, and there was sometimes a reversal after the war. Thus numbers of Easter Day communicants in the Church of England fell from 2.3 million in 1913 to 2.1 million in 1917; but recovered to 2.2 million in 1921 and nearly 2.4 million in 1925. Total Methodist membership in Great Britain fell from 829,565 in 1913 to 801,721 in 1920, but rose to 843,825 in 1928. Other figures, such as Anglican Sunday School attendances, never regained prewar levels, but downward trends were usually in evidence before the war. In general the longer term patterns examined in Chapter 3 appear more significant.[88]

Nevertheless behind the statistical, institutional and ritual continuities there was considerable upheaval in the life of official religion. Churches became short-staffed as clergy and ministers of military age left for the forces; pastoral resources were stretched by the need for ministry to the bereaved and the suffering. The conflict came to influence the content of worship and devotion and the programmes of voluntary organizations were restructured in order to assist the war effort.[89] Under such circumstances further blending of the Christian and the national was inevitable. A Church of Scotland clergyman later recalled with some embarrassment how 'the church . . . had become an instrument of the State', and how he had himself displayed 'a huge Union jack and the national flag of Scotland . . . upon the east wall of the church'.[90]

It is noteworthy that this tendency appears to have been as true of the Nonconformist and Presbyterian Churches as of the Church of England. The war effort received influential support from men such as A. T. Guttery, President of the Primitive Methodist Conference in 1916–17 and Robertson Nicoll, editor of the influential *British Weekly*, whose background was in the Free Church of Scotland. The leading Baptist, F. B. Meyer, saw a transcendental significance in the war, and in 1915 threw his weight behind the campaign for military recruitment.[91] Although the Free Churches had already steadily been growing closer to the state, the war marked a culmination of this process.

The response of Christians to the war as it went on can be illustrated from the pages of *The Churchman* magazine, whose moderate Anglican evangelicalism was probably broadly representative of opinion. In September 1914 the nation was unequivocally judged to have gone to war in a righteous cause and, although the exact place of the war in the divine purposes might be unclear, it was still possible to believe that God was overruling the clash of armies. In October the favourable course of the war was seen as the triumph of righteousness over evil through which God was speaking to the nation. By the late summer of 1915 a note of perplexity at the lack of rapid success had crept in, but there was acceptance of the need to take 'long views' and to trust 'in the ultimate triumph of Right over Might' and satisfaction at widespread acceptance of the 'sacrificial principle'. As the war wore on there were continuing signs that *The Churchman* saw it as a spiritual as well as military struggle: hopes for religious revival at home were closely linked with desire for victory in France. January 1917 saw unbroken resolution to continue the war 'until, by God's good help, the forces of the King and his Allies have crushed the infamy of German militarism', and at the end of 1918 eventual victory was hailed as an answer to prayer and a working out of God's purposes through human means.[92]

There were always voices among the clergy who sought to qualify militaristic impulses. In November 1914 the Archbishop of York, Cosmo Gordon Lang, anxious to check crude hatred, made an impromptu reference at a public meeting to his 'sacred memory' of the Kaiser at the funeral of Queen Victoria. Although the general tone of his speech had been strongly anti-German he was still widely denounced and complained at the difficulty of getting a hearing even 'for some faint voices of the Christian spirit'.[93] As the conflict continued naïve enthusiasm increasingly gave way to a combination of resolution and resignation, and the overwhelming presence of the war exposed Christian difficulties when specific issues were faced. The Archbishop of

Canterbury, Randall Davidson, endeavoured with cautious courage to balance patriotic loyalty with a wider Christian vision. More junior clergy and ministers faced the personal dilemma of whether to enlist, and if so whether to choose non-combatant roles. When conscription was introduced in 1916 this raised the question of the attitude of the churches to conscientious objectors. Others agonized over whether reprisals for German air-raids were justified, or struggled to maintain an internationalist Christian vision in the face of the conflict.[94]

On the other hand those numerous Christian leaders who in 1914 had publicly hailed the war as a clear-cut conflict of good and evil in which God was self-evidently on the side of Britain now worked through the logic of their position. The Bishop of London stressed that he had no hatred for those 'thousands of humble believing Christians' in Germany who had been misled by their leaders, but he still characterized the conflict as one between 'Christ and Odin'. When casualties began to mount he saw their lives as offered in the cause of Christ as well as of Britain:

> You have lost your boys, but what are they? Martyrs – martyrs as really as St Stephen was a martyr – martyrs dying for their faith as really as St Stephen, the first martyr, died for his. They looked up when they died in the trenches, or in the little cottage where they were carried, they looked up and they saw JESUS standing on the right hand of GOD. And he is keeping them safe for you there when the time comes. Covered with imperishable glory they pass to deathless life.

Many other clergy dwelt on the theme of martyrdom making a striking contrast with the more limited significance accorded to death in battle by nineteenth-century preachers.[95]

If an Anglican bishop could use such language it was inevitable that others would pursue further the spiritual nature of war and sacrifice. The poet F. W. Orde Ward wrote that,

> Our Lord is crucified in France
> In Belgium's holy places.

According to the poem, what Christ felt most deeply was

> That Luther's sons should be the first to hound
> Luther's great master to the slaughter ground.[96]

Kipling, whose son was killed in the war, in one of his poems translated the garden of Gethsemane to Picardy. Such connections were evoked on canvas by *The Great Sacrifice*, a popular picture by James Clark which shows the crucified Christ hanging above a dead soldier. Similar associations were made in verse by Sir John Arkwright in the hymn 'O valiant hearts', later widely used in Armistice Day services in the interwar period. Arkwright seemed to link Christ's cross to our 'lesser Calvaries', and asserted that the war dead, having drunk 'His cup of sacrifice', were 'following through death the martyred Son of God'.[97]

During the war music provided a powerful medium for the blending of religious and patriotic impulses. Music was regarded by one army chaplain as a 'powerful means' of 'spiritual treatment', while the Church was hailed as the most secure stronghold of national music.[98] In 1915 Elgar sketched out the music for a setting of three of Laurence Binyon's war poems, but for the moment did not publish it. He had been troubled over the stanza in the 'Fourth of August' which referred to the Germans:

> She fights the fraud that feeds desire on
> Lies, in a lust to enslave or kill,
> The barren creed of blood and iron,
> Vampire of Europe's wasted will.

In 1917, however, the composer, his sense of moral polarization reinforced by intervening events, at last completed the work by a calculated re-use of the music from *The Dream of Gerontius* which had related to the demons. During the war *Gerontius* itself enjoyed a revival, and the allusion could hardly have been lost on contemporary audiences. The full song cycle, 'The Spirit of England', conveyed a fervent and spiritual patriotism and was received with great enthusiasm.[99]

Meanwhile the feeling among churchmen that the war had a spiritual dimension encouraged efforts for the revival and extension of evangelism and pastoral care. On the home front, the National Mission of Repentance and Hope was held by the Church of England in the autumn of 1916, but it suffered from confused objectives and brought no substantial success.[100] A similar indictment can be made of much of the work of the chaplains with the forces. Despite high expectations from their work, their leadership was deficient, and their activities initially unduly constrained. To many soldiers they seemed remote and aloof. The situation improved as the war went on, and there were numerous individual chaplains, for example, Geoffrey Studdert-Kennedy ('Woodbine Willie') and Philip ('Tubby') Clayton, who had most effective ministries. Roman Catholic chaplains appear to have been particularly successful, perhaps because their administration of the sacraments gave them a well-defined and comforting role among frightened, suffering and dying men.[101]

The religious condition of the men at the front was a matter of controversy and varied interpretation at the time, and has remained so ever since. On the one hand one can point to the shock of the chaplains at the ignorance of basic Christian teaching among the troops and their failure to achieve any general turning to the churches despite the close links that were made between military and spiritual warfare. Perhaps such associations were part of the problem: men who had seen their comrades slaughtered in their thousands at the Battle of the Somme naturally found it less easy to believe in the war as part of the divine purpose. When unburied bodies had to be left to rot in no man's land, and human flesh and bones protruded in macabre fashion from the ground and from the sides of trenches, glib teaching about the Resurrection could not be readily assimilated.[102]

However, even while official religion appeared to make inadequate sense of the sufferings of war, some unofficial beliefs flourished. For example, early in the war there were accounts of soldiers who claimed to have seen strange lights, or mysterious figures tending the wounded, the so-called 'angels of Mons'. Although the rumours could be traced back to an avowedly fictional short story in the *Evening News*, knowledge of such a prosaic origin did not check their spread. Evidently there were many, at home as well as on the front, who *wanted* to believe in such indications of supernatural involvement. Significantly, though, the supposed miraculous intervention was perceived not in traditional Protestant terms as a manifestation of the providential power of God, but rather as the activity of intermediate agency. In this respect the 'angels of Mons' story provides a revealing insight into the spiritual world of the trenches, where fatalism and semi-magical beliefs were stronger than orthodox Christianity. The growth of spiritualism during the war added a further dimension, and was stimulated not only by active attempts to contact the dead with the assistance of mediums, but also by combatants who had disconcertingly vivid dreams of encounters with friends who had been killed. Such trends were reinforced by the advocacy of Sir Oliver Lodge, a leading physicist, who in 1916 published communications with his son since his death at Ypres; and Sir Arthur Conan Doyle, the creator of Sherlock Holmes, who saw the meaning of the conflict as 'essentially religious' in that it was a spur to the reform of decadent Christianity.[103]

When Christian ideas were taken up by soldiers they were often set in an unofficial context. The singing of hymns to mocking or bawdy words was an obvious illustration of this, although 'Abide with me', whose original words provided a powerful answer to fear of death, appears to have enjoyed significant popularity.[104] The consciousness of men in France and Belgium was touched by the numerous roadside crucifixes and, although these could arouse distaste from those of a Protestant disposition, they also appear to have stirred respect for the person of Christ, though more as an archetype of human suffering than as an incarnate Saviour. At Albert near the Somme a statue of the Virgin and Child left balancing precariously on the tower of a badly damaged church became a focus for a considerable body of superstition and unofficial theologizing. Some believed that the war would end when the Virgin fell; others that whichever side knocked it down would lose the conflict. A further instance of men drawing on the Christian tradition to provide some sense of meaning and purpose in the trenches was in the widespread use of imagery drawn from Bunyan's *Pilgrim's Progress*, such as the equation of no man's land with the Slough of Despond, or Christian's journey with the dreary march up to Ypres.[105]

The extent and depth of such religious associations among the rank and file remains uncertain, but it is undeniable that some cultural responses to the war reflected strongly held, if individual, versions of Christianity. In 'They' Siegfried Sassoon displayed his bitter cynicism towards the Church's presenting the war as a spiritual crusade, but in 'The Redeemer' he could also say of a soldier that 'He was Christ'.[106] This tendency was strongest in the writings of Wilfred Owen who had been a pious churchman until he became disillusioned with conventional Christianity in 1912. In May 1917, however, he wrote to his mother from the Somme that he felt himself 'more and more Christian as I walk the unchristian ways of Christendom'. He criticized the belligerence of national churches, and asserted that 'pure Christianity will not fit in with pure patriotism'.[107] Such views found expression in his poetry, notably in 'At a Calvary near the Ancre' (1917/18):

> One ever hangs where shelled roads part.
> In this war He too lost a limb,
> But His disciples hide apart;
> And now the Soldiers bear with Him.
>
> Near Golgotha strolls many a priest,
> And in their faces there is pride
> That they were flesh-marked by the Beast
> By whom the gentle Christ's denied.[108]

In other words the true followers of Christ were not his professed ecclesiastical representatives, but the soldiers who were genuinely sharing in his sufferings. Not for Owen was Bishop Winnington-Ingram's simplistic identification between death in battle and martyrdom. For him *'Dulce et decorum est pro patria mori'* was 'the old Lie', while in his chilling parody of the story of Abraham and Isaac he dwelt not on the sacrifice of young men, but on the twisted pride of their elders who sent them to their deaths. Notably too his 'Strange meeting' with a dead adversary occurs not in heaven but in hell.

Owen was killed in November 1918, and the intensity of his poetry expressed the situation of a man who never had the opportunity to set the acute anguish of the war in any kind of longer perspective. By contrast, Stanley Spencer's artistic statement on the war, painted on the walls of the Sandham Memorial Chapel at Burghclere in Hampshire between 1927 and 1932, offered a rather more optimistic, although still unconventional, Christian statement. The pictures recall Spencer's own experiences as a medical orderly in Bristol and Macedonia, but imbued with Christian symbolism. Thus a kit inspection evokes the last judgement and reveille the resurrection. The theme of resurrection is most powerfully explored in the enormous central painting of the cycle on the east wall of the chapel, in which soldiers rise from their graves, adjust their clothing, greet comrades, and present their crosses to the Risen Christ, just as a living soldier hands in his rifle at the close of his service.[109]

The Sandham Memorial Chapel was one of the more distinctive products of the general desire to commemorate the war dead which was a strong feature of British, as indeed of European consciousness, and an important point of contact between official, unofficial and quasi-religion. The earliest war memorials to the mass of the fallen (as opposed to individual leaders) date from the Crimean War, but examples from this conflict and from the Boer War were relatively rare. In the First World War a sense of a need for visible commemoration of the dead was strong and very widespread. Steps were sometimes taken even before the war had finished: at Exeter School a memorial reredos for the chapel was proposed as early as December 1915, and erected a year later. During the years immediately after the Armistice countless monuments were erected, although some projects were not completed for a decade or more. An individual could be commemorated in several different places, at his church, his school, his place of employment and on a municipal monument.[110]

The style of monuments and the content of inscriptions varied widely, but the linking of the Christian and the patriotic was frequently explicit. This was consistent with the iconography of war cemeteries themselves where a sword is contained within a central cross, and the stone of Remembrance has the appearance of an altar.[111] The memorial cloisters at Winchester College are adorned with the following inscription:

> Thanks be to God for the service of the five hundred Wyke-hamists who were found faithful unto death amid the manifold chances of the Great War. In the day of battle they forgat not God, who created them to do His will, nor their country, the stronghold of freedom, nor their school, the mother of godliness and discipline. Strong in this threefold faith they went forth from home and kindred to the battlefields of the world, and treading the path of duty and sacrifice laid down their lives for mankind. Thou therefore, for whom they died, seek not thine own, but serve as they served, and in peace or in war bear thyself ever as Christ's soldier, gentle in all things, valiant in action, steadfast in adversity.[112]

Here at least it seemed that ideals of Christian militarism had not been broken by the war, but rather served to make sense of the slaughter. Elsewhere, on church and village war memorials, the connections were seldom spelt out so fully, but the simple words 'For God, for King, for Country', conveyed the same message. This was reinforced by the widespread use of crosses, a distinctive feature of English village war memorials. There were even instances of calvaries – with a figure of Christ carved on the cross – and of designs inspired by medieval shrines, but, probably as a result of suspicion of such Catholic motifs, these were relatively rare.[113]

In some cases local arguments about the form of a memorial resulted in two being built, as at Ampthill in Bedfordshire where clergy and others objected to the village council's plans for a monument and ex-serviceman's club, and erected their own cross in the churchyard. However, the village council's memorial was still dedicated by the chaplain-general of the forces.[114] In Scotland sculptures of soldiers with no specific Christian reference were widespread, perhaps reflecting continuing Protestant suspicion of images. But the national memorial in Edinburgh was not without a certain ecclesiastical flavour which led to it being (inaccurately) described in 1931 as the only cathedral built in Scotland since the Reformation.[115] All over Britain large municipal monuments tended to draw their symbolism from secular or classical sources, but there were significant exceptions to this in cities with strong Anglican traditions, such as Bath, Oxford and Lincoln. The avoidance of Christian reference elsewhere implied a desire for inclusiveness in communities which were conscious of becoming increasingly pluralistic. Nevertheless memorials appear always to have been dedicated with a religious service: when fears of sectarianism led to this tradition being broken in Liverpool in 1930 considerable controversy and a partial reversal of the decision ensued.[116]

As well as being an expression of individual and corporate grief at the slaughter, war memorials were symbols of the pride of the institutions and communities that erected them. This tendency was nowhere more apparent than in the national Scottish and Welsh memorials in Edinburgh and Cardiff which served as symbols of national aspiration within an imperial framework. By contrast a projected memorial in Dublin to the 50,000 Irishmen who fell in the war was never completed, although a Northern Ireland memorial was built in Belfast after the Second World War.[117]

When war memorials were sited inside churches and cathedrals a Christian linkage was implied even when it was not made explicit. Often, though, an unofficial religious significance was clearly conveyed. Thus at Long Sutton (Lincolnshire) a memorial obelisk in the street carries the inscription 'For King and Country', while a tablet inside the church also lists those from the village who fell and is accompanied by a picture of the Virgin and Child and the legend, 'For God, King and Country'; 'R.I.P.'; 'May Light Perpetual Shine Upon Them'. In the Chapel at Clumber Park (Nottinghamshire), then the property of the devoutly Anglo-Catholic Duke of Newcastle, the memorial consists of a crucifixion, surmounted with the words 'For God, King and Empire' and 'Greater love hath no man than this' (John 15:13) and underneath carrying the lettering *Per crucem ad lucem* (To light by way of the cross). At St Nicholas Church in Durham the memorial carries the text, 'Be thou faithful unto death and I will give thee a crown of life' (Revelation 2:10) which in its original context specifically referred to Christian martyrdom. Beneath the names of the fallen is inscribed the prayer: 'O God for England these strong souls have passed – grant we may make her worthy them at last'. Nor did the Church of England have a monopoly on patriotic motifs in war memorials. At Westminister (Roman Catholic) Cathedral the dead are commemorated in the Chapel of St George and the English Martyrs around a sculptured figure of England's patron saint. The Latin inscription, with what appears to be a deliberate ambiguity between spiritual and physical warfare, prays for

Christ to call his soldiers into the celestial country. At Wesley's Chapel, regarded as the Methodist Mother Church, the memorial stained-glass window shows a soldier sheltered by the Risen Christ and standing on a roundel of St George and the dragon flanked by the arms of the Dominions.[118]

The blending of patriotism and Christianity evident in war memorials was also apparent in the annual ceremonies of Armistice Day as they developed after 1918. In October 1919 the King and government responded favourably to a suggestion that the war dead should be commemorated by everyone observing a period of two minutes silence at 11 a.m. on Armistice Day, 11 November. The innovation proved immensely successful and appears to have been universally observed. The ceremonies developed much further on 11 November 1920 when the King unveiled the Cenotaph in Whitehall. Following on a suggestion originating with David Railton, an army chaplain, and Dean Ryle of Westminster Abbey, there then ensued the burial of the 'Unknown Warrior': an unidentified body had been brought from one of the battlefields to represent all those killed, was accorded an elaborate Anglican funeral with the King as chief mourner, and was interred just inside the west door of Westminster Abbey. When a Jew complained at the inscribing of the text 'In Christ shall all be made alive' on the grave when the religion of the deceased was not known, Ryle declined to change it on the grounds that the text expressed not the faith of the dead man but that of those who had buried him.[119]

This set the tone for the co-operation of Church and state in the annual ceremonies at the Cenotaph and at local war memorials and churches up and down the land. The proximity of All Saints' Day (1 November) served to heighten the link, in popular perception if not in clerical intention, between Christian and patriotic martyrdom. War memorials and Armistice Day rituals were successful in gaining a wide popular appeal because they were malleable symbols, capable of a wide range of interpretation. On the one hand they could focus the view that 'it must never happen again'; on the other they could help to steel nerves and inspire patriotism for the possibility of another conflict. Both these perspectives were expressed in the newsreels of the interwar period. In terms of religion, Armistice Day could be at the same time both the focus of a system of patriotic symbols to which Christianity was marginal; and a basis for the endeavour to give Christian theological and spiritual meaning to the suffering and bereavement that was the legacy of war. This latter challenge, however, was one to which the churches never fully responded: they were content with their success in giving a

Christian dimension to unofficial religious aspirations and did not seek to push their influence further.

The Great War severely dented the naïve self-assurance that had lain behind the Christian imperialism and militarism of the prewar decades, and it reshaped the linkages between Christianity and patriotism. Nevertheless popular imperialism, continued to be a potent force, albeit a somewhat more sober one than hitherto, in the interwar period. Lord Meath's Empire Day movement continued to grow, and it was claimed that in 1928 some 5 million children participated in the ceremonies. Religious services were a prominent feature of its proceedings: a crowd estimated at 90,000 attended one at Wembley Stadium in 1925. In 1937 a service of Empire Youth was held at Westminster Abbey as part of the Coronation celebrations for George VI. Subsequently a new organization, the Empire Youth Movement was formed. This body fostered Empire Youth Sunday and Empire Youth Week and later drew inspiration from John Buchan's conviction that 'civilisation . . . must ultimately rest on the Christian Church'. This strand in the celebration of Empire was interwoven with a continuation of chivalric symbolism and the cultivation of patriotism, duty and discipline.[120]

The continuing power of the idea of Empire as a focus of religious and quasi-religious devotion was reinforced by its relationships with both the monarchy and the BBC. Sir John Reith, the first Director General of the BBC, was an enthusiastic supporter of the ideals of Empire Day and ensured that they were given generous air time. Religious services remained an uncontroversial feature of such broadcasts even when other aspects of them became a matter of dispute. In 1932 George V began the tradition of Christmas Day broadcasts to the Empire, which linked a major Christian festival to an imperial (later Commonwealth) vision and were to be assiduously maintained by George VI and Elizabeth II. For the remainder of George V's reign the broadcast was linked to a celebratory programme about the Empire, which normally included relays from the Holy Land and in 1934 the singing of the hymn 'All hail the power of Jesus' name'. From 1935 the Irish Free State, still formally part of the Empire, refused to participate. The imperial context of the Christmas broadcast was dropped in the early years of George VI's reign, but revived on the outbreak of war in 1939.[121] In the meantime, after the trauma of the abdication, the coronation of George VI in 1937 saw a climax in the broadcast and filmed linking of religious and imperial symbolism, a process assisted by the revision of the form of the Oath to accommodate the new order of self-government in the Dominions.[122]

The interwar period also saw the heyday of the British-Israelite movement, which despite its small size (5,000 to 10,000 active members) is significant in the present context because it showed the extreme to which identification of Christianity and the Empire could be pushed. This group, with its origins in the late nineteenth century, taught that descendants of the lost ten tribes of Israel had migrated through Europe and eventually came to Britain at the Norman conquest. Through them Britain as a nation inherited the Covenant promises made by God in the Old Testament. Moreover, a lecturer declared in 1928:

> We know something of the mighty growth of the British Empire; no human power could have made these Islands what they are at the present time . . . the British Empire fulfilled absolutely and accurately the promises God gave to Abraham and his descendants.

British Israelism found its support particularly among middle-class Anglican evangelicals, including a goodly sprinkling of clergy.[123]

Imperial administrators seldom saw matters in such simplistically visionary terms, but the Christian influences on policy were not insignificant. The growth of John Buchan's religious ideas in the last decade of his life coincided with his increasing prominence as an imperial figure and his appointment as Governor General of Canada in 1935. There were still missionaries and others in India who saw Britain as having a providential Christianizing and civilizing mission in the sub-continent. At the same time, connections were more double-edged than they had been before the First World War. Mahatma Gandhi gained respect in the churches for his 'Christlike' stance, which also facilitated his relations with the devoutly Anglican Lord Irwin, viceroy from 1926 to 1931. In Kenya missionaries and their converts played a significant role in the emergence of nationalist movements.[124]

In the meantime at home there were also contrasting religious tendencies. *Pacifism* in the absolute sense of refusing to participate in any recourse to force, as opposed to *pacificism*, the desire to use peaceful means as far as possible to resolve international disputes, had hardly existed except among Quakers before 1914, at least since the mid-nineteenth century high point in the activity of the Peace Society. Even a substantial minority of Quakers fought in the First World War. But in December 1914 the Fellowship of Reconciliation was formed as a discreet focus for a somewhat imprecise Christian pacifism. It had 8,000 members by 1918. During the 1920s the high hopes of a new peaceful world order centred on the League of Nations meant that the sense of a need for a firm pacifist stand retreated. However, as the international scene darkened in the early 1930s there was a proliferation of Christian pacifist groups. Most significantly, the charismatic leadership of Dick Sheppard, formerly Vicar of St Martin's-in-the-Fields in Trafalgar Square, in 1936 brought into being the Peace Pledge Union. Despite its Christian inspiration this organization also appealed to a liberal humanist constituency and had 87,000 members by 1937 and 136,000 in 1940.[125]

In general, official Christianity in the interwar period reacted firmly against the militarist tendencies of the pre-1918 era. As the challenge from the dictators grew during the 1930s Hensley Henson, now Bishop of Durham, was almost a lone ecclesiastical voice urging that a firm stand should be taken. Even Bishop Winnington-Ingram of London, whose militancy had been such a feature of the First World War, now saw it as 'the Christian thing' to seek peaceful relations with Germany.[126] In some cases, notably among Roman Catholics and Frank Buchman's revivalist Oxford Group movement, there was genuine sympathy for fascism or Nazism, which could reflect a more or less latent anti-Semitism. Sometimes, as in the case of A. C. Headlam, Bishop of Gloucester and chairman of the Church of England's Council on Foreign Relations, there was a culpable failure properly to investigate the issues. More commonly, though, there was an understandable ignorance of the horrific dimensions of Nazi policy and a sense of guilt over the treatment of Germany at Versailles.[127]

Christian leaders were thus ready supporters of the policy of appeasement. Indeed Irwin, now Viscount Halifax, Neville Chamberlain's foreign secretary in the final two years before the war, provided a strong personal link between the churches and the heart of government. When Chamberlain seemingly averted war by agreeing to the dismemberment of Czechoslovakia at Munich in September 1938 Lang, now Archbishop of Canterbury, saw this outcome as providential:

> We cannot, we dare not, doubt that this sudden uplifting of the cloud which for the last few weeks has darkened and oppressed our life is an answer to the great volume of prayer which with a most impressive unity and reality has been rising to God.[128]

There were a few dissenting voices, but it was only after the German annexation of the remainder of Czechoslovakia in March 1939 that there was sombre acceptance of the need for the 'massing of might on the side of right' and talk of the role of Britain as the defender of Christian civilization.[129]

Just as at the outbreak of the First World War it had been unclear where Christian militarism ended and secular patriotism began, in the years leading up to the Second World War the distinction between the preaching of peace by the churches and the general public's distaste for another conflict was an uncertain one. After September 1939 when the nation found itself, reluctant but resolute, once again at war, there were renewed signs of convergence between patriotism and religion. The King's Christmas broadcasts during the war contained explicitly Christian references, which led one clergymen to add to the 'comfortable words' in the Holy Communion liturgy a quotation introduced by 'Hear also what King George VI saith . . .'[130] In his famous broadcast in June 1940 Winston Churchill associated the 'Battle of Britain' with 'the survival of Christian civilization'.[131] In 1941 Viscount Bledisloe, president of the Empire Day movement, declared that 'It is against the Powers of Darkness that we are fighting, and the fate of the Empire, and with it that of civilization, are at stake'.[132]

Nevertheless there were important differences. Clergy and ministers were generally much more cautious than they had been in the First World War. Although Bishop Winnington-Ingram spoke of a 'Second Day of God', portraying the war as 'a fight between the spirit of Christ and the spirit of anti-Christ' he acknowledged that it was 'easy to mistake patriotism for Christianity'.[133] The man of the hour was now William Temple, Archbishop of York at the outbreak of war and Archbishop of Canterbury from 1942 until his death in 1944. In a broadcast in October 1939 he portrayed Britain as 'a dedicated nation', defending the 'traditional excellencies of European civilization . . . against the deified nation of the Nazis'.[134] Broadcasting on the National Day of Prayer on 26 May 1940 he stressed that:

> when we turned to prayer it could not be as Britons who happened to be Christians; it must be as Christians who happened to be British. Otherwise we fell into the error of our enemies, whose distinctive sin it was that they put their nationality first.[135]

While Temple thus saw considerable spiritual and moral significance in the war he presented it not in crudely nationalistic terms as a conflict between a 'good' Britain and an 'evil' Germany, but as a wider struggle in the cause of the whole of mankind against the excesses of Nazism. This was the tone of much of the Christian response to the war, in which condemnation of Nazism was prominent, but claims that Britain had a unique divinely appointed mission loomed much less large. Among combatants there was a notable absence of the high moral and spiritual purpose that had initially been apparent in the First World War. There was even direct criticism of the conduct of the war from George Bell, Bishop of Chichester, who strongly condemned the indiscriminate bombing of German cities.[136]

Although the Second World War, like the First, saw no dramatic changes in the statistical trends towards generally declining participation in church life, there were still signs of a transient religious vitality. People at home were affected by the war in an unprecedented manner, above all through bombing and evacuation. Such experiences could evoke religious responses: some resumed the churchgoing habit and the National Day of Prayer in May 1940 was very well supported.[137] Military chaplains, like their predecessors in the First World War, were painfully aware of the gulf that separated many from the churches, but there were still reports of men in POW camps taking comfort from religion, while the Commander-in-Chief of the Home Fleet could write to Archbishop Temple in 1942 of his 'firm conviction that throughout the Service and on shore there is a deeper religious feeling and a greater longing to live a more Christian life than ever before in my lifetime'.[138] Among existing Christians too there were signs of increased fervour and new beginnings: some of T. S. Eliot's and C. S. Lewis's most memorable writing dates from the war years; while 1940–1 saw the development of the 'Sword of the Spirit', a Roman Catholic initiative which attracted warm support from other churches, and was intended to point the way forward to a Christian democratic order after the war. The significance of all this must not be overstated or misunderstood. There was certainly no general or sustained Christian revival. Nevertheless there does appear to have been a stronger tendency than in the First World War for religious responses to the conflict to be channelled in official rather than unofficial directions.[139]

On a spring morning in 1946 Bishop Winnington-Ingram, who had resigned the see of London in 1939, died peacefully at his niece's home in rural Worcestershire. At his funeral was sung the hymn, 'The strife is o'er, the battle done'.[140] Both the choice of hymn and the time of his passing from the scene were symbolic. In the aftermath of the Second World War, even more than during the conflict itself, the kind of patriotic Christian militarism which the bishop in his prime had so conspicuously represented, had become an anachronism. After atomic bombs had been dropped on Hiroshima and Nagasaki, if any biblical imagery of warfare still had a relevance to actual and potential wars, it seemed to be that of the Apocalypse of St John, not the Christian soldier of St Paul's Epistle to the Ephesians. At a national thanksgiving service in August 1945 the Archbishop of Canterbury, Geoffrey Fisher, spoke of the use of 'weapons of darkness' in order to defeat darkness.[141] Moreover, as the full horror of the Jewish Holocaust in the Nazi death camps became known, even the theological rationalizations of suffering and sacrifice that had served for some in the First World War seemed to have become hollow.

At the same time the war presaged the end of the Empire. The almost indecent haste with which Britain left India in 1947 was a striking testimony to a collapse of confidence in providential imperial mission, which even in the interwar period had helped to legitimize British rule. The suddenness of the transition is graphically illustrated by the imperial grandeur of New Delhi as constructed to Sir Edwin Lutyens's designs during and after the First World War. Here it had seemed was the heart of an eastern empire that was to endure for the forseeable future. Britain's African empire was to survive for another fifteen years after which it too was given up with almost equal rapidity. Within a quarter of a century from the end of the Second World War the Empire had passed into memory, apart from anomalous territories such as Rhodesia, Hong Kong and the Falkland Islands.

Against this background the role of religion continued uncertain. If anything, the movements promoting the Empire gained a more Christian tone in their last years of viable existence in the 1950s.[142] The same was true of the continuing commemoration of the war dead. In 1946 the proceedings were to be moved to the nearest Sunday to 11 November: this arguably reduced their intensity as they no longer interrupted weekday life, but reinforced their identification with the practice of Christian worship. The Coronation of Elizabeth II in 1953, like that of her father sixteen years before, was a very public and spectacular reaffirmation of the religious significance of the monarchy and its links with the Empire.[143]

Nevertheless such continuities were deceptive. Shortly before Nurse Edith Cavell was executed in Brussels by the Germans in 1915 for helping allied soldiers she said to the chaplain who gave her Communion, 'I realise that patriotism is not enough. I must have no hatred or bitterness towards anyone'. A monument was erected to her near Trafalgar Square shortly after the end of the First World War, but only after several years were these words added to the inscription.[144] Even at the end of our period the second half of her utterance remained deeply challenging, but in the face of the suffering of the First World War, the hopes and fears of the interwar period, and the horrors of the struggle against Nazism and its allies, British patriotism had lost much of that fervent association with religion that had caused many to link it with ultimate moral and spiritual claims. On Second World War military gravestones the cross and the regimental badge were separated. No longer did patriotism so readily seem to be 'enough'.

9

CONCLUSION

Nationalism and secularization

In the autumn and winter of 1940, as German bombs rained down on the City of London, St Paul's Cathedral stood amidst the devastation, not unscathed but substantially intact. At the height of incendiary raids on the night of 29 December, Winston Churchill sent a message to the Lord Mayor that the cathedral must at all costs be saved.[1] Implicit in the Prime Minister's concern was an awareness that St Paul's had become a powerful symbol of national resistance to the attacks of the Luftwaffe and that its destruction would have been a serious blow to morale. The visual image of the cathedral during the blitz that is reproduced on the cover of this book is complemented by reflections in a commemorative volume published by *The Times*:

> In recalling the war years at St Paul's it will be necessary constantly to remind ourselves that it was at all times a living spiritual centre in the life of the City, of the nation, and, indeed, of the entire free world. There were long months when the way in which the dome of St Paul's emerged from the smoke and darkness after each successive raid, apparently indestructible however great the devastation around it, seemed like a miracle. Londoners came to regard it as a symbol of their own endurance and continuing faith in the future. That was the time of 'their finest hour'.[2]

At first sight it might appear paradoxical that, at a time when organized religion was in decline, a conspicuous expression of traditional Christianity could nevertheless become so central a focus of popular sentiment. The analysis carried out in the preceding pages, however, has provided many clues as to why and how such symbols continued to be important. It remains in this concluding chapter to bring together the main threads in the book and to relate the discussion to other interpretations of the pattern of religious change and national development in the United Kingdom and Ireland.[3]

Religious influences unquestionably retreated. Participation in organized official religion declined, as measured by attendance figures, membership statistics and the like. In the case of some groups this began as early as the late nineteenth century, at least in relative terms, but in other quarters, as we noted in Chapter 3, there was no clear evidence of absolute decline until well into the twentieth century. Nevertheless for much of the twentieth century the trends for most denominations have usually been downwards. Active participants were a much smaller proportion of the population in 1945 than they had been in 1851, and were to decrease in number still further during the ensuing decades. Meanwhile the role of official religion in everyday life substantially contracted. Whereas the early Victorian churches had had central roles in education, social welfare and, in effect, local government, their mid-twentieth-century counterparts found that most of these roles had been taken over by the agencies of a greatly expanded state. Moreover, whereas nineteenth-century politics had at times seemed to revolve around religious issues, by the Second World War, if not earlier, these had become much more marginal. Frameworks of ideas which offered an explicitly supernaturalist interpretation of the world commanded much less general cultural acceptance than they had done. Science seemed to explain more; the Bible less. Even among those who remained committed to institutional religion, beliefs about the spiritual realm now differentiated it much less sharply from the material. The fearful hope of cataclysmic divine intervention in human history receded; concepts of heaven and hell were reinterpreted where they were not rejected. Heaven became an idealized recreation of the Victorian family; hell changed from a place of very literal fire and torture to a kind of negative apotheosis of English suburbia on a wet February afternoon, as portrayed by C. S. Lewis in 1945.[4]

The evidence that such historical trends have taken place in Britain is, broadly speaking, irrefutable. However, the concept of 'secularization', often used to define and explain them, is more contentious. According to this hypothesis it is argued that in the Middle Ages there was a high point of the identification of the structures of official religion with the bases of political, cultural and social power. This system was weakened by the new ideas associated with the Renaissance and by the division of Western Christendom at the Reformation. It took a further dent from the more rigorous scepticism of Enlightenment philosophers. But 'the great discontinuity'[5] did not come until industrialization in the nineteenth century. This led to 'the emergence in England of a society pluralistic, urbanised and relatively affluent, whose rhythm of life was dominated by the artificial rationality of an industrialized economy'.[6] In the long run, it is argued, all the features of 'modern' industrial society proved to be inimical to religion. Pluralism and urbanization precluded the kind of social and ideological coherence which could exist in a pre-industrial rural community and hence religious institutions could no longer enjoy an uncriticized ascendancy over the popular mind. Affluence meant that alternative forms of leisure increasingly became available, while general access to satisfactory medical care, social security and insurance removed much of the insecurity which had led people to turn to religion in the past. The last unknown enemy, death, had admittedly not been conquered, but it had been removed from the regular social experience of younger people. The ordered patterns of industrial mass-production and bureaucratic administration brought rationality to people's lives, which implied that there was little or no need to invoke the supernatural to explain the unpredictable.[7]

The plausibility of this line of argument conceals questionable assumptions. Talk of 'secularization' implies a dichotomy between the spheres of the 'secular' and the 'religious' but, as we have seen, this separation was seldom clear cut. The definition of religion is itself problematic: a certain degree of argumentative slight of hand makes it possible to represent the same society and culture as being at very different stages in the process of secularization. Was the engagement of the churches with nationalism and imperialism in the twenty years before the First World War a sign that they had themselves become 'secularized'; or was it, on the other hand, an indication of the permeation of 'religious' influences through society? In the face of such definitional difficulties it seems more helpful and precise to think rather of changes in ways of being religious, of shifts in the relative importance of official religion, unofficial religion and quasi-religion. Such an approach does not preclude the acknowledgement that consistently 'secular' outlooks existed and, arguably, became more widespread during our period, but it does point up the need for care and precision in making such judgements.

The claim that 'secularization' was associated with 'industrialization' and 'modernization'[8] begs questions about the identification of the beginning and end points of this process. The era of most rapid industrialization and urbanization in the nineteenth century closely corresponded to the height of Victorian religious resurgence. It is true that there were negative consequences for traditional forms of unofficial religion, but organized religion demonstrated a capacity to flourish in an urban environment and to diffuse its teachings to a substantial proportion of the population. Moreover the twentieth-century recession in religion in Britain has closely paralleled what Martin Wiener has called the 'decline of the industrial spirit',[9] an indication that if industrialism and religion are connected historically they have if anything tended to reinforce rather than to undermine each other.

The exceptions to the pattern of religious decline are too numerous and varied to be readily accommodated by the secularization hypothesis. It has been suggested that in a 'secular' society those groups that wish to maintain a full-blooded religious commitment are forced to become sub-cultures, technically *sects*, with strong alternative structures of authority and ideology.[10] This hypothesis would explain, for example, the growth of Pentecostalism in the twentieth century, and the continued vigour of some hardline Baptist, Presbyterian and ultra-orthodox Jewish groups within a limited constituency. The theory is put under strain, however, when it is faced with the continuing strength of more numerously supported religious groups during the twentieth century. In particular, as indicated by the figures in Chapter 3, Roman Catholic numbers in Britain were still growing in the 1930s and 1940s, both absolutely and relatively. Granted that they were in some respects still isolated from the main currents of British life, they were geographically concentrated in some of the most industrialized and urbanized areas of Britain – the west of Scotland, Lancashire, the West Midlands and London – and could hardly have been immune from those forces allegedly at the root of secularization.

Then there is the question of Scotland, Wales and, above all, Ireland. As we noted in Chapter 3, Scotland and Wales had substantially higher levels of religious affiliation than England in the first half of the twentieth century. If this could be explained merely by reference to remote rural areas, such as the Cambrian Mountains and the West Highlands, this could plausibly, if patronizingly, be dismissed as a function of 'backwardness'. But it was also true of industrial South Wales and the urbanized belt of central Scotland. The argument applies with even more force in relation to Ireland. It is true that the persistence of religious observance in rural areas is consistent with the theory, but does it adequately explain the signs of *resurgence* in both Catholic and Protestant churches in the later nineteenth century? Moreover until well into the second half of the twentieth century very high levels of religious practice were a feature of life in the cities of Dublin and Belfast as well as in the countryside.

The case of Ireland serves as a bridge to wider international comparisons. France in the nineteenth and early twentieth centuries was much less industrialized than Britain, but there was more widespread complete rejection of religion. Some of the exceptions to this were certainly in largely rural areas, such as Brittany and the Vendée, but the geographical pattern of religion and irreligion generally showed little clear relationship to economic and social factors. Towns could sometimes show a higher level of religious practice than their rural hinterlands.[11] On the other hand in the United States, surely the archetype of a modernized, industrialized society, religious practice and reference remained in the twentieth century considerably higher than in Britain. This has been frequently attributed to the availability of a plurality of religious options, mirroring the pluralism of contemporary social structures. However, in Britain too a wide range of religious groups existed, but the capacity to sustain commitment was much more limited.[12] Indeed, after the Roman Catholics and sectarian groups, the groups that have fared least badly in Britain have been the Established Churches, so often derided as anomalous survivals from an age of religious monopoly, out of place in a pluralistic order.

The secularization hypothesis has been refined in the face of awareness of such counter-examples. In particular it has been suggested that religion has flourished as a means of 'cultural defence', providing resources 'for the defence of a national, local, ethnic, or status-group culture'. Ireland is cited as an obvious example of this process, while the cases of Scotland and Wales are also relevant. A second refinement is to suggest that religion may retain significance in periods of 'cultural transition': thus it is accepted that the Industrial Revolution was a period of religious strength, and that decline only set in with the maturing of the industrial economy at the end of the nineteenth century.[13] It is rather hard to see, however, how either approach can readily be used to explain the case of the United States.

The extent to which the secularization hypothesis has had to be modified and qualified by its protagonists suggests that it is in reality too blunt an instrument for conceptualizing and explaining the complexities of religious change in the nineteenth and twentieth centuries. A more constructive approach is to treat as 'not proven' the hypothesis that social and cultural processes in the 'modern' era have *inevitably* eroded religion and to look for more contingent and less all-encompassing explanations of religious decline.

Jeffrey Cox, in his study of the churches in Lambeth in the late nineteenth and early twentieth centuries, argues that there is no necessary conflict between religion and a particular kind of social structure, but the very fact of social change can frequently be disruptive of previous patterns of observance. Thus he writes:

> Steelmakers are not intrinsically hostile to Christianity because of their nearness to the heart of modern technology. But steelmaking does involve drastic changes in social relationships, and the voluntary nature of modern religion has greatly increased the chances that a particular church will find itself the victim of unanticipated social changes.[14]

This point can be developed further by observing that such 'unanticipated social changes' could also provide points of opportunity for religion, as for Methodists in the early British Industrial Revolution and for Roman Catholics in the aftermath of the Great Famine in Ireland. Also, to pursue Cox's example, the decline of steelmaking, perhaps even more than its rise, implied substantial social change, and consequent difficulties for the churches. Cox locates the beginnings of pronounced decline in the Lambeth churches around the turn of the twentieth century and attributes this particularly to the perception that the state was taking over social functions previously performed by the churches, and among Nonconformists to an increase in life opportunities which distracted them from the chapels. There was nothing inevitable about this trend, but the manner in which the churches had assumed social and philanthropic roles as well as strictly religious tasks rendered them vulnerable to competition. They were ill-equipped to resist because of an internal crisis of morale and a readiness implicitly to accept that they had become an irrelevance to the mainstream of life. This internal lack of confidence, perhaps a kind of collective 'morning after' reaction to the energy and ambivalent achievements of Victorian religion meant that there was little will to counteract a cultural tendency to agnosticism and a feeling that organized Christianity was 'old-fashioned'.[15]

The merit of Cox's approach is that he provides a focused explanation of the objective historical facts of church decline without resorting to debatable sociological generalization. Where the contingent circumstances were different, it follows that outcomes varied. For example, in Wales the Revival of 1904–5 and the achievement of disestablishment in 1920 appear to have prevented – or at least delayed – the kind of crisis of morale that Cox perceives in early twentieth-century Lambeth. In

Ireland, political circumstances ensured that official religion maintained its relevance to social life.

My intention in the present book has been similarly to emphasize particular historical changes in the nature and significance of religion, while remaining sceptical about the applicability of the secularization hypothesis. The trend during the late nineteenth and early twentieth centuries was for the dominant religious tone of Britain to change from an ethos of doctrinally hard-edged and tightly disciplined churches to a more diffuse and varied shifting kaleidoscope of beliefs. Doctrinal rigour and ministerial authoritarianism survived, but it became more the exception than the rule. The significance of the newer and more liberal ideas which came with advances in science, history and biblical studies, was not so much that they generated a 'crisis of plausibility' as the advocates of secularization theory are prone to suggest, but that they opened the way to a much wider range of ways of being religious. This trend was accentuated by the very vigour of Victorian religion, the desire of the churches to exert influence in all areas of life, which led to symbiotic relationships with culture and politics as well as with the social life of local communities. At the same time the unofficial religion of pre-Victorian rural culture was being modified, especially in the urban setting, into something closer to a diffuse shadow of official religion.[16]

The particular focus has been on the relationship of religion to the formation and projection of national identity, patriotism and nationalism. The diffuse nature of late Victorian and Edwardian religion, coinciding as it did with the summit of national self-confidence as manifested in the literature, popular imperialism and state ceremonial of the period, was an important factor in giving ideological legitimacy to the national mood. Patriotism acquired an edge of absolute spiritual claims which led it to the threshold of a nationalism that equated the cause of Britain with the cause of God. This mood was at its height in the first decade and a half of the twentieth century, before the chastening experience of the Great War, but it continued in more muted form into the middle decades of the twentieth century. The patriotism in question drew strength rather than division from the unresolved tensions between 'England' and 'Britain', associated respectively with Anglican and Protestant frameworks of belief. While those with broad and high church Anglican sympathies could contemplate 'England' from their vantage points at Westminster, in country rectories, cathedral cities, and Oxford halls, 'Britain' could inspire Nonconformists, Scottish and Irish Presbyterians and Welsh chapel-goers. This latter appeal was undergirded by the sense of mission and opportunity provided by the Empire. Faced with this powerful construction of patriotic identity, Scottish and Welsh alternatives faltered. Even in Catholic Ireland nationalists struggled before the First World War to find sufficiently powerful ideological and spiritual legitimacy to mount an effective challenge to British rule.

Comparison with the United States is enlightening. Callum Brown suggests that there has been a pattern of rise and decline in adherence to official religion in the United States following about sixty-five years behind the corresponding trends in Britain. The peaks occurred in 1904–5 and in 1970.[17] There is a correlation with the stabilization of the proportion of the population living in cities, but the two dates can also be linked to turning points in national self-confidence. The years after 1904 saw Britain withdrawing from much of Ireland and bogged down in war in France; while around 1970 the United States was experiencing bloody humiliation in Vietnam, and subsequently saw faith in public probity at home undermined by the Watergate scandal. In general it has been observed that nations enjoying a period of international hegemony have often simultaneously experienced vigorous religious activity.[18] Such an interpretation would occasion no surprise among those Victorian Christians who saw the British Empire as the divine reward for their own faithfulness to the Gospel; more prosaically, one might ponder the interplay between strong religious commitment, cultural self-assurance and high-profile action on the world stage.

From 1914 the stress of war and revolution severely checked the ascendancy of God and Greater Britain. If a specific watershed can be identified it is in the events of the spring and summer of 1916. Early in May in Dublin the leaders of the Easter Rising were executed by the British; two months later 20,000 British soldiers died on the first day of the Battle of the Somme. British bullets gave martyrs to Ireland; German bullets rendered martyrdom for Britain disconcertingly commonplace. Contemporaries were not to know that Sir Douglas Haig, commanding the British forces at the Somme, had written to his wife on the eve of the battle, 'I feel that every step in my plan has been taken with the Divine help', but the appalling nature of the outcome was to weaken severely the credibility of ready associations between national interest and the will of God.[19]

Within little more than five years the south of Ireland had become a virtually independent state. The pressure for Home Rule on the Irish side has often been analysed; but also very significant was the lack of will on the British side to resist it, buying off the Unionists with the partition of Ulster, a 'solution' that was barely on the political agenda before the war. It implies a serious denting of imperial Protestant self-assurance, brought about, it might be noted, under a government headed by a Welsh Nonconformist.

In Britain, meanwhile, revulsion against the militarism associated with the war and the pastoral failures brought to light during the conflict contributed to the heightening of that 'crisis of morale' which Cox detects in the early twentieth-century churches. The tailspin of support for appeasement noted in the previous chapter, and initiatives such as the Conference on Politics, Economics and Citizenship in 1924 were in the long run rather less significant than an increasing tendency of clergy at the grass roots to feel that the churches no longer had anything relevant to say to society as a whole, and that they should concentrate rather on their specifically 'religious' functions.[20] The 1920s and 1930s proved to be quite fertile decades for Christian intellectual and artistic restatement, but pointing the way to a religion disengaged from secular trends. At the same time the cultural deposit left by official religious activity in earlier decades continued to be significant in the interwar period. The quasi-religious interrelationships between Christianity, nation, Empire and monarchy remained and revived powerfully in the face of the crisis of 1940.

The decades after 1945 saw pronounced changes in the nature of British nationalism and in the position of religion. There is an intriguing parallel between the position of religion and the fate of the Empire: both seemed to enjoy an element of stability in the 1950s, but the loss of the African colonies in the 1960s coincided with a decade of widespread and sharp decline in official religious observance. Both were symptoms of wider conditions of social, cultural and political change, but in the light of the states of mind explored in this book it seems not unreasonable to speculate that there were more specific linkages in popular consciousness. This period also saw the passing from the scene of the generation whose consciousness had been formed before and during the First World War.

In Scotland and Wales a period of limited cultural nationalism in the mid-twentieth century gave way after the Second World War, and particularly from the 1960s, to more organized movements with a substantial popular base. In the interwar period it would seem that the continuing significant strength of official religion worked in favour of the British connection: both the disestablished Church in Wales and the reunited Church of Scotland had credibility as genuinely indigenous institutions while pointing their adherents and sympathizers to wider frameworks of, respectively, Anglican and Protestant imperial unity.

Their postwar decline, however, coinciding as it did with the loss of the imperial framework for British unity, opened the door to more secular and more uncompromising expressions of nationhood. The outbreak of open sectarian confrontation in Northern Ireland in the late 1960s reinforced this process by associating Britishness with a harsh and unfashionable Protestant militancy at the very time that England reverted from the role of partner in imperial mission to that of oppressive southern and eastern neighbour.

Other developments indicated that a reshaping of national and religious identities was forseeable. From the 1950s there was extensive migration to Britain from the Indian subcontinent and elsewhere of people adhering to religions other than Christianity. By the mid-1980s both Sikhs and Hindus in Britain numbered several hundred thousand and the Muslim total was approaching a million.[21] It is not insignificant that these groups perceived themselves as coming to a Christian country, but as it became clear that they were to be a permanent and growing proportion of the population, their presence began in some quarters to stir a rethinking of traditional assumptions of what it meant to be British or English. During the same period closer ties with Europe also began to have an impact on public consciousness in both Britain and Ireland. There were signs that resistance to this trend owed something to a continued association of Britishness with Protestantism, but counter-currents, especially among younger people, were also apparent.

Nevertheless the echoes of the past remained. In 1852 the Duke of Wellington had been laid to rest in St Paul's Cathedral,

> Under the cross of gold
> That shines over city and river . . .[22]

When the field marshals of the Second World War died, memorial tablets to them were placed in the crypt around Wellington's sarcophagus. It was in St Paul's in 1977 that Elizabeth II gave thanks for the silver jubilee of her reign and in 1981 that the Prince of Wales was married. Both events evoked memories of imperial splendour and were enthusiastically received affirmations of the links between Church, monarchy and nation. In 1982, however, after the Falklands War with Argentina, St Paul's was the setting for an event that suggested that traditional assumptions were now increasingly being questioned. The order of service eschewed triumphalism, and the Archbishop of Canterbury, Robert Runcie, clearly delineated in his sermon the boundaries of Christian patriotism. Although praising the courage of the British forces, he described war as a sign of human failure and stressed the importance of accepting other peoples as brothers and sisters. He went on:

> That is one reason why those who interpret God's will must never claim him as an asset for one nation or group rather than another. War springs from the love and loyalty which should be offered to God being applied to some God substitute, one of the most dangerous being nationalism.[23]

The complaint of one Conservative MP that 'cringeing clergy' had misused St Paul's was an indication that the role of 'the parish church of the Empire'[24] was now, in the absence of an empire, rather less than clear cut. Wider uncertainty about the nature of British national and religious identity in the late twentieth century also found expression in a growing public agnosticism towards the monarchy.

The prognosis for both religion and nationhood in Britain is unclear. It is possible to postulate a further advance of secularity, a restructuring of residual religious impulses, or a resurgence of a modified official religion. One might envisage the break-up of the United Kingdom, the attainment of a new sense of identity within Europe, or a successful if divisive reassertion of 'Britishness'. Whatever the outcomes, the legacy of the historic interlinking of religion and nationhood needs to be understood and addressed.

NOTES

1 INTRODUCTION: RELIGION AND NATIONHOOD IN MODERN BRITAIN

1 Public Record Office, Kew, Returns of the Census of Religious Worship HO/129/501/7, Leeds, St Peter.
2 Jim Obelkevich, Lyndal Roper and Raphael Samuel, *Disciplines of Faith: Studies in Religion, Politics and Patriarchy* (London, 1987), p. 7.
3 Peter Lake in 'What is religious history?', *History Today* 35 (August 1985), p. 47; Patrick Collinson, *The Religion of Protestants: The Church in English Society 1559–1625* (Oxford, 1982), p. 189.
4 Richard C. Trexler, 'Reverence and profanity in the study of early modern religion', in Kaspar von Greyerz, ed., *Religion and Society in Early Modern Europe* (London, 1984), pp. 245–69.
5 John Bossy, 'Some elementary forms of Durkheim', *Past and Present* 95 (1982), pp. 4–8.
6 Nottingham University Library, Department of Manuscripts, Newcastle Diary, Ne2F3, 15 November 1828.
7 Fourth Duke of Newcastle, *Thoughts in Times Past, Tested by Subsequent Events*, (London, 1837), p. xx.
8 R. Key, *The Gospel Among the Masses* (?1866), reprinted in James Moore, ed., *Religion in Victorian Britain: Vol. III Sources* (Manchester, 1988), p. 250.
9 Newcastle Diary, Ne2F3, 15 November 1828; *Punch*, 17 September 1892.
10 J. M. Barrie, *The Little Minister* (London, 1892), pp. 240–1.
11 William James, *The Varieties of Religious Experience* (First published 1902; Harmondsworth, Penguin edn 1982), p. 31.
12 Emile Durkheim, *The Elementary Forms of The Religious Life*, trans. J. W. Swain (London, 1915), p. 47; Steven Lukes, *Emile Durkheim, His Life and Work: A Historical and Critical Study* (London, 1913), p. 233; Bossy, op. cit., p. 3.
13 D. Mackenzie Brown, *Ultimate Concern: Tillich in Dialogue* (London, 1965), pp. 4–5; Paul Tillich (ed. Terence Thomas), *The Encounter of Religions and Quasi-Religions* (Lampeter, 1990), pp. 31–6.
14 Nehemiah Curnock, ed., *The Journal of the Rev. John Wesley, A.M.* (8 vols, London, 1911), Vol. II, p. 257n.

15 Trexler, op. cit., p. 250; Eamon Duffy, *The Stripping of the Altars: Traditional Religion in England c.1400–1580* (New Haven, 1992), pp. 2–3.

16 Tillich (ed. Thomas), op. cit., pp. 6–7.

17 Ibid., pp. 7–8; Keith Thomas, *Religion and the Decline of Magic* (London, 1971), pp. 51–77.

18 N. Abercrombie *et al.*, 'Superstition and religion: the God of the gaps', *A Sociological Yearbook of Religion in Britain* 3 (1970), pp. 93–129.

19 S. J. Connolly, 'The "blessed turf": cholera and popular panic in Ireland, June 1832', *Irish Historical Studies* 23 (1981), pp. 214, 230–1.

20 The official text is in Irish, but this English version had emotive associations with the Easter Rising of 1916. See Ruth Dudley Edwards, *Patrick Pearse: The Triumph of Failure* (London, 1977), pp. 302–3.

21 It should be noted that these categories are defined with reference to ecclesiastical organizations rather than secular ones. It will be apparent that quasi-religions can have close links to the official structures of the state, a situation further confused by the existence of Established Churches in Britain, another instance of the fluidity of the categories here developed.

22 Alan Wilkinson, *The Church of England and First World War* (London, 1978), pp. 298–9. It is worth noting that the extent to which the different dimensions of religion were intermingled in the British form of this ceremony was greater than in most other countries. The French Unknown Warrior, for example, was buried not in a great church, but under the Arc de Triomphe. See also below, pp. 246–7.

23 Rosemary O'Day in 'What is religious history?', *History Today* 35 (August 1985), p. 48.

24 For examples of such approaches see, respectively, Rosemary O'Day, *The English Clergy* (Leicester, 1979) and Martin Ingram, 'Religion, communities and moral discipline in late sixteenth and early seventeenth-century England: case studies', in von Greyerz, op. cit., pp. 177–93.

25 Bernard Ward, *The Dawn of the Catholic Revival in England, 1781–1803* (2 vols, London, 1909); *The Eve of Catholic Emancipation* (3 vols, London, 1911–12); *The Sequel to Catholic Emancipation* (2 vols, London, 1915).

26 John Kent, *The Unacceptable Face. The Modern Church in the Eyes of the Historian* (London, 1987), pp. 98–9.

27 For examples see Obelkevich, Roper and Samuel, op. cit. and for a survey David Hempton, '"Popular religion", 1800–1986', in Terence Thomas, ed., *The British: Their Religious Beliefs and Practices 1800–1986* (London, 1988), pp. 181–210.

28 For a notable recent example of work on social history that gives considerable prominence to religion see Leonore Davidoff and Catherine Hall, *Family Fortunes: Men and Women of the English Middle Class, 1780–1850* (London, 1987).

29 Examples include M. Cowling, *Religion and Public Doctrine in Modern England* (Cambridge, 1980, 1985); Boyd Hilton, *The Age of Atonement: The Influence of Evangelicalism on Social and Economic Thought 1785–1865* (Oxford, 1988); J. P. Parry, *Democracy and Religion: Gladstone and the Liberal Party 1867–1875* (Cambridge, 1986).

30 'National consciousness' is used here as the most general category, incorporating all these three.

31 Thomas Arnold, *Introductory Lectures on Modern History* (London, 1843), pp. 23–4.
32 Thomas Flanagan, 'Literature in English, 1801–91', in W. E. Vaughan, ed., *Ireland Under the Union, 1801–70* (Oxford, 1989), p. 510.
33 *Missionary Hymns for Children* (Sheffield, 1851), p. 7.
34 Gerald Newman, *The Rise of English Nationalism: A Cultural History 1740–1830* (London, 1987), pp. 52–3.
35 Hugh Cunningham, 'The Language of Patriotism, 1750–1914', *History Workshop Journal* 12 (Autumn 1981), p. 12.
36 John Cumming, *Christian Patriotism; or the Claims of Home and Country to Christian Consideration* (London, 1839).
37 Cunningham, op. cit., p. 21.
38 Linda Colley, *Britons: Forging the Nation 1707–1837* (New Haven and London, 1992), p. 372.
39 John Breuilly, *Nationalism and the State* (Manchester, 1982), p. 1; Benedict Anderson, *Imagined Communities: Reflections on the Origin and Spread of Nationalism* (London, 1983), p. 16.
40 A serious attempt to trace the emergence of English nationalism has been made by Gerald Newman in *The Rise of English Nationalism*, but this has little to offer on religion, nor does it explore the wider British dimension.
41 For example, see D. G. Boyce, *Nationalism in Ireland* (London, 1982).
42 Carlton J. H. Hayes, *Essays on Nationalism* (New York, 1966; reissue of 1926 work), pp. 93–125.
43 Boyce, op. cit., pp. 16–17; Peter Alter, *Nationalism* (London, 1989), pp. 9–10.
44 George L. Mosse, 'Mass politics and the political liturgy of nationalism', in Eugene Kamenka, ed., *Nationalism: The Nature and Evolution of an Idea* (London, 1973), pp. 38–54. A somewhat different approach to phenomena of this kind is represented by the concept of 'civil religion' which has been applied particularly to the United States (see, for example, Russell E. Richey and Donald G. Jones, eds, *American Civil Religion* (New York, 1974). For discussion of the concept and its applicability to Britain see John Wolffe, 'The Religions of the Silent Majority', in Gerald Parsons, ed., *The Growth of Religious Diversity: Britain from 1945: Vol. I Traditions* (London, 1993), pp. 317–27.
45 Ninian Smart, 'Lands of hope and glory', *The Times Higher Education Supplement*, 2 February 1990, p. 15.
46 Hans Kohn, *The Idea of Nationalism: A Study in its Origins and Background*, (New York, 1944), pp. 165–8; Colley, op. cit., pp. 11–54, 368–9.
47 G. Croly, *England the Fortress of Christianity* (London, 1839).
48 G. S. Faber, *The Primitive Doctrine of Election* (London, 1836), p. 20.
49 Hugh McNeile, *Nationalism in Religion* (London, 1839), pp. 2–4.
50 J. H. Newman, *Historical Sketches*, 2nd series (London, 1873), pp. 203–4.
51 F. G. Lee, *The Church Under Queen Elizabeth. An Historical Sketch* (London, 1880), p. 164.

2 A STRANGE WARMING? THE FORMATION OF VICTORIAN RELIGION

1 Nehemiah Curnock, ed., *The Journal of the Rev. John Wesley, A.M.* (3 vols, London, 1909), Vol. I, pp. 475–6.

2 Quoted in John Walsh, 'Origins of the Evangelical Revival', in G. V. Bennett and J. D. Walsh, eds, *Essays in Modern English Church History in Memory of Norman Sykes* (London, 1966), p. 134.

3 Arthur Fawcett, *The Cambuslang Revival: The Scottish Evangelical Revival of the Eighteenth Century* (London, 1971), pp. 105–7.

4 John Wesley, ed., *A Collection of Hymns for the Use of the People Called Methodists* (London, 1821), p. 197.

5 For a fuller analysis of evangelical characteristics see D. W. Bebbington, *Evangelicalism in Modern Britain: A History from the 1730s to the 1980s* (London, 1989), pp. 2–17.

6 Richard Carwardine, 'The Welsh Evangelical Community and "Finney's Revival"', *Journal of Ecclesiastical History* 29 (1978), p. 471.

7 Bebbington, op. cit., pp. 34–50.

8 John Walsh, 'Religious societies: Methodist and evangelical 1738–1800', in W. J. Sheils and Diana Wood, eds, *Voluntary Religion: Studies in Church History* 23 (Oxford, 1986), pp. 279–302.

9 Marilyn J. Westerkamp, *Triumph of the Laity: Scots-Irish Piety and the Great Awakening, 1625–1760* (New York, 1988).

10 W. R. Ward, *The Protestant Evangelical Awakening* (Cambridge, 1992), p. 312 and *passim*.

11 J. W. Massie, *The Evangelical Alliance: Its Origins and Development* (London, 1847), p. 100. See also (especially for analysis of the relationship between evangelicalism and Protestantism), John Wolffe, 'The Evangelical Alliance in the 1840s', in Sheils and Wood, op. cit., pp. 333–46.

12 Robert Currie, Alan Gilbert and Lee Horsley, *Churches and Churchgoers: Patterns of Church Growth in the British Isles Since 1700* (Oxford, 1977), pp. 40, 139–41, 148.

13 John Henry Newman, *Apologia Pro Vita Sua* (London, 1881 edn; first published 1864), p. 4.

14 J. Wesley Bready, *England Before and After Wesley* (London, 1938).

15 Fawcett, op. cit., pp. 113–15.

16 John Walsh, 'Methodism and the mob in the eighteenth century', in G. J. Cuming and Derek Baker, eds, *Popular Belief and Practice: Studies in Church History* 8 (Cambridge, 1972), pp. 213–27.

17 Bebbington, op. cit., p. 11.

18 Deborah Valenze, *Prophetic Sons and Daughters: Female Preaching and Popular Religion in Industrial England* (Princeton, NJ, 1985).

19 Walsh, 'Evangelical Revival', op. cit., pp. 136–7.

20 Elie Halévy, *The Birth of Methodism in England*, trans. and ed. by Bernard Semmel (Chicago, 1971). For an assessment of Halévy's thesis see J. D. Walsh, 'Elie Halévy and the birth of Methodism', *Transactions of the Royal Historical Society*, 5th series, 25 (1975), pp. 1–20.

21 Alan D. Gilbert, *Religion and Society in Industrial England: Church, Chapel and Social Change 1740–1914* (London, 1976), pp. 87–93.

22 E. P. Thompson, *The Making of the English Working Class* (Harmondsworth, 1968; first published 1963), p. 405.

23 Currie, Gilbert and Horsley, op. cit., p. 105.

24 Eric Hopkins, 'Religious dissent in Black Country industrial villages in the first half of the nineteenth century', *Journal of Ecclesiastical History* 34 (1983), pp. 411–24.

25 Fawcett, op. cit., pp. 102–3; David Luker, 'Revivalism in theory and practice: the case of Cornish Methodism', *Journal of Ecclesiastical History* 37 (1986), pp. 617–18.

26 Fawcett, op. cit., p. 175.

27 Christopher B. Turner, 'Revivalism and Welsh Society in the nineteenth century', in Jim Obelkevich, Lyndal Roper and Raphael Samuel, *Disciplines of Faith: Studies in Religion, Politics and Patriarchy* (London, 1987), pp. 314–15.

28 Bebbington, op. cit., p. 7; Fawcett, op. cit., pp. 116–17.

29 Derec Llwyd Morgan (trans. Dyfnallt Morgan), *The Great Awakening in Wales* (London, 1988), pp. 48–9.

30 Luker, op. cit., pp. 613–14; David Hempton and Myrtle Hill, *Evangelical Protestantism in Ulster Society 1740–1890* (London, 1992), pp. 13–14; David Clark, *Between Pulpit and Pew: Folk Religion in a North Yorkshire Fishing Village* (Cambridge, 1982), pp. 146–51. Important further evidence of the relationship between Methodism and popular culture is to appear in a forthcoming book by Peter Lineham.

31 R. Porter and M. Teich, eds, *The Enlightenment in National Context* (Cambridge, 1981), p. 6.

32 Bebbington, op. cit., pp. 50–5.

33 Stewart J. Brown, *Thomas Chalmers and the Godly Commonwealth in Scotland* (Oxford, 1982), pp. 218–19.

34 Bebbington, op. cit., pp. 80–3.

35 John Bossy, *The English Catholic Community 1570–1850* (London, 1975) pp. 182–94; James Darragh, 'The Catholic population of Scotland since the year 1680', *Innes Review* 4 (1953), p. 55.

36 Bossy, op. cit., pp. 391–401.

37 For further discussion of the comparison between Roman Catholicism and dissent see Eamon Duffy, *Peter and Jack: Roman Catholics and Dissent in Eighteenth-century England* (London, 1982).

38 Linda Colley, *Britons: Forging the Nation 1707–1837* (New Haven and London, 1992), pp. 19–24, 46; Edward Norman, *Roman Catholicism in England* (Oxford, 1985), p. 41; Christine Johnson, *Developments in the Roman Catholic Church in Scotland 1789–1829* (Edinburgh, 1983), pp. 7–8.

39 George F. E. Rudé, 'The Gordon Riots: a study of the rioters and their victims', *Transactions of the Royal Historical Society*, 5th series, 6 (1956), pp. 99–100.

40 Patrick J. Corish, *The Irish Catholic Experience: A Historical Survey* (Dublin, 1985), p. 123.

41 Ibid., pp. 127, 130.

42 The estimates used are those of Currie, Gilbert and Horsley, op. cit., p. 25. They estimate Catholic numbers at 129,000 in 1800 and 846,000 in 1850. Population was 10.5 million in 1801 and 20.8 million in 1851 (B. R. Mitchell

and Phyllis Deane, *Abstract of British Historical Statistics* (Cambridge, 1962), p. 6).

43 Bossy, op. cit., pp. 317–18.
44 Ibid., pp. 299, 338–54.
45 Darragh, op. cit., pp. 55, 59.
46 Bossy, op. cit., pp. 423–7.
47 Ibid., pp. 382–5; G. Connolly, 'The transubstantiation of myth: towards a new popular history of Roman Catholicism in England', *Journal of Ecclesiastical History* 30 (1984), pp. 78–104.
48 Donal A. Kerr, *Peel, Priests and Politics: Sir Robert Peel's Administration and the Roman Catholic Church in Ireland, 1841–1846* (Oxford, 1982), pp. 1–67.
49 For a list of members of the Hackney Phalanx see Clive Dewey, *The Passing of Barchester* (London, 1991), pp. 149–68.
50 [W. Palmer], *A Narrative of Events Connected with the Publication of the Tracts for the Times* (Oxford and London, 1843), p. 107.
51 J. H. Newman, *The Via Media of the Anglican Church* (2 vols, London, 1877), Vol. I, p. 17.
52 J. H. Newman, *Sermons Preached on Various Occasions* (Westminster, Md, 1968), pp. 171–2, 176–7.
53 Bossy, op. cit., p. 297.
54 John Wolffe, *The Protestant Crusade in Great Britain, 1829–1860* (Oxford, 1991), pp. 29–64 and *passim*.
55 W. J. Conybeare, 'Church parties', *The Edinburgh Review* 98 (1853), p. 275.
56 For fuller explanation and discussion of the concept of 'Establishment', see Chapter 6, below.
57 Norman Sykes, *Church and State in England in the Eighteenth Century* (Cambridge, 1934), pp. 319ff.; J. C. D. Clark, *English Society 1688–1832* (Cambridge, 1985), pp. 139–41, 229.
58 Edmund Burke (ed. Conor Cruise O'Brien), *Reflections on the Revolution in France* (Harmondsworth, 1968), p. 198.
59 F. C. Mather, 'Georgian churchmanship reconsidered: some variations in Anglican public worship 1714–1830', *Journal of Ecclesiastical History* 36 (1985), pp. 255–83. Cf. F. C. Mather, *High Church Prophet: Bishop Samuel Horsley (1733–1806) and the Caroline Tradition in the Later Georgian Church* (Oxford, 1992).
60 Peter Virgin, *The Church in an Age of Negligence: Ecclesiastical Structure and the Problems of Church Reform 1700–1840* (Cambridge, 1989), pp. 131–70, 191–214; Gordon Rupp, *Religion in England 1688–1791* (Oxford 1986), p. 511. See above, Chapter 1, pp. 5–13.
61 R. B. Sher, *Church and University in the Scottish Enlightenment* (Edinburgh, 1985), pp. 151–2.
62 Dominic Bellenger, 'The emigré clergy and the English Church, 1789–1815', *Journal of Ecclesiastical History* 34 (1983), pp. 392–410.
63 Johnson, op. cit., pp. 119–29.
64 Deryck Lovegrove, 'English evangelical dissent and the European conflict, 1780–1815', in W. J. Sheils, ed., *The Church and War: Studies in Church History* 20 (Oxford, 1983), pp. 263–76.
65 N. U. Murray, 'The Influence of the French Revolution on the Church of England and its rivals, 1789–1802', Oxford DPhil thesis, 1975, pp. 276–8.

66 Anon., *A Sermon Preached on the Sunday after the Funeral of the Right Honourable Lord Viscount Nelson* (Chelsea, 1806), pp. 7, 12.

67 John Styles, *A Tribute to the Memory of Nelson: A Sermon Delivered at West Cowes, November 10 1805* (Newport, IOW, 1806), Preface, pp. 6–7, 21, 24.

68 John Townsend, *Lord Nelson's Funeral Improved in A Discourse Delivered the 12th of January 1806* (London, 1806), p. 33 and *passim.*

69 John Gardiner, *A Tribute to the Memory of Lord Nelson* (Bath, 1805), pp. 15, 19; Colley, op. cit., p. 180.

70 Colley, op. cit., pp. 222, 231, 270–3.

71 See below, pp. 153–8.

72 S. C. Orchard, 'English Evangelical Eschatology, 1790–1850', Cambridge PhD. thesis, 1968, pp. 32–63.

73 William Wilberforce, *An Appeal to the Religion, Justice and Humanity of the Inhabitants of the British Empire, in Behalf of the Negro Slaves in the West Indies* (London, 1823), pp. 74–5.

74 Quoted in Marianne Elliott, *Partners in Revolution: The United Irishmen and France* (New Haven, 1982), p. 23.

75 Ibid., pp. 238–9.

76 Hempton and Hill, op. cit., pp. 20–44.

77 Wolffe, *Protestant Crusade,* op. cit., *passim.*

78 Nottingham University Library, Department of Manuscripts, Newcastle Diary, Ne2F2, 31 December 1829.

79 Cf. Colley, op. cit., p. 334. Colley points out, however, that 'Protestant patriotism remained powerful and widespread' after 1829, as will also be argued in later chapters of the present book.

80 See, for example, *Speech of the Rev. Hugh McNeile in defence of the Established Church at the Second Annual Meeting of the Protestant Association. . . . May 10 1837* (3rd edn, London, 1839).

81 Brown, op. cit., pp. 222ff. See below, Chapter 5, pp. 99–102.

82 Wolffe, 'Evangelical Alliance', op. cit., p. 341.

83 Cf. Bernard M. G. Reardon, *Religious Thought in the Victorian Age: A Survey from Coleridge to Gore* (London, 1980); Ruth Roberts, *Arnold and God* (Berkeley, 1983), p. 57.

84 This view has been advanced by Richard Brent in *Liberal Anglican Politics: Whiggery, Religion and Reform, 1830–1841* (Oxford, 1990) and criticized by R. W. Davis, 'The Whigs and religious issues', in R. W. Davis and R. J. Helmstadter, eds, *Religion and Irreligion in Victorian Society* (London, 1992), pp. 29–50.

3   GOD MADE THEM HIGH OR LOWLY? OFFICIAL RELIGION

1 See above, pp. 8–12.

2 Sean Connolly, *Religion and Society in Nineteenth Century Ireland* (Dundalk, 1985), p. 3.

3 Edward Royle, *The Victorian Church in York* (York, 1983), p. 9.

4 Ibid., pp. 27–31.

5 Nigel Yates, 'The religious life of Victorian Leeds', in Derek Fraser, ed., *A History of Modern Leeds* (Manchester, 1980), pp. 255–6.

6 Borthwick Institute of Historical Research, York, 'Report upon the state of the Rural Deanery of the City and Ainsty of York, December 1845' (RD.AIN 2).

7 E. T. Davies, *Religion in the Industrial Revolution in South Wales* (Cardiff, 1965), p. 32.

8 P. M. H. Bell, *Disestablishment in Ireland and Wales* (London, 1969), pp. 32–3.

9 David Hempton and Myrtle Hill, *Evangelical Protestantism in Ulster Society 1740–1890* (London, 1992), pp. 108–9.

10 For a fuller discussion of the Disruption and the events which led to it, see below, Chapter 5.

11 Callum G. Brown, 'The costs of pew-renting: church management, church-going and social class in nineteenth-century Glasgow', *Journal of Ecclesiastical History* 38 (1987), pp. 347–61.

12 Peter Hillis, 'Presbyterianism and social class in mid-nineteenth-century Glasgow: a study of nine churches', *Journal of Ecclesiastical History* 32 (1981), pp. 47–64.

13 Patrick Joyce, *Work, Society and Politics: The Culture of the Factory in Late Victorian England* (London, 1982), pp. 253–4. The indications that there was *some* working-class support for the Established Churches are not of course inconsistent with evidence of the apathy of the majority, especially the unskilled, which will be examined further below.

14 R. H. Inglis, *Church Extension: Substance of a Speech delivered in the House of Commons, 30 June 1840* (London, 1840), p. 69.

15 A. D. Gilbert, *Religion and Society in Industrial England* (London, 1976), p. 130.

16 Callum G. Brown, *The Social History of Religion in Scotland since 1730* (London, 1987), pp. 142, 150–1.

17 Davies, op. cit., pp. 97ff.

18 Ieuan Gwynedd Jones, 'Ecclesiastical economy: aspects of church building in Victorian Wales', in R. R. Davies, Ralph A. Griffiths, Ieuan Gywnedd Jones and Kenneth O. Morgan, eds, *Welsh Society and Nationhood* (Cardiff, 1984), p. 218.

19 D. H. Akenson, *The Church of Ireland: Ecclesiastical Reform and Restoration, 1800–1855* (New Haven and London, 1971), p. 218 and *passim*.

20 Clyde Binfield, *So Down to Prayers: Studies in English Nonconformity 1780–1920* (London, 1977), p. 21.

21 For a convenient survey of Nonconformist groups in the Victorian period see Gerald Parsons, ed., *Religion in Victorian Britain: Vol. I Traditions* (Manchester, 1988), pp. 75–86.

22 A. A. MacLaren, *Religion and Social Class: The Disruption Years in Aberdeen* (London, 1974), pp. 69–94.

23 Brown, *The Social History of Religion*, op. cit., pp. 105–12.

24 W. R. Lambert, 'Some working-class attitudes towards organized religion in nineteenth-century Wales', in Gerald Parsons, ed., *Religion in Victorian Britain: Vol. IV Interpretations* (Manchester, 1988), p. 101.

25 Colin Spencer, *The History of Hebden Bridge* (Hebden Bridge, 1991), pp. 57–62, 69.

26 There remained those rumps of both the Free Church (Wee Frees) and the United Free Church who were unable to accept these unions, as well as the

Free Presbyterian Church which left the Free Church of Scotland in 1892 because of its perceived declension from Calvinist standards and ideals.

27 Gilbert, op. cit., p. 42.

28 David Englander, 'Anglicized not Anglican: Jews and Judaism in Victorian Britain', in Gerald Parsons, ed., *Religion in Victorian Britain: Vol. I Traditions*, pp. 240, 253.

29 Ibid., pp. 255–6.

30 M. M. Ally, 'History of Muslims in Britain', Birmingham MA thesis, 1981, pp. 1–82.

31 David Clark, *Between Pulpit and Pew: Folk Religion in a North Yorkshire Fishing Village* (Cambridge, 1982), pp. 66–90.

32 Kew, Public Record Office, Returns of the Census of Religious Worship, HO/129/500/8, Farnley Iron Works.

33 R. Currie, A. Gilbert and L. Horsley, *Churches and Churchgoers: Patterns of Church Growth in the British Isles Since 1700* (Oxford, 1977), p. 216.

34 Englander, op. cit., p. 255.

35 B. I. Coleman, *The Church of England in the Mid-Nineteenth Century* (London, 1980), p. 40.

36 John D. Gay, *The Geography of Religion in England* (London, 1971), p. 223.

37 Brown, *The Social History of Religion*, op. cit., p. 61.

38 *Parliamentary Papers*, 1854, lix, p. 18. It should be reiterated that this figure – like the Glasgow and Edinburgh figures quoted above – probably reflects something of an undercalculation of the proportion of Church of Scotland attendances due to missing returns.

39 For two geographically widely separated illustrations see Hillis, op. cit.; and David Luker, 'Revivalism in theory and practice: the case of Cornish Methodism', *Journal of Ecclesiastical History* 37 (1986), pp. 603–19.

40 It might be objected that the communicant figures could reflect stronger liturgical emphasis on Holy Communion as much as widening commitment to the Church. On the other hand when, from 1924, electoral roll figures began to be available they exceeded communicant numbers by a ratio of approximately 5 to 3, thus giving grounds for the reverse argument that the numbers given here understate Anglican strength. The problem is a good example of the caution necessary in interpreting such statistics, but they are the best indicator available to us.

41 Currie, Gilbert and Horsley, op. cit., p. 135.

42 In order to permit the calculations in this paragraph Roman Catholics have been notionally assigned to England and Wales in proportion to total population.

43 These figures have been obtained by summing up all the figures in Currie, Gilbert and Horsley, op. cit., Tables A1 to A5, pp. 128–55. As the smaller churches listed in Table A6 (pp. 156–60) have had to be omitted because Great Britain totals have not been disaggregated, and figures for other small groups are not available at all, the percentages given are a slight underestimate.

44 Connolly, op. cit., p. 6.

45 Ibid., p. 42; Emmet Larkin, 'The Devotional Revolution in Ireland, 1850–75', *American Historical Review* 77 (1972), p. 636.

4 OUTSIDE THE SHEEPFOLD? UNOFFICIAL RELIGION

1 G. W. E. Russell, *Arthur Stanton: A Memoir* (London, 1917), p. 72. Cf. John Kent, 'Feelings and festivals: an interpretation of some working-class religious attitudes', in H. J. Dyos and Michael Wolff, eds, *The Victorian City: Images and Realities* (2 vols, London, 1973), Vol. II, pp. 865–6.

2 Keith Thomas, *Religion and the Decline of Magic* (London, 1971).

3 J. Obelkevich, *Religion and Rural Society, South Lindsey: 1825–1875* (Oxford, 1976); David Clark, *Between Pulpit and Pew: Folk Religion in a North Yorkshire Fishing Village* (Cambridge, 1982).

4 S. J. Connolly, *Priests and People in Pre-Famine Ireland* (Dublin, 1982).

5 A. W. Smith, 'Popular Religion', *Past and Present* 40 (1968), p. 183; Clark, op. cit., pp. 118–19; Obelkevich, op. cit., p. 272.

6 Obelkevich, op. cit., p. 131.

7 Borthwick Institute, York, Archbishop's Visitation Returns for 1900 (B.Bp.Vis.1900), 167, Holy Trinity, Heworth; 278, All Saints', North Ferriby; and *passim*.

8 Obelkevich, op. cit., p. 264.

9 Roderick Floud and Donald McCloskey, eds, *The Economic History of Britain Since 1700* (2 vols, Cambridge, 1981), Vol. I, p. 27; B. R. Mitchell and Phyllis Deane, *Abstract of British Historical Statistics* (Cambridge, 1962), p. 28.

10 Borthwick Institute, B.Bp.Vis.1900/208, Kirby Misperton. This might be compared with Thomas Hardy's fictional version of the development of such a relationship in *Jude the Obscure* (Harmondsworth, 1978; first published 1896), pp. 80–119.

11 The percentages given have been calculated from the figures in Mitchell and Deane op. cit., pp. 28–33. For a case of 'antenuptial fornication' in Govan, Scotland, in 1855 see Peter Hillis, 'Presbyterianism and social class', *Journal of Ecclesiastical History* 32 (1981), p. 61.

12 Connolly, op. cit., pp. 191–3, 200–13.

13 Obelkevich, op. cit., p. 296.

14 Clark, op. cit., pp. 128–9; Obelkevich, *Religion and Rural Society*, p. 297.

15 Connolly, op. cit., pp. 148–59: Lynn Hollen Lees, *Exiles of Erin: Irish Migrants in Victorian London* (Manchester, 1979), pp. 186–7.

16 Obelkevich, op. cit., pp. 266–7.

17 Ibid., pp. 269–70; Clark, op. cit., pp. 107–8; Erik Routley, *The English Carol* (New York, 1959), pp. 50–2.

18 Clark, op. cit., pp. 91–5.

19 Obelkevich, op. cit., pp. 268–9.

20 Clark, op. cit., pp. 106–7.

21 Connolly, op. cit., pp. 105–9; Lees, op. cit., pp 167–8.

22 Obelkevich, op. cit., p. 275; Connolly, op. cit., pp. 116–19.

23 Ibid., pp. 135–48.

24 Obelkevich, op. cit., pp. 283–7.

25 Connolly, op. cit., p. 101.

26 Peter Mathias, *The First Industrial Nation: An Economic History of Britain 1700–1914* (London, 1960), pp. 198–9, 246, 249. A town is here defined as a community with a population of more than 5,000.

27 W. R. Ward, *Religion and Society in England 1790–1850* (London, 1972), pp. 78–9; Robert Colls, 'Primitive Methodists in the northern coalfields', in Jim Obelkevich, Lyndal Roper and Raphael Samuel, eds, *Disciplines of Faith* (London, 1987), pp. 323–34.

28 James Hunter, *The Making of the Crofting Community* (Edinburgh, 1976), pp. 94–106.

29 R. W. Ambler, 'The Transformation of Harvest Celebration in nineteenth-century Lincolnshire', *Midland History* 3 (1975–6), p. 301.

30 A. C. Benson, *The Life of Edward White Benson* (2 vols, 1900), Vol. I, p. 484. Benson was later Archbishop of Canterbury.

31 Richard Mudie-Smith, ed., *The Religious Life of London* (1904), p. 30; Jeffrey Cox, *The English Churches in a Secular Society: Lambeth, 1870–1930* (New York, 1982), pp. 102–3.

32 Donald M. Lewis, *Lighten Their Darkness: The Evangelical Mission to Working-Class London, 1828–1860* (Westport, Conn., 1986), pp. 120–1.

33 Olive Checkland, *Philanthropy in Victorian Scotland* (Edinburgh, 1980), p. 67; Peter Hillis, 'Education and evangelization: Presbyterian missions in mid-nineteenth-century Glasgow', *Scottish Historical Review* 66 (1987), pp. 46–62.

34 Leslie Howsam, *Cheap Bibles: Nineteenth-Century Publishing and the British and Foreign Bible Society* (Cambridge, 1991), pp. 49–51.

35 Edwin Hodder, *The Life and Work of the Seventh Earl of Shaftesbury K.G.* (3 vols, London, 1887), Vol. II, p. 359.

36 Quoted Hillis, op. cit., p. 53.

37 Cox, op. cit., pp. 95–6.

38 For Nonconformist attitudes to the 1902 Act, and its political context see below, pp. 126–7.

39 Adrian Hastings, *A History of English Christianity 1920–1985* (London, 1986), p. 105. This figure includes an unknown proportion of adult participants.

40 Peter G. Forster, 'Residual religiosity on a Hull council estate', *Sociological Review* 37 (1989), p. 491.

41 Callum G. Brown, *The Social History of Religion in Scotland Since 1730* (London, 1987), p. 85.

42 Quoted by Stephen Yeo, *Religion and Voluntary Organisations in Crisis* (London, 1976), p. 163.

43 Lees, op. cit., pp. 191–2.

44 Bernard Aspinwall, 'The Welfare State within the State: the Saint Vincent de Paul Society in Glasgow, 1848–1920', in W. J. Sheils and Diana Wood, eds, *Voluntary Religion: Studies in Church History* 23 (Oxford, 1986), pp. 445–59.

45 Lewis, op. cit., pp. 129–31; James R. Moore, *Religion in Victorian Britain: Vol. III Sources* (Manchester, 1988), pp. 269–71, quoting the contemporary account by C. M. Davies of Stanton's ministry.

46 Emmet Larkin, 'The devotional revolution in Ireland, 1850–75', *American Historical Review* 77 (1972), pp. 625–52.

47 Larkin, op. cit., pp. 648–9.

48 Michael J. F. McCarthy, *Priests and People in Ireland* (Dublin, 1902), p. 251; K. Theodore Hoppen, *Ireland since 1800: Conflict and Conformity* (London, 1989), p. 152.

49 Sheridan Gilley, 'Vulgar piety and the Brompton Oratory, 1850–1860', in R. Swift and S. Gilley, eds, *The Irish in the Victorian City* (London, 1985), pp. 255–66.

50 Quoted by David Englander, 'Anglicized not Anglican: Jews and Judaism in Victorian Britain', in Gerald Parsons, ed., *Religion in Victorian Britain: Vol. I Traditions* (Manchester, 1988), p. 253.

51 Edward Royle, *Victorian Infidels: The Origins of the British Secularist Movement 1791–1866* (Manchester, 1974), pp. 229–44.

52 Susan Budd, 'The loss of faith: reasons for unbelief among members of the secular movement in England, 1850–1950', *Past and Present* 36 (1967), pp. 106–25.

53 Lewis, op. cit., pp. 128–49.

54 Quoted by Cox, op. cit., p. 94.

55 John Burnett, *Destiny Obscure: Autobiographies of Childhood, Education and Family from the 1820s to the 1920s* (London, 1982), pp. 36–43; Hugh McLeod, 'New perspectives on Victorian class religion: the oral evidence', *Oral History* 14, 1 (1986), pp. 33–4.

56 George Lansbury, *My Life* (London, 1928), pp. 29–30.

57 Cf. Brian Harrison, 'Religion and Recreation in Nineteenth-Century England', *Past and Present* 38 (1967), pp. 123–5.

58 Cox, op. cit., p. 93.

59 McLeod, op. cit., p. 33.

60 Cox, op. cit., p. 95.

61 C. F. G. Masterman, *The Condition of England* (London, 1909), p. 268. Cf. E. R. Wickham, *Church and People in an Industrial City* (London, 1957), p. 180; Hugh McLeod, *Class and Religion in the Late Victorian City* (London, 1974), pp. 246–50.

62 Borthwick Institute York, Archbishop's Visitation Returns for 1931 (Bp. V.1931/RET), St Lawrence, York.

63 Mass Observation, *Puzzled People* (London, 1947), pp. 21, 42–4, 50–1, 56–7, 86, 96.

64 Ibid., pp. 72–4.

65 Nicholas Abercrombie *et al.*, 'Superstition and religion: the God of the Gaps', *A Sociological Yearbook of Religion in Britain* 3 (1970), p. 124 and *passim.* The foregoing discussion of course begs the questions of how the beliefs of official Christianity were also changing during the period, a point which will be addressed in Chapter 7.

66 For further development and substantation of this analysis see John Wolffe, *The Protestant Crusade in Great Britain 1829–60* (Oxford, 1991), D. G. Paz, *Popular Anti-Catholicism in Mid-Victorian England* (Stanford, 1992) and David Hempton and Myrtle Hill, *Evangelical Protestantism in Ulster Society, 1740–1890* (London, 1992), p. 44 and *passim.*

67 Wolffe, op. cit., p. 75; David A. Roberts 'The Orange Order in Ireland: a religious institution?', *British Journal of Sociology* 22 (1971), pp. 269–82.

68 Tom Gallagher, *Glasgow: The Uneasy Peace* (Manchester, 1987), p. 99.

69 Patrick Joyce, *Work, Society and Politics: The Culture of the Factory in Later Victorian England* (Brighton, 1980), p. 174.

70 Quoted ibid., pp. 249–50.

5   HIGH TIDE OF FAITH? RELIGION AND NATIONHOOD AROUND 1850

1 T. Brown, *Annals of the Disruption, with Extracts from the Narratives of Ministers who left the Scottish Establishment in 1843* (Edinburgh, 1893), pp. 90–2.

2 Stewart J. Brown, *Thomas Chalmers and the Godly Commonwealth in Scotland* (Oxford, 1982), p. 335.

3 G. I. T. Machin, *Politics and the Churches in Great Britain 1832 to 1868* (Oxford, 1977), p. 114.

4 Brown, op. cit., pp. 324–6.

5 New College Library, Edinburgh, bound volume of tributes to Thomas Chalmers, X13b 4/1, poem by Wm M'Comb.

6 *The Times*, 27 May 1843, p. 7.

7 *The Times*, 17 August 1843, pp. 6–7; 18 August 1843, p. 6.

8 *Free Church Magazine* 42 (June 1847), pp. 189–90, quoting *Inverness Courier*.

9 *The Times*, 17 August 1843, p. 6.

10 Quoted by Oliver MacDonagh, *The Emancipist: Daniel O'Connell 1830–47* (London, 1989), p. 235.

11 Richard Davis, *The Young Ireland Movement* (Dublin, 1987), pp. 35, 38.

12 Jacqueline R. Hill, 'Nationalism and the Catholic Church in the 1840s: Views of Dublin Repealers', *Irish Historical Studies* 19 (1975), pp. 371–95.

13 Quoted by E. D. Steele, 'Cardinal Cullen and Irish nationality', *Irish Historical Studies* 19 (1975), p. 240.

14 Trinity College Library, Dublin, Irish Ballads Collection, 189. t, Vol. I, No. 143, Lines to the Memory of Daniel O'Connell.

15 *Parliamentary Papers*, 1847, Vol. XXVII, Part I, pp. i, 3–5.

16 Ibid., Part III, pp. 59–60, 63.

17 Ibid., Part III, pp. 58.

18 Ibid., Part I, p. 6.

19 Prys Morgan, 'From Long Knives to Blue Books', in R. R. Davis, Ralph A. Griffiths, Ieuan Gywnedd Jones and Kenneth O. Morgan, eds, *Welsh Society and Nationhood* (Cardiff, 1984), pp. 199–200.

20 Prys Morgan, 'From a death to a view: the hunt for the Welsh past in the Romantic period', in Eric Hobsbawm and Terence Ranger, eds, *The Invention of Tradition* (Cambridge, 1983), pp. 43–100.

21 Morgan, 'Long Knives to Blue Books', op. cit., p. 208.

22 See above, p. 60.

23 *The Protestant Watchman* (1850), p. 274.

24 Printed in E. R. Norman, *Anti-Catholicism in Victorian England* (London, 1968), p. 160.

25 G. M. Young and W. D. Handcock, eds *English Historical Documents 1833–1844* (London, 1956), p. 365.

26 'Puseyism' was a widely used term of abuse, derived from Edward Pusey, one of the movement's most prominent leaders.

27 *The Protestant Watchman* (1850), p. 274; Norman, op. cit., p. 160.

28 *The Times*, 26 November 1850, p. 7. See also ibid., 29 November 1850, p. 5; 30 November 1850, p. 6; 7 December 1850, p. 5.

29 *The Times*, 30 November 1850, p. 6. See also ibid., 26 November 1850, p. 7; 3 December 1850, p. 8; 5 December 1850, p. 5.

30 *The Times*, 6 December 1850, p. 6.

31 Young and Handcock, op. cit., p. 366.

32 J. H. Newman, *Sermons Preached on Various Occasions* (Westminster, Md, 1968), pp. 170, 174–9.

33 *The Works of Alfred Lord Tennyson* (London, 1897), p. 218.

34 See, for example, S. M. Anderson, *Every Man the Bearer of his own Burden* (London, 1852); Henry N. Barrett, *The Victor Vanquished* (London, 1852).

35 The *Leeds Intelligencer*, 20 November 1852.

36 *Works of Tennyson*, op. cit., p. 221.

37 Bodleian Library, Oxford, Napier MSS (MS Eng. Misc. b.96), ff. 333–41.

38 *The Times*, 12 November 1852, p. 8; 19 November 1852, p. 5.

39 Peter Burman, *St Paul's Cathedral* (London, 1987), pp. 155–6.

40 See, for example, *The Eclectic Review*, November 1852, p. 641.

41 The *Leeds Intelligencer*, 20 November 1852.

42 The *Freeman's Journal*, 20 November 1852.

43 Dublin City Hall, Minutes of the Municipal Council of the City of Dublin, Vol. 16, 1 November 1852.

44 Edinburgh City Chambers, Edinburgh Town Council Minutes, Vol. 259, p. 38, 30 November 1852.

45 Olive Anderson, 'The Reactions of Church and Dissent towards the Crimean War', *Journal of Ecclesiastical History* 16 (1965), pp. 209–20.

46 Ibid., pp. 214–17.

47 G. S. Bull, *Home and How to Make it Happy* (Birmingham, 1854).

48 [Catherine Marsh], *Memorials of Captain Hedley Vicars, Ninety-Seventh Regiment* (London, 1904 edn), pp. x, 288–91. Cf. Olive Anderson, 'The Growth of Christian Militarism in mid-Victorian Britain', *English Historical Review* 86 (1971), pp. 48–9.

6 THINE IS THE KINGDOM? POLITICS, COMMUNITY AND THE MONARCHY

1 Quoted by William H. Mackintosh, *Disestablishment and Liberation* (London, 1972), p. 28.

2 Roundell Palmer, Earl of Selborne, *A Defence of the Church of England against Disestablishment* (5th edn, London, 1911), p. 74.

3 *'Church and Queen' – Five Speeches delivered by the Rt Hon. B. Disraeli M.P.*, 1860–1864 (London, 1865), p. 18.

4 Quoted by P. M. H. Bell, *Disestablishment in Ireland and Wales* (London, 1969), p. 158.

5 Dissenters (but not Roman Catholics) had in practice been able by the early nineteenth century to circumvent the provisions of the penal legislation excluding them from Parliament, but its repeal was still a change of considerable symbolic importance.

6 Callum G. Brown, *A Social History of Religion in Scotland since 1730* (London, 1987), pp. 99, 197.

7 J. P. Parry, 'Religion and the collapse of Gladstone's first government, 1870–1874', *The Historical Journal* 25 (1982), pp. 85–95.

8 For a detailed account of its history see William H. Mackintosh, *Disestablishment and Liberation: The Movement for the Separation of the Anglican Church from State Control* (London, 1972).

9 St Deiniol's Library, Hawarden, Glynne Gladstone MSS, 1039, Geo. J. Knight to Mrs. Gladstone; D. W. Bebbington, 'Gladstone and the Nonconformists: a religious affinity in politics', in D. Baker, ed., *Church, Society and Politics: Studies in Church History* 12 (Oxford, 1975), pp. 369–82; Eugenio F. Biagini, *Liberty, Retrenchment and Reform: Popular Liberalism in the Age of Gladstone 1860–1880* (Cambridge, 1992), pp. 390–1.

10 The pattern of legislation was somewhat different in Ireland, where the 1867 Reform Act did not apply, but there had been significant changes in 1829 and 1850. The effect was broadly to enfranchise the more substantial farmers. See K. Theodore Hoppen, *Ireland since 1800: Conflict and Conformity* (London, 1989), p. 86.

11 J. P. D. Dunbabin, 'Electoral reforms and their outcome in the United Kingdom 1865–1900', in T. R. Gourvish and Alan O'Day, eds, *Later Victorian Britain 1867–1900* (1988), p. 102.

12 It might be objected here that the men who could vote were less exposed to religious influences than the as yet unenfranchised women. However, as will be argued below, loyalties were mediated as much by the general ethos of a community as by the specific teaching of the churches.

13 Quoted by H. J. Hanham, *Elections and Party Management: Politics in the Time of Disraeli and Gladstone* (London, 1959), p. 19.

14 P. F. Clarke, *Lancashire and the New Liberalism* (Cambridge, 1971), pp. 254–7, 267.

15 Hanham, op. cit., pp. 117–21.

16 Hugh McLeod, 'New Perspectives on Victorian class religion: the oral evidence', *Oral History* 14, no. 1 (1986), p. 36.

17 Hanham, op. cit., pp. 314, 317; Patrick Joyce, *Work, Society and Politics: The Culture of the Factory in Later Victorian England* (London, 1982), pp. 253–5.

18 Joyce, op. cit., pp. 256–61.

19 Martin Pugh, *The Tories and the People 1880–1935* (Oxford, 1985), pp. 13, 20–4, 28–36, 47–53, 81–7 and *passim*.

20 Biagini, op. cit., p. 37.

21 *British Library General Catalogue of Printed Books.*

22 Biagini, op. cit., pp. 31–5.

23 Glynne-Gladstone MSS, 1037, Cissy Rawlins to Mrs Gladstone, 20 May 1898. Cf. Biagini, op. cit., pp. 395–405.

24 Roy Jenkins, *Asquith* (London, 1964), pp. 14, 18–19; John Grigg, *The Young Lloyd George* (London, 1973), pp. 33–5. For an example of Lloyd George's use of biblically resonant language, see below, p. 236.

25 Eileen Yeo, 'Christianity in Chartist struggle, 1838–42', *Past and Present* 91 (1981), pp. 109–39.

26 Charles Kingsley, *The Message of the Church to Labouring Men* (London, 1851), p. 20.

27 Robert Moore, *Pitmen, Preachers and Politics* (Cambridge, 1974), p. 59; Clarke, op. cit., p. 263.

28 George Lansbury, *My Life* (London, 1928), pp. 38–9.

29 Paul Thompson, *Socialists, Liberals and Labour: the Struggle for London 1885–1914* (London, 1967), p. 31.

30 Moore, op. cit., pp. 169–82; E. T. Davies, *Religion in the Industrial Revolution in South Wales* (Cardiff, 1965), pp. 160–1; Kenneth D. Brown 'Nonconformity and the British Labour Movement: A Case Study', *Journal of Social History* 8 (1975), pp. 113–20.

31 A. Ainsworth, 'Religion in the working class community, and the evolution of socialism in late nineteenth century Lancashire: A case of working class consciousness', *Histoire Sociale/Social History* 10 (1977), pp. 364–5.

32 Stanley Baldwin, *On England* (London, 1926), pp. 195–6.

33 Stephen Yeo, 'A new life: the religion of Socialism in Britain, 1883–1896', *History Workshop Journal* 4 (1977), pp. 6, 9–18, 34; Thompson, op. cit., pp. 209–10.

34 Lansbury, op. cit., p. 78.

35 Biagini, op. cit., p. 352.

36 Thompson, op. cit., p. 293.

37 Quoted by Stephen Yeo, op. cit., pp. 5–6, 20.

38 Lansbury, op. cit., pp. 281–8.

39 Stephen Yeo, op. cit., p. 6.

40 Ieuan Gwynedd Jones, *Communities: Essays in the Social History of Victorian Wales* (Llandysul, 1987), pp. 81–4, 262–313.

41 Kenneth O. Morgan, 'The Welsh in English politics, 1868–1982', in R. R. Davies, Ralph A. Griffiths, Ieuan Gwynedd Jones and Kenneth O. Morgan, eds, *Welsh Society and Nationhood* (Cardiff, 1984), p. 235.

42 Quoted by G. I. T. Machin, *Politics and the Churches in Great Britain, 1869 to 1921* (Oxford, 1987), p. 168.

43 *The Times*, 14 September 1892, p. 4. Cf. Kenneth O. Morgan, *Wales in British Politics 1868–1922* (3rd edn, Cardiff, 1980), pp. 122–3.

44 Morgan, *Wales in British Politics*, op. cit., p. 162.

45 Ibid., pp. 303–4; Keith Robbins, 'Religion and Identity in Modern British History', in Stuart Mews, ed., *Religion and National Identity: Studies in Church History* 18 (Oxford, 1982), pp. 476–7.

46 H. J. Hanham, 'Mid-century Scottish nationalism: romantic and radical', in R. Robson, ed., *Ideas and Institutions of Victorian Britain* (London, 1967), pp. 150–4.

47 D. W. Bebbington, 'Religion and national feeling in nineteenth-century Wales and Scotland', in Mews, ed., op. cit., pp. 500–1.

48 *Proposed National Monument to Dr Chalmers* (Edinburgh, 1869); Michael T. R. B. Turnbull, *Monuments and Statues of Edinburgh* (Edinburgh, 1989), pp. 48–9.

49 Hanham, 'Mid-century Scottish nationalism', op. cit., pp. 143–73.

50 Graham Walker, 'Protestantism and political culture, 1890–1990', in Graham Walker and Tom Gallagher, eds, *Sermons and Battle Hymns: Protestant Popular Culture in Modern Scotland* (Edinburgh, 1990), pp. 90–1. Walker stresses the inherent ambivalences of Scottish political identity as related to Protestantism.

51 Stewart J. Brown, '"Outside the Covenant": The Scottish Presbyterian churches and Irish immigration, 1922–1938', *The Innes Review* 42 (1991), pp. 19–45.

52 Christopher Harvie, *Scotland and Nationalism: Scottish Society and Politics 1707–1977* (London, 1977), p. 51; Tom Gallagher, *Glasgow: The Uneasy Peace* (Manchester, 1987), p. 165.

53 Quoted by Henry R. Sefton, 'The Church of Scotland and Scottish nationhood' in Mews, ed., op. cit., p. 550.

54 Bebbington, 'Religion and national identity', op. cit., pp. 501–3; John Wolffe, *The Protestant Crusade in Great Britain 1829–1860* (Oxford, 1991), pp. 310–11.

55 Desmond Bowen, *The Protestant Crusade in Ireland, 1800–70* (Dublin, 1978), p. 313.

56 See also below, pp. 195–8 for discussion of the contribution of nominal Protestants such as W. B. Yeats to Irish culture.

57 Archbishop John MacHale of Tuam was an important exception to this trend, but an increasingly isolated one.

58 Hoppen, op. cit., pp. 158–60.

59 David Hempton, '"For God and Ulster": Evangelical Protestantism and the Home Rule Crisis of 1886', in Keith Robbins, ed., *Protestant Evangelicalism: Britain, Ireland, Germany and America c. 1750–1950: Studies in Church History*, Subsidia 7 (Oxford, 1990), pp. 225–54; Joseph Lee, *The Modernisation of Irish Society 1848–1918* (Dublin, 1973), pp. 132–3.

60 David Hempton and Myrtle Hill, *Evangelical Protestantism in Ulster Society 1740–1890* (London, 1992), pp. 172–85; I. G. C. Hutchinson, *A Political History of Scotland 1832–1924* (Edinburgh, 1986), p. 162.

61 A. T. Q. Stewart, *The Ulster Crisis: Resistance to Home Rule, 1912–14* (London, 1967), pp. 62, 66. The exact number of signatories was 471,414, which included 234,046 women who signed a parallel document.

62 R. F. G. Holmes, ' "Ulster will fight and Ulster will be right": the Protestant churches and Ulster's resistance to Home Rule, 1912–14', in W. J. Sheils, ed., *The Church and War: Studies in Church History* 20 (Oxford, 1983), pp. 329–30.

63 Mark Tierney, *Croke of Cashel: The Life of Archbishop Thomas William Croke, 1823–1902* (Dublin, 1976), pp. 76–8, 139–40 and *passim.*

64 Hoppen, op. cit., pp. 160–6; Tom Garvin, 'Priests and patriots: Irish separatism and the fear of the modern, 1890–1914', *Irish Historical Studies* 25 (1986), pp. 67–81.

65 Quoted by John Newsinger, 'I bring not peace but a sword': the religious motif in the Irish War of Independence', *Journal of Contemporary History* 13 (1978), p. 614. Cf. Sheridan Gilley, 'Pearse's sacrifice: Christ and Cuchulain crucified and risen in the Easter Rising, 1916', in J. Obelkevich, L. Roper and Raphael Samuel, eds, *Disciplines of Faith* (London, 1987), pp. 479–97.

66 Michael Fogarty, *The Great Bishop of Limerick* (Dublin, 1917), p. 15; Hoppen, op. cit., p. 167.

67 Quoted by Newsinger, op. cit., p. 622.

68 Newsinger, op. cit., p. 623.

69 J. H. Whyte, *Church and State in Modern Ireland 1923–1979* (Dublin, 1980), pp. 10–12.

70 Ibid., pp. 24–61.

71 John A. Murphy, 'The Achievement of Eamon de Valera', in John P. O'Carrol and John A. Murphy, eds, *De Valera and His Times* (Cork, 1986), pp. 5–9.

72 J. P. O'Carroll, 'Eamon de Valera, charisma and political development', in O'Carroll and Murphy, op. cit., pp. 17–33; M. A. G. O'Tuathaigh, 'De Valera and sovereignty', in ibid., p. 67.

73 Steve Bruce, *God Save Ulster: The Religion and Politics of Paisleyism* (Oxford, 1986), pp. 14–17, 84–5.

74 J. H. Whyte, *Interpreting Northern Ireland* (Oxford, 1990), pp. 18–22; John Wolffe, '"And There's Another Country. . .", Religion, the state and British identities', in G. Parsons, ed., *The Growth of Religious Diversity: Britain from 1945: Vol. II Issues* (London, 1994), pp. 107–15.

75 *The Times*, 10 July 1911, pp. 9–10.

76 *The Times*, 14 July 1911, pp. 9–11.

77 *The Times*, 20 July 1911, p. 9.

78 David Cannadine, 'The context, performance and meaning of ritual: the British monarchy and the "Invention of Tradition" c. 1820–1977', in E. Hobsbawm and T. Ranger, eds, *The Invention of Tradition* (Cambridge, 1983), pp. 108–20. Linda Colley, *Britons: Forging the Nation 1707–1837* (New Haven and London, 1992), pp. 217–36 draws attention to a previous phase of royal popularity in the later years of George III's reign, but readily acknowledges (p. 230) that it proved to be transient.

79 William M. Kuhn, 'Ceremony and politics: the British monarchy, 1871–1872', *Journal of British Studies* 26 (1987), pp. 133–62.

80 John Wolffe, 'Secular saints: Church and civic commemoration in the United Kingdom, 1874–1910', *Hispania Sacra* 42 (1990), pp. 435–43.

81 A. C. Benson, *The Life of Edward White Benson* (2 vols, 1900), Vol. II, pp. 130, 135.

82 Leviticus 25.

83 Malcolm Chase, 'From millenium to anniversary: the concept of jubilee in late eighteenth- and nineteenth-century England', *Past and Present* 128 (1990), pp. 132–47; Kingsley, op. cit., p. 8.

84 Hugh Cunningham, 'The language of patriotism', in R. Samuel, ed., *Patriotism: The Making and Unmaking of British National Identity: Vol. I History and Politics* (London, 1989), pp. 57–89.

85 This conclusion broadly reflects the analysis of D. Cannadine and E. Hammerton, 'Conflict and consensus on a ceremonial occasion: the diamond jubilee in Cambridge', *Historical Journal* 24 (1981), pp. 111–46 and Ross McKibbin, 'Why was there no Marxism in Great Britain?', *English Historical Review* 99 (1984), pp. 310–16.

86 John Wolffe, 'The end of Victorian values? Women, religion and the death of Queen Victoria', in W. J. Sheils and Diana Wood, eds, *Women in the Church: Studies in Church History 27* (Oxford, 1990), pp. 481–504; Colley, op. cit., p. 272.

87 This point must obviously be qualified by recognition of the ambivalent status of the Church of England in relation to Scotland, Wales and Northern Ireland. However, not the least remarkable feature of British religious history for much of the twentieth century was the failure of this to become an emotive issue.

88 *The Queen's Best Monument: A Memorial Report from the Spectator* (London, 1901); Wolffe, 'End of Victorian Values?', op. cit.

7 THE REAL FREE CHURCH? CULTURE AND BELIEF

1 John Cumming, *Apocalyptic Sketches* (London, 1849). The work went through numerous editions in a short space of time.

2 William Feaver, *The Art of John Martin* (Oxford, 1975), pp. 200–4; Jeremy Maas, *Holman Hunt and the Light of the World* (London, 1984).

3 W. Holman Hunt, *Pre-Raphaelitism and the Pre-Raphaelite Brotherhood* (2 vols, London, 1905), Vol. II, p. 493.

4 It must be stressed that in the discussion of changes in theology in this chapter no pretence to comprehensiveness is made. The aim rather is briefly to highlight developments of particular relevance to the wider argument of this book. The reader who requires a more detailed and nuanced account should refer to the footnotes and Further Reading.

5 Cited Bernard M. G. Reardon, *Religious Thought in the Victorian Age: A Survey from Coleridge to Gore* (London, 1980), pp. 197–8.

6 E. Williams, *The Life and Letters of Rowland Williams, DD* (2 vols, London, 1874), Vol. I, p. 133.

7 John Wolffe, 'Evangelicalism in mid-nineteenth-century England', in Raphael Samuel, ed., *Patriotism: The Making and Unmaking of British National Identity: Vol. I History and Politics* (1989), pp. 188–200.

8 John Morley, *The Life of William Ewart Gladstone* (2 vols, London, 1908), Vol. I, p. 283.

9 W. F. Monypenny and G. E. Buckle, *The Life of Benjamin Disraeli Earl of Beaconsfield* (6 vols, London 1910–20), Vol. III, pp. 247–8. For fuller accounts of the Gorham Case and its context see Owen Chadwick, *The Victorian Church* (2 vols, London, 1966–70), Vol. I, pp. 250–71 and J. R. Wolffe, 'Bishop Henry Phillpotts and the administration of the diocese of Exeter 1830–1869', *Transactions of the Devonshire Association* 114 (1982), pp. 99–113.

10 *Essays and Reviews* (London, 1860), p. 180.

11 For a sensitive but powerful contemporary Nonconformist assessment of the implications of Anglican diversity see R. W. Dale's *Nonconformity in 1662 and 1862* (London, 1862), an extract from which is reprinted in James R. Moore, ed., *Religion in Victorian Britain: Vol. III Sources* (Manchester, 1988), pp. 134–7.

12 Mark D. Johnson, *The Dissolution of Dissent, 1850–1918* (New York, 1987), pp. 6–7, 63–114.

13 Technically in 1900 it was the majority who joined the United Free Church, rather than the small minority who continued as the Free Church, who were the seceders. This important point of principle was settled by a House of Lords' judgement in 1904.

14 F. Kingsley, *Charles Kingsley: His Letters and Memories of His Life* (2 vols, London, 1876), Vol. II, p. 171; Reardon, op. cit., p. 292; James R. Moore, *The Post-Darwinian Controversies* (Cambridge, 1979).

15 *The Times*, 1 May 1882, p. 6; James R. Moore, 'Freethought, secularism, agnosticism: the case of Charles Darwin', in G. Parsons, ed., *Religion in Victorian Britain: Vol. I Traditions* (Manchester, 1988), pp. 289–315.

16 Charles Gore, ed., *Lux Mundi: A Series of Studies in the Religion of the Incarnation* (1889), pp. 211, 293, 354; Cf. Boyd Hilton, *The Age of*

Atonement: The Influence of Evangelicalism on Social and Economic Thought 1785–1860 (Oxford, 1988), pp. 253–339.

17 *The Church Hymnary* (Edinburgh, 1898), pp. 670–2.

18 W. G. Fallows, *Mandell Creighton and the English Church* (London, 1964), pp. 22–3, 58; R. T. Shannon, 'John Robert Seeley and the idea of a national Church', in Robert Robson, ed., *Ideas and Institutions of Victorian Britain*, (London, 1967), p. 239; Owen Chadwick, *Hensley Henson: A Study in the Friction between Church and State* (Oxford, 1983), pp. 80–1, 97.

19 Keith W. Clements, *Lovers of Discord: Twentieth Century Theological Controversies in England* (London, 1988), pp. 52–8.

20 Alan M. G. Stephenson, *The Rise and Decline of English Modernism* (London, 1984), pp. 7–10.

21 Ibid., pp. 116–18, 123.

22 G. K. A. Bell, *Randall Davidson Archbishop of Canterbury* (2 vols, London, 1935), Vol. II, pp. 1140–2; F. A. Iremonger, *William Temple Archbishop of Canterbury* (London, 1948), pp. 490–2; Adrian Hastings, *A History of English Christianity 1920–1985* (London, 1986), pp. 232–3.

23 Herbert Hensley Henson, *Bishoprick Papers* (Oxford, 1946), pp. 40–9; Chadwick, *Henson*, op. cit., pp. 204–7.

24 *Liberal Evangelicalism* (London, [1923]), p. v.

25 D. W. Bebbington, *Evangelicalism in Modern Britain* (London, 1989), pp. 198–202, 220.

26 Quoted by K. T. Hoppen, *Ireland since 1800* (London, 1989), p. 240.

27 Steve Bruce, *No Pope of Rome* (Edinburgh, 1985), pp. 39–41; *The Protestant Truth Society: Report for the Year 1896–97* (London, ?1897), p. 12.

28 Bebbington, op. cit., pp. 217–23; Hastings, op. cit., pp. 293–4.

29 Reardon, op. cit., pp. 256–8, 269–83.

30 Derek Jarrett, *The Sleep of Reason* (1988), pp. 32–4, 116–18; J. M. Winter, 'Spiritualism and the First World War', in R. W. Davis and R. J. Helmstadter, eds, *Religion and Irreligion in Victorian Society* (London, 1992), pp. 185–200.

31 Chadwick, *Victorian Church*, op. cit., Vol. I, pp. 533–9; Gerald Parsons, 'On speaking plainly', in G. Parsons, ed., *Religion in Victorian Britain: Vol. II Controversies* (Manchester, 1988), pp. 205, 215–17.

32 G. K. Chesterton, *G. F. Watts* (London, 1904), p. 8.

33 Ruth Roberts, *Arnold and God* (Berkeley and Los Angeles, 1983), pp. 107, 198–9.

34 Quoted, ibid., p. 258.

35 Matthew Arnold, (ed. J. Dover Wilson) *Culture and Anarchy* (Cambridge, 1932), pp. 12–14, 34 and *passim*. Cf. Roberts, op. cit., pp. 143–53.

36 Shannon, op. cit., pp. 236–67; Reba N. Soffer, 'History and religion: J. R. Seeley and the burden of the past', in Davis and Helmstadter, op. cit., pp. 133–50.

37 Thomas Arnold, *Lectures in Modern History* (London, 1843), pp. 23–4; Arnold, op. cit., pp. 27–8; Shannon, op. cit., p. 257.

38 Cf. D. W. Bebbington, 'Religion and national identity in nineteenth-century Wales and Scotland', in Stuart Mews, ed., *Religion and National Identity: Studies in Church History* 18 (Oxford, 1982), pp. 501–3.

39 Nicholas Temperley, *Jonathan Gray and Church Music in York* (York, 1977), pp. 9–10.

40 Bernarr Rainbow, *The Choral Revival in the Anglican Church, 1839–1872* (London, 1970), pp. 58–74.

41 Lionel Adey, *Class and Idol in the English Hymn* (Vancouver, 1988), p. 18.

42 Andrew L. Drummond and James Bulloch, *The Church in Victorian Scotland 1843–1874* (Edinburgh, 1975), pp. 184–9.

43 Adey, op. cit., pp. 76–80.

44 Erik Routley, *The English Carol* (New York, 1959), pp. 160, 173–4, 186–7. See above, Chapter. 4, p. 84.

45 Adey, op. cit., pp. ix-xi; Bernarr Rainbow, 'Parochial and Nonconformist church music', in Nicholas Temperley, ed., *The Romantic Age 1800–1914* (London, 1981), pp. 165–6; Henry James Garland, *Henry Francis Lyte and the Story of 'Abide with me'* (Manchester, 1956), pp. 125–6.

46 For a brief survey of literature of this kind see Margaret M. Maison, *Search Your Soul, Eustace: A Survey of the Religious Novel in the Victorian Age* (London, 1961).

47 On Warboise see Elisabeth Jay, *The Religion of the Heart* (Oxford, 1979), pp. 244–60.

48 Georgina Battiscombe, *Charlotte Mary Yonge: The Story of an Uneventful Life* (London, 1943), pp. 14, 73.

49 Cf. David Newsome, *Godliness and Good Learning* (London, 1961), pp. 55–7.

50 Colin Manlove, 'George MacDonald's Early Scottish Novels', in Ian Campbell, ed., *Nineteenth Century Scottish Fiction* (Manchester, 1979), p. 69; F. R. Hart, *The Scottish Novel: A Critical Survey* (London, 1978), p. 101.

51 Stephen Prickett, *Romanticism and Religion: The Tradition of Coleridge and Wordsworth in the Victorian Church* (Cambridge, 1976), pp. 223–48; Hilton, op. cit., pp. 314–15; Kathy Triggs, *The Stars and the Stillness: A Portrait of George MacDonald* (Cambridge, 1986), pp. 93, 108, 164; William Raeper, *George MacDonald* (Tring, 1987), pp. 250, 255, 314–15.

52 Leslie Parris, ed., *Pre-Raphaelite Papers* (London, 1984), pp. 23–43, 114–15; Maas, op. cit., pp. 73ff., 83–4.

53 Holman Hunt, op. cit., Vol II, p. 409; Norman Vance, *The Sinews of the Spirit: The Ideal of Christian Manliness in Victorian Literature and Religious Thought* (Cambridge, 1985), pp. 4–6.

54 Maurice Frost, ed., *Historical Companion to Hymns Ancient and Modern,* (London, 1962), p. 329; Maas, op. cit., p. 78.

55 Nicholas Temperley, 'Cathedral music', in Temperley, *The Romantic Age,* op. cit., pp. 200–1.

56 Holman Hunt, op. cit, Vol. I, p. 307; Mary Lago, ed., *Burne-Jones Talking: His Conversations 1895–1898* (London, 1982), p. 27.

57 Quoted, John Dixon Hunt, *The Wider Sea: A Life of John Ruskin* (London, 1982), p. 117.

58 Kenneth Clark, *The Gothic Revival* (London, 1928, 1974), pp. 192–213.

59 Michael Day, *Modern Art in English Churches* (London, 1984), p. 12.

60 See above, p. 1.

61 Clyde Binfield, *So Down to Prayers: Studies in English Nonconformity 1780–1920* (London, 1977), pp. 145–61.

62 Drummond and Bulloch, op. cit., pp. 191–2.

63 J. G. Lockhart, *Cosmo Gordon Lang* (London, 1949), p. 3.

64 John Betjeman *Ghastly Good Taste* (London, 1933, 1970); John Maddison, 'Basil Champneys and the John Rylands Library', in John H. G. Archer, ed., *Art and Architecture in Victorian Manchester* (Manchester, 1985), pp. 240–3.

65 Temperley, *Jonathan Gray*, op. cit., pp. 28–9.

66 Colley, op. cit., p. 32.

67 Arthur Jacobs, *Arthur Sullivan: A Victorian Musician* (Oxford, 1984), p. 72; Charles L. Graves, *Hubert Parry: His Life and Works* (2 vols, London, 1926), Vol. II, pp. 148–58; Jeremy Dibble, *C. Hubert H. Parry: His Life and Music* (Oxford, 1992), pp. 109–13.

68 J. H. Moore, *Edward Elgar: A Creative Life* (Oxford, 1984), pp. 57, 65–7, 423.

69 Percy Dearmer, *Art and Religion* (London, 1924), pp. 8, 25; Day, op. cit., pp 16–17.

70 G. Parsons, 'On Speaking Plainly: "Honest Doubt" and the Ethics of Belief', in G. Parsons, ed., *Religion in Victorian Britain: Vol. II Controversies* (Manchester, 1988), pp. 192–3; H. M. Butler, *A Sermon Preached in . . . Reference to the Death of Lord Tennyson* (Cambridge, 1892), pp. 14–15; Charles F. G. Masterman, *Tennyson as Religious Teacher* (London, 1900), pp. 188–9, 194–215; *The Works of Alfred Lord Tennyson* (London, 1897), pp. 274, 475.

71 Robert and Vineta Colby, 'Mrs Oliphant's Scotland: the romance of reality', in Campbell, ed., op. cit., pp. 89–104.

72 Eric Anderson, 'The Kailyard revisited', in Campbell, ed., op. cit., pp. 130–47.

73 George Blake, *Barrie and the Kailyard School* (London, 1951); Thomas D. Knowles, *Ideology, Art and Commerce: Aspects of Literary Sociology in the Late Victorian Scottish Kailyard* (Gothenburg, 1983), pp 50–63.

74 Quoted by Valentine Cunningham, *Everywhere Spoken Against: Dissent in the Victorian Novel* (Oxford, 1975), p. 62.

75 Anderson, op. cit., pp. 135–6.

76 S. Lee, ed., *Dictionary of National Biography 1901–11* (London, 1912), Vol. III, pp. 73–4; Jeanne Sheehy, *The Rediscovery of Ireland's Past: the Celtic Revival 1830–1930* (London, 1980), pp. 121–45.

77 Jay, op. cit., pp. 207–43; M. Bartholomew, 'The moral critique of Christian orthodoxy' in G. Parsons, ed., *Religion in Victorian Britain: Vol. II* (Manchester, 1988), p. 170.

78 *Poems by Matthew Arnold* (London 1905), p. 16.

79 *Culture and Anarchy*, pp. 10–16, 44–8.

80 Chesterton, op. cit., p. 11; Graves, op. cit., Vol II, p. 157; Mrs Russell Barrington, *G.F. Watts: Reminiscences* (London, 1905), pp. 9, 19, 189–91.

81 Derek Jarrett, *The Sleep of Reason* (London, 1988), pp. 4–6, 18.

82 John Christian, ed., *The Last Romantics* (London, 1989).

83 Read, op. cit., p. 364; Mark Girouard, *The Return to Camelot* (New Haven, 1981), p. 2.

84 Rudyard Kipling (ed. Thomas Pinney), *Something of Myself and Other Autobiographical Writings* (Cambridge, 1990), pp. xxiii–iv, 6; Philip Mason, *Kipling: The Glass, the Shadow and the Fire* (London, 1975), pp.

113, 140–1, 248–9; T. S. Eliot, *A Choice of Kipling's Verse* (London, 1941), p. 20.

85 Ibid., p. 107.

86 Rudyard Kipling, *Stalky and Co* (London, 1899), pp. 212–13; *Puck of Pook's Hill* (London, 1906), pp. 305–6; J. S. Bratton, 'Of England, home and duty', in J. M. Mackenzie, ed., *Imperialism and Popular Culture* (Manchester, 1986), p. 75.

87 Eliot, op. cit., p. 140.

88 Moore, op. cit., pp. 238, 365, 521 and *passim*; Jeremy Crump, 'The identity of English music: the reception of Elgar 1898–1935' in Robert Colls and Philip Dodd, eds, *Englishness: Politics and Culture* (London, 1986), pp. 165–71.

89 Quoted by Peter Brooker and Peter Widdowson, 'A literature for England', in Colls and Dodd, op. cit., p. 131; *Poems by Rupert Brooke* (London, 1931), p. 63.

90 Adey, op. cit., pp. 168, 189 and *passim*.

91 F. D. How, *Bishop Walsham How* (London, 1898), pp. 351–8.

92 Wilfrid Mellers, *Vaughan Williams and the Vision of Albion* (1989), pp. 5–6; Dibble, op. cit., pp. 483–5. See above, p. ix.

93 Thomas Flanagan, 'Literature in English, 1801–91', in W. E. Vaughan, ed., *Ireland Under the Union: Vol. I 1801–70* (Oxford, 1989), pp. 495–509.

94 Sheehy, op. cit., pp. 41–9, 177.

95 Temperley, *Romantic Age*, op. cit., p. 204.

96 Sheehy, op. cit., pp. 58–60, 144–5. The original plans for the O'Connell memorial at Glasnevin were even more elaborate and evocative than the scheme eventually realized.

97 Flanagan, op. cit., pp. 512–14; Herman J. Heuser, *Canon Sheehan of Doneraile* (London, 1917), p. 229.

98 Quoted F. S. L. Lyons, *Culture and Anarchy in Ireland 1890–1939* (Oxford, 1979) p. 80; cf. John Hutchinson, *The Dynamics of Cultural Nationalism: The Gaelic Revival and the Creation of the Irish Nation State* (London, 1987), pp. 120–7.

99 Sheridan Gilley, 'Pearse's sacrifice: Christ and Cuchulain crucified and risen in the Easter Rising 1916', in J. Obelkevich, L. Roper and R. Samuel, eds, *Disciplines of Faith: Studies in Religion, Politics and Patriarchy* (London, 1987), pp. 483–4; Ruth Dudley Edwards, *Patrick Pearse: The Triumph of Failure* (London, 1977), pp. 261–4.

100 Dudley Edwards, op. cit., pp. 335–44; Lyons, op. cit., pp. 129–32, 136–7. See above, p. 151–2.

101 Flanagan, op. cit., pp. 515–20.

102 Henry Summerfield, *That Myriad-Minded Man – AE* (Gerrards Cross, 1975), pp. 79, 112.

103 G. S. Watson, *Irish Identity and the Literary Revival* (London, 1979), pp. 94, 96, 98. Cf. Lyons, op. cit., p. 49; M. C. Flannery, *Yeats and Magic: The Earlier Works* (Gerrards Cross, 1977).

104 Watson, op. cit., pp. 87–9; W. B.Yeats: 'Man and the Echo', in *Last Poems and Plays* (London, 1940); Elizabeth Cullingford, *Yeats, Ireland and Fascism* (London, 1981), p. 53.

105 Watson, op. cit., pp. 37, 46; Lyons, op. cit., pp. 68–70.

106 Watson, op. cit., pp. 154–5.

107 Sheehy, op. cit., pp. 41, 177; Kenneth McConkey, *A Free Spirit: Irish Art 1860–1960* (London, 1990), pp. 27–43.

108 McConkey, op. cit., pp. 46–7.

109 Sheehy, op. cit., pp. 178–9.

110 *Rudyard Kipling's Verse 1885–1918* (3 vols, London, 1920), Vol I, p. 307.

111 Summerfield, op. cit., p. 156.

112 The marriage collapsed within two years, but its nationalist credentials were impressive. John MacBride was among the leaders of the Easter Rising shot by the British in 1916; Sean, Gonne's only child by MacBride, was later to become chief of staff of the IRA (Samuel Levenson, *Maud Gonne* (London, 1976), pp. 204, 228–9 and *passim*).

113 Gonne to Yeats, 10 February 1903, printed in Anna MacBride White and A. Norman Jeffares, *The Gonne-Yeats Letters 1893–1938* (London, 1992), p. 166.

114 The intention is not to deny the existence of other constructions of identity – for example Anglo-Irish, English Catholic, Scottish, Ulster or Welsh – but rather to indicate that at this period of the early twentieth century these lacked an emotive and spiritual power comparable to the three alignments given in the text.

115 G. I. T. Machin, 'British Churches and the Cinema in the 1930s', in Diana Wood, ed., *The Church and the Arts: Studies in Church History*, 28 (1992), pp. 477–88.

116 Dearmer, op. cit.; Day, op. cit., p. 16.

117 Judith Nesbitt, ed., *Stanley Spencer: A Sort of Heaven* (Liverpool, 1992), pp. 13, 38–9.

118 Jane Alison, ed., *Stanley Spencer: The Apotheosis of Love* (London, 1991).

119 Nesbitt, op. cit., p. 45; Day, op. cit., p. 28; A. K. Walker, 'Stanley Spencer – Christian visionary?', *Modern Churchman* 24 (1981), pp. 14–16.

120 Eric Gill, *Autobiography* (London, 1940), p. 200.

121 Hastings, op. cit., pp. 285–6.

122 Jeffrey Meyes, *D. H. Lawrence: A Biography* (London, 1990), pp. 352–3, 363–5.

123 John Buchan, *Memory Hold-the-Door* (London, 1940), pp. 15–18 and *passim*; J. F. Kruse, *John Buchan and the Idea of Empire*, (University of Miami PhD thesis, 1982), p. 217.

124 Janet Adam Smith, *John Buchan* (London, 1965), pp. 141–5, 256–60.

125 Vance, op. cit., pp. 174–6.

126 Smith, op. cit., pp. 274–80.

127 Kruse, op. cit., pp. 202, 216; Buchan, op. cit., pp. 292–3.

128 Smith, op. cit., pp. 463–4.

129 John Buchan, *What the Union of the Churches Means to Scotland* (Edinburgh, 1929), pp. 14–15.

130 Buchan, *Memory Hold-the-Door*, op. cit., pp. 231–3.

131 John Buchan, *The Kirk in Scotland* (Dunbar, 1985), pp. 130–1, 135–7.

132 Buchan, *Memory Hold-the-Door*, op. cit., p. 248; Gavin Wallace in Cairns Craig, ed., *The History of Scottish Literature: Vol. 4 Twentieth Century* (Aberdeen, 1987), p. 247.

133 Quoted by Michael Ffinch, *G. K. Chesterton* (London, 1986), p. 281.

134 Ibid., pp. 89–91.

135 Ibid., pp. 255–6, 291–2.

136 Lyndall Gordon, *Eliot's Early Years* (Oxford, 1977); Maurice Cowling, *Religion and Public Doctrine in Modern England* (Cambridge, 1980), pp. 100–1; Hastings, op. cit., pp. 236, 259.

137 C. S. Lewis, *The Great Divorce* (London, 1972), pp. 59–60.

138 C. S. Lewis, *Surprised by Joy: The Shape of my Early Life* (London, 1955), pp. 65, 74–9, 169–71, 210–1.

139 T. S. Eliot, *Collected Poems 1909–1962* (London, 1963), p. 215.

140 Lyndall Gordon, *Eliot's New Life* (Oxford, 1988), p. 137.

141 T. S. Eliot, *The Idea of a Christian Society and Other Writings* (London, 1982), pp. 74–7, 125–6.

142 C. S. Lewis, *The Horse and his Boy* (Harmondsworth, 1954), p. 142.

143 C. S. Lewis, *The Last Battle* (Harmondsworth, 1956), p. 170.

144 Gwyn Jones, ed., *The Oxford Book of Welsh Verse in English* (Oxford, 1977), pp. xxiv–vi.

145 Thomas Parry (trans. H. Idris Bell), *A History of Welsh Literature* (Oxford, 1955), pp. 411, 491–2.

146 English translation in Jones, op. cit., p. 202; Parry, op. cit., p. 414.

147 Quoted Ned Thomas, *The Welsh Extremist* (London, 1971), p. 46.

148 Geraint Davies, 'A tale of two Thomases – reflections on two Anglo-Welsh poets', in Horst W. Drescher and Hermann Völkel, eds, *Nationalism in Literature* (Frankfurt am Main, 1989), p. 292; Paul Ferris, *Dylan Thomas* (London, 1977), p. 43; Rushworth M. Kidder, *Dylan Thomas: The Country of the Spirit* (Princeton, 1973).

149 See, for example, Daniel Jones, ed., *Dylan Thomas: The Poems* (London, 1971), p. 174.

150 Alan Bold, *MacDiarmid: Christopher Murray Grieve: A Critical Biography* (London, 1988), pp. 33, 180–224.

151 Hugh MacDiarmid, *A Drunk Man Looks at the Thistle* (Edinburgh, 1987), pp. 96, 124.

152 Edwin Muir, *An Autobiography* (London, 1954), pp. 246–7.

153 Edwin Muir, *Collected Poems* (London, 1963), p. 116.

154 Andro Linklater, *Compton MacKenzie: A Life* (London, 1987), pp. 227, 266–7 and *passim*.

155 W. B. Yeats, 'Easter 1916', in *Collected Poems* (London, 1933), p. 204. Yeats further explored the motif of blood sacrifice in the Easter Rising in 'The Rose Tree' *(Collected Poems*, p. 206).

156 Sheehy, op. cit., pp. 178–9.

157 Hutchinson, *Dynamics of Cultural Nationalism*, pp. 308–10.

158 Summerfield, op. cit., p. 229; Cullingford, *Yeats*, p. 193; W. B. Yeats, *A Full Moon in March* (London, 1935), p. 47.

159 Louis MacNeice, *Zoo* (1938), reprinted in Patricia Craig, ed., *The Rattle of the North: An Anthology of Ulster Prose* (Belfast, 1992), p. 245.

160 Garth Turner, '"Aesthete, impressario, and indomitable persuader": Walter Hussey at St Matthew's, Northampton and Chichester', in Diana Wood, ed., *The Church and the Arts: Studies in Church History* 28 (1992), pp. 523–35.

161 Day, op. cit., pp. 12, 17, 19–24; Mellers, op. cit., pp. 249–51; Hastings, op. cit., pp. 491–504.

162 Cf. Hastings, op. cit., pp. 288–95.

163 Dearmer, op. cit., p. 17.

164 Adey, Class and Idol, op. cit., pp. 218–19, 222–40.

8 ONWARD CHRISTIAN SOLDIERS? THE EMPIRE AND WAR

1 Bickford H. C. Dickinson, *Sabine Baring-Gould: Squarson, Writer and Folklorist* (Newton Abbot, 1970), pp. 43–7.
2 Maurice Frost, ed., *Historical Companion to Hymns Ancient and Modern* (London, 1962), p. 290.
3 Dickinson, op. cit., pp. 49–50.
4 T. S. Eliot, *A Choice of Kipling's Verse* (London, 1941), p. 137. Cf. Numbers 14.
5 A. L. Drummond and J. Bulloch, *The Church in Victorian Scotland 1843–1874* (Edinburgh, 1975), pp. 145–50.
6 B. Stanley, *The Bible and the Flag: Protestant Missions and British Imperialism in the Nineteenth and Twentieth Centuries* (Leicester, 1990), pp. 85–90, 98–101.
7 See above, p. 42.
8 Stanley, op. cit., pp. 100–1.
9 E. Hodder, *The Life and Work of the seventh Earl of Shaftesbury, K. G.* (3 vols, London, 1887), Vol. I, pp. 463–77; Vol. II, pp. 5–16.
10 Stanley, op. cit., pp. 70–4; B. Stanley, '"Commerce and Christianity": providence theory, the missionary movement and the imperialism of free trade, 1842–1860', *Historical Journal* 26 (1983), pp. 71–94. The connection between commerce and Christianity is given a lesser and more transient significance by A. Porter, '"Commerce and Christianity": the rise and fall of a nineteenth-century missionary slogan', *Historical Journal* 28 (1985), pp. 597–621.
11 Westminster Abbey monument; J. M. Mackenzie, 'David Livingstone: the construction of the myth', in G. Walker and T. Gallagher, eds, *Sermons and Battle Hymns: Protestant Popular Culture in Modern Scotland* (Edinburgh, 1990), pp. 24–42.
12 R. Baird, *The Progress and Prospects of Christianity in the United States of America* (1851), pp. 44–8, 56, 58.
13 D. A. Lorimer, *Colour, Class and the Victorians: English Attitudes to the Negro in the Mid-nineteenth Century* (Leicester, 1978), pp. 69–91.
14 B. Stanley 'Christian responses to the Indian mutiny of 1857', in W. J. Sheils, ed., *The Church and War: Studies in Church History* 20 (Oxford, 1983), pp. 277–90.
15 B. Porter, *The Lion's Share: A Short History of British Imperialism 1850–1983* (London, 1984), pp. 37–9.
16 S. Neill, *A History of Christian Missions* (London, 1986), pp. 308–9; D. Kooiman, *Conversion and Social Equality in India: The London Missionary Society in South Travancore in the 19th Century* (New Delhi, 1989).
17 Neill, op. cit., p. 303; B. D. Metcalf, *Islamic Revival in British India: Deoband 1860–1900* (Princeton, 1982).
18 E. J. Sharpe, *Faith Meets Faith: Some Christian Attitudes to Hinduism in the Nineteenth and Twentieth Centuries* (London, 1977), pp. 24–32; M. Maw, *Visions of India: Fulfilment Theology, The Aryan Race Theory and the Work*

of British Protestant Missionaries in Victorian India (Frankfurt am Main, 1990).

19 Porter, op. cit., pp. 39–41; Stanley, *Bible and the Flag*, op. cit., p. 103.

20 B. S. Cohn, 'Representing authority in Victorian India', in E. Hobsbawm and T. Ranger, eds, *The Invention of Tradition* (Cambridge, 1983), pp. 165–210; *The Times*, 1 January 1877, p. 5; 8 January 1877, p. 5.

21 S. Wheeler, *History of the Delhi Coronation Durbar held on the First of January 1903 to Celebrate the Coronation of His Majesty King Edward VII Emperor of India* (London, 1904), pp. 127–34, 144–7.

22 *The Historical Record of the Imperial Visit to India* (London, 1911), pp. 256–68, 270–4.

23 Stanley, *Bible and the Flag*, op. cit., pp. 116–32.

24 T. Ranger, 'The Invention of Tradition in Colonial Africa', in Hobsbawm and Ranger, eds, op. cit., pp. 214, 226, 229–32.

25 James Munson, *The Nonconformists: In Search of a Lost Culture* (London, 1991), pp. 185–6; C. T. Bateman, *John Clifford: Free Church Leader and Preacher* (London, 1904), pp. 204–19; John Clifford, *God's Greater Britain* (London, 1899).

26 J. Maas, *Holman Hunt and the Light of the World* (London, 1984), pp. 141–203. Only in Canada was the picture relatively unsuccessful.

27 For some case-studies see W. J. Sheils and Diana Wood, eds, *The Churches, Ireland and the Irish: Studies in Church History* 25 (Oxford, 1989).

28 Stanley, *Bible and the Flag* op. cit., pp. 116–21, 132.

29 Neill, op. cit., pp. 282–4.

30 Munson, op. cit., pp. 186–203.

31 For examination of these changes in attitude see R. Koebner and H. D. Schmidt, *Imperialism: The Story and Significance of a Political Word, 1840–1960* (Cambridge, 1964) and C. C. Eldridge, *England's Mission: The Imperial Idea in the Age of Disraeli and Gladstone* (London, 1973).

32 D. W. Bebbington, *The Nonconformist Conscience: Chapel and Politics, 1870–1914* (London, 1982), pp. 106–126.

33 Ibid., pp. 108–9; R. T. Shannon, *Gladstone and the Bulgarian Agitation 1876* (London, 1963), pp. 160–8; John Morley, *The Life of William Ewart Gladstone* (London, 1908), Vol. II, p. 152.

34 C.C. Eldridge, 'Sinews of Empire: changing perspectives', in C. C. Eldridge, ed., *British Imperialism in the Nineteenth Century* (London, 1984), pp. 184–5.

35 *At Rest-Read at a Memorial Meeting of the Society of American Women in London* (London, 1901).

36 J. Ellison and G. H. S. Walpole, eds, *Church and Empire: A Series of Essays on the Responsibilities of Empire* (London, 1907), pp. v-vi, xiii, 21–41.

37 Eliot, op. cit., pp. 187–9.

38 For detailed analysis see John M. Mackenzie, *Propaganda and Empire: The Manipulation of British Public Opinion 1880–1960* (Manchester, 1984) and John M. Mackenzie, ed., *Imperialism and Popular Culture* (Manchester, 1986).

39 Mackenzie, *Propaganda and Empire*, op. cit., pp. 206, 213–15, 220–1.

40 Quoted, ibid., p. 180.

41 Ibid., pp. 231–40.

42 Quoted by J. A. Hobson, *The Psychology of Jingoism* (London, 1901), p. 54.

43 *Memorials of Captain Hedley Vicars Ninety-Seventh Regiment* (London, 1904), pp. x-xi; O. Anderson, 'The growth of Christian militarism in mid-Victorian Britain', *English Historical Review* 86 (1971), pp. 48–9.

44 See above, p. 41; C. I. Hamilton, 'Naval Hagiography and the Victorian Hero', *The Historical Journal* 23 (1980), pp. 392–4.

45 Anderson, op. cit., 49–52; J. M. Mackenzie, 'Heroic myths of Empire', in J. M. Mackenzie, ed., *Popular Imperialism and the Military 1850–1950* (Manchester, 1992), pp. 116–121.

46 Mackenzie, 'Heroic Myths', op. cit., pp. 125–30; D. H. Johnson, 'The Death of Gordon: A Victorian Myth', *The Journal of Imperial and Commonwealth History* 10 (1982), pp. 285–310.

47 I am indebted to Mr Warwick Burton for drawing this window to my attention.

48 Mark Girouard, *The Return to Camelot* (New Haven, 1981), pp. 2–14; Henry James Garland, *Henry Francis Lyte and the Story of "Abide with Me"* (Manchester, 1956), pp. 82–3.

49 Lionel Adey, *Class and Idol in the English Hymn* (Vancouver, 1988), pp. 202–8; Anderson, op. cit., pp. 69–71; Derek Jarrett, *The Sleep of Reason*, (London, 1988), p. 82.

50 C. Kingsley, *Brave Words for Brave Soldiers and Sailors* (London, 1855), p. 10.

51 Anderson, op. cit., pp. 52–66; H. J. Hanham, 'Religion and nationality in the mid-Victorian army', in M. R. D. Foot, ed., *War and Society* (London, 1973), pp. 167–70.

52 A. Wilkinson, *The Church of England and the First World War* (London, 1978), pp. 124–5.

53 Hanham, op. cit., pp. 179–81.

54 *Imperial Visit to India*, op. cit., p. 274.

55 Cf. D. Newsome, *Godliness and Good Learning* (London, 1961), pp. 195–239; N. Vance, *The Sinews of the Spirit* (Cambridge, 1985), pp. 166–206; J. A. Mangan, 'Social Darwinism and upper-class education in late Victorian and Edwardian England', in J. A. Mangan and J. Walvin, eds, *Manliness and Morality: Middle-class Masculinity in Britain and America 1800–1940* (Manchester, 1987), pp. 135–159.

56 J. A. Mangan, '"The grit of our forefathers": invented traditions, propaganda and imperialism', in Mackenzie, ed., *Imperialism and Popular Culture*, op. cit., pp. 117–21.

57 Quoted in J. A. Mangan, 'Social Darwinism', op. cit., p. 156.

58 H. Cunningham, *The Volunteer Force: A Social and Political History 1859–1908* (London, 1975), pp. 12, 19, 69, 74.

59 C. Kingsley, *A Sermon at the Volunteer Camp, Wimbledon* (London, 1867), p. 7.

60 E. Hodder, *John MacGregor ('Rob Roy')* (London, 1894), pp. 230–49; D. Jamie, *John Hope: Philanthropist and Reformer* (Edinburgh, 1900), pp. 385–405.

61 J. Springhall, *Youth, Empire and Society: British Youth Movements, 1883–1940* (London, 1977), pp. 22–52.

62 Ibid., p. 40; J. Springhall, 'Building character in the British boy: the attempt to extend Christian manliness to working-class adolescents, 1880–1914', in Mangan and Walvin, op. cit., pp. 53–61.

63 Springhall, *Youth, Empire and Society*, op. cit., pp. 53–70, 90–3; Wilkinson, op. cit., p. 36.

64 B. Harrison, 'For, Church, Queen and family: The Girls' Friendly Society 1874–1920', *Past and Present* 61 (1983), pp. 107–11; J. Wolffe, 'The end of Victorian values? Women, religion and the death of Queen Victoria', in W. J. Sheils and D. Wood, eds, *Women in the Church: Studies in Church History* 27 (Oxford, 1990), pp. 493–5.

65 M. Heath-Stubbs, *Friendship's Highway: Being the History of the Girls' Friendly Society, 1875–1935* (London, 1935), p. 82; Springhall, *Youth, Empire and Society*, op. cit., pp. 129–33.

66 S. Mews, 'The General and the bishops: alternative responses to dechristianisation', in T. R. Gourvish and A. O'Day, eds, *Later Victorian Britain 1867–1900* (London, 1988), pp. 209–28; O. Chadwick, *The Victorian Church* (2 vols, London, 1966–70), Vol. II, pp. 287–99.

67 Springhall, 'Building character in the British boy', op. cit., pp. 61–70.

68 J. Rowbotham, *Good Girls Make Good Wives: Guidance for Girls in Victorian Fiction* (London, 1989), pp. 191–2; Springhall, 'Building character in the British boy', op. cit., p. 65.

69 Adey, op. cit., pp. 175–85; Springhall, 'Building character in the British boy' op. cit.; M. D. Blanch, 'British society and the war', in P. Warwick, ed., *The South African War: The Anglo-Boer War 1899–1902* (London, 1980), p. 210–38; J. A. Hobson, *The Psychology of Jingoism* (London, 1901), pp. 41–62.

70 Kingsley, *Brave Words*, op. cit., p. 8.

71 O. Anderson, 'The reactions of Church and dissent towards the Crimean War', *Journal of Ecclesiastical History*, 16 (1965), pp. 209–20; A. Tyrrell, 'Making the millennium: the mid-nineteenth century peace movement', *The Historical Journal* 20 (1978), pp. 75–95.

72 N. W. Summerton, 'Dissenting attitudes to foreign relations, peace and war', *Journal of Ecclesiastical History* 28 (1977), pp. 151–78.

73 S. Koss, *The Anatomy of an Antiwar Movement: The Pro-Boers* (Chicago, 1973), pp. 225–6; Bebbington, *Nonconformist Conscience*, pp. 121–4; B. Porter, 'The Pro-Boers in Britain', in Warwick, ed., op. cit., pp. 246–8.

74 J. Clifford, *The War and the Churches* (London, 1914), p. 8. Cf. Summerton, op. cit., pp. 177–8; Wilkinson, op. cit., pp. 13–31.

75 M. Ceadel, 'Christian pacifism in the era of two World Wars', in W. J. Sheils, ed., *The Church and War: Studies in Church History* 20 (1983), p. 395.

76 R. F. G. Holmes, '"Ulster will fight and Ulster will be right": the Protestant churches and Ulster's resistance to Home Rule 1912–14', in Sheils, op. cit., pp. 334–5; Ruth Dudley Edwards, *Patrick Pearse: The Triumph of Failure* (London, 1977), p. 179.

77 K. Theodore Hoppen, *Ireland Since 1800: Conflict and Conformity* (London, 1989), pp. 65–6.

78 S. D. Henry, 'Scottish Baptists and the First World War', *The Baptist Quarterly* 31 (1985), pp. 55–6.

79 Peter C. Matheson 'Scottish war sermons 1914–1919', *Records of the Scottish Church History Society* 17 (1972), p. 207.

80 Kenneth O. Morgan, *Rebirth of a Nation: Wales 1880–1980* (Oxford, 1981), pp. 159–67.

81 W. E. Henley in C. S. Evans, ed., *Our Glorious Heritage. A Book of Patriotic Verse for Boys and Girls* (London, 1914), p. 19.

82 A. F. Winnington-Ingram, *A Day of God, Being Five Addresses on the Subject of the Present War* (London, 1914), p. 23.

83 Rupert Brooke, *1914 and Other Poems* (London, 1915), p. 11.

84 Quoted in Stuart P. Mews, 'Religion and English Society in the First World War', (Cambridge PhD thesis 1973), pp. 50, 54, 176.

85 Mangan, 'Social Darwinism' op. cit.; P. M. Kennedy, *The Rise of the Anglo-German Antagonism 1860–1914* (London, 1980), pp. 361–85.

86 Stephen Humphris, *Hooligans or Rebels? An Oral History of Working Class Childhood and Youth 1859–1939* (London, 1981), pp. 38, 134–5.

87 Quoted by Wilkinson, *Church of England and the First World War*, op. cit., pp. 29–30; Alan Wilkinson, *Dissent or Conform? War, Peace and the English Churches 1900–1945* (London, 1986), pp. 26–7.

88 R. Currie, A. Gilbert and L. Horsley, *Churches and Churchgoers: Patterns of Church Growth in the British Isles Since 1700* (Oxford, 1977), pp. 128, 164, 167.

89 Wilkinson, *Church of England and the First World War*, op. cit., pp. 57–62; Clyde Binfield, *So Down to Prayers*, pp. 232–48.

90 Quoted by A. J. Hoover, *God, Germany and Britain in the Great War: A Study in Clerical Nationalism* (New York, 1989), p. 129.

91 Wilkinson, *Dissent or Conform?*, op. cit., pp. 24–5, 30ff.; Mews, 'Religion and English society', op. cit., pp. 91–2.

92 *The Churchman* 28 (1914), pp. 641–5, 721–4; 29 (1915), pp. 561–8, 641–4; 31 (1917), pp. 1–2; 32 (1918), pp. 689–70.

93 J. G. Lockhart, *Cosmo Gordon Lang* (London, 1949), pp. 248–9.

94 Wilkinson, *Church of England and the First World War*, op. cit., pp. 32–56, 98–102, 197–229.

95 Winnington-Ingram, op. cit., pp. 30, 75; Matheson, op. cit., p. 209. See above, p. 41.

96 F. W. Orde Ward, *The Last Crusade: Patriotic Poems* (London, n.d.), pp. 19–20.

97 Eliot, op. cit., pp. 50–1; Wilkinson, *Church of England and the First World War*, op. cit., plate 2, p. 191; Adey, op. cit., pp. 217–18. For a more positive assessment of these controversial stanzas see Wilkinson, ibid. p. 192.

98 Stuart Mews, 'Music and religion in the First World War', in Diana Wood, ed., *The Church and the Arts* (Oxford, 1992), pp. 465–75.

99 J. H. Moore, *Edward Elgar: A Creative Life* (Oxford, 1984), pp. 674–82, 705; Jeremy Crump, 'The identity of English music: the reception of Elgar 1898–1935' in Robert Colls and Philip Dodds, eds, *Englishness: Politics and Culture* (London, 1986), pp. 175–7.

100 David M. Thompson, 'War, the nation and the Kingdom of God: the origins of the national mission of repentance and hope 1915–16', in W. J. Sheils, ed., *The Church and War: Studies in Church History* 20 (1983), pp. 337–50; Wilkinson, *Church of England*, pp. 72–9.

101 Wilkinson, *Church of England and the First World War*, op. cit., pp. 109–52.

102 Ibid., pp. 152–68; David Cannadine, 'War and death, grief and mourning in modern Britain', in Joachim Whaley, ed., *Mirrors of Mortality: Studies in the Social History of Death* (London, 1981), pp. 202–12; 218–19.

103 J. M. Winter, 'Spiritualism and the First World War', in R. W. Davis and R. J. Helmstadter, eds, *Religion and Irreligion in Victorian Society: Essays in Honor of R. K. Webb* (London, 1992), pp. 185–200; Mews, 'Religion and English society', op. cit., pp. 96–108.

104 Wilkinson, *Church of England and the First World War*, op. cit., pp. 156–9; Crump, op. cit., p. 174.

105 Paul Fussell, *The Great War and Modern Memory* (Oxford, 1975), pp. 117–44.

106 Siegfried Sassoon, *Collected Poems* (London, 1947), pp. 16–17, 23–4.

107 Jon Stallworthy, *Wilfred Owen* (Oxford, 1974), pp. 85, 185–6.

108 E. Blunden, ed., *The Poems of Wilfred Owen* (London, 1931), p. 108.

109 The National Trust, *Stanley Spencer at Burghclere* (London, 1991); Winter, op. cit., pp. 195–7. It seems to me, however, that Winter's treatment of Spencer's paintings as 'spiritualist' renders this concept problematically diffuse.

110 *Exeter School 1880–1983* (Exeter, 1984), p. 35; Derek Boorman, *At the Going Down of the Sun: British First World War Memorials* (York, 1988).

111 George L. Mosse, *Fallen Soldiers: Reshaping the Memory of the World Wars*, (New York, 1990), pp. 82–4.

112 Quoted Boorman, op. cit., p. 14.

113 Examples are given by Boorman, op. cit., pp. 74–5.

114 Ibid., p. 71.

115 Ibid., pp. 59–64; 161–3; K. S. Inglis, 'To the glorious dead: imperial war memorials 1918–1939' (unpublished paper), p. 18. I am much indebted to Professor Inglis for sending me a copy of this paper.

116 Boorman, op. cit., pp. 144–8, 154.

117 Ibid., pp. 159–63; Inglis, op. cit., pp. 18–19.

118 Descriptions in this paragraph are from personal observation.

119 Cannadine, 'War and death', op. cit., pp. 219–26; Wilkinson, *Church of England and the First World War*, op. cit., 298–300.

120 Mackenzie, *Propaganda and Empire*, op. cit., pp. 233–8; Mangan, 'The grit of our forefathers', op. cit., p. 132.

121 John M. Mackenzie, '"In touch with the infinite": the BBC and the Empire, 1922–53', in Mackenzie, *Imperialism and Popular Culture*, op. cit., pp. 163–91.

122 Lockhart, op. cit., pp. 408–13; Cannadine, 'British monarchy', op. cit., pp. 143–4, 152.

123 Gerald Studdert-Kennedy, *British Christians, Indian Nationalists and the Raj* (Delhi, 1991), pp. 190–8.

124 Ibid., *passim*; Stanley, *Bible and the Flag*, op. cit., pp. 146–55.

125 Martin Ceadel, 'Christian pacifism in the era of two World Wars', in Sheils, ed., *Church and War*, op. cit., pp. 391–408; Wilkinson, *Dissent or Conform?*, op. cit., pp. 101–36; Hastings, op. cit., pp. 330–6.

126 Wilkinson, *Dissent or Conform?*, op. cit., pp. 166–7, 176.

127 Hastings, op. cit., pp. 319–29; D. W. Bebbington, 'The Oxford Group Movement between the Wars', in W. J. Sheils and Diana Wood, eds, *Voluntary Religion: Studies in Church History* 23 (1986), pp. 505–6.

128 Quoted by Wilkinson, *Dissent or Conform?*, op. cit., p. 174.

129 Ibid., pp. 184–5.

130 Ibid., p. 279.

131 Keith Robbins, 'Britain, 1940 and "Christian civilization"', in Derek Beales and Geoffrey Best, eds, *History, Society and the Churches* (Cambridge, 1985), p, 279.

132 Quoted Mackenzie, *Propaganda and Empire*, op. cit., p. 234.

133 A. F. Winnington-Ingram, *A Second Day of God* (London, 1940), pp. 2, 3.

134 Quoted F. A. Iremonger, *William Temple Archbishop of Canterbury* (London, 1948), p. 540.

135 *The Times*, 27 May 1940, p. 3.

136 Robbins, 'Christian civilization', op. cit., pp. 285–95; Hastings, op. cit., pp. 373–81; Paul Fussell, *Wartime: Understanding and Behavior in the Second World War*, (New York, 1989), pp. 129–43.

137 *The Times*, 27 May 1940, p. 7; 30 November 1940, p. 5.

138 Iremonger, *Temple*, pp. 553–4.

139 Hastings, op. cit., pp. 382–400; Wilkinson, *Dissent or Conform?*, op. cit., pp. 276–86.

140 S. C. Carpenter, *Winnington-Ingram: the Biography of Arthur Foley Winnington-Ingram Bishop of London 1901–1939* (1949), pp. 352–3.

141 Wilkinson, *Dissent or Conform?*, op. cit., p. 307.

142 Mackenzie, *Propaganda and Empire*, op. cit., pp. 238–9.

143 Cannadine, 'The British monarchy', op. cit., pp. 153–4.

144 Wilkinson, *Church of England and the First World War*, op. cit., p. 223; Boorman, op. cit., p. 6.

9 CONCLUSION: NATIONALISM AND SECULARIZATION

1 *St Paul's in War and Peace* (*The Times*, London, 1960), p. 51.

2 Ibid., p. 36. I am grateful to my mother, who lived through the London blitz, for drawing the symbolic significance of St Paul's to my attention. Cf. Linda Colley, *Britons: Forging the Nation 1707–1837* (New Haven and London, 1992), p. 29.

3 It is important to acknowledge at the outset that these are less clear cut from a Scottish, Welsh or, above all, Irish perspective than from an Anglo-centric one, a point to which we shall return below.

4 C. S. Lewis, *The Great Divorce* (London, 1945), pp. 13–14.

5 Alan D. Gilbert, *The Making of Post-Christian Britain: A History of the Secularization of Modern Society* (London, 1980), p. 42.

6 Alan D. Gilbert, *Religion and Society in Industrial England* (London, 1976), p. 203.

7 Gilbert, *Post-Christian Britain*, op. cit., pp. 47–99.

8 For an explanation of these terms see Gilbert, *Post-Christian Britain*, op. cit., pp. 42–5.

9 Martin J. Wiener, *English Culture and the Decline of the Industrial Spirit 1850–1980* (London, 1981).

10 Gilbert, *Post-Christian Britain*, op. cit., pp. 135–7 and *passim*.

11 Ralph Gibson, *A Social History of French Catholicism 1789–1914* (London, 1989), pp. 170–80.

12 Roger Finke, 'An unsecular America', in Steve Bruce, ed., *Religion and Modernization: Sociologists and Historians Debate the Secularization Thesis*

(Oxford, 1992), pp. 145–69; Steve Bruce, 'Pluralism and religious vitality', in ibid., pp. 170–94.

13 Roy Wallis and Steve Bruce, 'Secularization: the orthodox model', in S. Bruce, ed., *Religion and Modernization*, op. cit., pp. 17–21. Cf. David Martin, *A General Theory of Secularization* (Oxford, 1978).

14 Jeffrey Cox, *The English Churches in a Secular Society: Lambeth 1870–1930* (New York, 1982), p. 267.

15 Ibid., pp. 270–6.

16 It may be instructive to compare Colin Campbell's suggestion ('Analysing the Rejection of Religion', *Social Compass* 24 (1977), pp. 339–46) that irreligion can emerge in what he calls either 'reactive' or 'developmental' forms. The former implies a radical rejection of religion, but the latter was 'as much originating within the religious tradition and extending its premises as arising in total denial of them'.

17 Callum G. Brown, 'A revisionist approach to religious change', in Bruce, ed., *Religion and Modernization*, op. cit., p. 50.

18 P. Smith, 'Anglo-American religion and hegemonic change in the world system, c. 1870–1980', *British Journal of Sociology*, 37 (1986), pp. 88–105.

19 Alan Wilkinson, *Church of England and the First World War* (London, 1978), pp. 169–70.

20 Cox, op. cit., p. 273.

21 Kim Knott, 'Other major religious traditions', in Terence Thomas, ed., *The British: Their Religious Beliefs and Practices 1800–1986* (London, 1988), pp. 139–44.

22 A. Tennyson, 'Ode on the Death of the Duke of Wellington' l. 49–50.

23 *The Times*, 27 July 1982, p. 12.

24 Ibid., p. 1.

FURTHER READING

1 INTRODUCTION: RELIGION AND NATIONHOOD IN MODERN BRITAIN

Religion

An accessible but inconclusive introduction to the various perspectives adopted by historians is provided by 'What is religious history?', *History Today* 35 (August 1985), 43–52. The view that religion was part of the essential fabric of eighteenth-century society was forcefully and controversially reasserted by J. C. D. Clark, *English Society, 1688–1832* (Cambridge, 1985). For theoretical perspectives see the works cited in the text and footnotes; also for recent surveys of the literature on definitional problems, Geoffrey Ahern and Grace Davie, *Inner City God: The Nature of Belief in the Inner City* (London, 1987) and Edward Bailey, '"Implicit religion": A bibliographical introduction', *Social Compass* 37 (1990), 499–509. For a stimulating, if idiosyncratic, survey of historical writing on the history of Christianity see John Kent, *The Unacceptable Face: The Modern Church in the Eyes of the Historian* (London, 1987).

Nationalism

General surveys include Hans Kohn, *The Idea of Nationalism* (New York, 1967); Ernest Gellner, *Nations and Nationalism* (Oxford, 1983); John Breuilly, *Nationalism and the State* (Manchester, 1982); Benedict Anderson, *Imagined Communities: Reflections on the Origin and Spread of Nationalism* (London, 1983), and E. J. Hobsbawm, *Nations and Nationalism Since 1780: Programme, Myth, Reality* (Cambridge, 1990). A wide range of perspectives on British patriotisms emerge from Linda Colley, *Britons: Forging the Nation 1707–1837* (New Haven and London, 1992) and Raphael Samuel, ed., *Patriotism: The Making and Unmaking of British National Identity* (3 vols, London, 1989). For richly varied empirical explorations of linkages between religion and national identity see Stuart Mews, ed., *Religion and National Identity: Studies in Church History* 18 (Oxford, 1982).

2   A STRANGE WARMING? THE FORMATION OF VICTORIAN RELIGION

Evangelicalism

The standard history is D. W. Bebbington, *Evangelicalism in Modern Britain: A History from the 1730s to the 1980s* (London, 1989). The social and religious context of early Methodism is explored in articles by John Walsh, notably, 'Origins of the Evangelical Revival', in G.V. Bennett and J. D. Walsh, eds, *Essays in Modern Church History in Memory of Norman Sykes* (London, 1966) and 'Elie Halévy and the birth of Methodism', *Transactions of the Royal Historical Society*, 5th series, 25 (1975), pp. 1–20. On revivalism see Richard Carwadine, *Transatlantic Revivalism: Popular Evangelicalism in Britain and America 1790–1862* (London, 1978); David Luker, 'Revivalism in theory and practice: the case of Cornish Methodism', *Journal of Ecclesiastical History* 37 (1986), 3–19 and (in its mid-Victorian phase) John Kent, *Holding the Fort: Studies in Victorian Revivalism* (London, 1978). Coverage of Ireland, Scotland and Wales is patchy: David Hempton and Myrtle Hill, *Evangelical Protestantism in Ulster Society 1740–1890* (London, 1992) is excellent; Arthur Fawcett, *The Cambuslang Revival: The Scottish Evangelical Revival of the Eighteenth Century* (London, 1971) and Derec Llwyd Morgan (trans. Dyfnallt Morgan), *The Great Awakening in Wales* (London, 1988) are useful, but less academically rigorous. For an international perspective see W. R. Ward, *The Protestant Evangelical Awakening* (Cambridge, 1992) and on the role of women: Deborah M. Valenze, *Prophetic Sons and Daughters: Female Preaching and Popular Religion in Industrial England* (Princeton, 1985) and Gail Malmgreen, ed., *Religion in the Lives of English Women, 1760–1930* (London, 1986).

Catholicism

John Bossy's treatment in *The English Catholic Community 1570–1850* (London, 1975) should be compared with that of Edward Norman in *Roman Catholicism in England from the Elizabethan Settlement to the Second Vatican Council* (Oxford, 1985) and *The English Catholic Church in the Nineteenth Century* (Oxford, 1984). There are two books on Scottish Catholicism, both stronger on narrative than analysis: Peter F. Anson, *Underground Catholicism in Scotland 1622–1878* (Montrose, 1970) and Christine Johnson, *Developments in the Roman Catholic Church in Scotland 1789–1829* (Edinburgh, 1983). On Ireland see Patrick J. Corish, *The Irish Catholic Experience: A Historical Survey* (Dublin, 1985) and for the implications of Irish immigration R. Swift and S. Gilley, eds, *The Irish in the Victorian City* (London, 1985). On anti-Catholicism see the items noted in the further reading for Chapter 5.

Developments 1789–1843

The most recent survey of the eighteenth-century Church, Gordon Rupp's *Religion in England 1688–1791* (Oxford, 1986), does not supersede Norman Sykes, *Church and State in England in the Eighteenth Century* (Cambridge,

1934). On Scotland see A. L. Drummond and J. Bulloch, *The Scottish Church 1688–1843: the Age of the Moderates* (Edinburgh, 1973). For the impact of the French Revolution see V. Kiernan, 'Evangelicalism and the French Revolution', *Past and Present* (1952), 44–56 and for differing aspects of evangelicalism in the early nineteenth century E. M. Howse, *Saints in Politics: The 'Clapham Sect' and the Growth of Freedom* (London, 1953), Doreen M. Rosman, *Evangelicals and Culture* (London, 1984) and David Hempton, *Methodism and Politics in British Society 1750–1850* (London, 1984). W. R. Ward's *Church and Society in England, 1790–1850* (London, 1972) is a heavy-going but worthwhile account of the challenge to the Anglican Establishment arising from the rise of Nonconformity. On Irish developments see G. C. Bolton, *The Passing of the Irish Act of Union* (Oxford, 1966) and Sean Connolly, *Religion and Society in Nineteenth Century Ireland* (Dundalk, 1985). The immediate context of Catholic Emancipation is examined by G. I. T. Machin, *The Catholic Question in English Politics 1820 to 1830* (Oxford, 1964) and its aftermath particularly as it related to evangelicalism, explored by John Wolffe, *The Protestant Crusade in Great Britain, 1829–1860* (Oxford, 1991). There is a vast literature on the Oxford Movement, but one might start with the classic near contemporary account, R. W. Church, *The Oxford Movement: Twelve Years 1833–1845* (London, 1891), or Geoffrey Rowell, *The Vision Glorious: Themes and Personalities of the Catholic Revival in Anglicanism* (Oxford, 1983).

3 GOD MADE THEM HIGH OR LOWLY? OFFICIAL RELIGION

Churches and their communities

There are chapters surveying all the main groups in Gerald Parsons, ed., *Religion in Victorian Britain: Vol. I Traditions* (Manchester, 1988). For a general account of the twentieth century see Adrian Hastings, *A History of English Christianity, 1920–1985* (London, 1986).

More detailed examination of the Church of England should start with Owen Chadwick's *The Victorian Church* (2 vols, London, 1966, 1970). For the reforms of the 1830s and afterwards see also G. F. A. Best, *Temporal Pillars* (London, 1964); P. T. Marsh, *The Victorian Church in Decline* (London, 1969); and K. A. Thompson, *Bureaucracy and Church Reform, 1800–1965* (Oxford, 1970). The personnel are analysed in Alan Haig, *The Victorian Clergy* (London, 1984). On Nonconformity Clyde Binfield's *So Down to Prayers* (London, 1977) is splendidly evocative of the atmosphere of the more socially élite chapels and the cousinhoods centred upon them, but for more structured analysis one could turn to James Munson, *The Nonconformists* (London, 1991). Working-class Methodism is explored by Robert Moore, *Pitmen, Preachers and Politics: The Effects of Methodism in a Durham Mining Community* (Cambridge, 1974). On Scotland see: Callum G. Brown, *The Social History of Religion in Scotland Since 1730* (London, 1987); on Wales E. T. Davies, *Religion in the Industrial Revolution in South Wales* (Cardiff, 1965) and on the north of Ireland, Peter Brooke, *Ulster Presbyterianism: The Historical Perspective 1610–1970* (New York, 1987).

The position of religious institutions on the ground is explored in a variety of local studies, including A. Allan MacLaren, *Religion and Social Class: The Disruption Years in Aberdeen* (London, 1974); Hugh McLeod, *Class and Religion in the Late Victorian City* (London, 1974); James Obelkevich, *Religion and Rural Society: South Lindsey 1825–1875* (Oxford, 1976); and Edward Royle, *The Victorian Church in York* (York, 1983) and *Nonconformity in Nineteenth-Century York* (York, 1985). There is relatively little material of this kind on the twentieth century, but David Clark, *Between Pulpit and Pew: Folk Religion in a North Yorkshire Fishing Village* (Cambridge, 1982) and Jeffrey Cox, *The English Churches in a Secular Society, Lambeth: 1870–1930* (New York, 1982) are both important and stimulating monographs.

Attendance and membership

On the 1851 Census, its limitations and implications, see K. S. Inglis, 'Patterns of religious worship in 1851', *Journal of Ecclesiastical History* 11 (1960), pp. 74–86; W. S. F. Pickering, 'The 1851 Religious Census – a useless experiment?', *British Journal of Sociology* 18 (1967), pp. 382–407 and B. I. Coleman, *The Church of England in the Mid-Nineteenth Century* (Historical Association pamphlet, 1980). A significant proportion of the original returns have now been published, including those for Lincolnshire, Oxfordshire and the whole of Wales. An essential source book for membership statistics, which also includes extensive evaluation of the evidence, is Robert Currie, Alan Gilbert and Lee Horsley, *Churches and Churchgoers: Patterns of Church Growth in the British Isles Since 1700* (Oxford, 1977). See also A. D. Gilbert, *Religion and Society in Industrial England: Church, Chapel and Social Change 1740–1914* (London, 1976); and John D. Gay, *The Geography of Religion In England* (1971); and David Martin, *A Sociology of English Religion* (1967).

4   OUTSIDE THE SHEEPFOLD? UNOFFICIAL RELIGION

For a general survey of lower-class attitudes to religion see Hugh McLeod, *Religion and the Working Class in Nineteenth-Century Britain* (1984). The older and more 'pessimistic' view is presented in K. S. Inglis, *Churches and the Working Classes in Victorian England* (1963). There is also much useful discussion, especially in sections relating to Roman Catholics and Jews, in Gerald Parsons, ed. *Religion in Victorian Britain Vol. I Traditions* (Manchester, 1988). There are no comparable studies of the twentieth century, but a certain amount can be inferred from Alan D. Gilbert, *The Making of Post-Christian Britain* (London, 1980) and David Martin, *A Sociology of English Religion* (London, 1967).

There is an overview of folk religion and its successors in David Hempton, '"Popular Religion", 1800–1986', in Terence Thomas, ed., *The British: Their Religious Beliefs and Practices 1800–1986* (London, 1988), pp. 181–210. For further detail the local studies already noted, particularly those by Clark and Obelkevich, are very important. For Ireland and the Irish see S. J. Connolly, *Priests and People in Pre-Famine Ireland* (Dublin, 1982) and Lynn Hollen Lees, *Exiles of Erin: Irish Migrants in Victorian London* (Manchester, 1979).

For examples of the various strategies of official religion in confronting perceived popular indifference see: Donald M. Lewis, *Lighten Their Darkness: The Evangelical Mission to Working-Class London 1828–1860* (Westport, Conn., 1986); Emmet Larkin, 'The devotional revolution in Ireland, 1850–75', *American Historical Review* 77 (1972), pp. 625–52; R. Swift and S. Gilley, eds, *The Irish in the Victorian City* (London, 1985); T. W. Laqueur, *Religion and Respectability: Sunday Schools and Working Class Culture 1780–1850* (New Haven, 1976); James Murphy, *Church, State, and Schools in Britain, 1800–1970* (London, 1971); Callum G. Brown, 'Religion, class and church growth', in W. Hamish Fraser and R.J. Morris, eds, *People and Society in Scotland: Vol. II 1830–1914* (Edinburgh, 1990); and Stephen Yeo, *Religion and Voluntary Organisations in Crisis* (London, 1976). The last named is a local study of Reading in the period 1890 to 1914.

The concept of 'diffusive Christianity' is most fully discussed in J. Cox's *The English Churches in a Secular Society, Lambeth: 1870–1930* (New York, 1982) but important additional insights are provided by Hugh McLeod, 'New perspectives on Victorian class religion: the oral evidence', *Oral History* 14, 1 (1986), pp. 31–49. McLeod here acknowledges that he had previously underestimated the role of religion in working-class life, an earlier view reflected in his *Class and Religion in the Late Victorian City* (1974). On secularism see the two books by Edward Royle, *Victorian Infidels: The Origins of the British Secularist Movement, 1791–1866* (Manchester, 1974) and *Radicals, Secularists and Republicans: Popular Freethought in Britain, 1866–1915* (Manchester, 1980). Studies of Protestant-Catholic sectarian conflict include: Frank Neal, *Sectarian Violence: The Liverpool Experience, 1819–1914* (Manchester, 1988); Steve Bruce, *No Pope of Rome: Militant Protestantism in Modern Scotland* (Edinburgh, 1985); A. C. Hepburn, 'Catholics in the north of Ireland, 1850–1921: the urbanization of a minority' in A. C. Hepburn, ed., *Minorities in History* (London, 1978); and John Darby, *Conflict in Northern Ireland: The Development of a Polarised Community* (Dublin, 1976). The division of communities among Anglican-Nonconformist lines is explored in Patrick Joyce, *Work, Society and Politics* (1980) and Paul T. Phillips, *The Sectarian Spirit: Sectarianism, Society and Politics in Victorian Cotton Towns* (Toronto, 1982).

5   HIGH TIDE OF FAITH? RELIGION AND NATIONHOOD AROUND 1850

Scotland, Ireland and Wales

For accounts of the Disruption see G. I. T. Machin, *Politics and the Churches in Great Britain, 1832 to 1868* (Oxford, 1977), Ch. IV, and Gerald Parsons, 'Church and state in Victorian Scotland: disruption and reunion', in Gerald Parsons, ed., *Religion in Victorian Britain: Vol. II Controversies* (Manchester, 1988). Chalmers's ideas and influence are discussed in depth in Stewart J. Brown, *Thomas Chalmers and the Godly Commonwealth in Scotland* (Oxford, 1982). For the development of national consciousness in Scotland see: Christopher Harvie, *Scotland and Nationalism: Scottish Society and Politics, 1707–1977* (London, 1977); Hugh Trevor-Roper, 'The invention of tradition: the Highland tradition of Scotland', in Eric Hobsbawm and Terence Ranger, eds, *The*

Invention of Tradition (Cambridge, 1983); and Rosalind Mitchison, 'Nineteenth century Scottish nationalism: the cultural background' in Rosalind Mitchison, ed., *The Roots of Nationalism: Studies in Northern Europe*, (Edinburgh, 1980). Links with religion are explored in D. W. Bebbington, 'Religion and national feeling in nineteenth-century Wales and Scotland', in Stuart Mews, ed., *Religion and National Identity: Studies in Church History* 18 (Oxford, 1982).

On the general context of the Repeal movement see J. C. Beckett, *The Making of Modern Ireland 1603–1923* (London, 1966), Ch. XVI. There are numerous biographies of O'Connell, but the fullest and most recent is Oliver Mac-Donagh's. The second volume, *The Emancipist: Daniel O'Connell 1830–47* (London, 1989) includes discussion of the 'monster meetings'. See also D. G. Boyce, *Nationalism in Ireland* (London, 1982); Richard Davis, *The Young Ireland Movement* (Dublin, 1987); and for the situation of the Roman Catholic Church, Donal A. Kerr, *Peel, Priests and Politics: Sir Robert Peel's Administration and the Roman Catholic Church in Ireland, 1841–1846* (Oxford, 1982).

The Welsh Blue Books controversy is analysed by Prys Morgan, 'From Long Knives to Blue Books', in R. R. Davies, Ralph A. Griffiths, Ieuan Gwynedd Jones and Kenneth O. Morgan, eds, *Welsh Society and Nationhood* (Cardiff, 1984). For the background see Jac L. Williams and Gwilym Rees Hughes, eds, *The History of Education in Wales* (Swansea, 1978) and Education Office for Wales, *Education in Wales, 1847–1947* (London, 1948). The revival of Welsh culture is surveyed by Prys Morgan, 'From a death to a view: the hunt for the Welsh past in the Romantic period', in E. Hobsbawm and T. Ranger, eds, *The Invention of Tradition* (Cambridge, 1983).

British dimensions

On the 'papal aggression' and its context see Gerald Parsons 'Victorian Roman Catholicism: Emancipation, Establishment and Achievement', in Parsons, ed., *Religion in Victorian Britain: Vol. I*, and W. Ralls, 'The Papal Aggression of 1850: a study in Victorian anti-Catholicism', *Church History* 43 (1974), pp. 242–56 (reprinted in Gerald Parsons, ed., *Religion in Victorian Britain: Vol. IV Interpretations* (Manchester, 1988). Wider ranging accounts of Victorian anti-Catholicism are provided by E. R. Noman, *Anti-Catholicism in Victorian England* (London, 1968) which includes reprinted documentary sources; John Wolffe, *The Protestant Crusade in Great Britain, 1829–60* (Oxford, 1991), and D. G. Paz, *Popular Anti-Catholicism in Mid-Victorian England* (Stanford, California, 1992). On Guy Fawkes celebrations see R. D. Storch, 'Please to remember the fifth of November', in R. D. Storch, ed., *Popular Culture and Custom in Nineteenth-Century Britain* (London, 1982), pp. 71–99.

The discussion of Wellington's funeral is derived primarily from the author's own as yet unpublished primary research, but there is an account of it in J. Morley, *Death, Heaven and the Victorians* (London, 1971). On the duke himself see Neville Thompson, *Wellington After Waterloo* (London, 1986). Relationships between religion and the Crimean War are explored in works by Olive Anderson: *A Liberal State at War: English Politics and Economics during the Crimean War* (London, 1967); 'The reactions of Church and dissent towards the Crimean War', *Journal of Ecclesiastical History* 16 (1965), pp. 209–20; and 'The growth of Christian militarism in mid-Victorian Britain', *English Historical Review* 86 (1971), pp. 46–72. On the development of evangelical ideas of the nation see John Wolffe, 'Evangelicalism in mid-nineteenth-century England', in R. Samuel, ed., *Patriotism: the Making and Unmaking of British National Identity: Vol. I History and Politics* (London, 1989), pp. 169–87.

6 THINE IS THE KINGDOM? POLITICS, COMMUNITY AND THE MONARCHY

For accounts of the political struggles concerning religion see G. I. T. Machin's two volumes, *Politics and the Churches in Great Britain 1832 to 1868* (Oxford, 1977) and *Politics and the Churches in Great Britain 1869 to 1921* (Oxford, 1987). These are a mine of detailed information. For particular important phases and developments Machin's work is complemented by P. M. H. Bell, *Disestablishment in Ireland and Wales* (London, 1969); J. P. Parry, *Democracy and Religion: Gladstone and the Liberal Party, 1867–1875* (Cambridge, 1986) and D. W. Bebbington, *The Nonconformist Conscience: Chapel and Politics, 1870–1914* (London, 1982).

There is no general account of the interrelationships between religion, elections and the development of political parties, but a good deal can be gleaned from H. J. Hanham, *Elections and Party Management: Politics in the Time of Disraeli and Gladstone* (London, 1959) and local studies, particularly P. F. Clarke, *Lancashire and the New Liberalism* (Cambridge, 1971) and Patrick Joyce, *Work, Society and Politics* (Brighton, 1980). The Primrose League is examined by Martin Pugh, *The Tories and the People 1880–1935* (Oxford, 1985). eFor Christian Socialism see E. R. Norman, *The Victorian Christian Socialists* (Cambridge, 1987) and P. d'A. Jones, *The Christian Socialist Revival, 1877–1914* (Princeton, 1968). The religious dimensions of early Socialism are explored by Stephen Yeo, 'A new life: the religion of Socialism in Britain, 1883–1896', *History Workshop Journal* 4 (1977), pp. 5–56.

The essential account of Welsh politics in the period is Kenneth O. Morgan, *Wales in British Politics 1868–1922* (3rd edn, Cardiff, 1980) while studies of interactions between religion and politics at the local level are provided by Ieuan Gywnedd Jones, *Communities: Essays in the Social History of Victorian Wales* (Llandysul, 1987). For the activities of the leading protagonist see John Grigg, *The Young Lloyd George* (London, 1973). On Scotland see: I. G. C. Hutchinson, *A Political History of Scotland 1832–1924: Parties, Elections and Issues* (Edinburgh, 1986); H. J. Hanham, 'Mid-century Scottish nationalism', in R. Robson, ed., *Ideas and Institutions of Victorian Britain* (London, 1967), and *Scottish Nationalism* (London, 1969). On the place of Protestantism in Scottish identity see Graham Walker and Tom Gallagher, eds, *Sermons and Battle Hymns: Protestant Popular Culture in Modern Scotland* (Edinburgh, 1990). The best short survey of recent Irish history is now K. Theodore Hoppen, *Ireland since 1800: Conflict and Conformity* (London, 1989), which is especially helpful in discussing links between religion and politics. See also: D. G. Boyce, ed., *The Revolution in Ireland 1879–1923* (London, 1988); A. T. Q. Stewart, *The Ulster Crisis: Resistance to Home Rule, 1912–14* (London, 1967); F. S. L. Lyons, *Culture and Anarchy in Ireland 1890–1939* (Oxford, 1979); and, on the post-partition period, J. H. Whyte, *Church and State in Modern Ireland 1923–1979*

(Dublin, 1980) and Steve Bruce, *God Save Ulster: The Religion and Politics of Paisleyism* (Oxford, 1986).

On state ceremonial the seminal article is David Cannadine, 'The context, performance and meaning of ritual: the British monarchy and the "Invention of Tradition"', c. 1820–1977' in E. Hobsbawm and T. Ranger, eds, *The Invention of Tradition* (Cambridge, 1983). This should be supplemented by the items noted in the footnotes, and by biographies of the sovereigns concerned, notably Stanley Weintraub, *Victoria: Biography of a Queen* (London, 1987).

7 THE REAL FREE CHURCH? CULTURE AND BELIEF

Theological trends

Bernard M. G. Reardon, *Religious Thought in the Victorian Age: A Survey from Coleridge to Gore* (London, 1980) effectively covers the field within the limits that it sets for itself. There is also much to be gleaned from Owen Chadwick's *The Victorian Church* (London, 1966, 1970) and from the two volumes of Gerald Parsons, ed., *Religion in Victorian Britain* (Manchester, 1988). Some of the more exotic varieties of belief are evoked in Derek Jarrett, *The Sleep of Reason* (London, 1988). On the twentieth century Adrian Hastings's *English Christianity 1920–1990* provides an elegant outline which might be filled out from Alan M. G. Stephenson, *The Rise and Decline of English Modernism* (London, 1984) and Keith W. Clements, *Lovers of Discord: Twentieth Century Theological Controversies in England* (London, 1988).

Literature

Accounts of religion in the nineteenth-century novel include: Valentine Cunningham, *Everywhere Spoken Against: Dissent in the Victorian Novel* (Oxford, 1975); Elisabeth Jay, *The Religion of the Heart: Anglican Evangelicalism and the Nineteenth Century Novel* (Oxford, 1979); R. L. Wolff, *Gains and Losses: Novels of Faith and Doubt in Victorian England* (New York, 1977); and Norman Vance, *The Sinews of the Spirit: The Ideal of Christian manliness in Victorian Literature and Religious Thought* (Cambridge, 1985). There is some helpful general discussion of the later part of the period in Hastings's *English Christianity*, but for more detail reference should be made to the biographies and writings of particular individuals, as cited in the notes. On Ireland Thomas Flanagan's chapter on 'Literature in English, 1801–91', in W. E. Vaughan, ed., *Ireland Under the Union: Vol. I 1801–70* (Oxford, 1989) is an excellent short survey. Subsequent developments are covered in F. S. L. Lyons, *Culture and Anarchy in Ireland 1890–1939* (Oxford, 1979) and G. J. Watson, *Irish Identity and the Literary Revival: Synge, Yeats, Joyce and O'Casey* (London, 1979). Douglas Gifford, ed., *The History of Scottish Literature: Vol. 3 Nineteenth Century* (Aberdeen, 1988) and Cairns Craig, ed., *Vol. 4 Twentieth Century* (Aberdeen, 1987) is invaluable; Thomas Parry (trans. H. Idris Bell), *A History of Welsh Literature* (Oxford, 1955) is useful, but comparatively dated. Horst W. Drescher and Hermann Völkel, eds, *Nationalism in Literature* (Frankfurt am

Main, 1989) is primarily concerned with Scotland, but also has some interesting material on Ireland and Wales.

Visual arts

The most accessible introduction to the Gothic Revival remains Kenneth Clark *The Gothic Revival* (London, 1974). There is an extensive literature on the Pre-Raphaelites, but in relation to the specific issues touched on in this chapter the most helpful starting point is Jeremy Maas, *Holman Hunt and the Light of the World* (London, 1984). On the nineteenth century see also Benedict Read, *Victorian Sculpture* (New Haven, 1982) and on the twentieth century Michael Day, *Modern Art in English Churches* (London, 1984); Tom Devonshire Jones, *Images of Christ: Religious Iconography in Twentieth Century British Art* (Northampton, 1993) and Judith Nesbitt, *Stanley Spencer: A Sort of Heaven* (Liverpool, 1992). On Ireland see Kenneth McConkey, *A Free Spirit: Irish Art 1860–1960* (London, 1990) and Jeanne Sheehy, *The Rediscovery of Ireland's Past: the Celtic Revival 1830–1930* (London, 1980).

Music

Nicholas Temperley, ed., *The Romantic Age 1800–1914* (London, 1981) is a thorough overview containing much that is relevant to relations between music and religion. Lionel Adey's *Class and Idol in the English Hymn* (Vancouver, 1988) is a stimulating analysis of its subject.

General

Mark Girouard, *The Return to Camelot: Chivalry and the English Gentleman* (New Haven, 1981) and Keith Robbins, *Nineteenth-Century Britain: Integration and Diversity* (Oxford, 1988) both suggest further interesting perspectives on the material surveyed in this chapter.

8 ONWARD CHRISTIAN SOLDIERS? THE EMPIRE AND WAR

Imperialism

The history of the British Empire in the period is surveyed in Bernard Porter, *The Lion's Share: A Short History of British Imperialism 1850–1983* (London, 1984), and related to the impact of missions in Brian Stanley, *The Bible and the Flag: Protestant Missions and British Imperialism in the Nineteenth and Twentieth Centuries* (Leicester, 1990). There is suggestive, if somewhat incidental, treatment of religion in John M. Mackenzie, *Propaganda and Empire: The Manipulation of British Public Opinion 1880–1960* (Manchester, 1984) and John M. Mackenzie, ed., *Imperialism and Popular Culture* (Manchester, 1986). For an interesting, if perhaps rather overstated, account of Christian influences on imperial policy in the twentieth century see Gerald Studdert-Kennedy, *British Christians, Indian Nationalists and the Raj* (Delhi, 1991).

Responses to war

Olive Anderson's important article 'The growth of Christian militarism in mid-Victorian Britain', *English History Review* 86 (1971), pp. 46–72, serves as a concise introduction to the states of mind explored in the text. More can be gleaned from Norman Vance, *The Sinews of the Spirit*, (Cambridge, 1985) and John Springhall, *Youth, Empire and Society: British Youth Movements, 1883–1940* (London, 1977). There is quite an extensive literature on religious responses to the First World War: Stuart Mews's Cambridge PhD thesis is excellent but sadly unpublished; Alan Wilkinson's, *The Church of England and the First World War* (London, 1978) and Albert Marrin's *The Last Crusade: The Church of England in the First World War* (Durham, NC, 1974) are more accessible. A welcome, relatively recent, addition is A. J. Hoover, *God, Germany, and Britain in the Great War: A Study in Clerical Nationalism* (New York, 1989) which is especially interesting in showing how the attitudes of the British were mirrored among their antagonists. The comparative perspective is also valuable in George L. Mosse, *Fallen Soldiers: Reshaping the Memory of the World Wars* (New York, 1990). Remembrance and war memorials have only recently begun to stir critical academic attention: Derek Boorman's useful, but solely descriptive survey, *At the Going Down of the Sun: British First World War Memorials* (York, 1988) might be read with reference to the more analytical questions raised in David Cannadine's 'War and death, grief and mourning in modern Britain', in Joachim Whaley, ed., *Mirrors of Mortality: Studies in the Social History of Death* (London, 1981). On pacifism see Martin Ceadel, *Pacifism in Britain 1914–1945: The Defining of a Faith* (Oxford, 1980). The Second World War is relatively poorly served by the literature, although Hastings's *English Christianity* provides a short survey and Alan Wilkinson's *Dissent or Conform? War, Peace and the English Churches 1900–1945* (London, 1986) offers some more detail. Paul Fussell's studies of the cultural impact of the two wars, *The Great War and Modern Memory* (New York, 1975) and *Wartime: Understanding and Behaviour in the Second World War* (New York, 1989), are both very stimulating, although the former provides more purchase than the latter on the themes of the present book.

9 CONCLUSION: NATIONALISM AND SECULARIZATION

The two works by Alan Gilbert cited in the notes provide the most accessible way into the secularization thesis from a historical point of view, but can be complemented by such sociological works as David Martin's *A General Theory of Secularization* (Oxford, 1978) and David Lyon's *The Steeple's Shadow: On the Myths and Realities of Secularization* (London, 1985). For up-to-date evaluations including some telling criticisms from non-English perspectives see Steve Bruce, ed., *Religion and Modernization: Sociologists and Historians Debate the Secularization Thesis* (Oxford, 1992).

Interrelationships between religion and nationality since 1945 are explored in Daniel Jenkins, *The British: Their Identity and Their Religion* (London, 1975);

Roger Hooker and John Sargent, eds, *Belonging to Britain: Christian Perspectives on Religion and Identity in a Plural Society* (London, 1991) and by John Wolffe in Gerald Parsons ed., *The Growth of Religious Diversity: Britain from 1945: Vol. II Issues* (1993).

INDEX